WHAT DO I WANT FROM THIS LIFE?
WHAT MAKES ME HAPPY ISN'T ENOUGH; ALL THOSE
THINGS THAT SATISFY OUR INSTINCTS COMPLETE ONLY
THE ANIMAL IN ALL OF US.

I WANT TO BE PROUD. I WANT SOMETHING MORE. I WANT
TO LOOK UP TO MYSELF AND WHEN I DIE I WANT TO BE
SMILING ABOUT THE THINGS I'VE DONE, NOT CRYING FOR
WHAT I HAVEN'T.

I GUESS I WANT TO BE SATISFIED I KNOW THE ANSWER
TO THIS QUESTION. EVERYONE WANTS TO BE DIFFERENT,
MAKE AN IMPACT, BE REMEMBERED.

TOM'S DIARY, NOVEMBER 2001

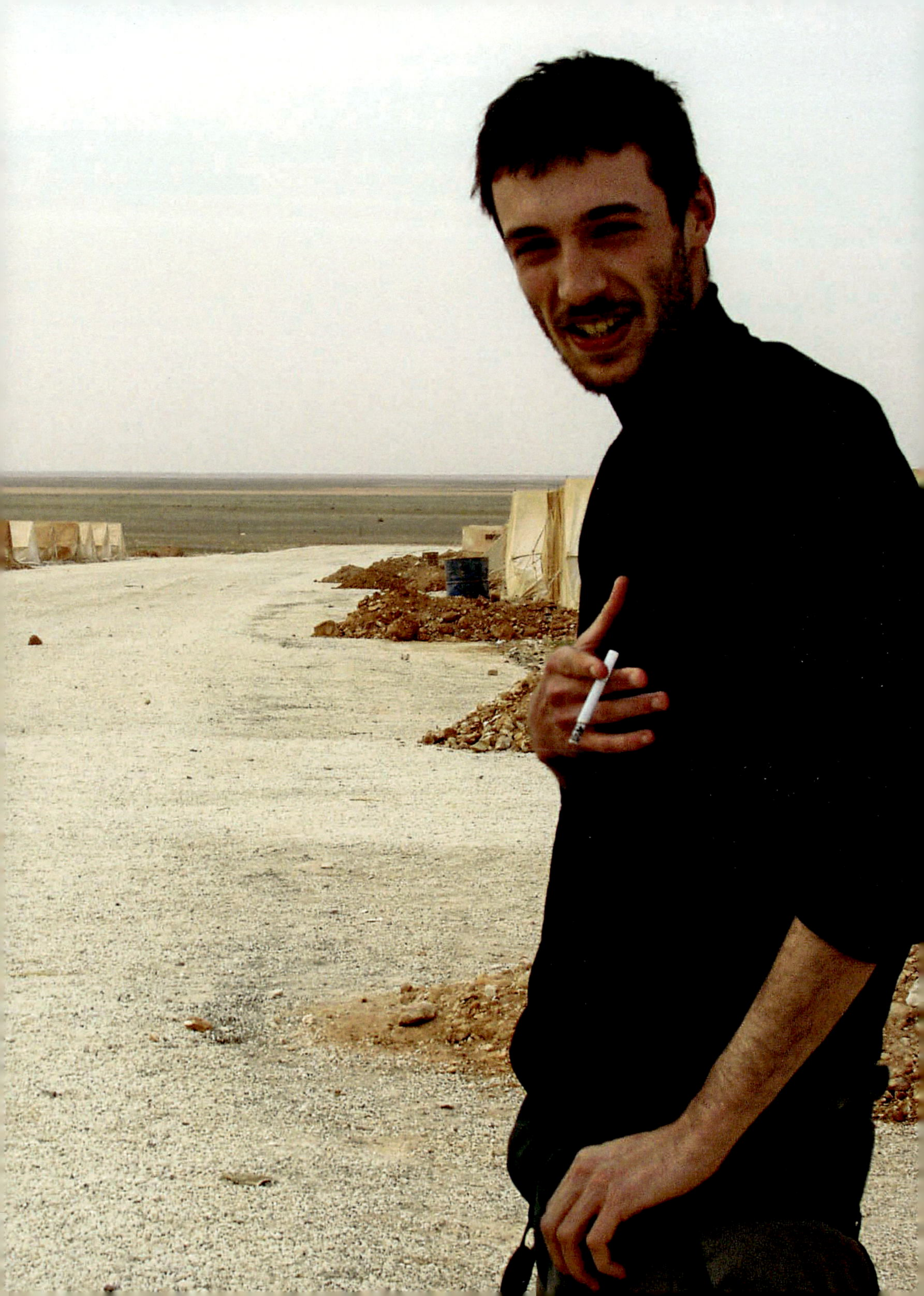

THE ONLY HOUSE LEFT STANDING

THE MIDDLE EAST JOURNALS OF
TOM HURNDALL

FOREWORD BY
ROBERT FISK

TROLLEY

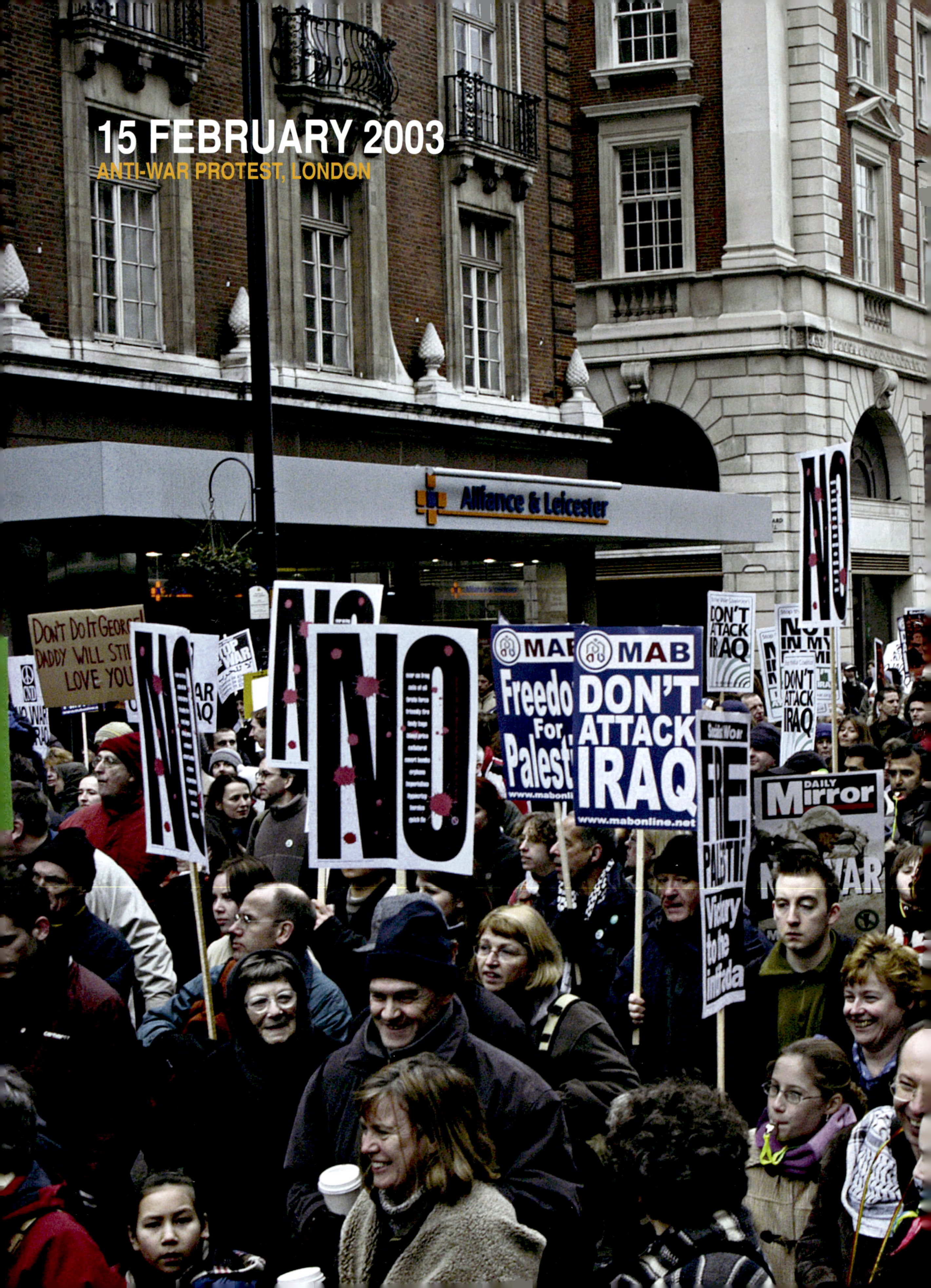

15 FEBRUARY 2003
ANTI-WAR PROTEST, LONDON
Alliance & Leicester
NO
NO
A NO
Don't Do It George!
Daddy will still
love you
STOP WAR
NO WAR IRAQ
MAB
Freedom For Palestine
www.mabonline.net
MAB
DON'T ATTACK IRAQ
www.mabonline.net
DON'T ATTACK IRAQ
DON'T ATTACK IRAQ
NOT IN MY NAME
FREE PALESTINE
Victory to the Intifada
DAILY Mirror
NO WAR

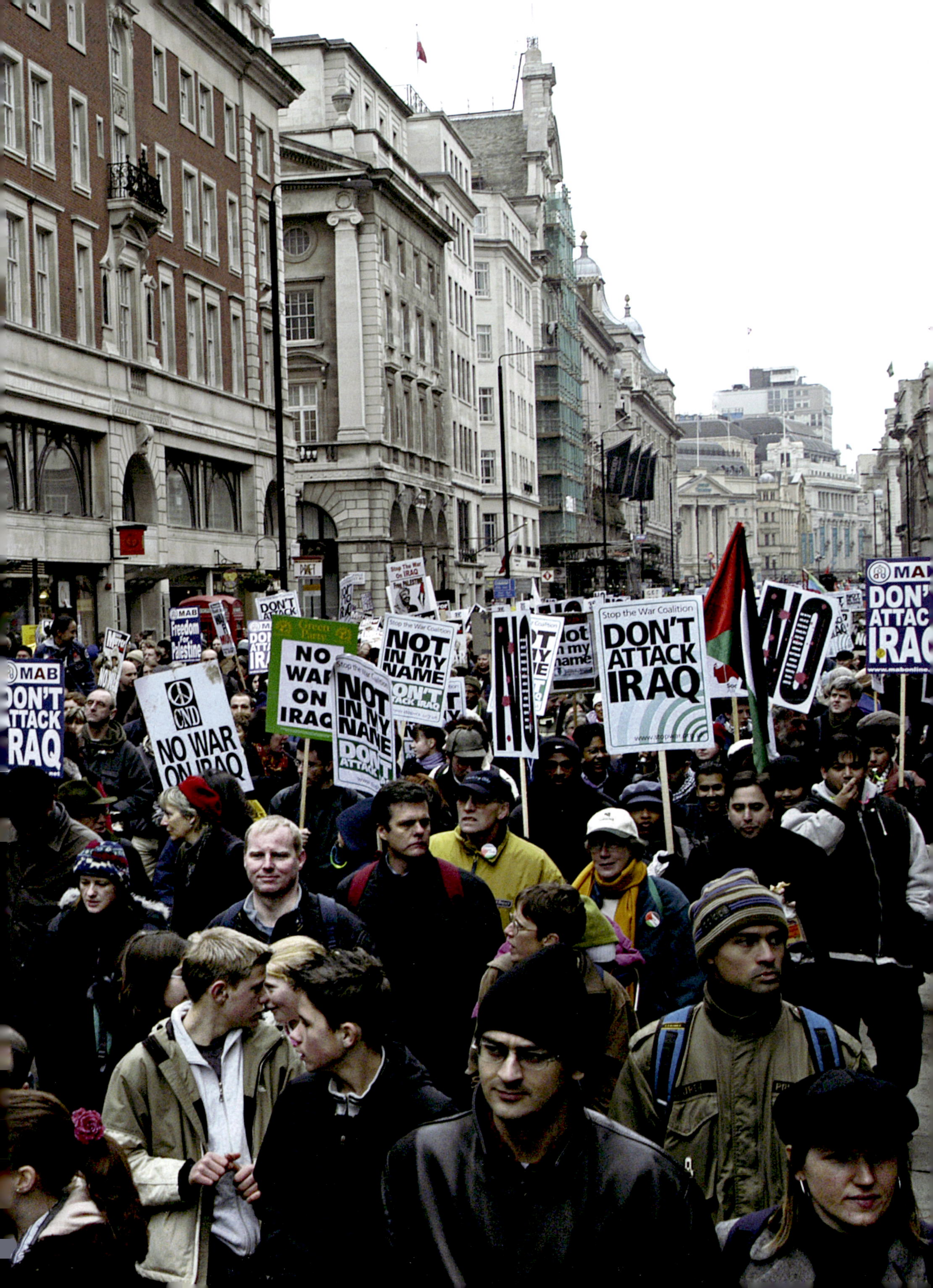
MAB
DON'T
ATTACK
IRAQ

CND
NO WAR
ON IRAQ

NO WAR
ON IRAQ

Freedom
for
Palestine

Green Party

NOT
IN MY
NAME
DON'T
ATTACK

Stop the War Coalition
NOT
IN MY
NAME

Stop The War
On IRAQ
Free PALESTINE

NOT
IN MY
NAME

NO

Stop the War Coalition
DON'T
ATTACK
IRAQ
www.stopwar.org

NO

MAB
DON'T
ATTACK
IRAQ
www.mabonline.net

My parting Shot

Of our lives gone past,
from our place in time,
We see nothing but our memories.
To lose them is to lose ourselves,
and our sight.

So when we lose our pasts in presence
they will live forever in our minds,
if we fire a parting shot;
a sign of definite closure,
to seal a stage in our life.

My stage was the need for stability,
a dependance on dependancy.
As excuses go, a gap is filled,
my break from the addiction,
and I go cold turkey.

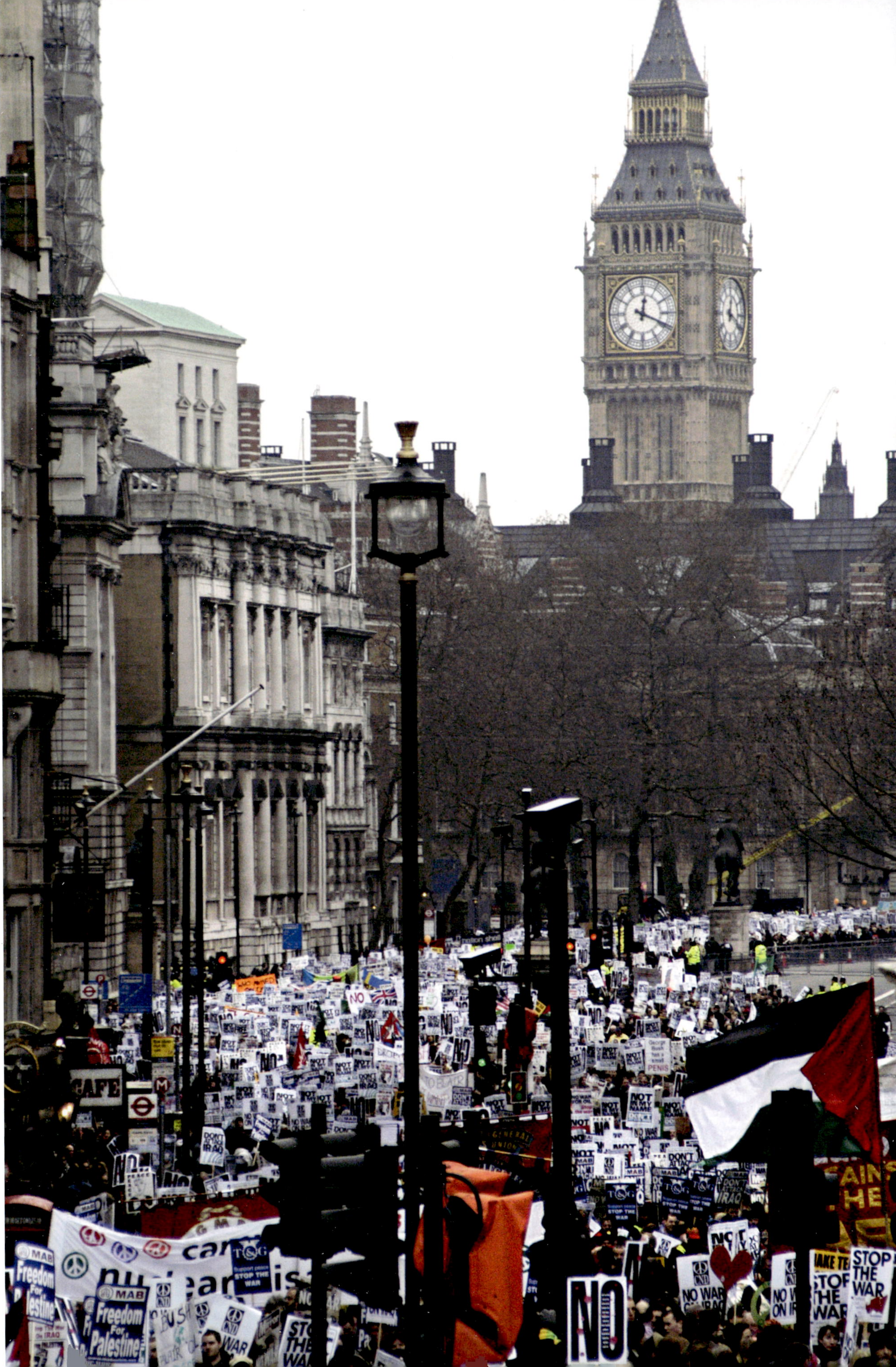

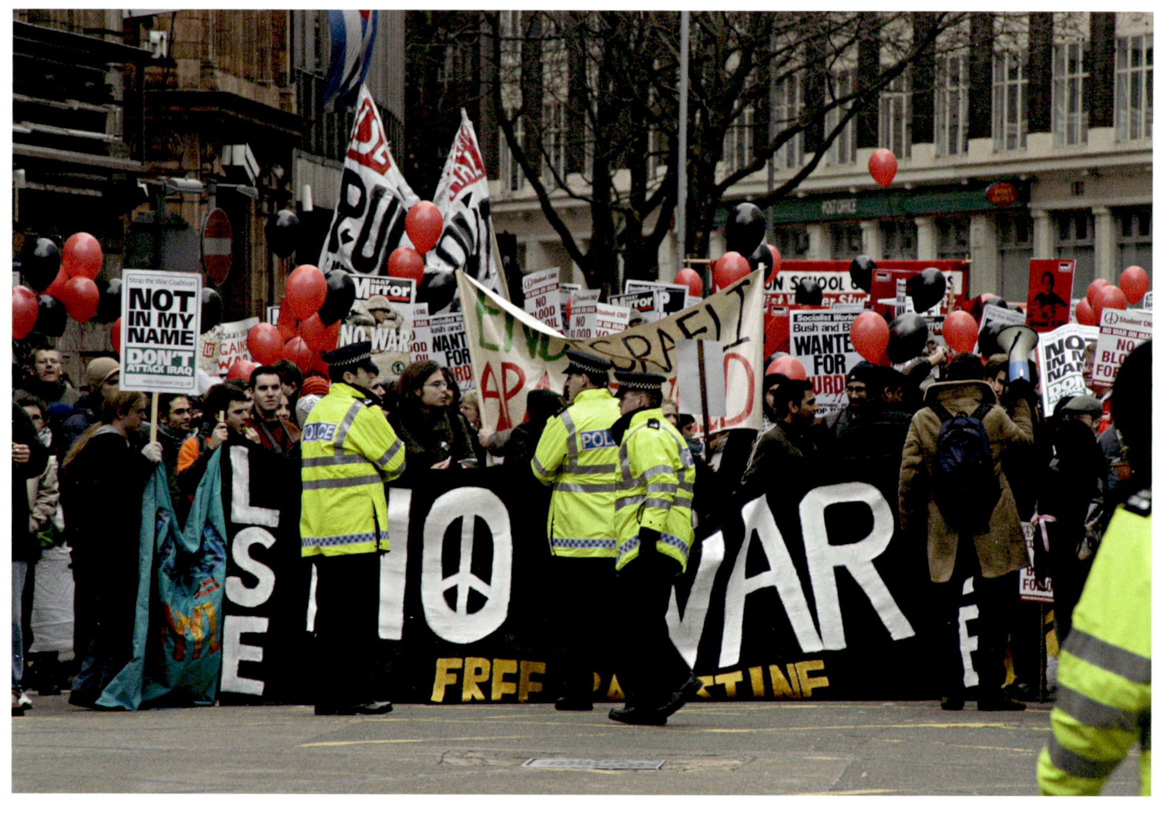
NOT IN MY NAME
DON'T ATTACK IRAQ
Stop the War Coalition
Daily Mirror
NO WAR FOR OIL
ISRAEL
LSE NO WAR
FREE PALESTINE
Socialist Workers
Bush and Blair
WANTED FOR MURDER
NO BLOOD FOR OIL
POLICE

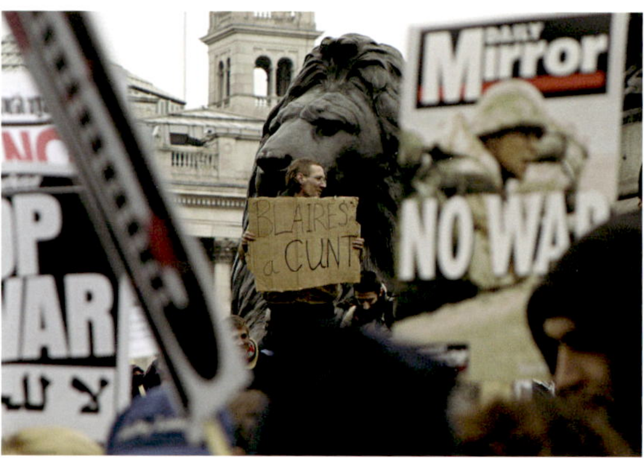
Daily Mirror
NO WAR
STOP WAR
BLAIRE'S a CUNT

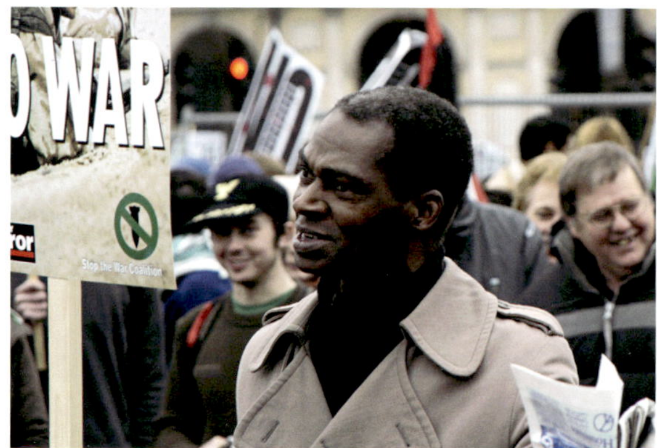
NO WAR
Stop the War Coalition

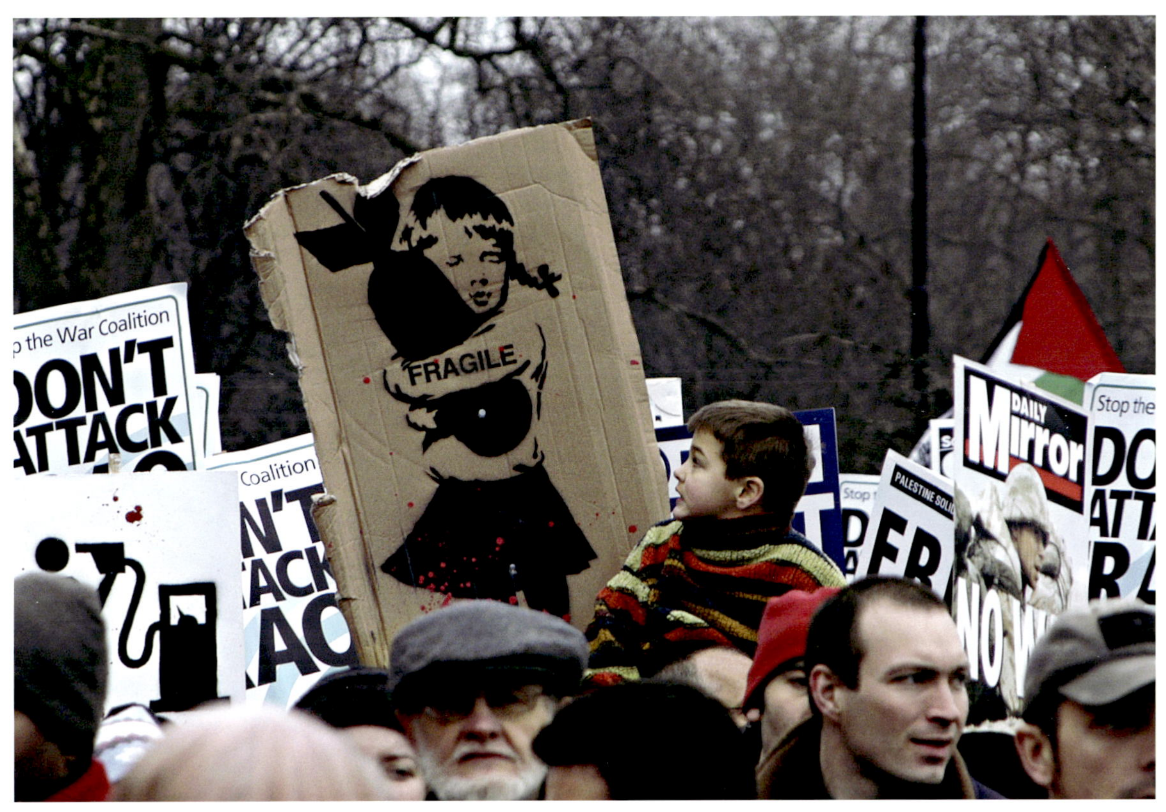
p the War Coalition
DON'T
ATTACK
Coalition
N'T
ACK
AQ
FRAGILE
DAILY
Mirror
Stop the
DO
ATT
PALESTINE SOLID
Stop t
NO W

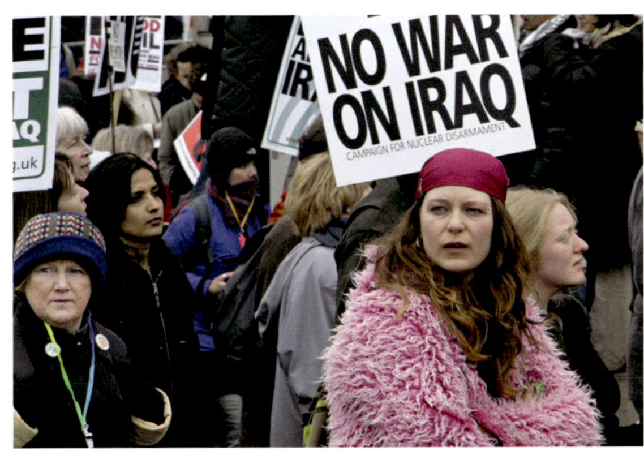
NO WAR
ON IRAQ
CAMPAIGN FOR NUCLEAR DISARMAMENT

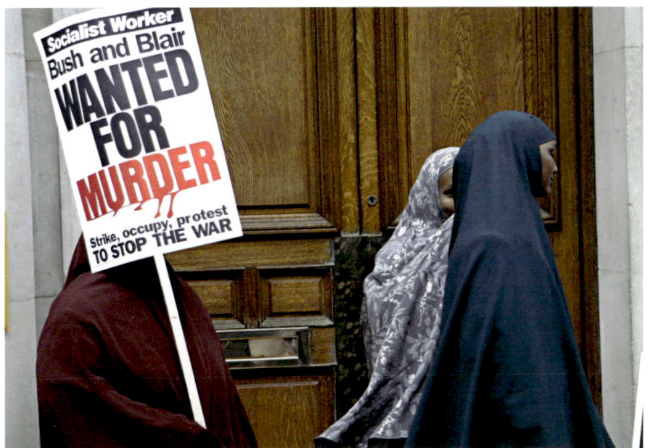
Socialist Worker
Bush and Blair
WANTED
FOR
MURDER
Strike, occupy, protest
TO STOP THE WAR

FOREWORD
BY ROBERT FISK

A brave man who stood alone. If only the world had listened to him.

I don't know if I met Tom Hurndall. He was one of a bunch of "human shields" who turned up in Baghdad just before the Anglo-American invasion in 2003, the kind of folk we professional reporters make fun of. Tree huggers, that kind of thing. Now I wish I had met him because – looking back over the history of that terrible war – Hurndall's journals show a remarkable man of remarkable principle. "I may not be a human shield," he wrote at 10.26 on 17 March from his Amman hotel. "And I may not adhere to the beliefs of those I have travelled with, but the way Britain and America plan to take Iraq is unnecessary and puts soldiers' lives above those of civilians. For that I hope that Bush and Blair stand trial for war crimes."

Hurndall got it about right, didn't he? It wasn't so simple as war/no war, black and white, he wrote. "Things I've heard and seen over the last few weeks prove what I already knew; neither the Iraqi regime, nor the American or British, are clean. Maybe Saddam needs to go but...the air war that's proposed is largely unnecessary and doesn't discriminate between civilians and armed soldiers. Tens of thousands will die, maybe hundreds of thousands, just to save thousands of American soldiers having to fight honestly, hand to hand. It is wrong." Oh, how many of my professional colleagues wrote like this on the eve of war? Not many.

We pooh-poohed the Hurndalls and their friends as groupies even when they did briefly enter the South Baghdad electricity station and met one engineer, Attiah Bakir, who had been horrifyingly wounded 11 years earlier when an American bomb blew a fragment of metal into his brain. "You can see now where it struck," Hurndall wrote in an email from Baghdad, "caving in the central third of his forehead and removing the bone totally. Above the bridge of his broken nose, there is only a cavity with scarred skin covering the prominent gap..."

A picture of Attiah Bakir stares out of the book, a distinguished, brave man who refused to leave his place of work as the next war approached. He was silenced only when one of Hurndall's friends made the mistake of asking what he thought of Saddam's government. I cringed for the poor man. "Minders" were everywhere in those early days. Talking to any civilian was almost criminally foolish. Iraqis were forbidden from talking to foreigners. Hence all those bloody "minders" (many of whom, of course, ended up working for Baghdad journalists after Saddam's overthrow).

Hurndall had a dispassionate eye. "Nowhere in the world have I ever seen so many stars as now in the western deserts of Iraq," he wrote on 22 February. "How can somewhere so beautiful be so wrought with terror and war as it is soon to be?" In answer to the questions asked of them by the BBC, ITV, WBO, CNN, al-Jazeera and others, Hurndall had no single reply. "I don't think there could be one, two or 100 responses," he wrote. "To each of us our own, but not one of us wants to die." Prophetic words for Tom to have written.

You can see him smiling selflessly in several snapshots. He went to cover the refugee complex at Al-Rowaishid and moved inexorably towards Gaza where he was confronted by the massive tragedy of the Palestinians. "I woke up at about eight in my bed in Jerusalem and lay in until 9.30," he wrote. "We left at 10.00... Since then, I have been shot at, gassed, chased by soldiers, had sound grenades thrown within metres of me, been hit by falling debris…"

Hurndall was trying to save Palestinian homes and infrastructure but frequently came under Israeli fire and seemed to have lost his fear of death. "While approaching the area, they (the Israelis) continually fired one- to two-second bursts from what I could see was a Bradley fighting vehicle… It was strange that as we approached and the guns were firing, it sent shivers down my spine, but nothing more than that. We walked down the middle of the street, wearing bright orange, and one of us shouted through a loudspeaker, 'We are International volunteers. Don't shoot!' That was followed by another volley of fire, though I can't be sure where from…"

Tom Hurndall had stayed in Rafah. He was only 21 where – in his mother's words – he lost his life through a single, selfless, human act. "Tom was shot in the head as he carried a single Palestinian child out of the range of an Israeli army sniper." Mrs Hurndall asked me to write a preface to Tom's book and this article is his preface, for a brave man who stood alone and showed more courage than most of us have dreamed of. Forget tree huggers. Hurndall was one good man and true.

Robert Fisk's World

A brave man who stood alone. If only the world had listened to him

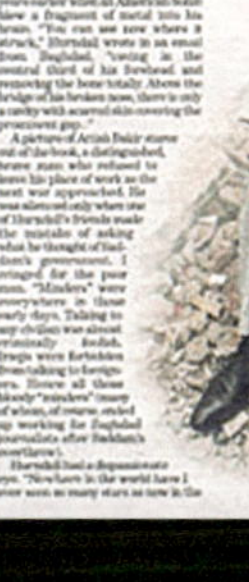

I wish I had met Tom Hurndall, a remarkable man of remarkable principle

AMMAN

21 - 24 FEBRUARY 2003

MAP OF THE MIDDLE EAST
TOM'S ITINERARY 21 FEBRUARY - 11 APRIL 2003

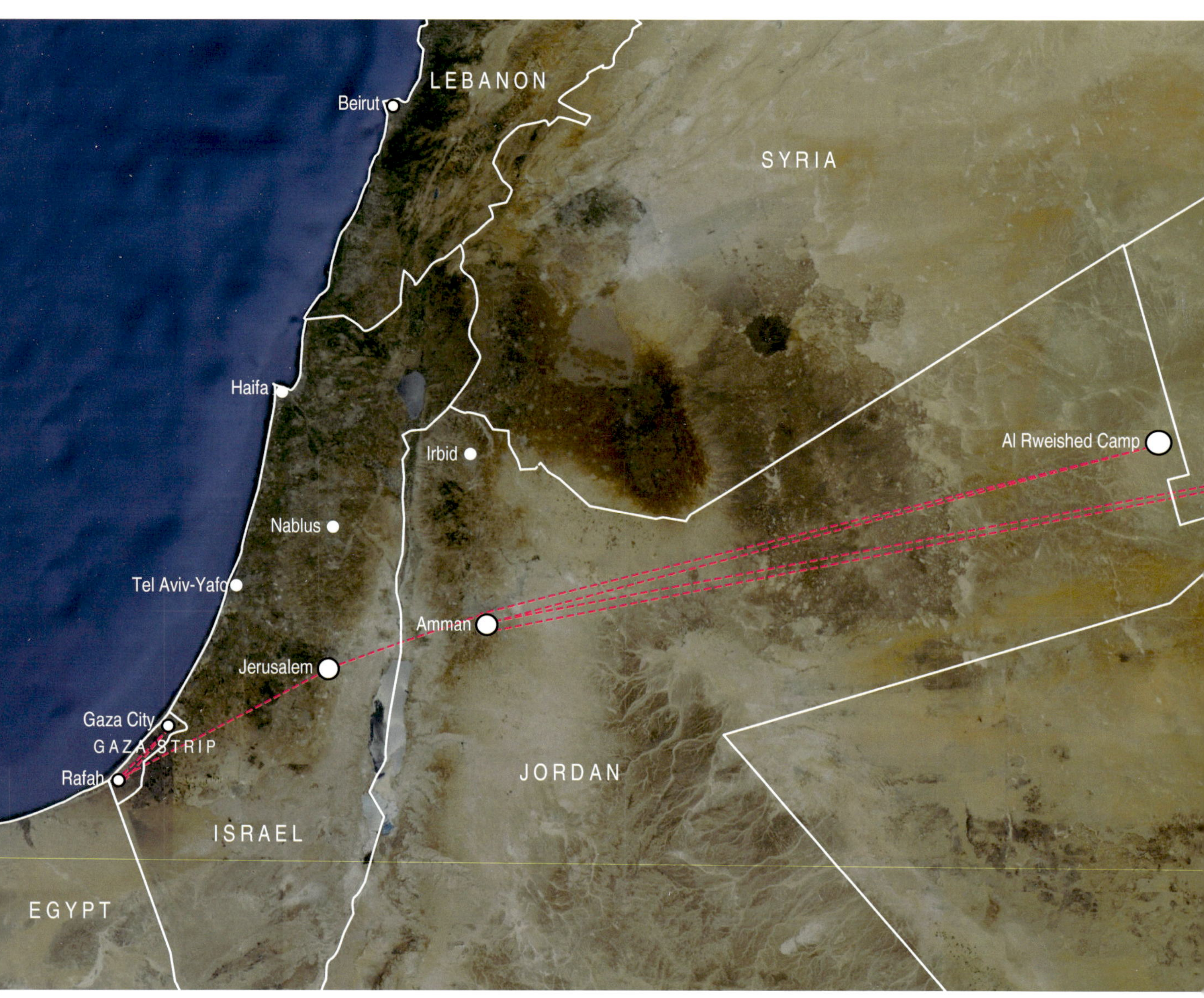

21 FEB LONDON - AMMAN, JORDAN
21 - 24 FEB AMMAN

24 FEB AMMAN - BAGHDAD, IRAQ
24 FEB - 3 MARCH BAGHDAD

3 MARCH BAGHDAD - AMMAN
4 - 21 MARCH AMMAN

21 MARCH AMMAN - AL-RWEISHED
REFUGEE CAMP, JORDAN
21 - 31 MARCH AL-RWEISHED RC

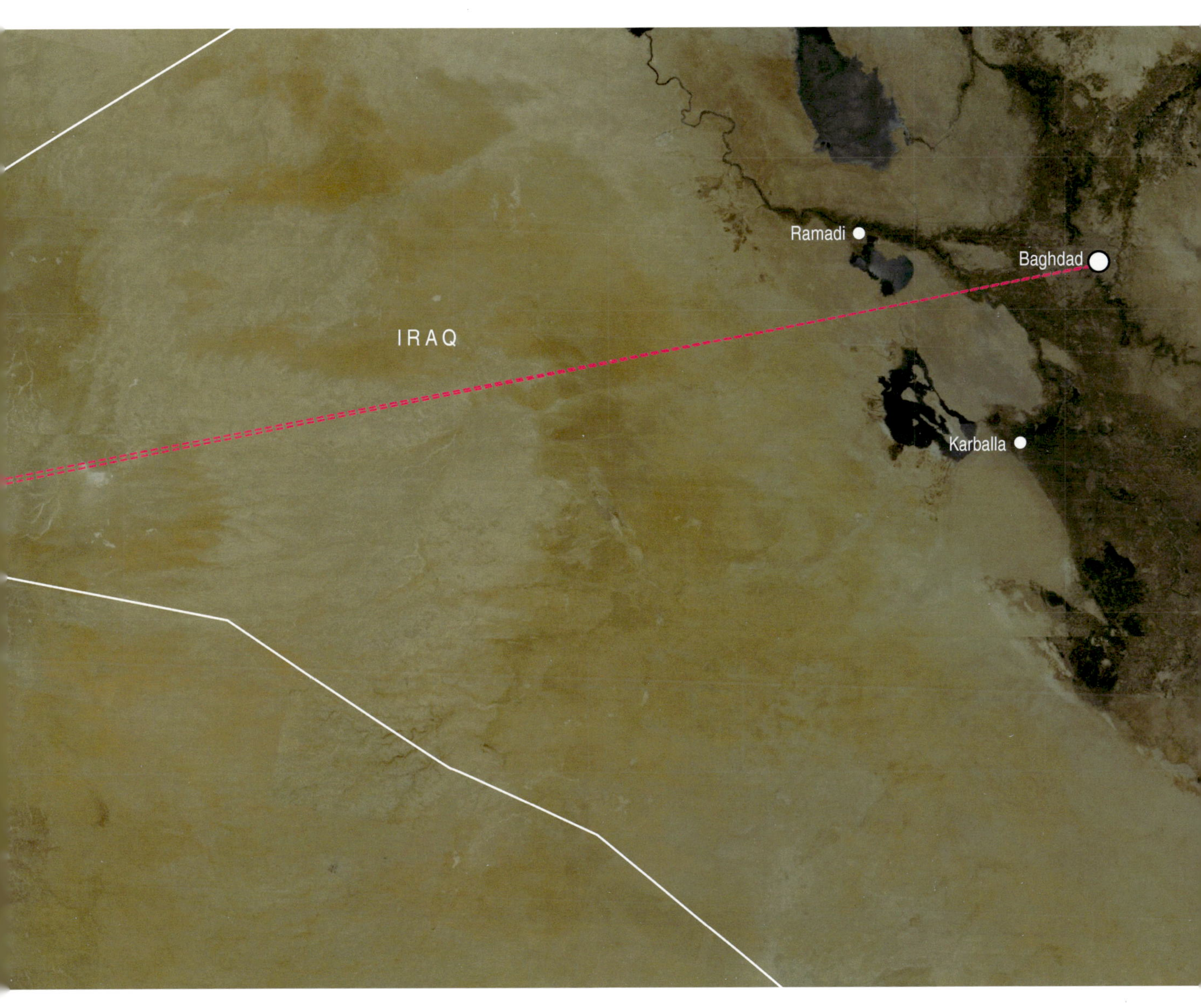

31 MARCH AL-RWEISHED RC - AMMAN
31 MARCH - 2 APRIL AMMAN

2 APRIL AMMAN - JERUSALEM
2 - 6 APRIL JERUSALEM
5 APRIL BEIT SAHOUR

6 APRIL JERUSALEM - RAFAH, GAZA
6 - 11 APRIL RAFAH
9 APRIL GAZA CITY

21 FEBRUARY

AMMAN

It wasn't what you would expect as we came in to land. Thick clouds sent the intermittent flashes from the wing thudding back up the fuselage, penetrating only a few metres, and the ground was only a wall of mist. You could see the raindrops momentarily frozen in their horizontal paths. Eventually, the ground came into contact, unexpectedly, but with a welcome bounce and we arrived.

In the queue for the visas the human shield group segregated at the end desk, all oblivious to where and what was supposed to come to pass only just beyond the arrivals lounge. The sporadic questions and answers were exchanged with a predictably nervous air, and everyone clung together as close as etiquette allowed. And then, with continuing disorder, we filed out into the open street.

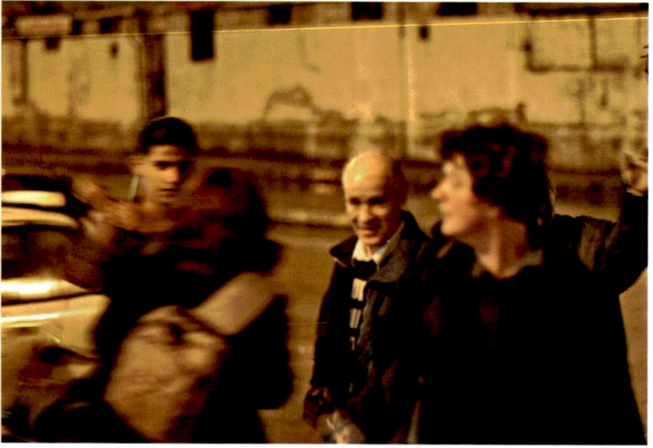

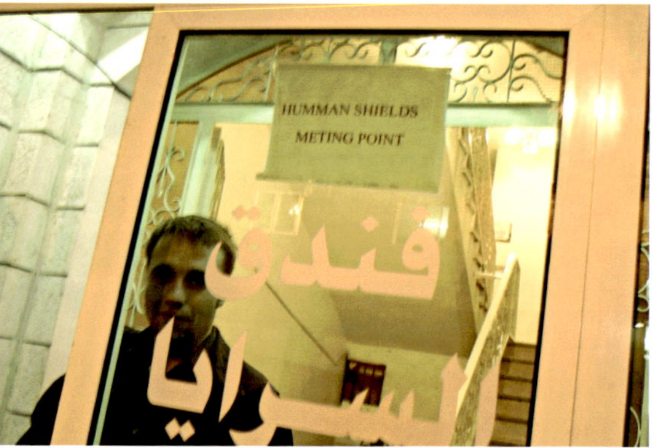

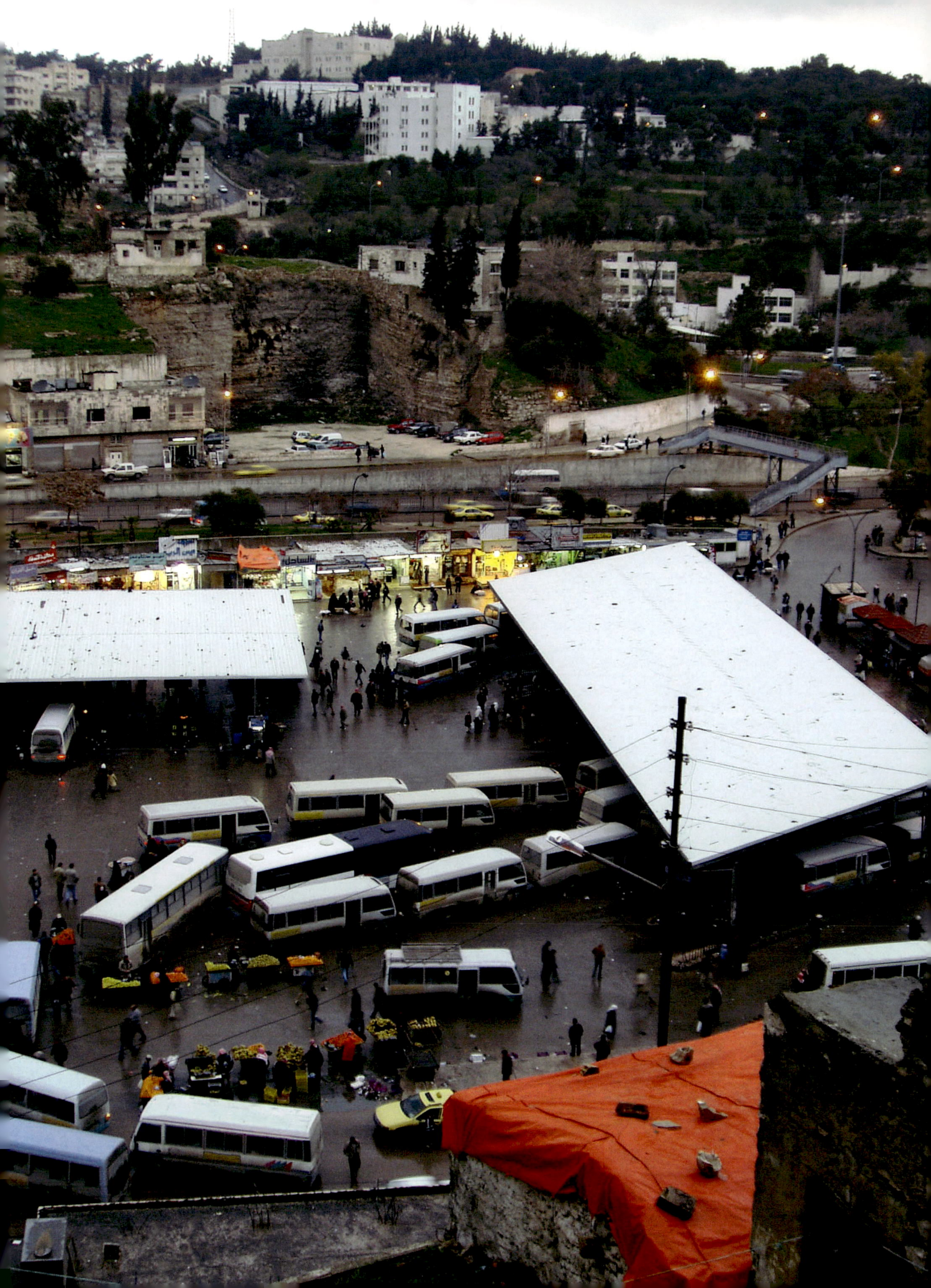

22 FEBRUARY

THIS IS IT. THIS IS WHEN REALISATION BEGINS TO SINK IN:
THE INEVITABLE. WHAT IF THE ONLY THING HAPPENS
THAT I'M SCARED OF?

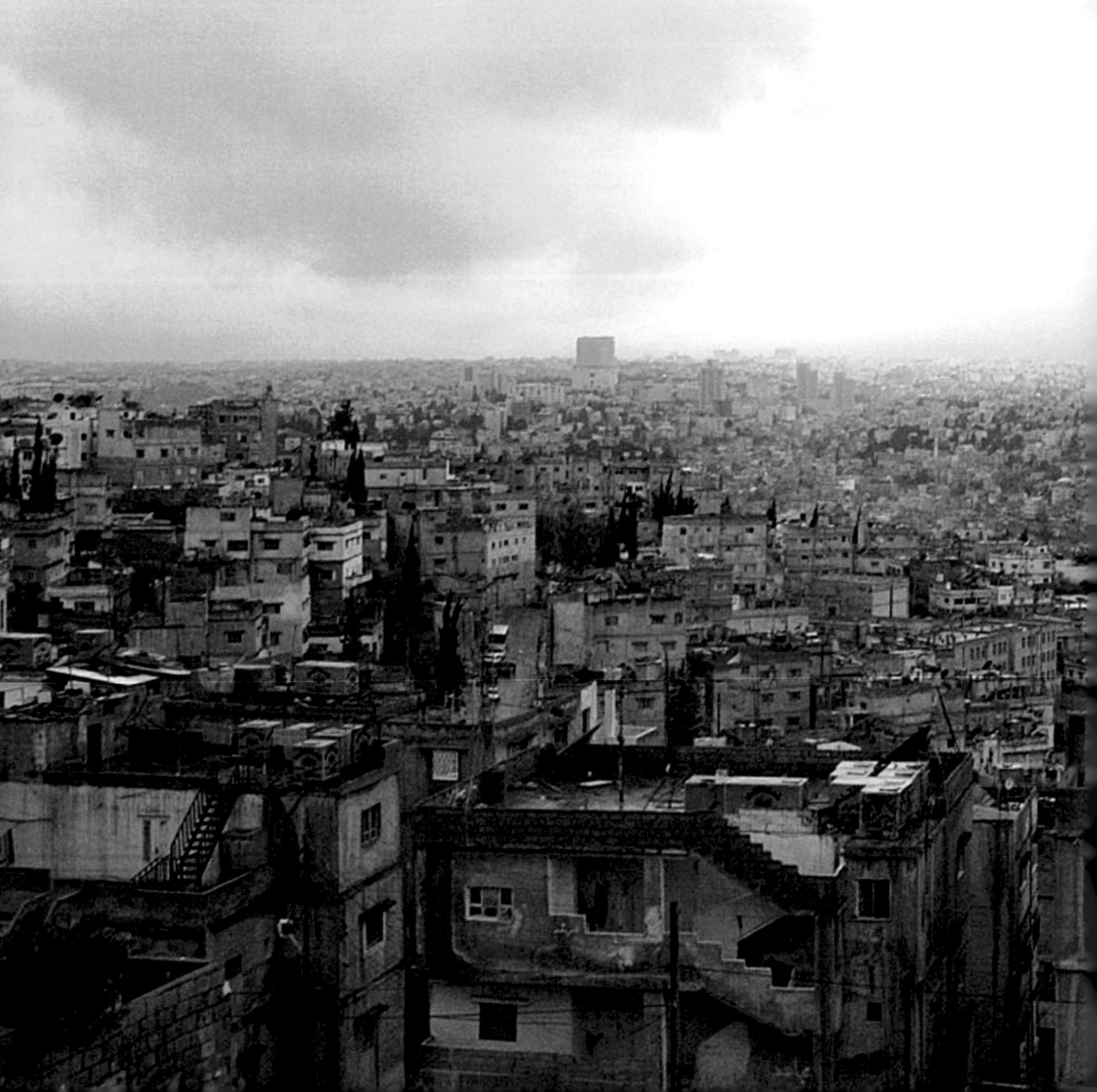

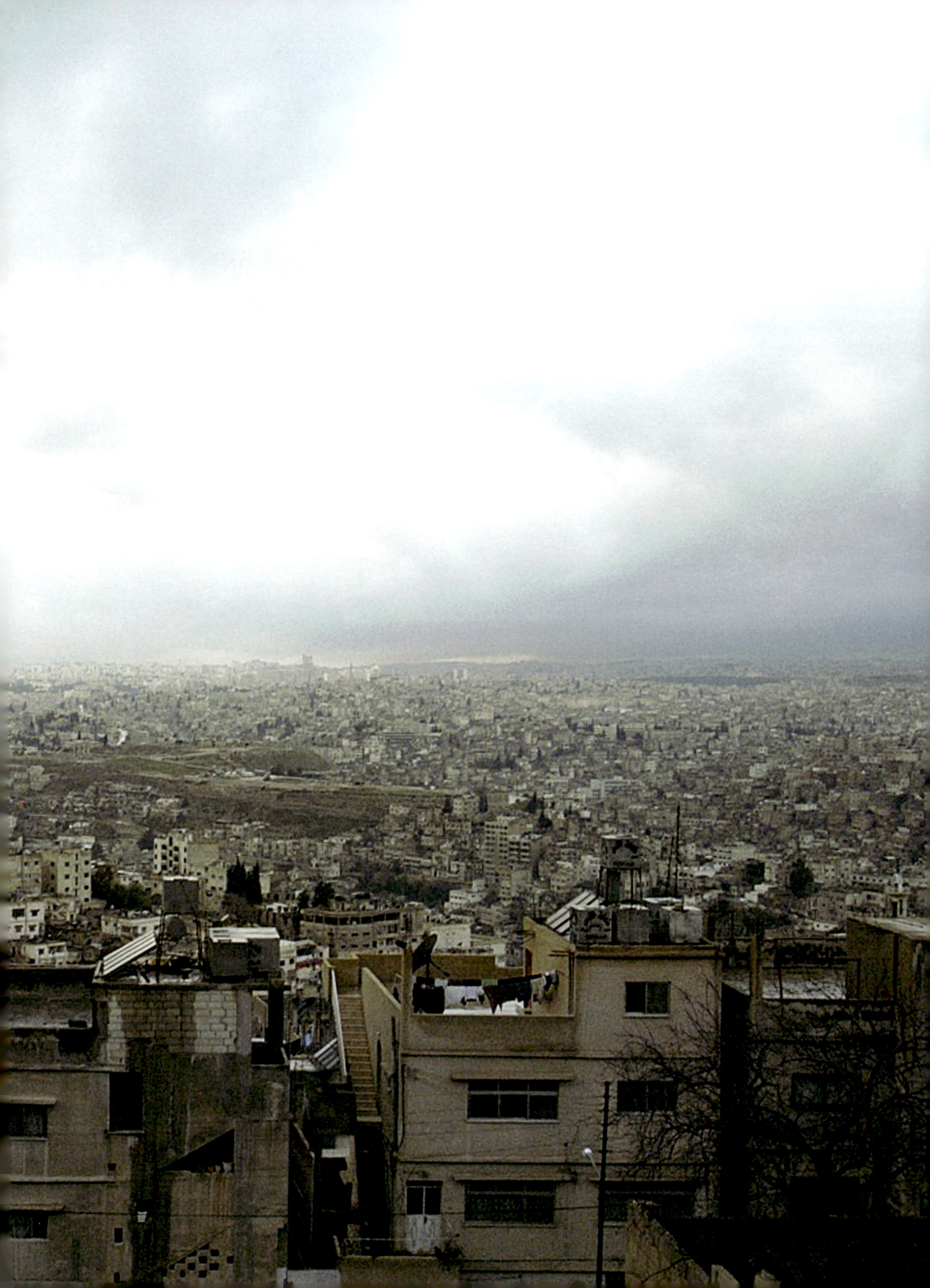

22 FEBRUARY

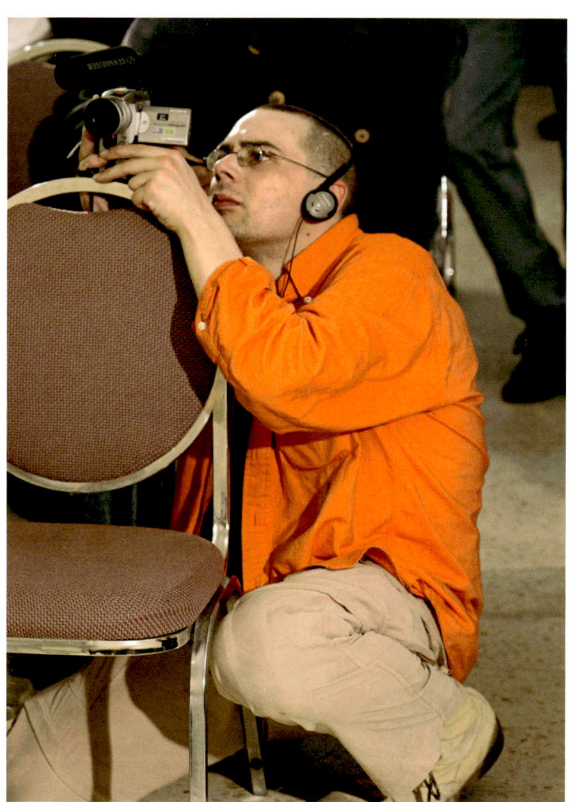

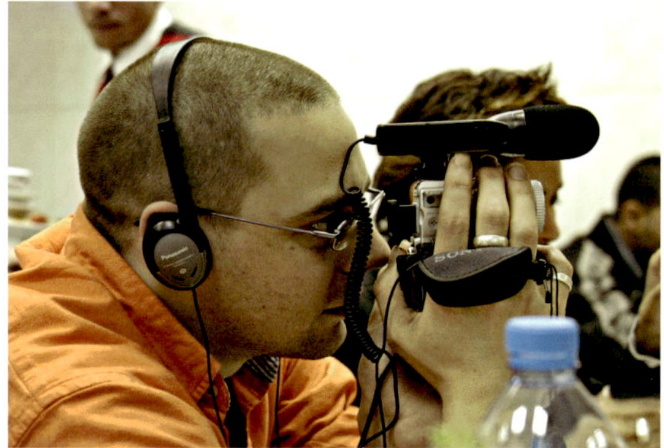

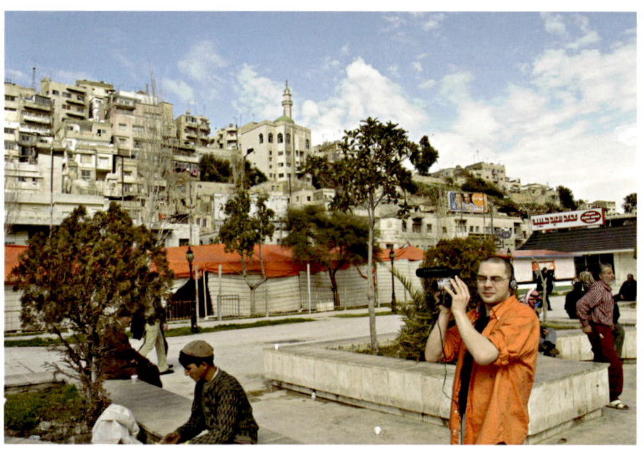

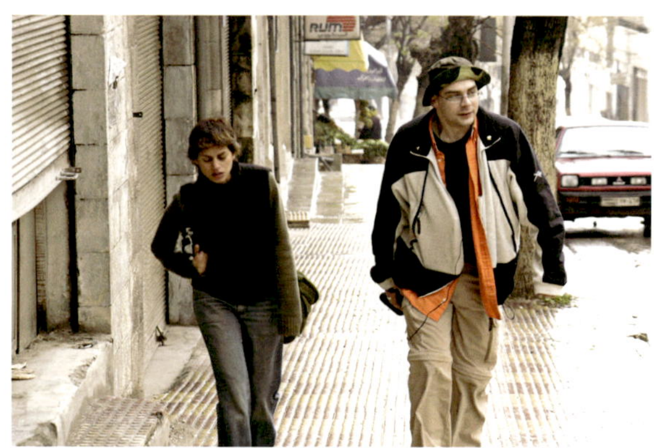

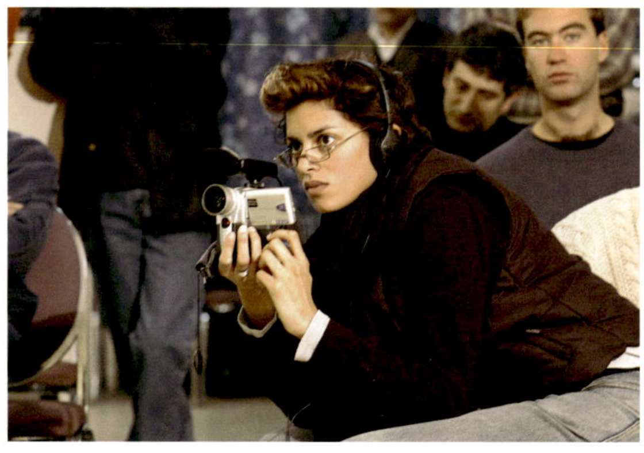

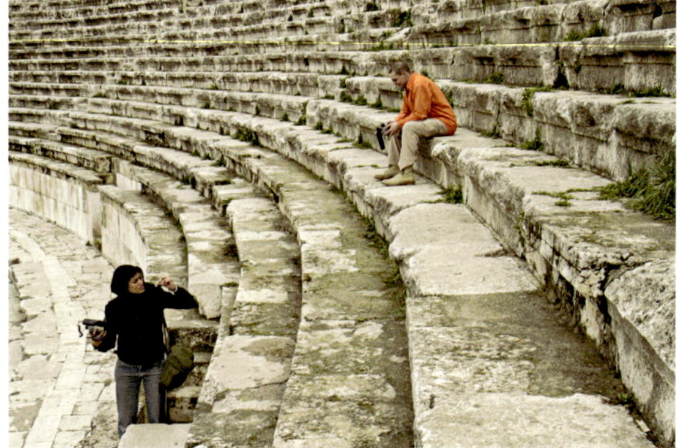

Ian,   22.02.03

Still in Amman, Jordan. Leaving on the 24th for Baghdad. Thought you might like to use these images of the human shields in preparation. Not much yet, but won't be able to get much to you for a while.

There is a huge amount of coverage that will stop when we crossover, though many of us have cameras & DV cameras. Everyone is in good spirits and optimistic, planning their accomodation in Baghdad, though I may try to take the train to Al-Basra after we arrive. Just so you know, the guy in orange is Deitar, the girl with the video cam is Michelle & the girl being interviewed is Uzma.

Hope your having fun in the sanctity of Manchester.

Tom Hurndall

22.02.03

Jocey,

Can you do me a favour and call Ian Holden, the editor of Pulp magazine in Manchester, find out the exact address of Pulp & forward this CD to him. His number is 0161 247 6502 & you will need to tell him who you are. Thanks.

Just so you know, I'm still in Amman and it's saturday night. We're leaving on Monday morning and should be there in the evening and we have accomodation already set up.

Everything is going great & the people all know exactly what they're doing.

See you soon,

Love

Tom

23 FEBRUARY
HUMAN SHIELDS PRESS CONFERENCE, AMMAN

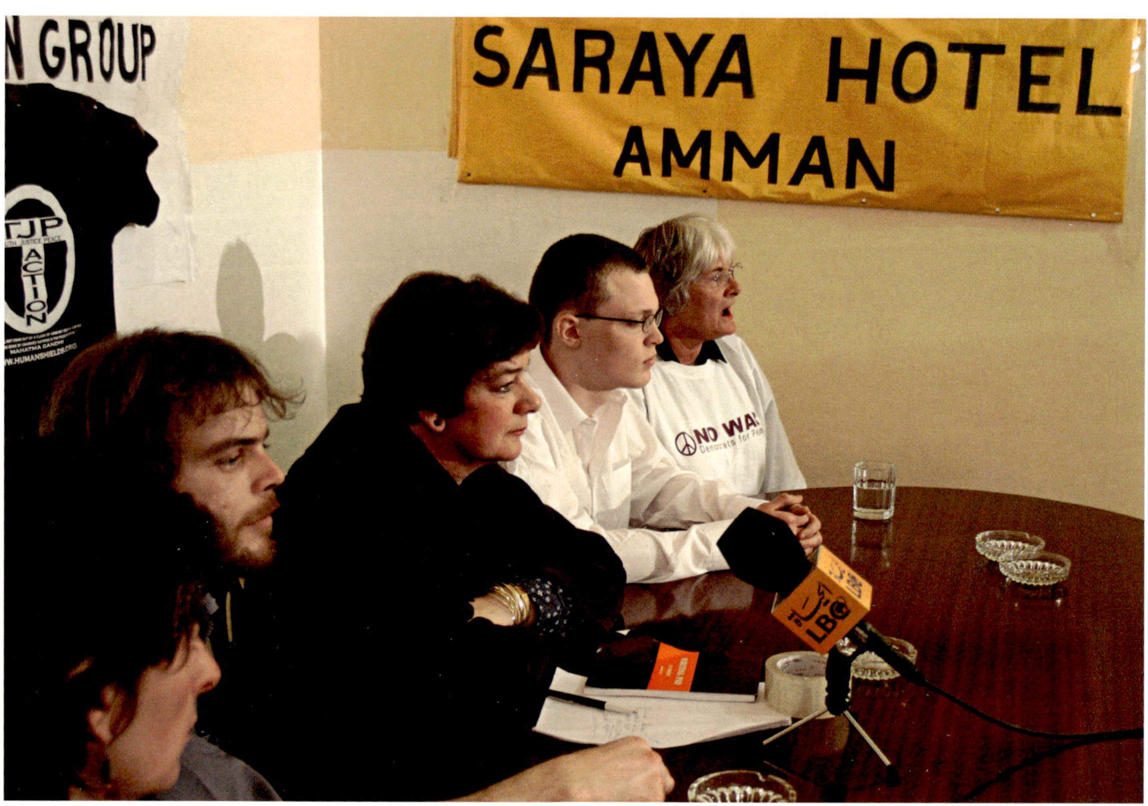

These forty-eight hours since that flight into Amman have ticked by with a sloth that I never thought possible.

Each second, encompassing a lifetime, has eroded slightly more into the will and strength of each of these kids who left so full of romantic ideals and faith.

I've watched as proud young men have waited, destroying themselves with doubts and fears they never knew they had, wilting under the heat.

And yet, never have I been so filled with respect for the courage of everyday people. What integrity it must have taken to stand forward; one amongst a seemingly endless line of indifferent faces, expressions only moved to disapproval.

How they walked, refusing to look back, while feeling the scowls of those around upon them, I will never know.

And on arrival, so full of optimism and self belief… I was proud to call myself one of them.

So, now, as they retreat one by one, can they really be blamed for their love of life?   It is not a choice, no matter their deliberations. It is a fear, and one they overcame until they themselves were overcome. For me they will never return to the masses and I feel blessed to have been offered these slow-moving hours in such company.

This is not their job, not their fight.

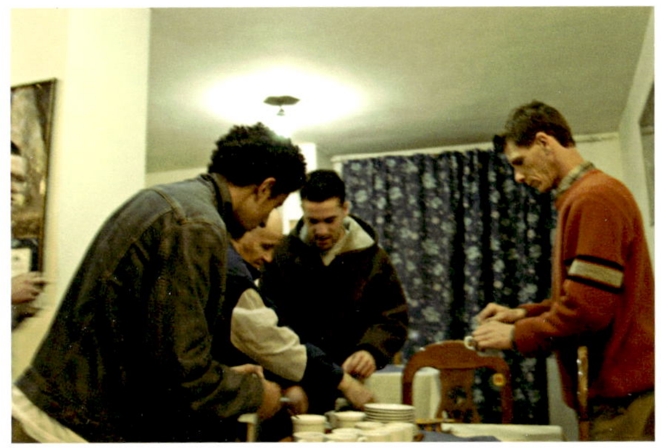
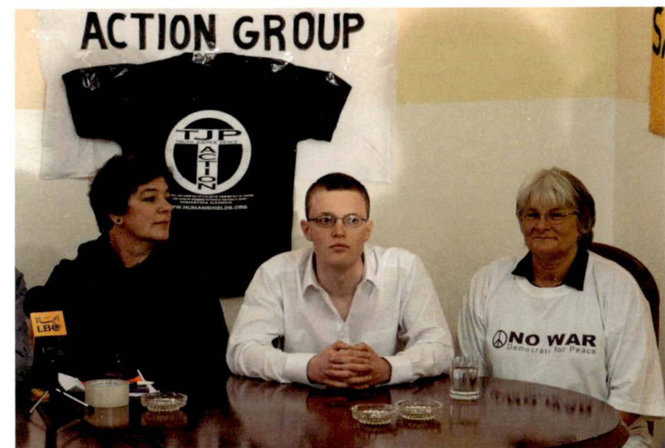

ACTION GROUP
S
NO WAR
Democrats for Peace

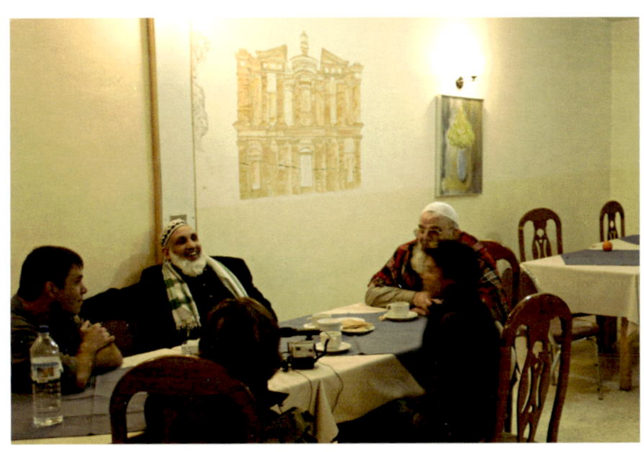
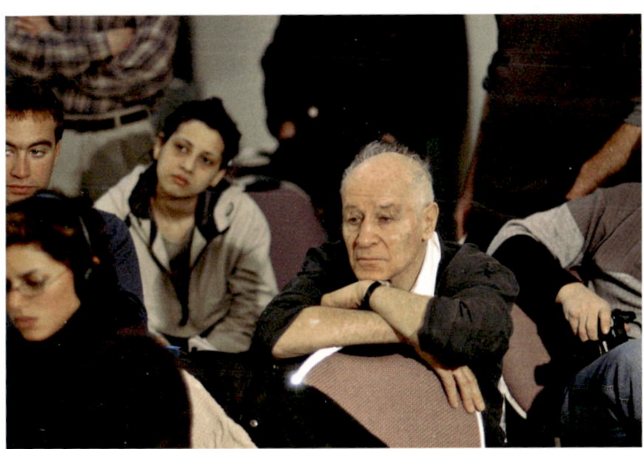

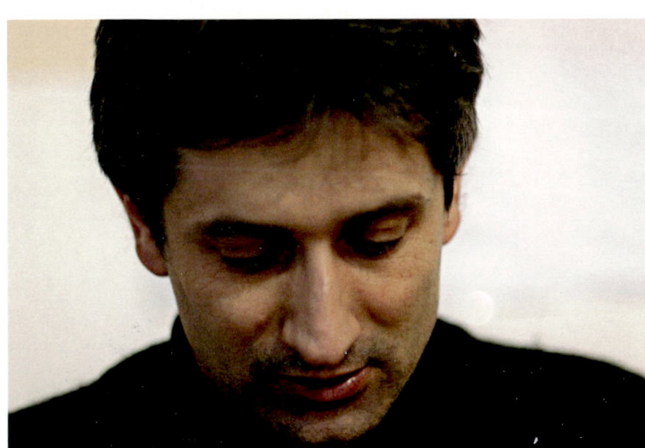
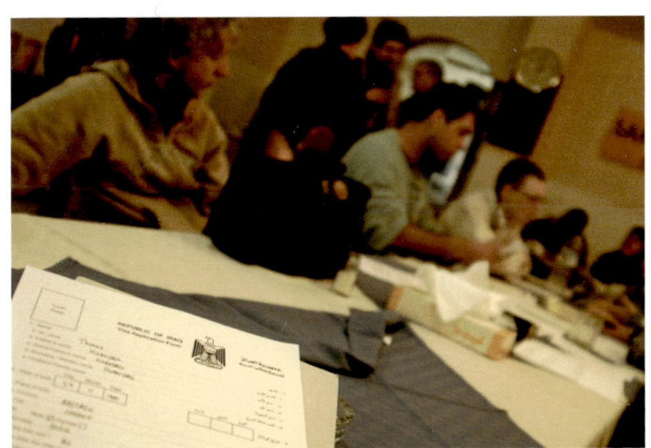

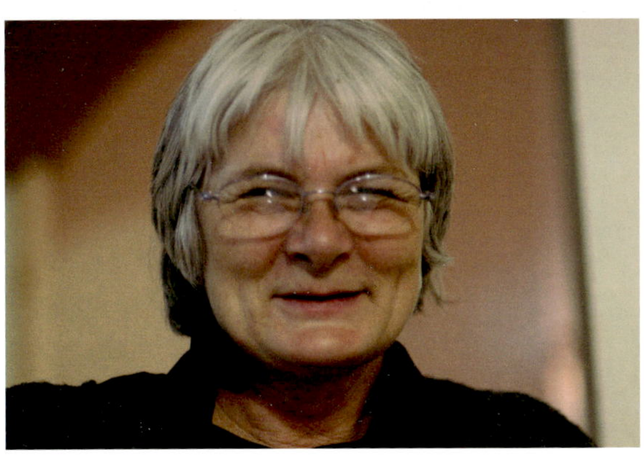
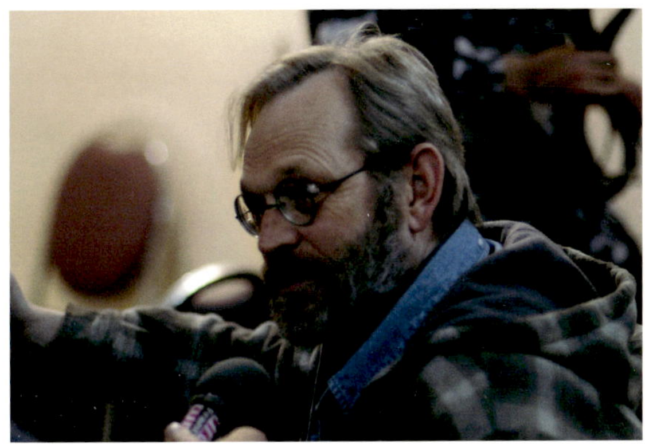

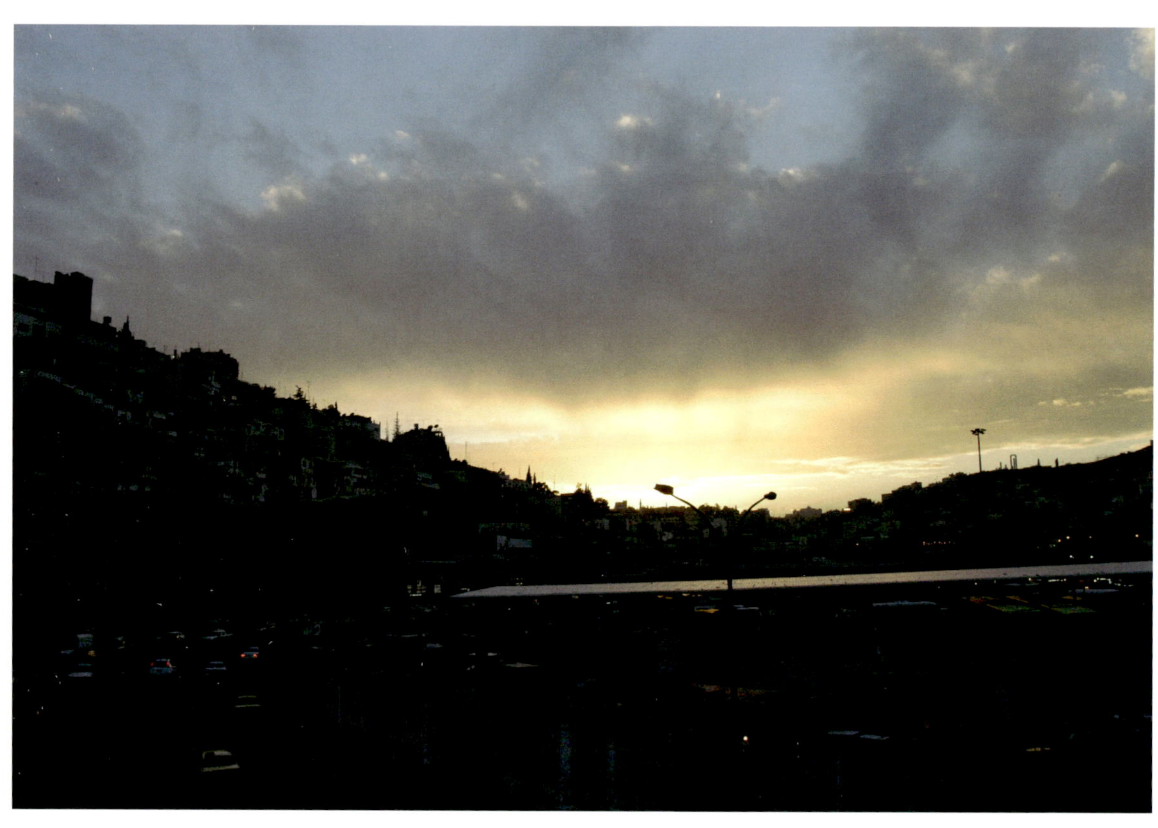

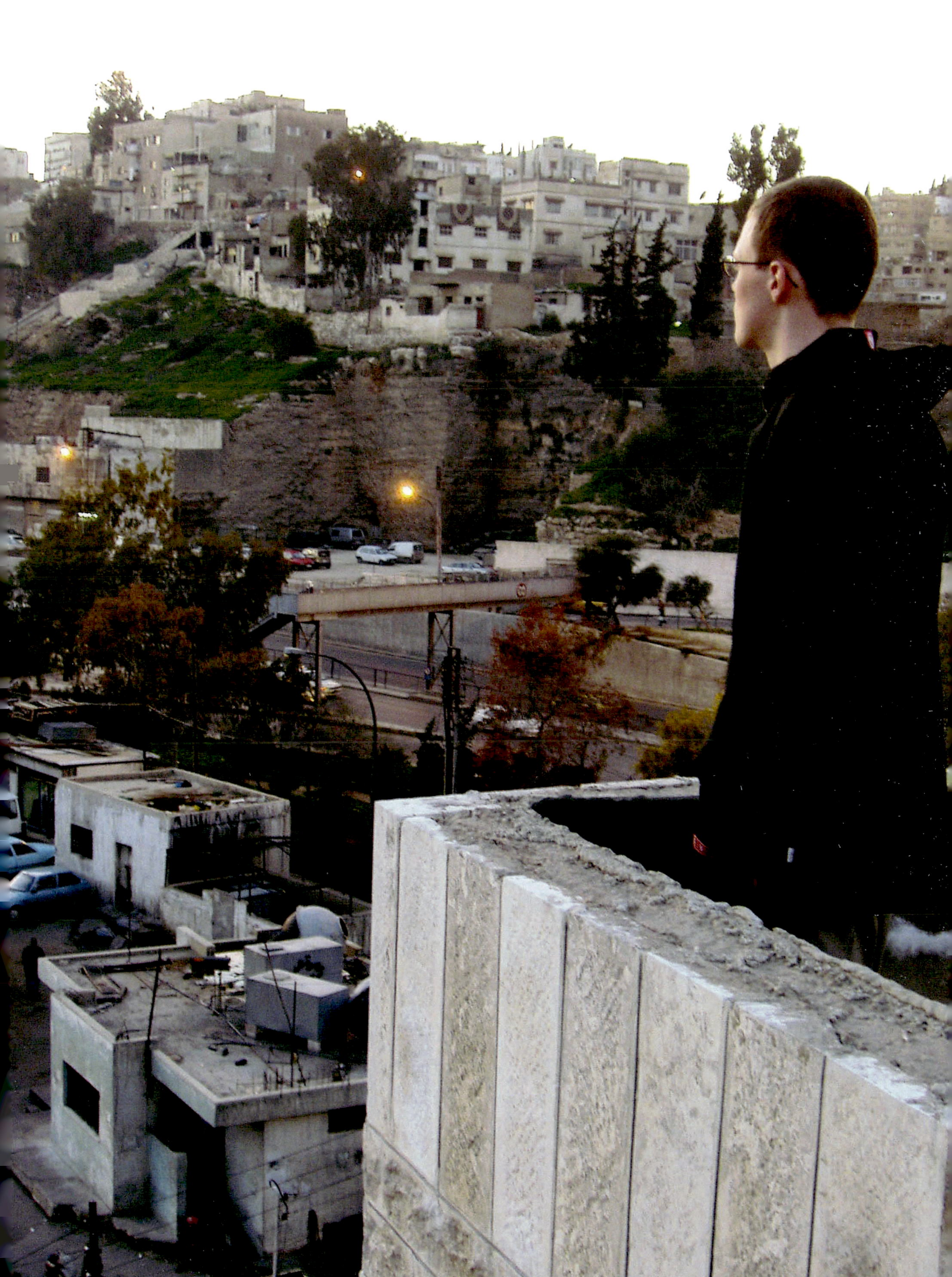

I came out here & I knew the risks.
I knew there would be others that I would travel
& live with & I knew some of them would
get hurt and maybe die. But I didn't imagine
it would get in the way.

BAGHDAD
24 FEBRUARY - 03 MARCH 2003

NOWHERE IN THE WORLD HAVE I EVER SEEN SO MANY
STARS AS NOW IN THE WESTERN DESERTS OF IRAQ.
HOW CAN SOMEWHERE SO BEAUTIFUL BE SO WROUGHT
WITH TERROR AND WAR AS IT IS SOON TO BE.

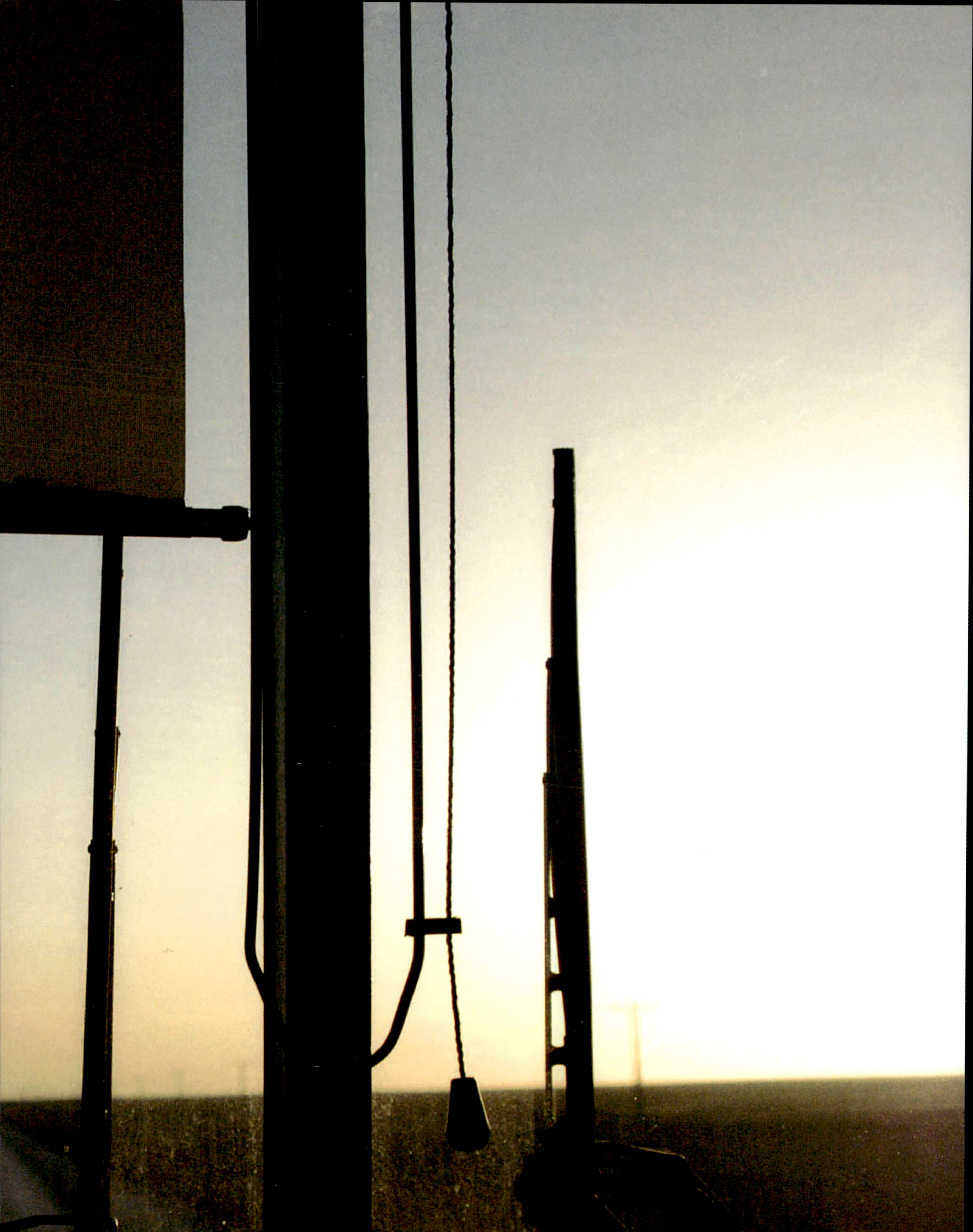

24 FEBRUARY
AMMAN - BAGHDAD

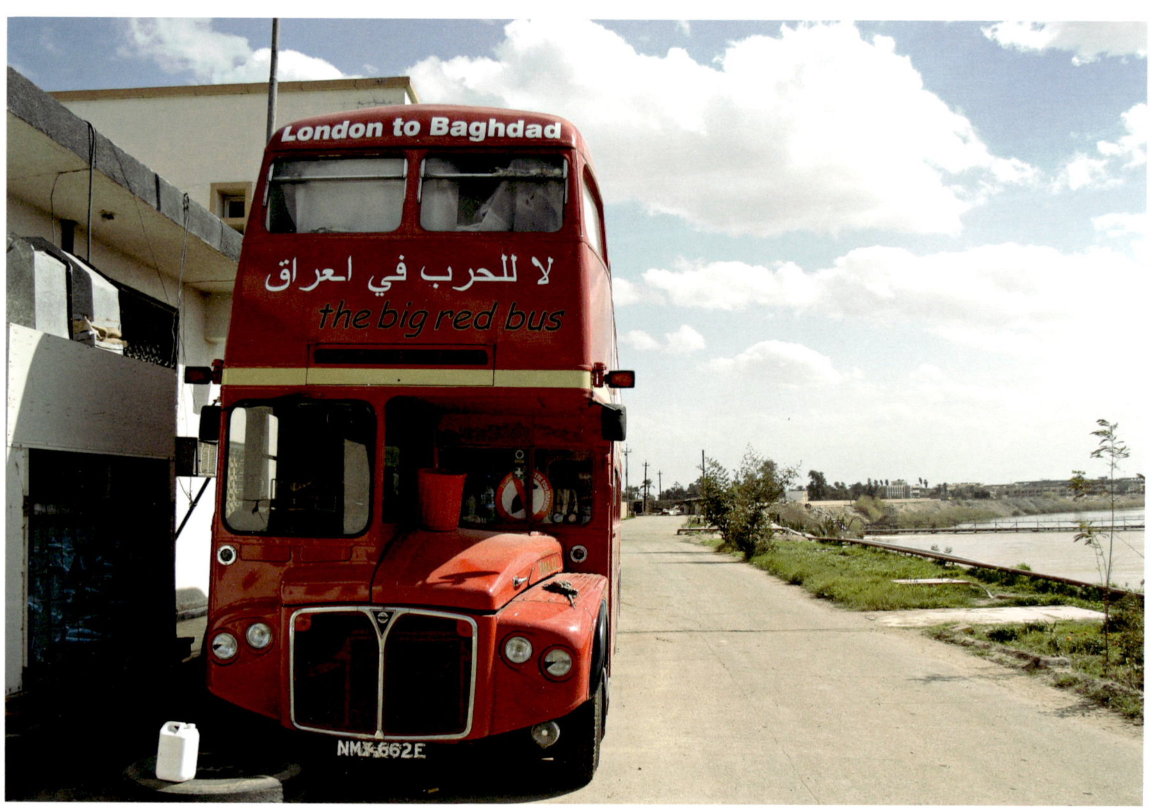

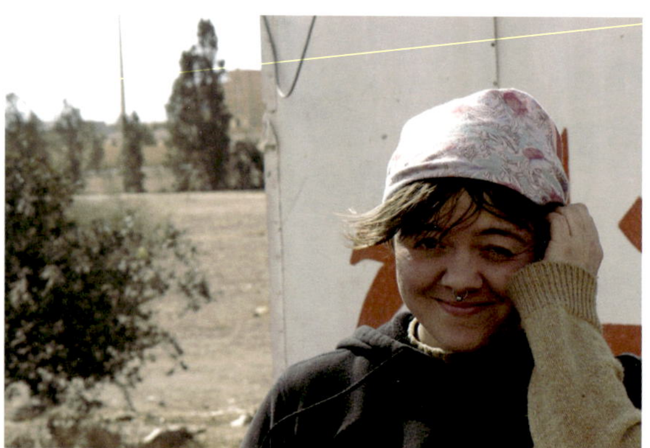

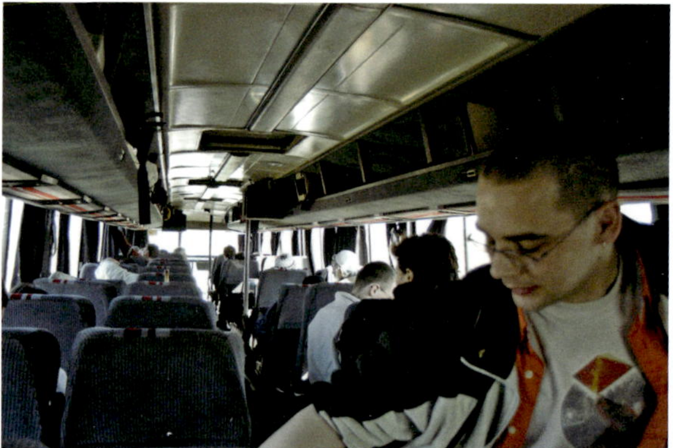

On the way into Baghdad they drank like fish.
There was neither wine nor beer, they drank only
vodka and scotch.

But it wasn't for the sake of celebration, or any
cause you could associate with their tree-hugging
reputation. This was the nervous, desperate drinking
you hope will blind you for just one blissful moment
to the likely fate that awaits you in 500km...400km…
300km...200km, and then, at any moment that you
will never see coming.

And that is the difference with the war we fight.
We have no SA80s or AK47s. We have no defence
and no control. We are caught in the middle. And
both sides hate us.

So how do we deal with it? We drink, in the face
of impotence. We laugh to distract ourselves, and as
we slur our words, we may be able to smile, true for
a moment, able to forget for only the next few hours.

Just one last word to the critics I know will read
this, to those who name us fools and worse. There
is not one of us who doesn't know we didn't eat
our last meal together in the early hours of this
morning. That on arrival we will separate and by
the end of this ordeal there will be more than a
handful of empty chairs and families in England,
Canada, Iceland, Spain, Italy, America, Germany,
Pakistan and others who will be inconsolable with
no answers to the questions they have. And, before
you judge, we love them very much. So much
more than it must seem by these words, and these
actions. We have no illusions and reality is far
harder to avoid for us, with the resonance of the
bombs we know will come, already in our ears.

So in answer to the questions we've all been asked
by the BBC, ITV, WBO, CNN, Al-Jazeera and
others, about why we are all still here, I don't think
there could be one, two, or a hundred responses.

To each of us our own, but not one of us wants to
die. We would lie down for our beliefs in ways
I've never seen before, not in the name of suicide
bombs, or killing, or even defence of who we love,
but for ideals, each our own. And that is how I
judge a person, by the convictions they have and
what is known as integrity.

Here, amongst these people, I swear to my family,
friends, critics and everyone, that I have never
felt such pride in friends' endurance. I call them
friends, though such a label would be to flatter
myself inexcusably.

These people sacrificed friendships to come, may
leave their parents childless and, beyond that, know
precisely what they are doing. One in a million
may have what they had to make it to Jordan,
but after the last 48 hours, stripping away at our
confidence, none but the elite are left. Elite in so
many ways.

The last 48 hours in Jordan have been the most
challenging test of my life and no doubt many
others'. Some could take it, but many stayed
behind. They were the few from a million. These,
now, are the only ones.

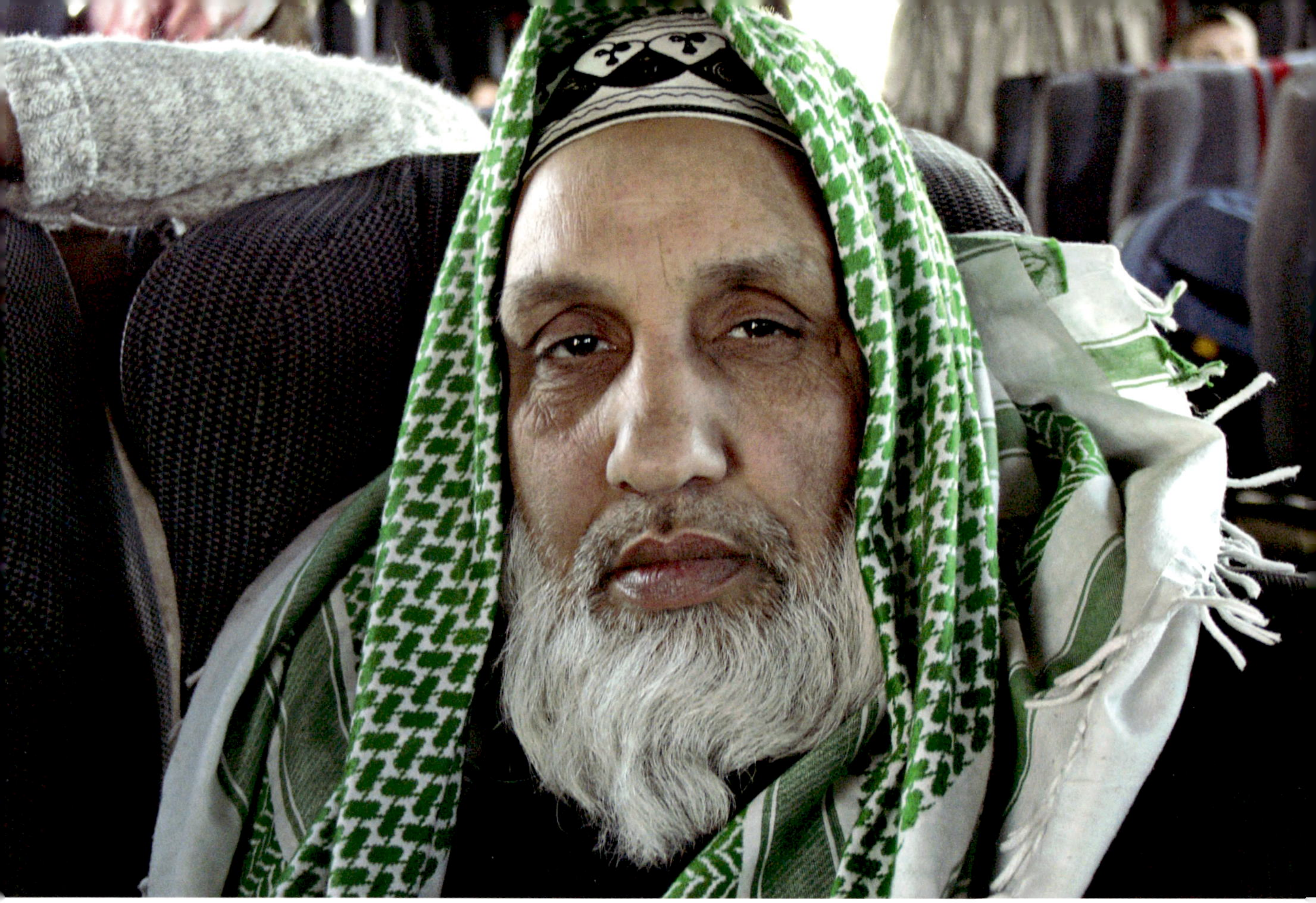

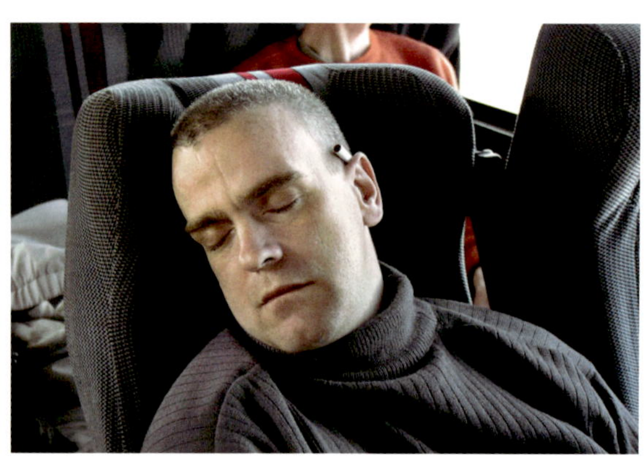

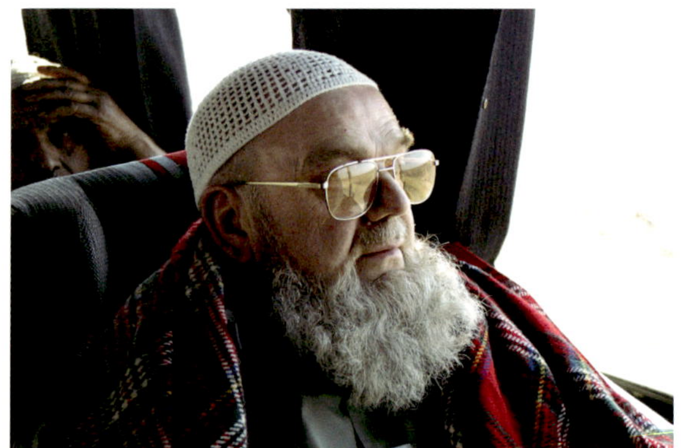

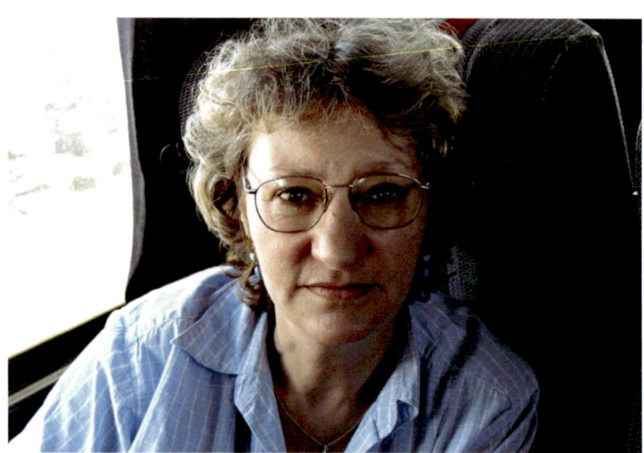

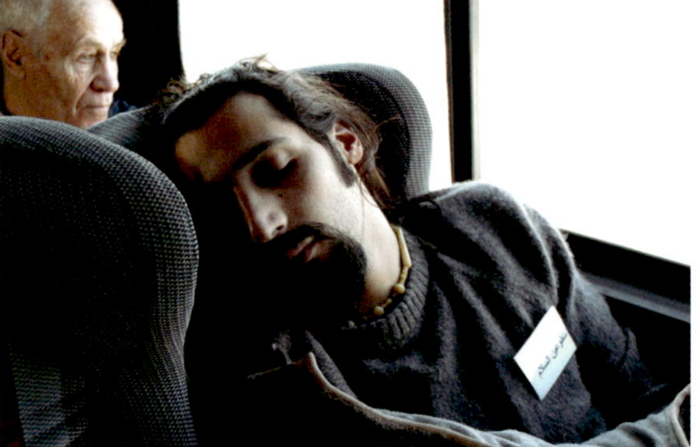

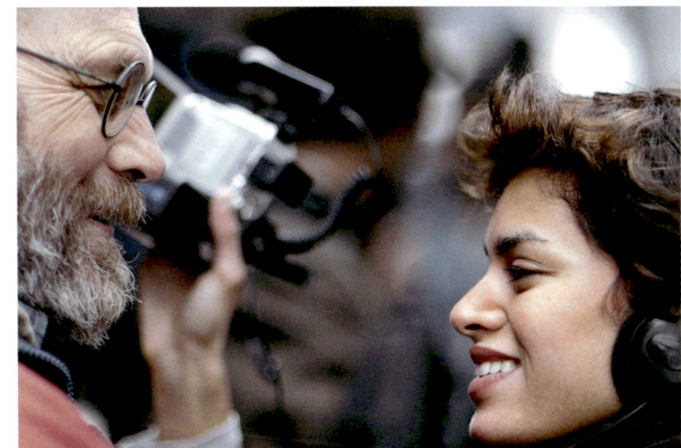

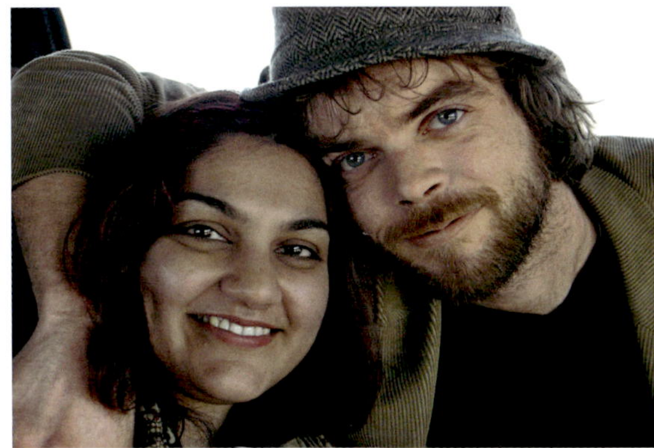

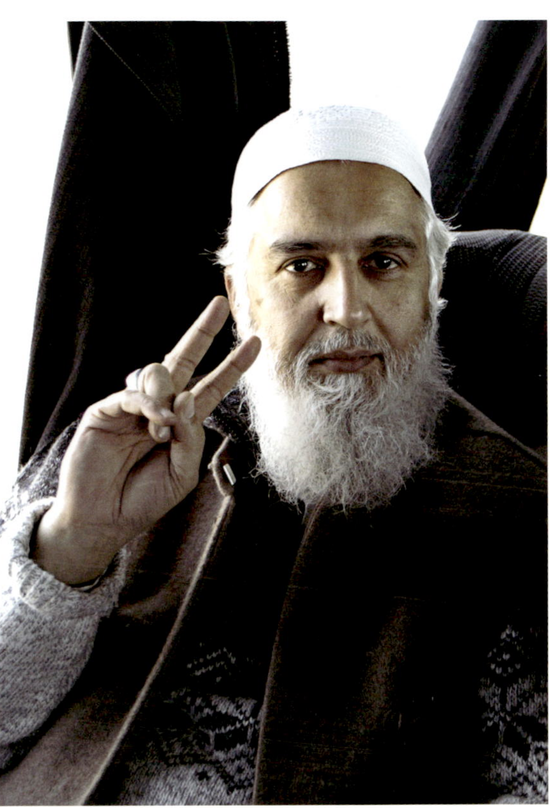

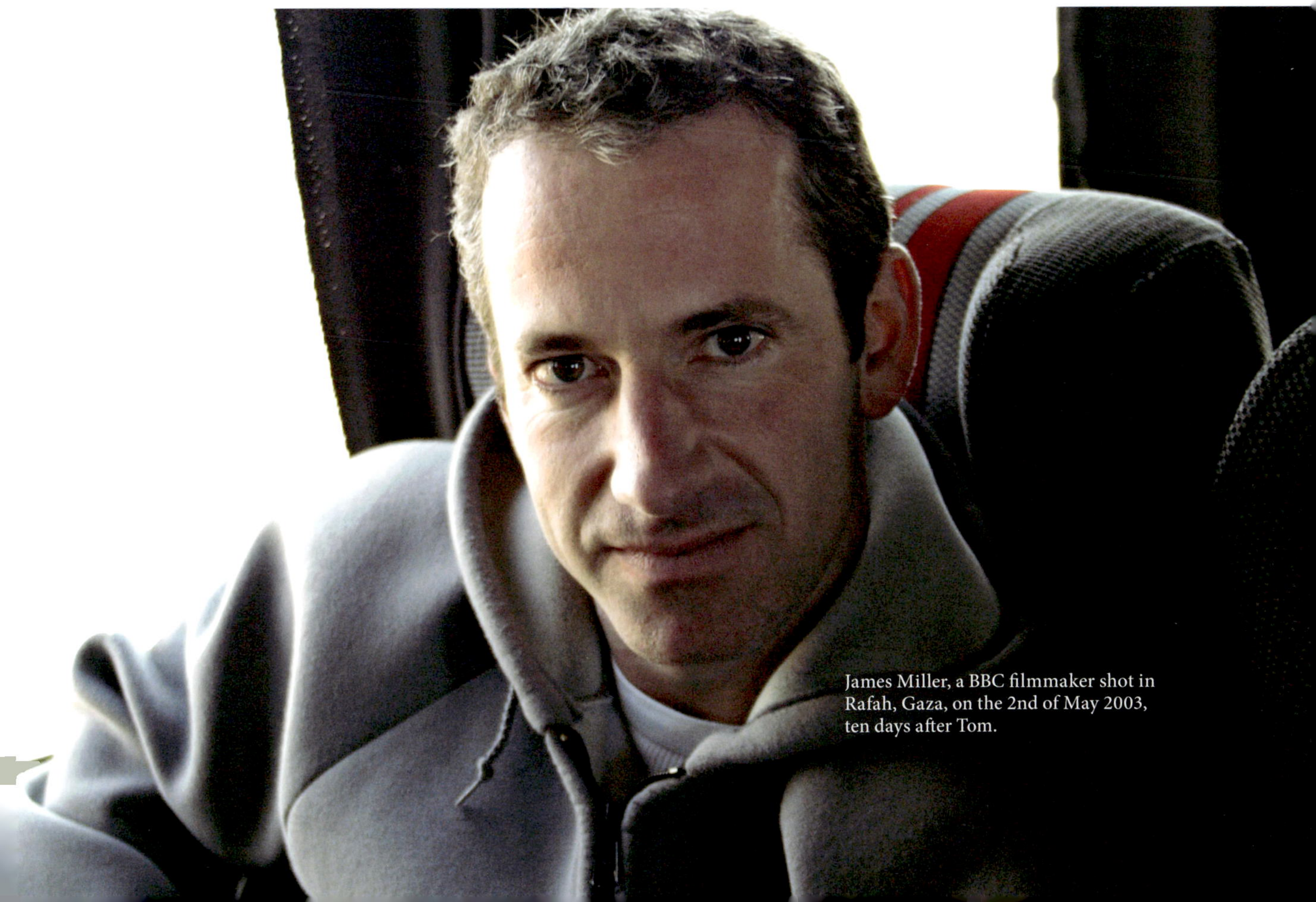

James Miller, a BBC filmmaker shot in Rafah, Gaza, on the 2nd of May 2003, ten days after Tom.

It's been four years since I first looked.
I saw, but didn't look.
On my own, I didn't know to be content,
for not having what I couldn't comprehend.
I just felt it was missing.

My eyes were opened by my friend,
who has always been there, my counsel and ladder.
I owe him all that I am, and he must see it.
Without his cowardice, I would still know fear.
But that's the way he is, and I respect his weakness.

Now I turn to see the past, for you must look
to what has been, and will be; both together.
The future holds the target I will never reach,
and the past, the loneliness I have lost.
In this pair, I know what I have now.

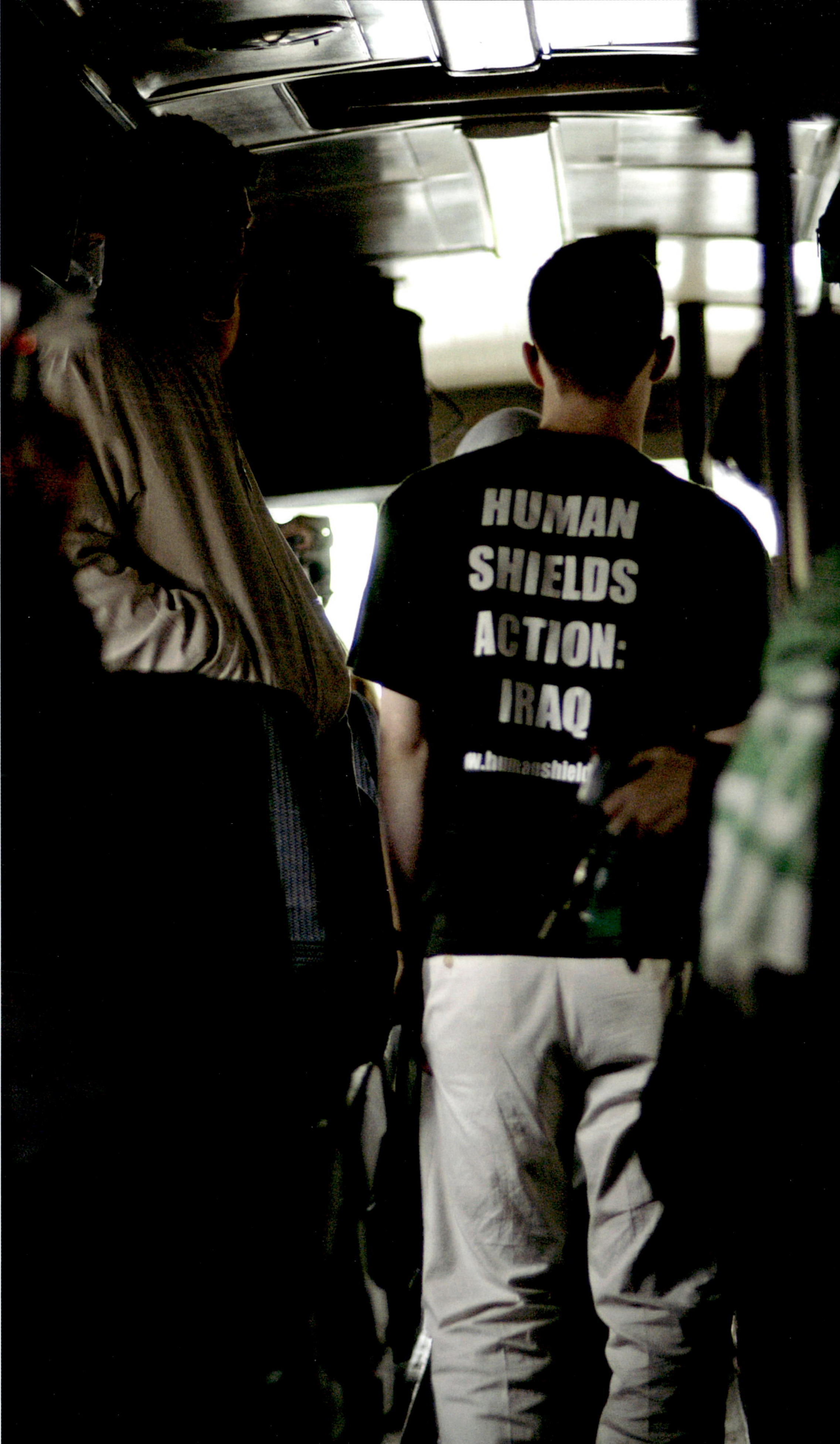

HUMAN
SHIELDS
ACTION:
IRAQ
w.humanshield

Possibly the two longest days of my life were spent two weeks ago in a hotel room in Amman, capital of the Jordanian Kingdom. You know the type, where you can use phrases like 'the seconds passed like hours' etc… And yet, strangely, I can remember little of my thoughts.

I spent around fifty-four hours in between touch-down at the airport and the coach leaving the Eastern border. You might even have called it a changeover, except I didn't close my eyes to sleep for a minute and every second was used in preparation. It was chaotic and rushed and nervous. I didn't own a moment for myself, so in that way, as you would expect, time flew by. But the strange thing was that, underneath, things were so different. In the obscure depths of my mind my thoughts ticked over with agonising patience. Fears, expectations, hopes and guilt. Every individual emotion I had ever experienced wracked my mind at some point, and their intensity didn't let up in the least.

Around me I watched men and women wilt under rumours that filtered through to us, and what they felt I could only imagine was on a parallel with myself. Some of the strongest minds I have ever met gave way and broke, their doubts eating away at their pride, at their courage. One by one they declared they wouldn't board the coach come Monday morning. But by the end, not one of them had failed to imagine the worst. Each had been to his/her own personal Hell, and only some had returned. I guess it is something you have to experience to know, but there is no metaphor in the statement that, from what we were hearing, to not board the coach would be the last chance to back out of a situation from which you stood a fifty-fifty evens chance of surviving.

With that in mind, come zero hour, the only way that I could leave my room was pure and true denial. When a man must lie to himself to do what he knows he should, that is when you know he is terrified. And I don't scare easily. I don't believe it takes 'the moment before death' to leave your life flashing before your eyes, only enough to make you contemplate it really ending. I only know that not a thought I ever had was left in its grave during the four hours to the border.   Everything came back to me, and as I wrote a letter to my youngest brother, apologizing and telling him how much I loved him, there was no way I could hold back the tears. So many sources had reported that on arrival we wouldn't be permitted to leave until killed by American bombs, or freed by American soldiers. The irony of our defence of Iraqi people and fear of Iraqi government was, in retrospect, highly amusing. It is only a shame that we were labouring under such false pretences as we entered Iraq.

By the end of the several-hour long ordeal that was Iraqi customs, the twenty-two left had known each other for around sixty-eight hours. For the first time since arrival I was able to relax. It's strange that when you know something is out of your control, you might as well sit back and enjoy the view. With that in mind, I began thinking of my company. It occurred to me that I had never been a part of a group of people that I respected so much. Few, if any, conformed to their tree-hugging image, none were political extremists and only a couple had ever before been any form of activists. It struck me that these were absolute representatives of those who attended the march the week before in London. They were normal in every way, except that they had the courage to take the protest one step further and still keep it peaceful. In that way, and through that courage,

I felt proud to be associated with them and guilty for my differing motives for being there. There was a paramedic, a lawyer, a photographer, a couple of students, a teacher, a preacher, a social-worker, and I am sure that there was one in particular who was CIA (human shields and aid groups are the only real means of obtaining an Iraqi visa, and the Central Intelligence Agency is no exception).

Among our group were the youngest and oldest that would enter into Iraq in any group associated with the Human Shields. Eric is seventy-four, and from Camden, London, and Nathan is twenty and lives just outside London. Simply, they were diverse. But it was not only their ages and professions that differed, but their ideals and motivations. Some were there to 'stop the war', some were there to 'defend' hospitals and schools, some were there to simply stand beside the Iraqi public (including a very select few to stand beside the 'regime'), and some, like myself, were there to document and provide coverage. Simply, they were the handful out of millions who had the courage to protest even when their lives and freedom were on the line, and, while my faith was mildly lacking before, when I return to Manchester, any suggestion of their 'stupidity' would result in a, probably violent, rebuttal from myself. Those who know me know that I do not give out praise easily, and I dislike people as much as most dislike me. But these people were heroes in my eyes, and those of anyone who knew them.

And that was where we stood as we began the eleven-hour journey from Amman to Baghdad. Four to the border and seven after.

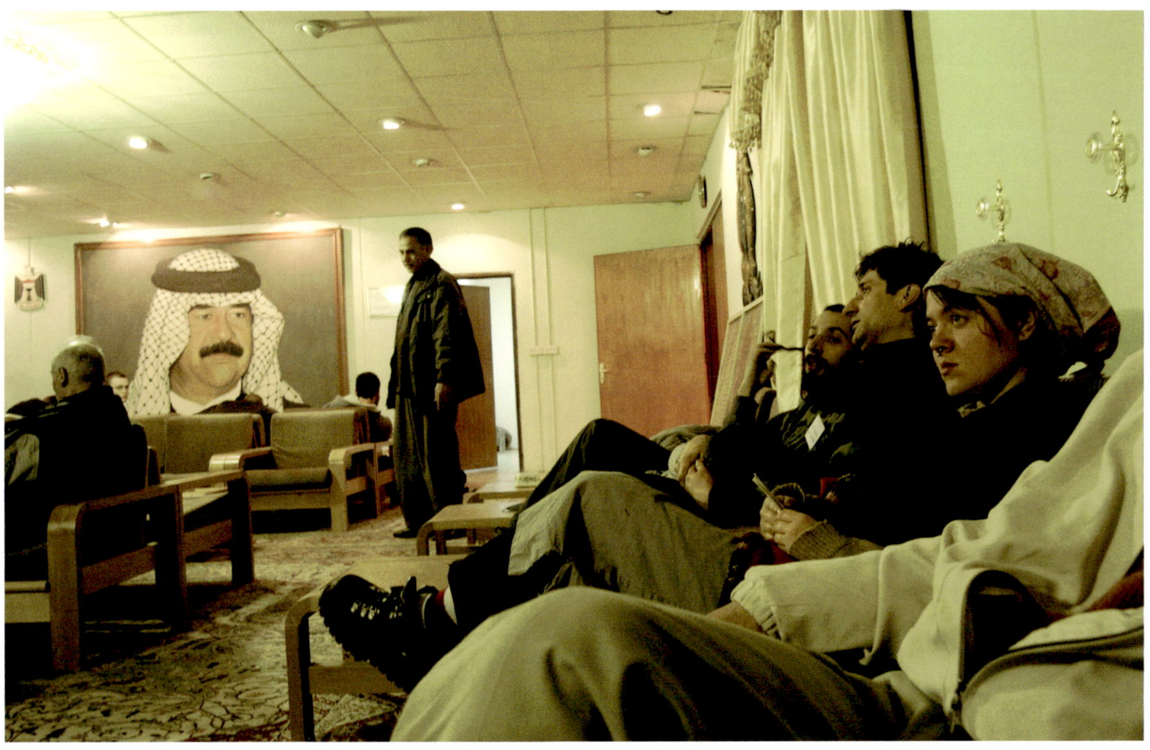

25 FEBRUARY

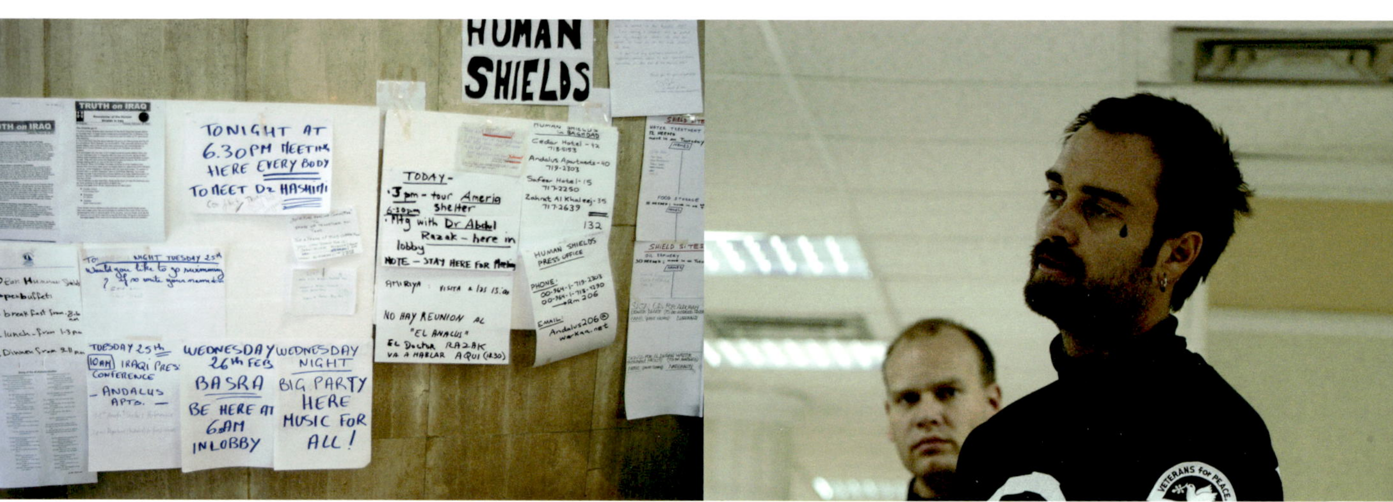

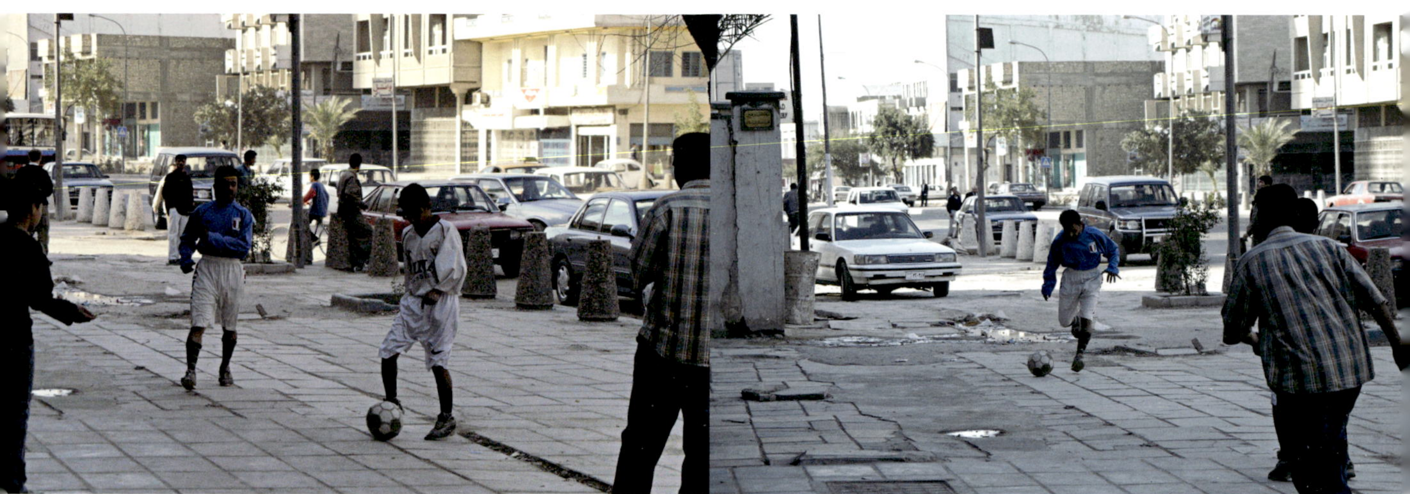

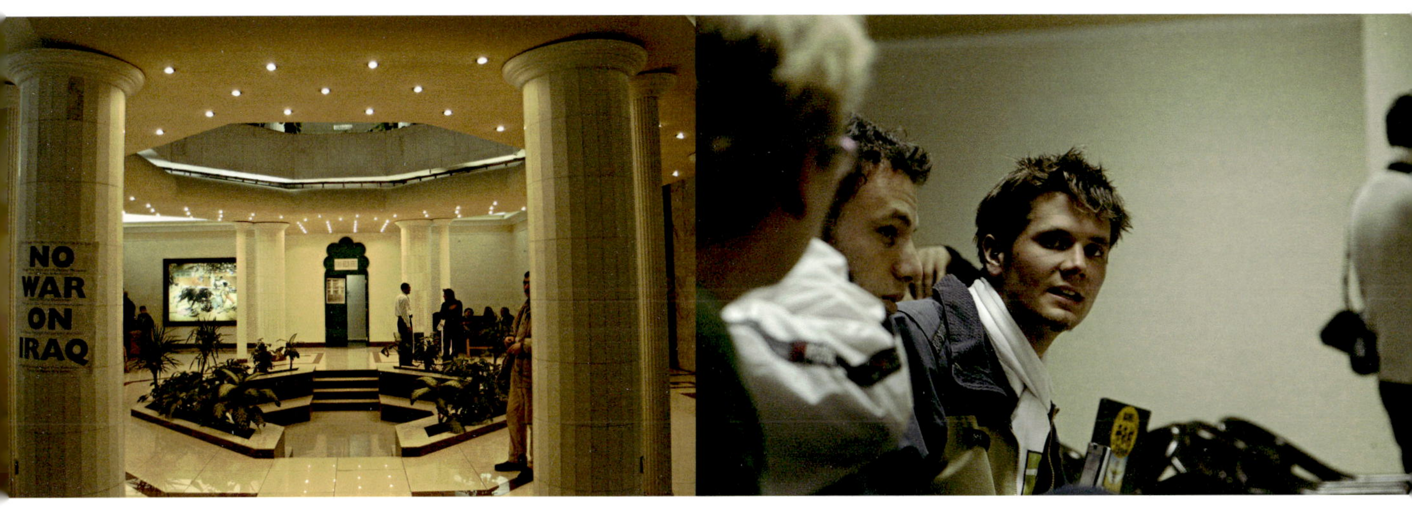

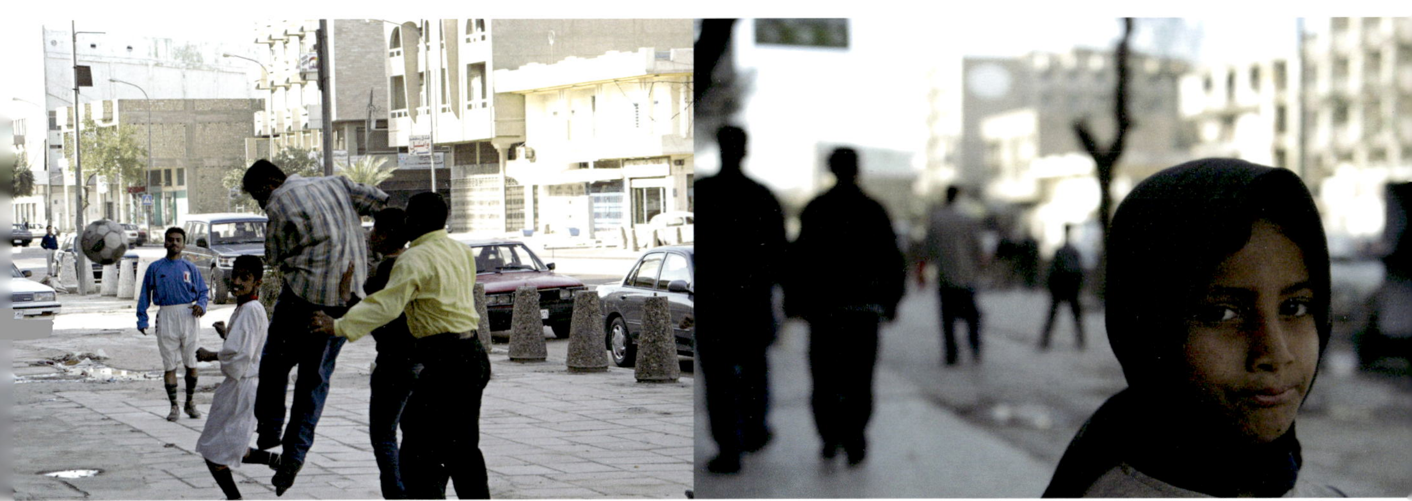

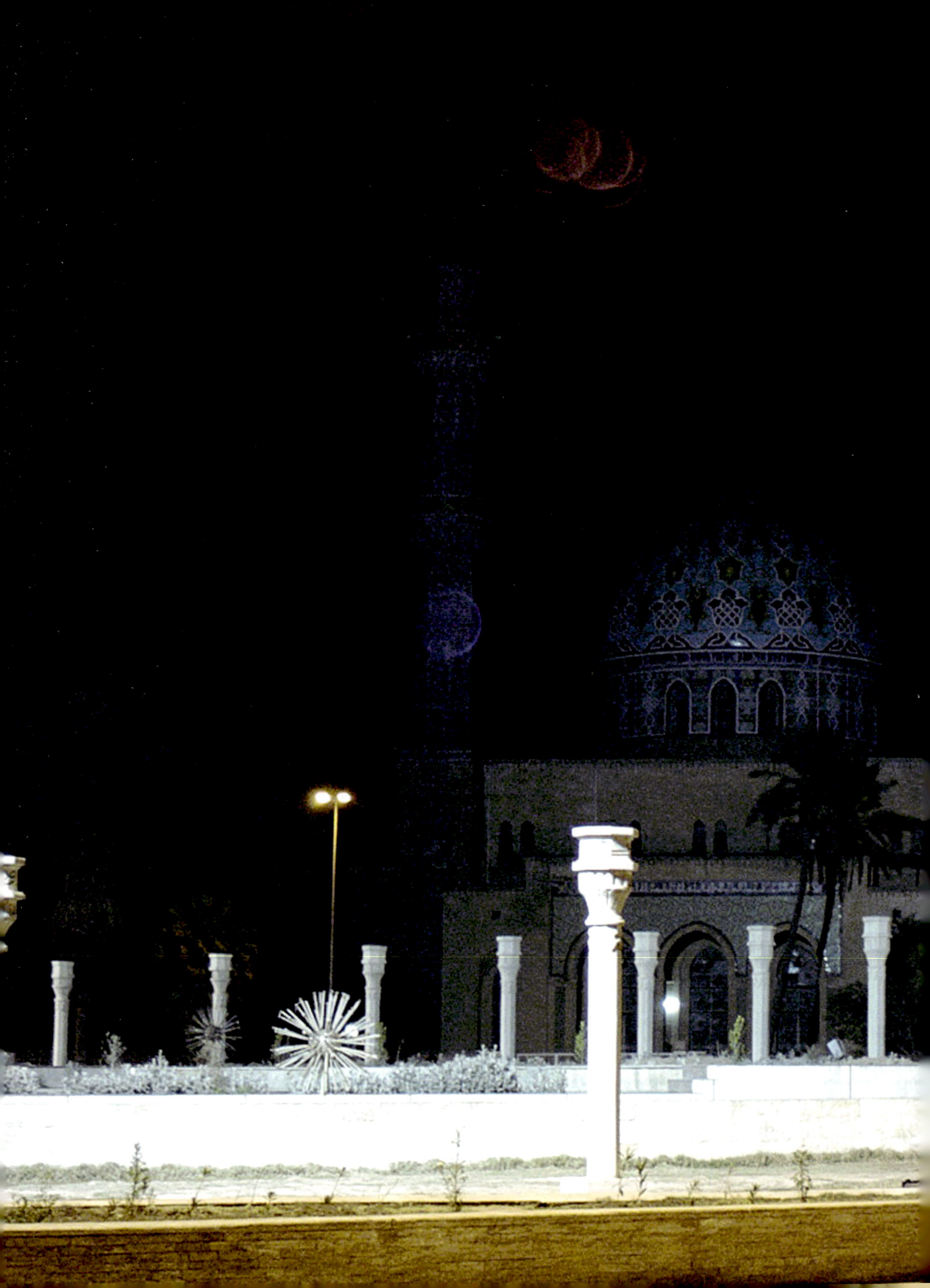

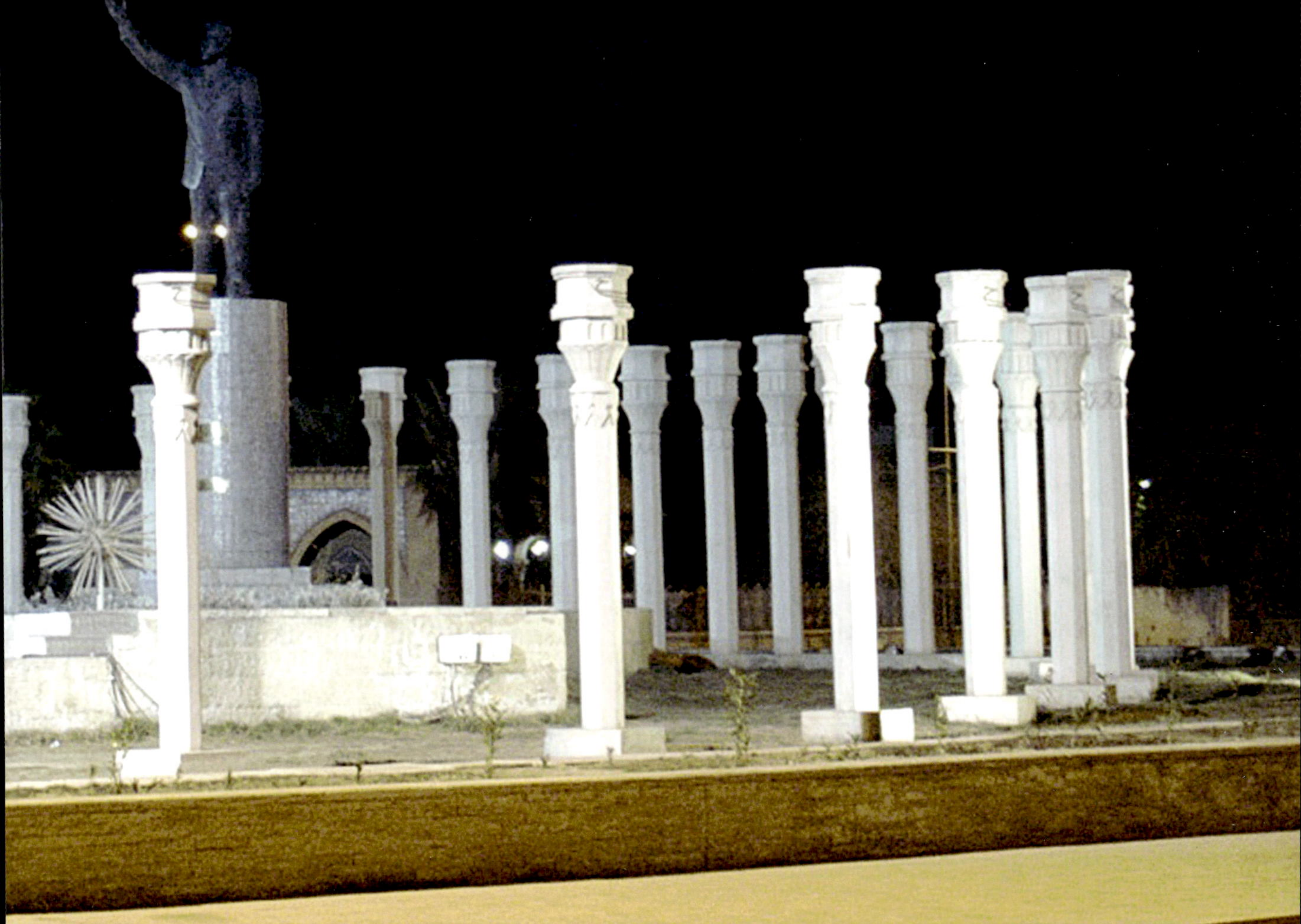

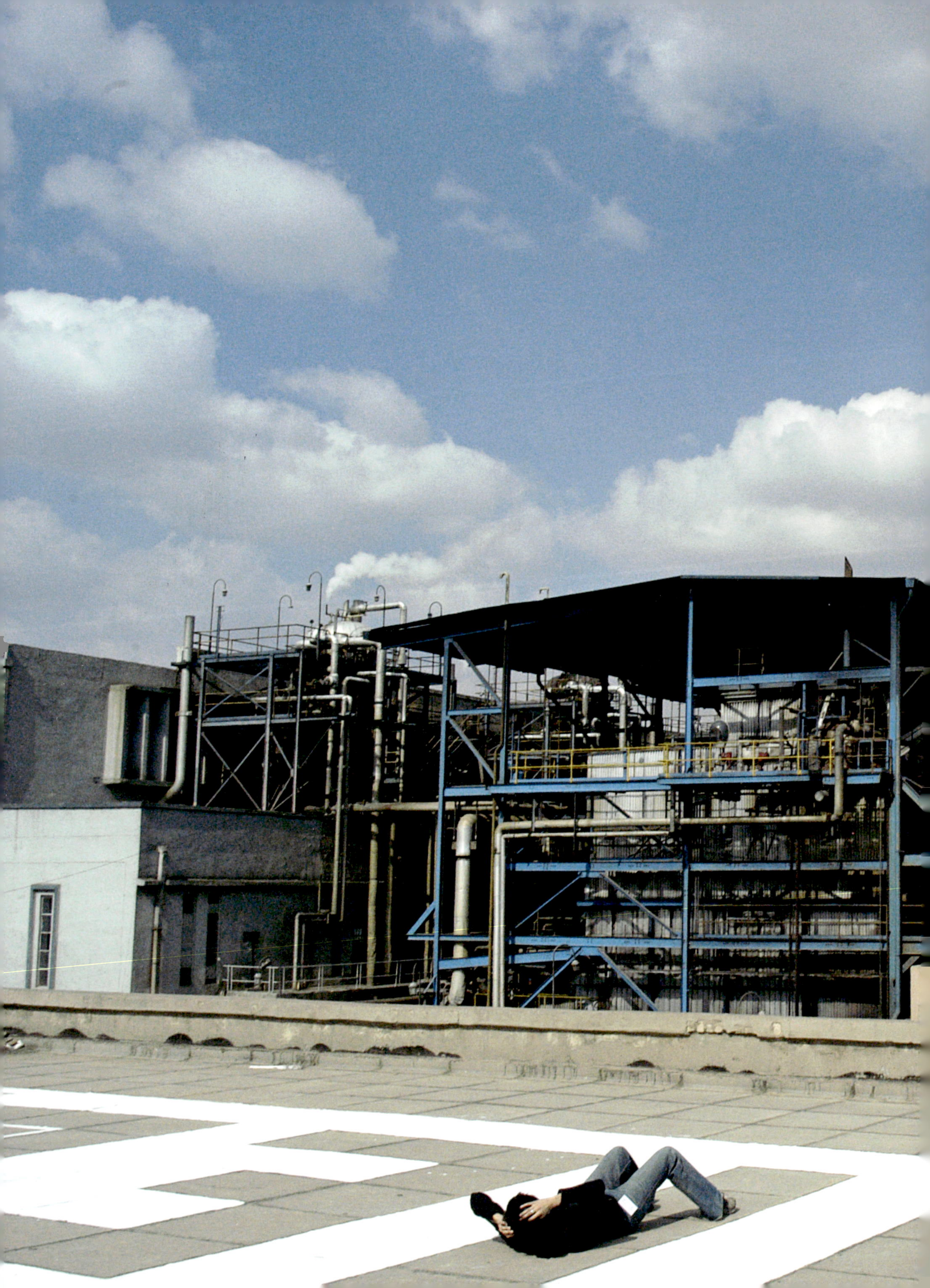

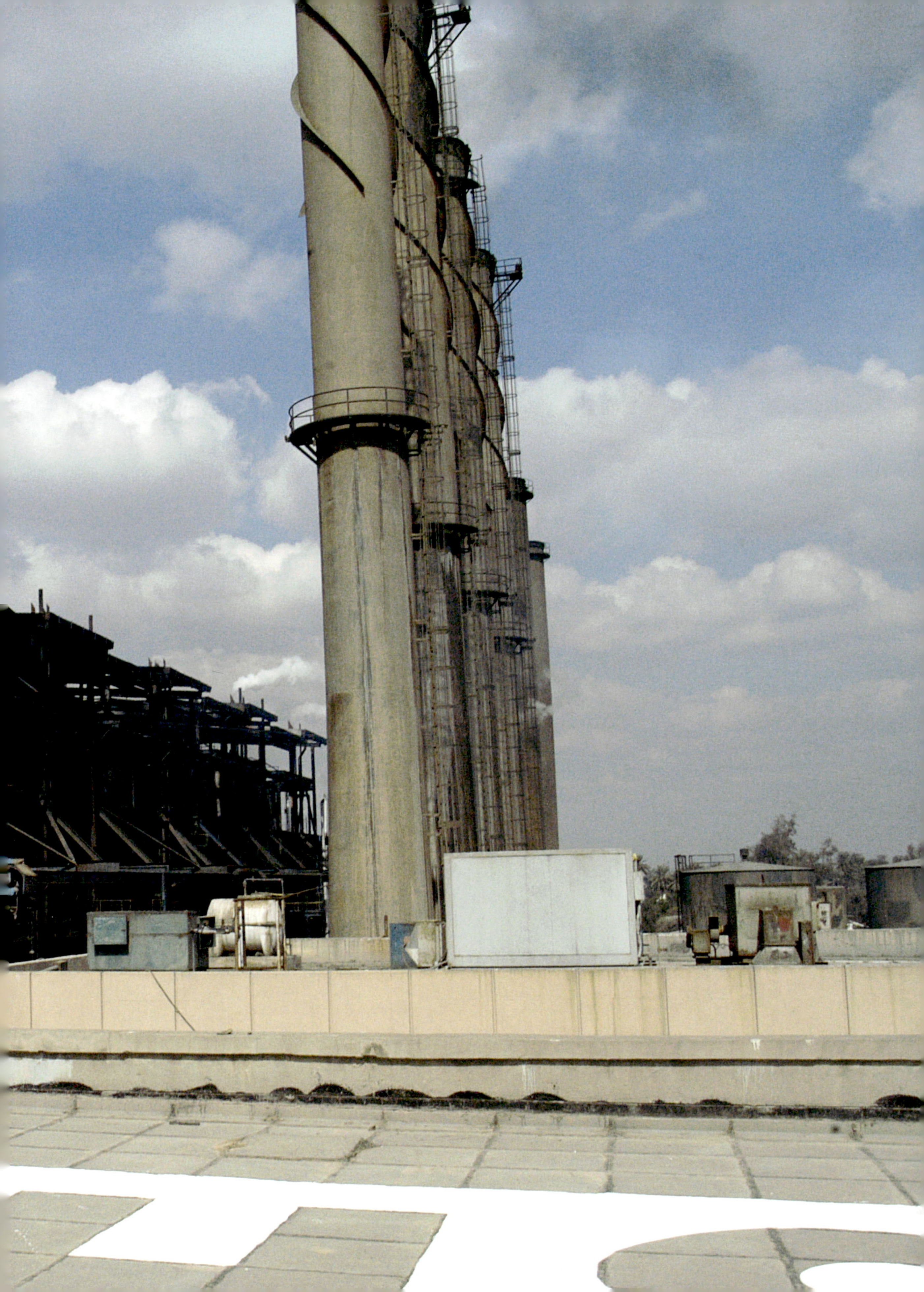

27 FEBRUARY

INTERVIEW AT SOUTH BAGHDAD POWER STATION, EMAILED TO PULP MAGAZINE

Attiah Bakir is a worker in the South Baghdad Power Station that provides, along with two others like it, most of the power throughout the Baghdad area. He is an engineer, is forty-eight years old, and has eight children. Although we interviewed several workers at the site, where there are human shields present, Attiah is slightly different.

Speaking through a government minder (posing as a convenient English-speaking technician), Attiah tells us how he was working the night-time shift eleven years ago when the power plant was bombed. He described four bombs hitting the area and where exactly they struck (the compound is quite extensive). He then described that he was working, and how a piece of metal was launched by the explosion towards him. It bounced off the metal work-desk and made contact with his head. After that he remembers little but his face being drenched in blood and his friends driving him to hospital. Indeed, you can now see where it struck, caving in the central third of his forehead and removing the bone totally. Above the bridge of his broken nose, there is only a cavity with scarred skin covering the prominent 'gap'. Soon after he arrived at the hospital he checked himself out, out of fear that it would be bombed too.

We asked him whether he is afraid, now that he will again be working, knowing that the Americans/British will certainly attack the site for the second time. He replied that he was not afraid, that he would go on like normal, and asked what he should do, get everyone to leave the power plant? He pointed out that without power the hospitals cannot work, neither can heating, cooking appliances or anywhere where there isn't a generator.

He did, however, mention that his children are terrified for him. After that, Michelle made the mistake of questioning his support of the government and 'the man' himself. From then on, the minder answered passionately for him.

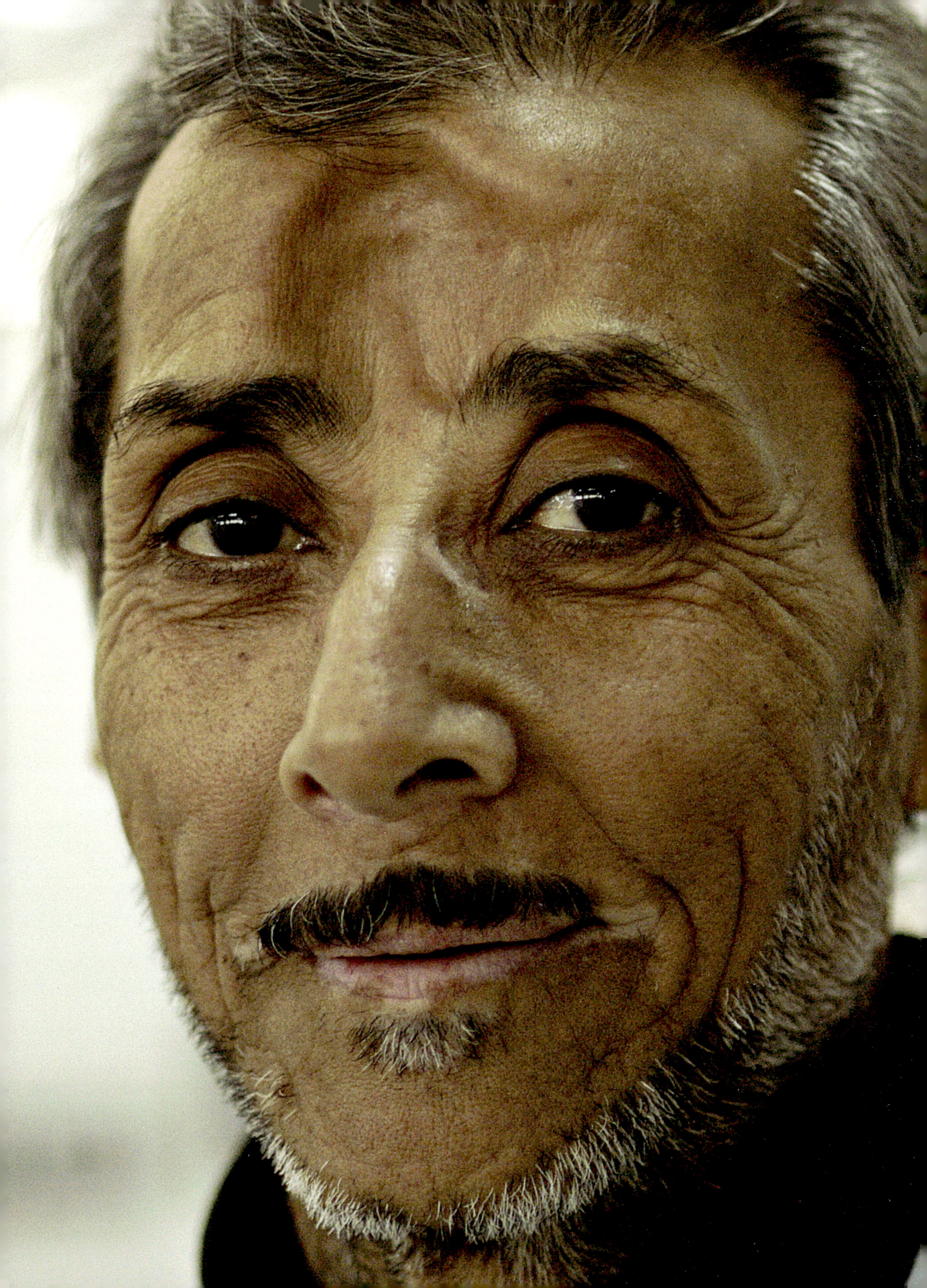

Over the last few weeks there has been a lot of media attention on the possible war on Iraq: when/if it will happen, what the motivation behind America and Britain's policies are, how they will proceed and who will be with them. This media attention has covered everything from Colin Powell's persuasive presentation to the UN security council, to the British Armed Forces feeling the need to purchase their own boots because army-issues would melt in the heat, and even the some 200 human shields (figures vary depending on publicists).

What I have come to realise, both by following popular media and discussing issues with experts (no offence to The Sun who probably expect such criticism, and The Times & co), is that the British public is being manipulated. OK, so to anyone who has a mind of his/her own this is an obvious fact, and nothing new. It is the extent of this that has caught me by surprise. Take, for example, the instance that many people have jumped upon as evidence of Iraq's material breach of 'International Law'; the Al-Samoud 2 rockets recently discovered to have a flight capability in excess of what was permitted by the UN. Initially, this was a clear-cut case of material breach, shown to all the world. What they didn't tell you (except by a small number of night-time news reports) is that they exceeded the 150km limit by exactly 12km, and the only way they could reach that far was through adapting the rockets to hold more fuel (in doing so, reducing the explosives capacity), and removing the heavy warhead and guidance systems totally (effectively taking the point away from firing it in the first place). Another example is so relevant to people's opinions of current affairs in the region that in its absence in popular press, I am sure that there has been some kind of (I hate to say the

word) conspiracy. It is the ongoing incursions into Iraqi airspace by British and, more commonly, American fighter-bombers to carry out air-surface rocket attacks and strategic bombing, specifically targeted at anti-aircraft installations and mobile anti-aircraft launch-pads ('large heavily-manned flatbed trucks with SAM launchers fixed on the back' for normal people) in southern Iraq, concentrated in and around Al-Basra. It is not common knowledge, but this war has already started, and the victims are everyday soldiers defending their country in no illegal way. So who am I to be in a position to write about such things when CNN, NBC, BBC & co have neglected to mention it? This answer is twofold. Firstly, public or private, all broadcasters rely heavily on ratings. I don't think I need to elaborate on the number of BBC directors, editors and department managers who have been 'relieved' due to a lack of viewer interest. And then you have to ask yourself what the viewers want to see and hear, plus the need of each to maintain a healthy relationship with the military, government, and others, just to be kept in the loop. Only last year I heard of a certain premier league football club refusing to circulate press releases or invitations to conferences to a national tabloid, seriously damaging their coverage out of retribution for an article.

The second, slightly more direct and relevant fact, is that unlike most of the media, I have been granted a visa for entry into Iraq and am at present on the ground on the east bank of the Tigris, in Baghdad. That is not to say that there are no journalists here. On the contrary, there are, according to official figures, the best part of three hundred and fifty (still a fraction of those who applied from all over the world). Unfortunately Iraq differs from the West in that for once, a journalist's pass gives you the privilege of your very own Iraqi minder wherever you go, and very, very limited access to anything you want to do. Ironically, with all the money these agencies throw at war-zone coverage (including Associated Press spending USD 1 million on erecting a crane to lift the entirety of their equipment, including a van, onto the roof of the Al-Rashid hotel, just for the view). They are just too closely watched. In stark contrast, I have a poor photocopy of a group visa, with twenty names on the back and 'HUMAN SHIELD' written in English and Arabic on the front.

For the cynics of the world, that will remove any credibility I may have had at the top of this page, and I am not going to do myself any favours by admitting having never written an article in my life. Now that I've succeeded in removing half of the readership, I can say why I am here. I am here to photograph. Not quite the image of a Hawaiian-T-Shirt clad tourist and, surprisingly, too modest to claim to be a photo-journalist. I am a twenty-one year old student of Manchester Metropolitan University. I differ from the rest of you drunken wasters in four ways relevant to where I am. <1> I have some experience of Middle-Eastern, or should I say Arabic, life. I am English, and white, but have spent a lot of time travelling and studying the region. <2> I have worked as a photo journalist before, in the dangerous, barbaric streets of Greater London, and am studying a photography course. <3> Although I have no intention of dying as a human shield, I share the same beliefs as many of them. In this, and any other article I am going to write, I will try my hardest to ignore my 'leanings' (which aren't actually very extreme anyway) and record only the facts. Suffice to say that in any war that comes to pass, I disagree with the approach adopted time and time again by the American military in respect to care, diligence and overall interest in civilian casualties. You only have to look back at the last Gulf War when the public bomb shelter in Al-Amiriyah was hit by two bombs; the first designed to open up the roof and the second was laser-guided to fall through the hole and send the modern-day equivalent of napalm, burning phosphoric anti-personnel chemicals in every direction. 400 women and children died because the men were protecting their homes from looters at the time.) I may, through my presence or subsequent photographs, help be the cause of 'relatively' surgical ground troops being utilised where otherwise bombs would simply wipe everything out. It's a simplification, and maybe totally futile, but I've met the workers in the '12th April Water Purification Plant' that lost friends there from bombs 12 years ago, and at least I'm trying. <4> Lastly, I am simply curious. I want to know what a war-time situation does to people. I want to know whether I can handle those type of circumstances. I want to know what type of people are the human shields - people prepared to go all the way. I want to see what inner-Iraq is really like and what the real consensus is among the Iraqi people in respect to concepts such as 'regime-change', 'weapons of mass destruction', 'oppression' and most importantly, 'war'. But most of all, I want to see first-hand what my government is proposing should be done with my hard-earned taxes.

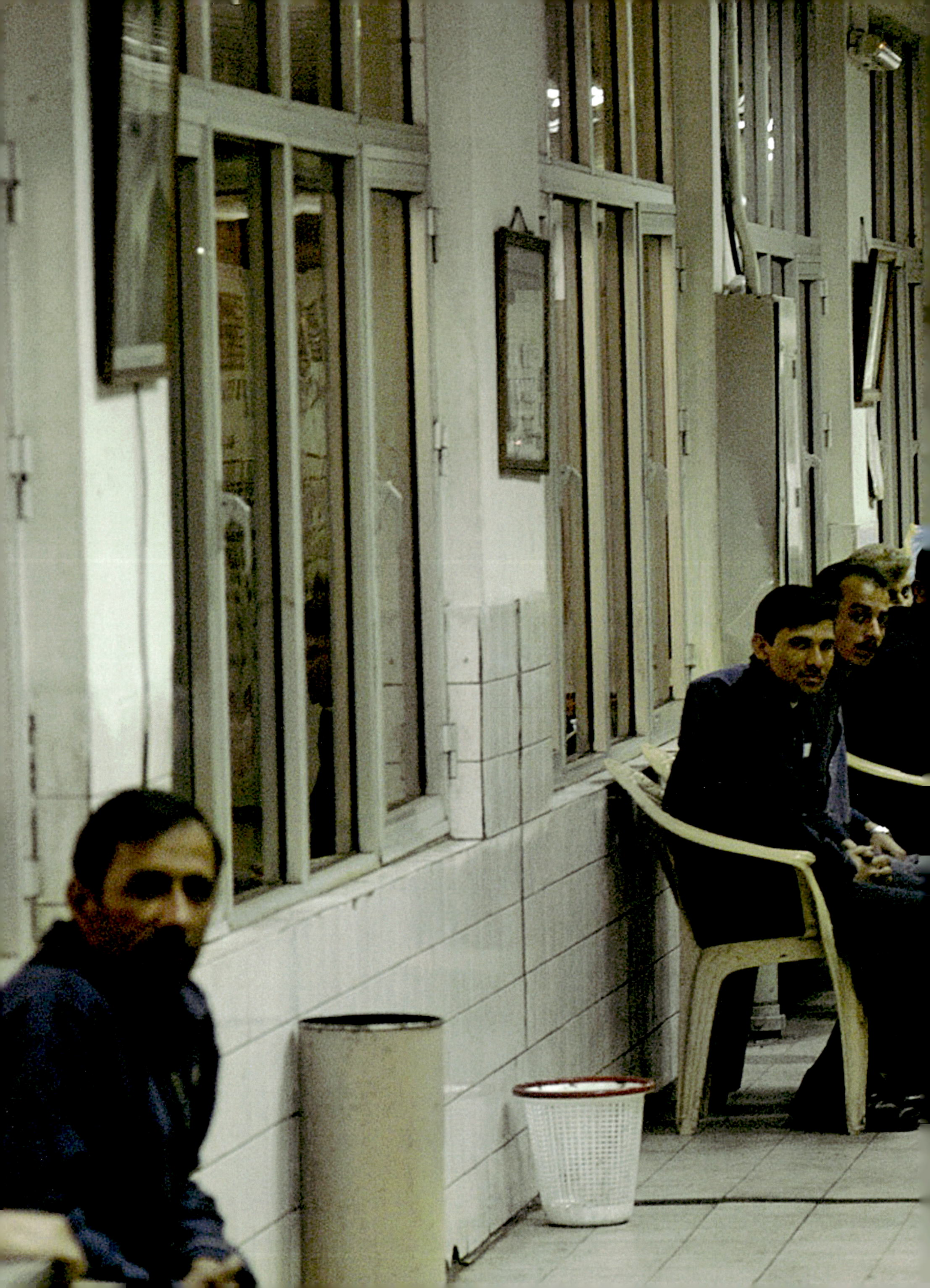

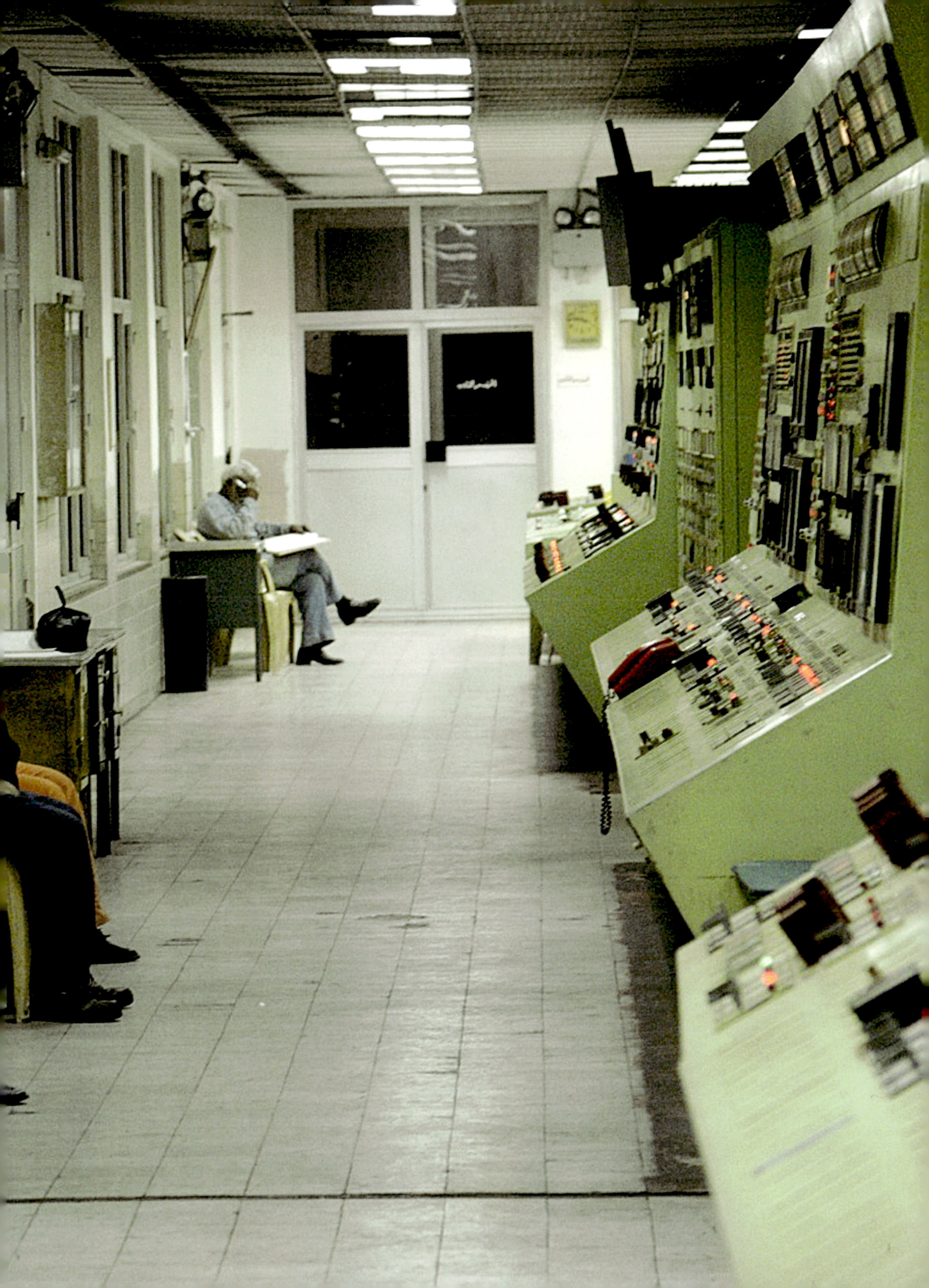

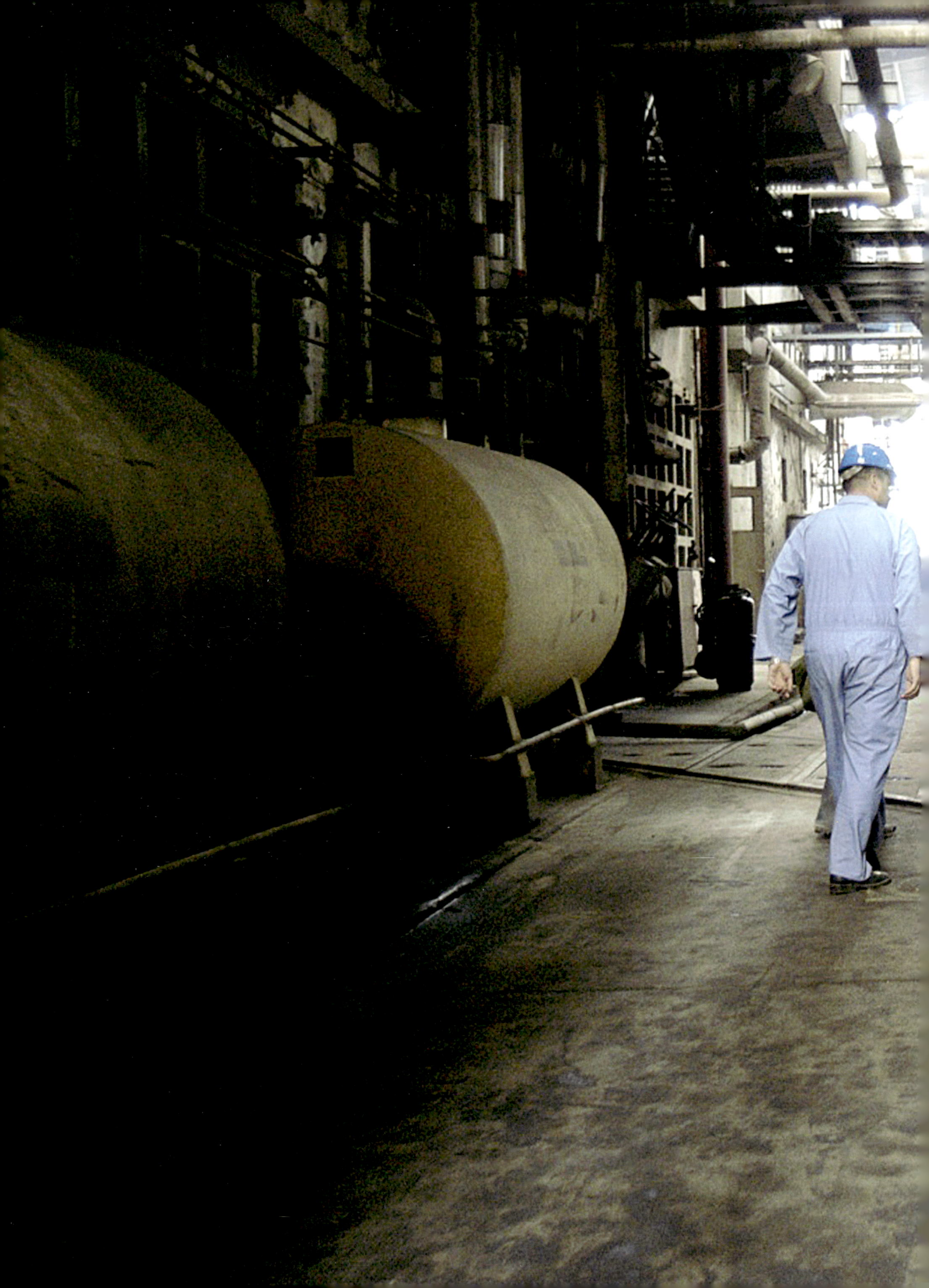

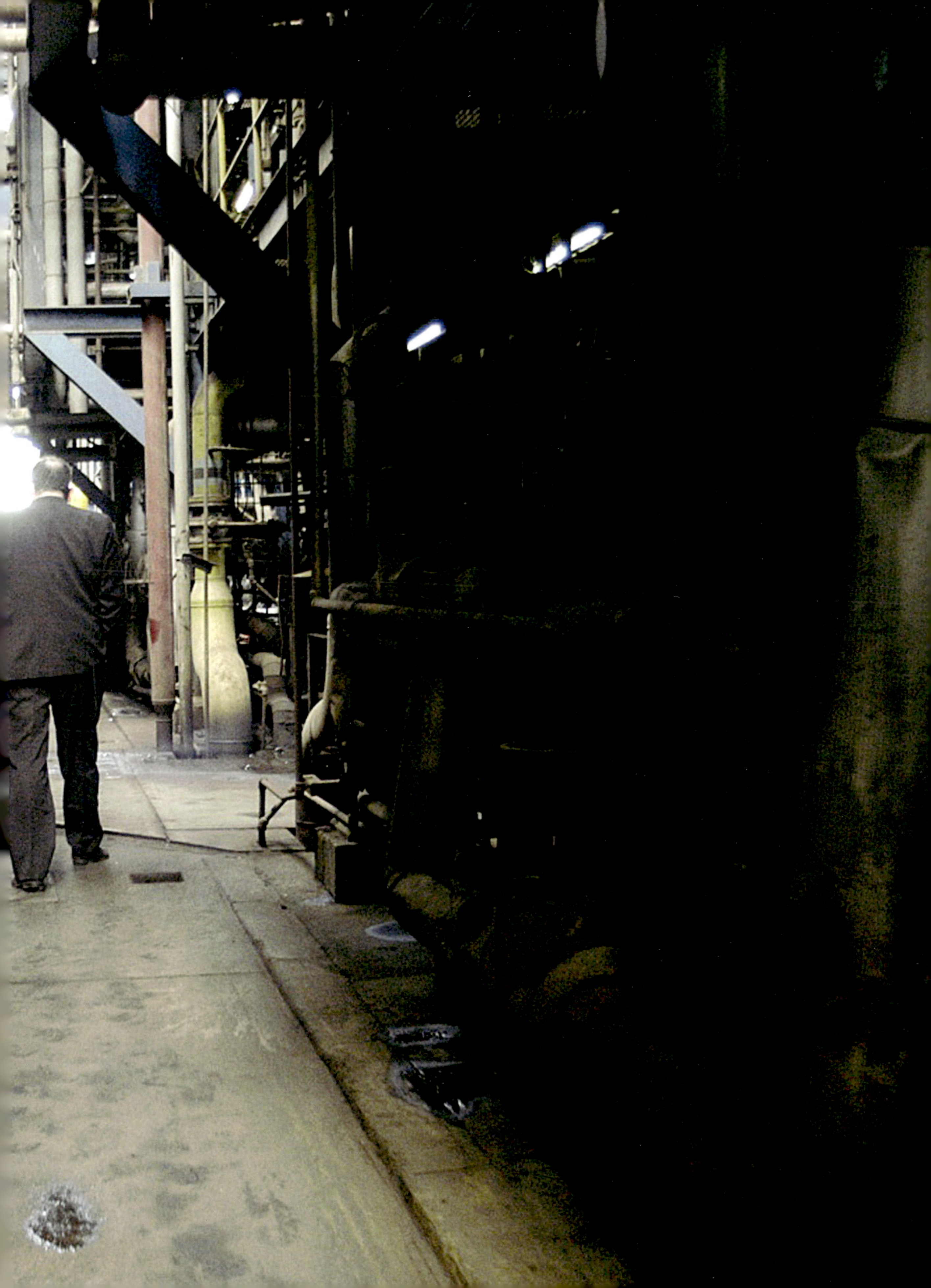

28 FEBRUARY

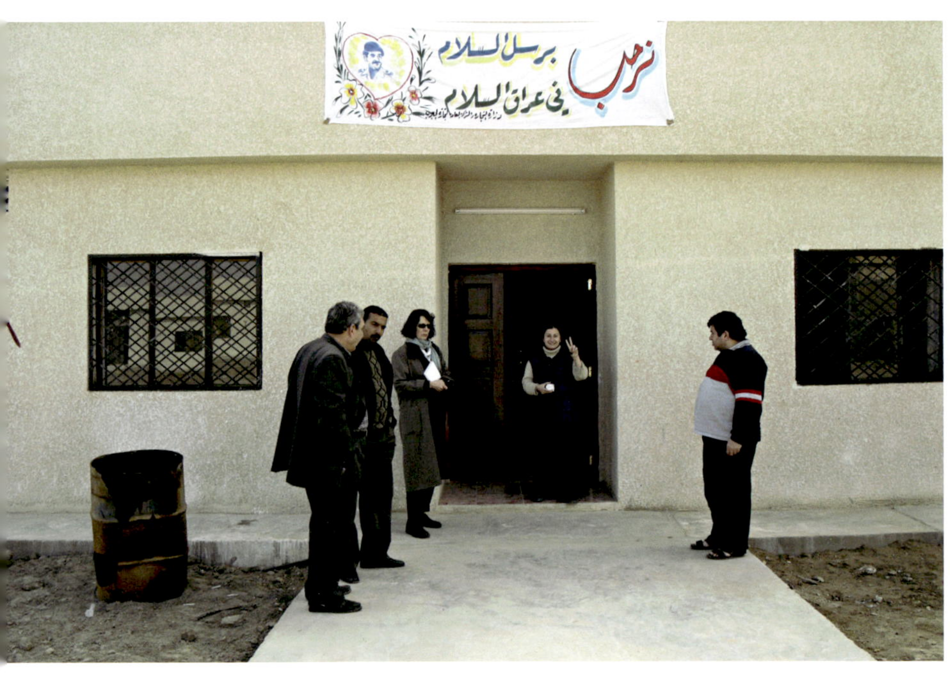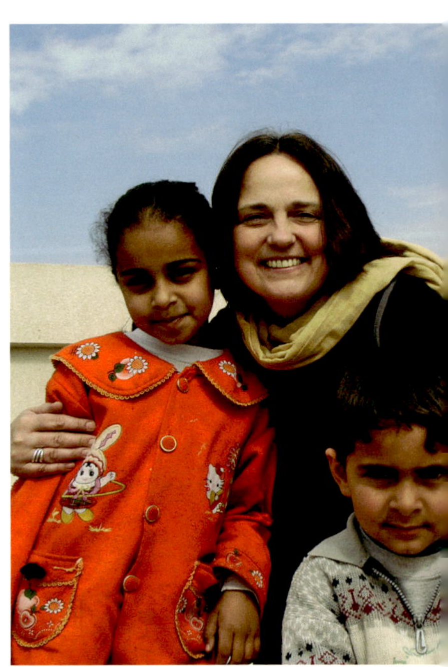

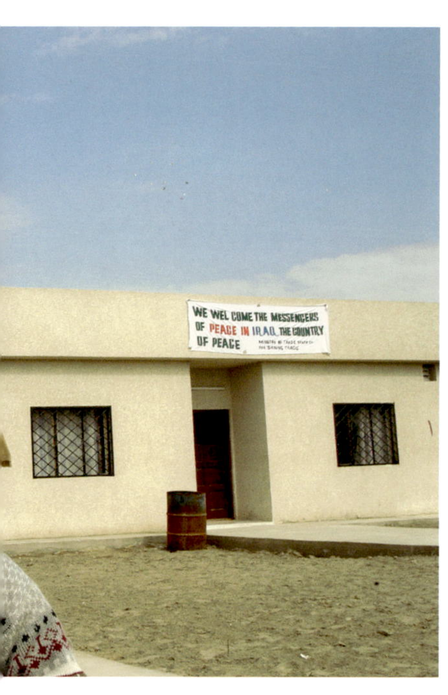
WE WEL COME THE MESSENGERS
OF PEACE IN IRAQ THE COUNTRY
OF PEACE

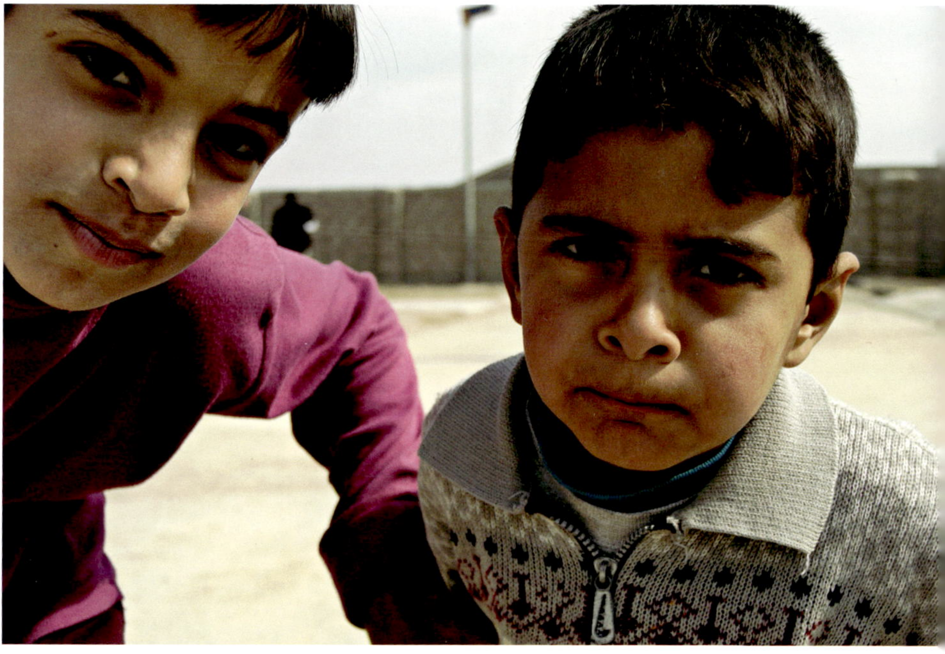

01 MARCH
BAGHDAD

We arrived last Tuesday, early in the morning and have stayed in the Khaleej apartments on Al-Sa'adun. They are funded by the government through FPS, so we are paying nothing.

Within the human-shield society tensions have started to run higher than I think is safe under these circumstances. Announcements today about sites and lack of available communication have sparked the built-up stress and led to many statements causing panic. Internal politics are ripping people apart and tempers are short.

Bruce, from Canada, "The children in the school look at us as if we are secret servicemen. We are not, but our drivers are, and they dictate the letters they write to American children".

This is the moment that I have decided to leave.

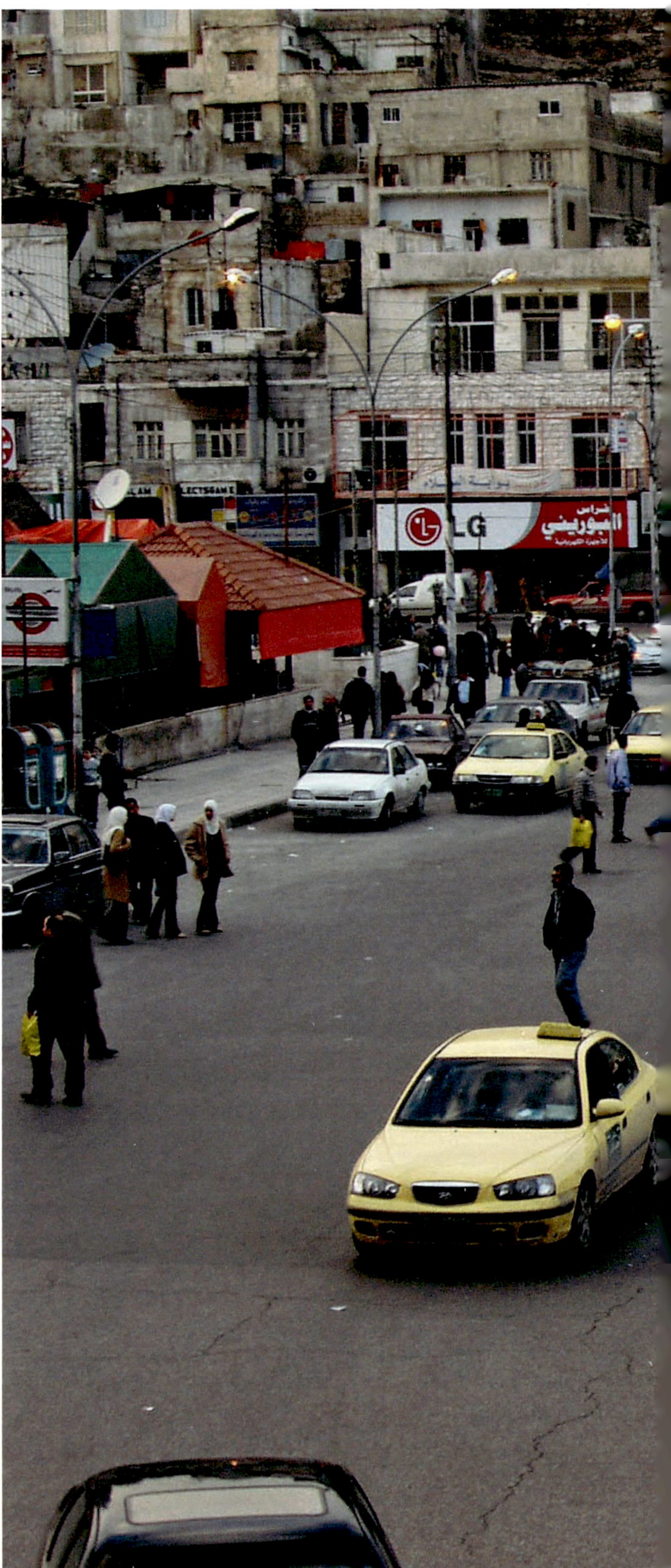

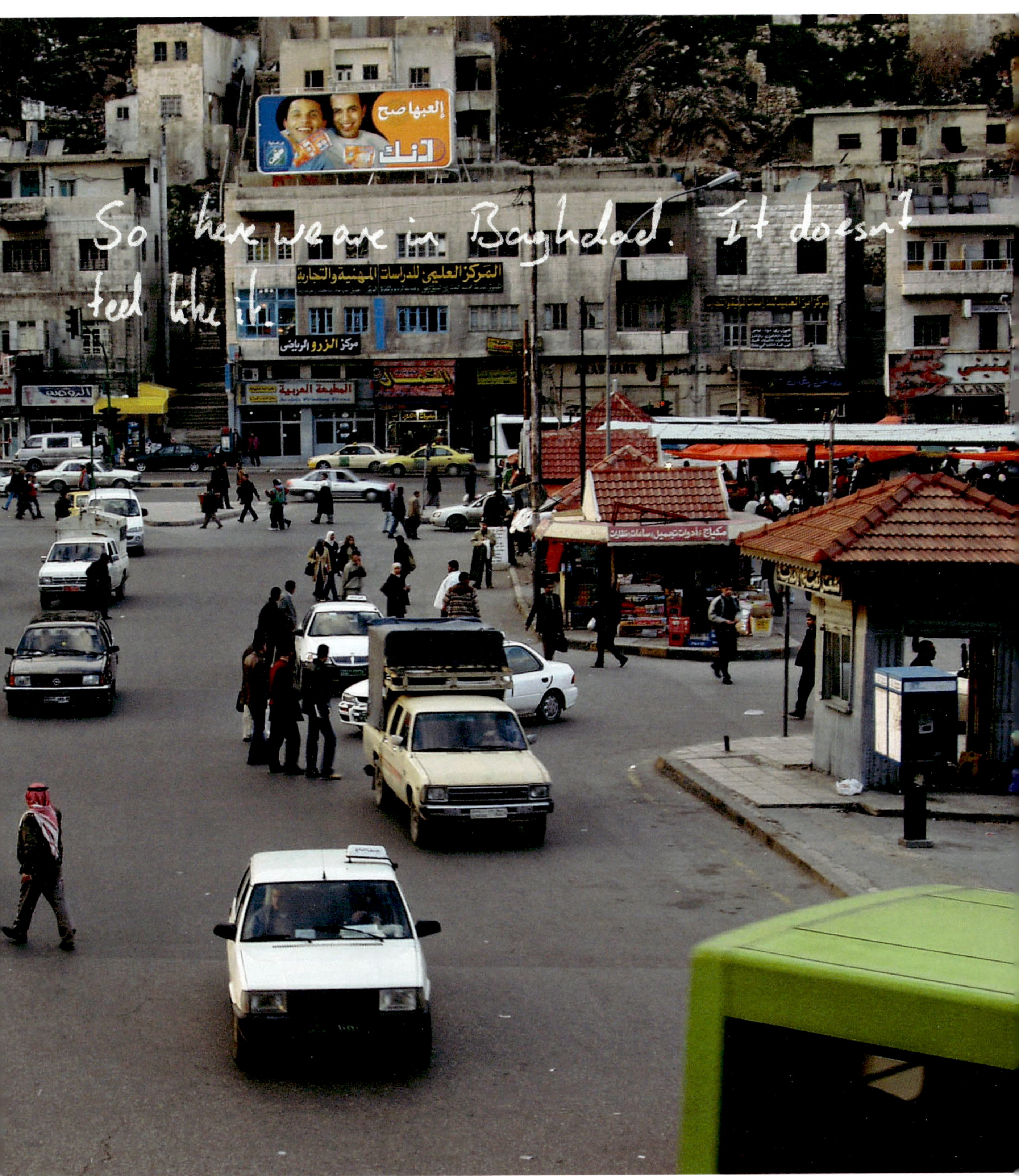

So here we are in Baghdad. It doesn't
feel like it.

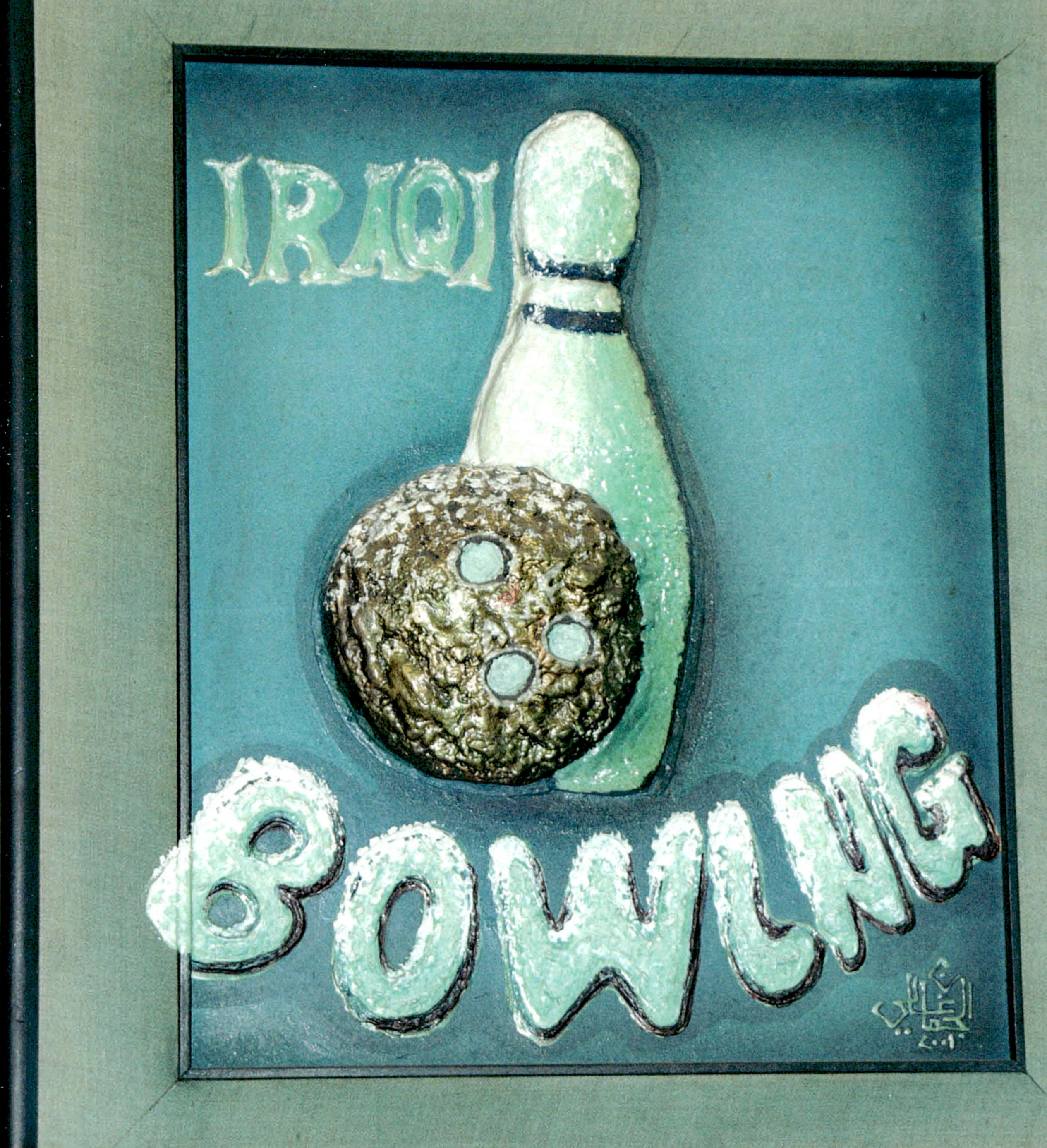
IRAQI
BOWLING

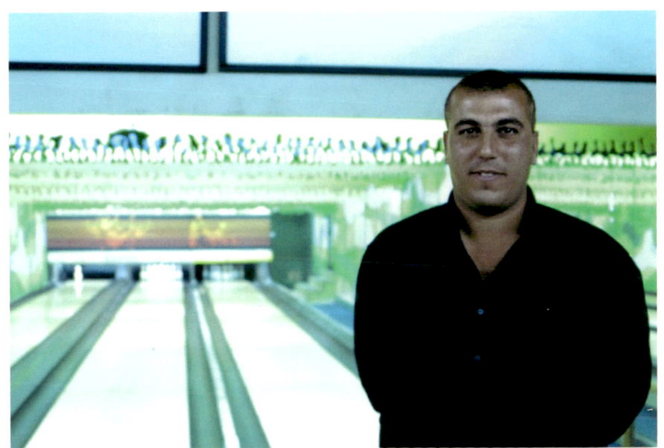 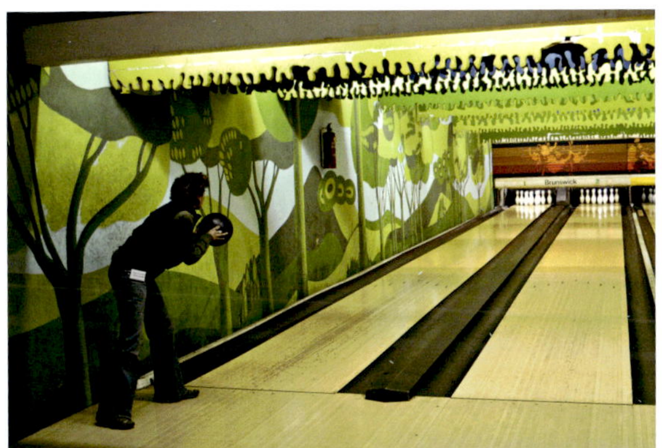

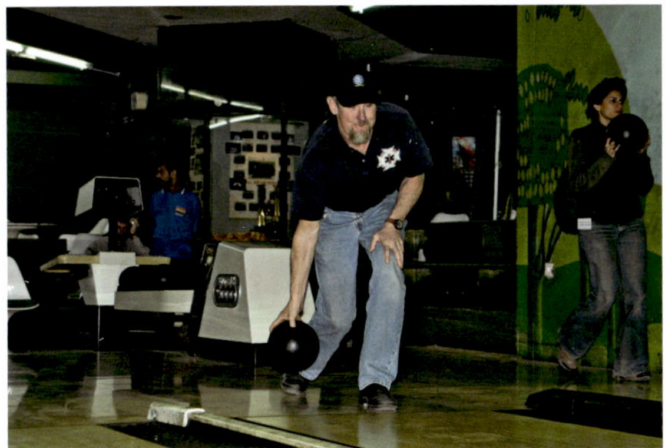 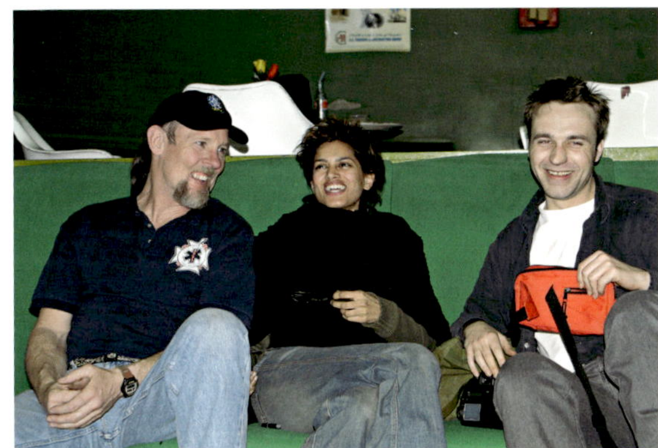

Maybe it's one of those surreal moments in time where groups of everyday people come together from two extremes and the most differing backgrounds you can imagine.

Like the tale of the British and German troops leaving their trenches on Christmas Day, 1914, only to join for a game of football on the frosted ground. Or, maybe, for the cynics, irony in the impoverished befriending the naïve for a quick buck before being invaded and the hard times ahead.

Whatever it was, it was nervous, and it was unsure ground. Basically, it was the essence of everything that we had done so far. But we enjoyed a moment of escape from media interviews, tours of industrial...

I think I've decided what I want to do, that will both help people here and let me do what I want to do.

03 MARCH
BAGHDAD

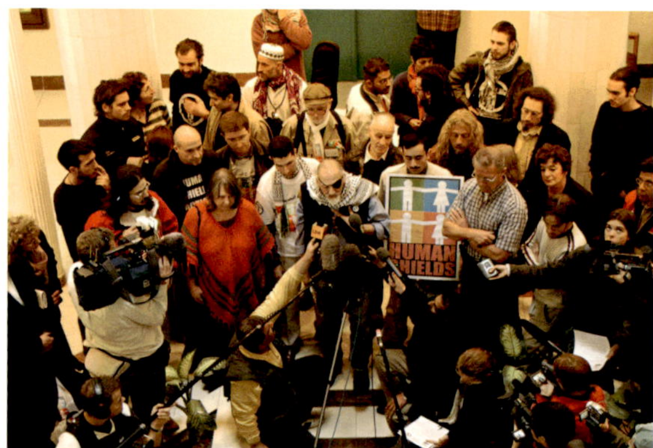

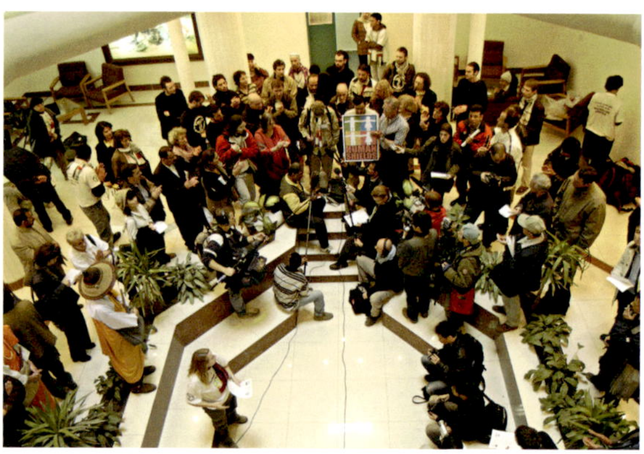

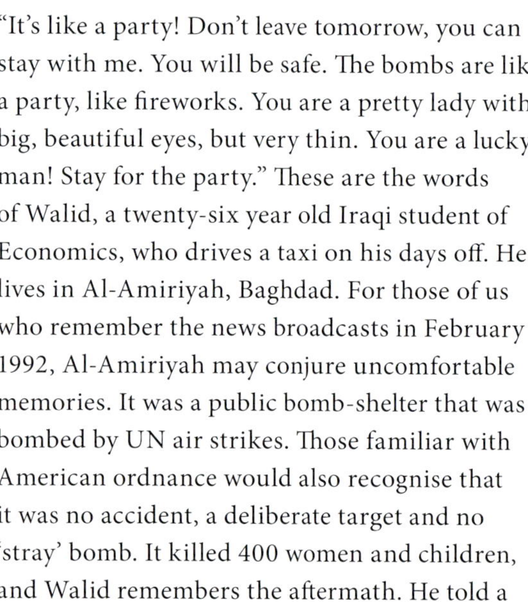

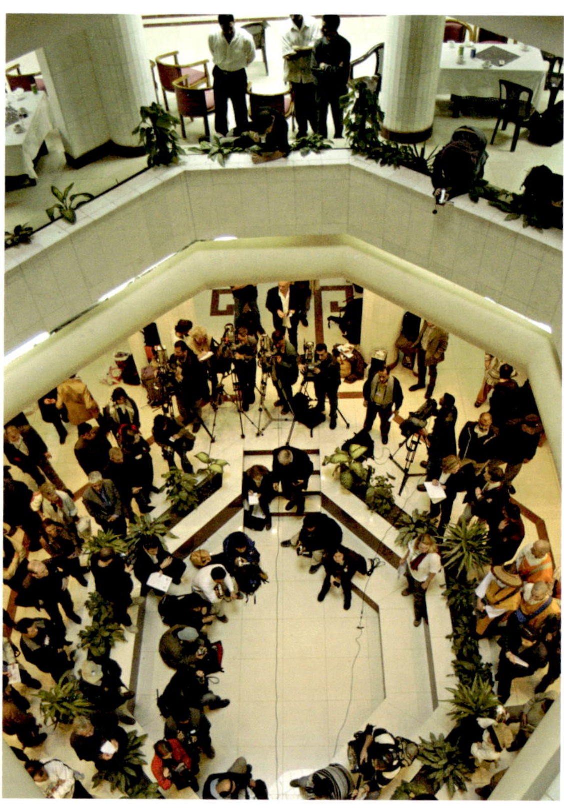

"It's like a party! Don't leave tomorrow, you can stay with me. You will be safe. The bombs are like a party, like fireworks. You are a pretty lady with big, beautiful eyes, but very thin. You are a lucky man! Stay for the party." These are the words of Walid, a twenty-six year old Iraqi student of Economics, who drives a taxi on his days off. He lives in Al-Amiriyah, Baghdad. For those of us who remember the news broadcasts in February 1992, Al-Amiriyah may conjure uncomfortable memories. It was a public bomb-shelter that was bombed by UN air strikes. Those familiar with American ordnance would also recognise that it was no accident, a deliberate target and no 'stray' bomb. It killed 400 women and children, and Walid remembers the aftermath. He told a friend and me, as we interviewed him, driving through the west of the city, how they couldn't open the shelter's doors to rescue those left alive. And then how he watched the charred bodies piled onto the back of a truck, with no hope of identification. But still, he describes the imminent bombardment of Iraq, and specifically Baghdad, as 'a party'. We asked him why.

"I don't remember the Iran war. I was alive, but it was a way of life. You couldn't point and say "that was when it was", because it was eight years long. And in 1991 we were used to it. It is normal. It is explosions and bombs, like a party." Ironically, it was his nonchalant attitude that may have saved his life eleven years ago, when he was only fifteen.

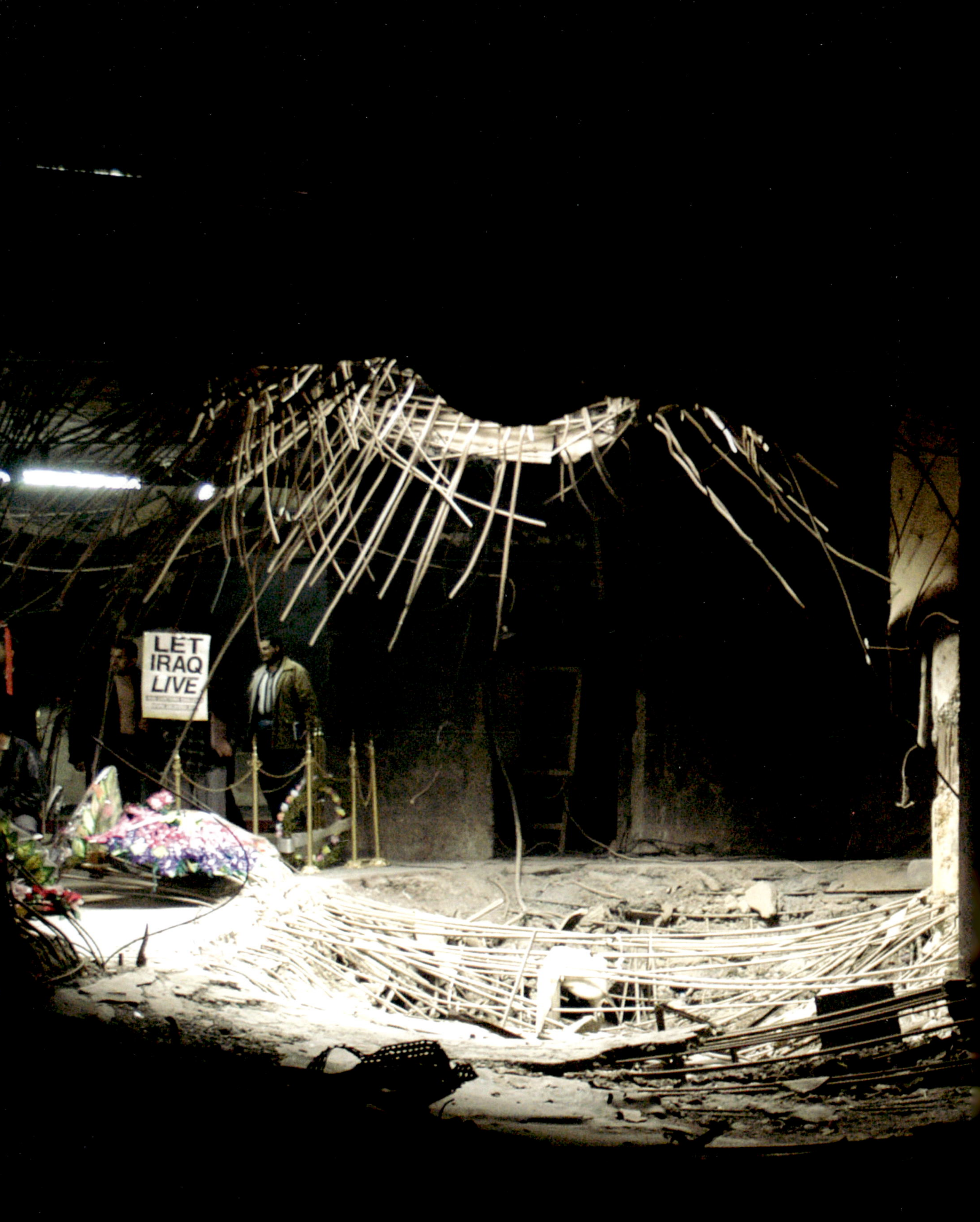
LET
IRAQ
LIVE

AMMAN

03 - 21 MARCH 2003

06 MARCH
AMMAN

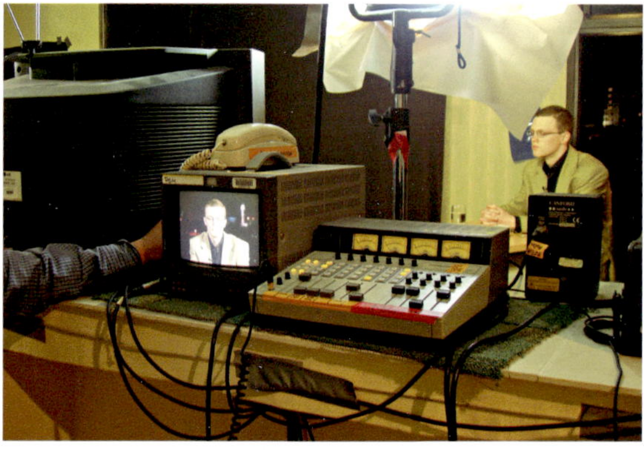

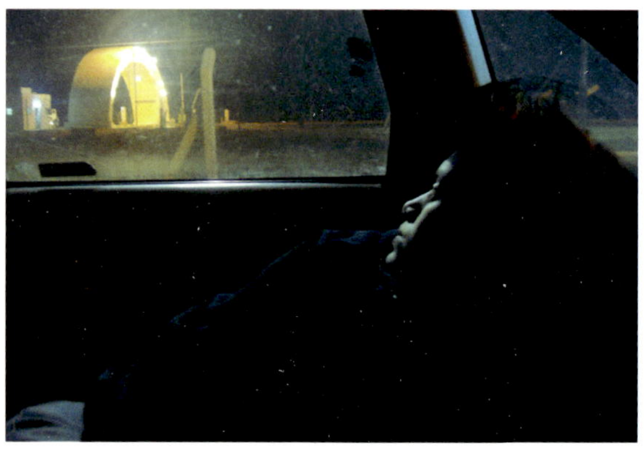

I think I've decided what I want
to do, that will both help people here & let
me do what I want to do.

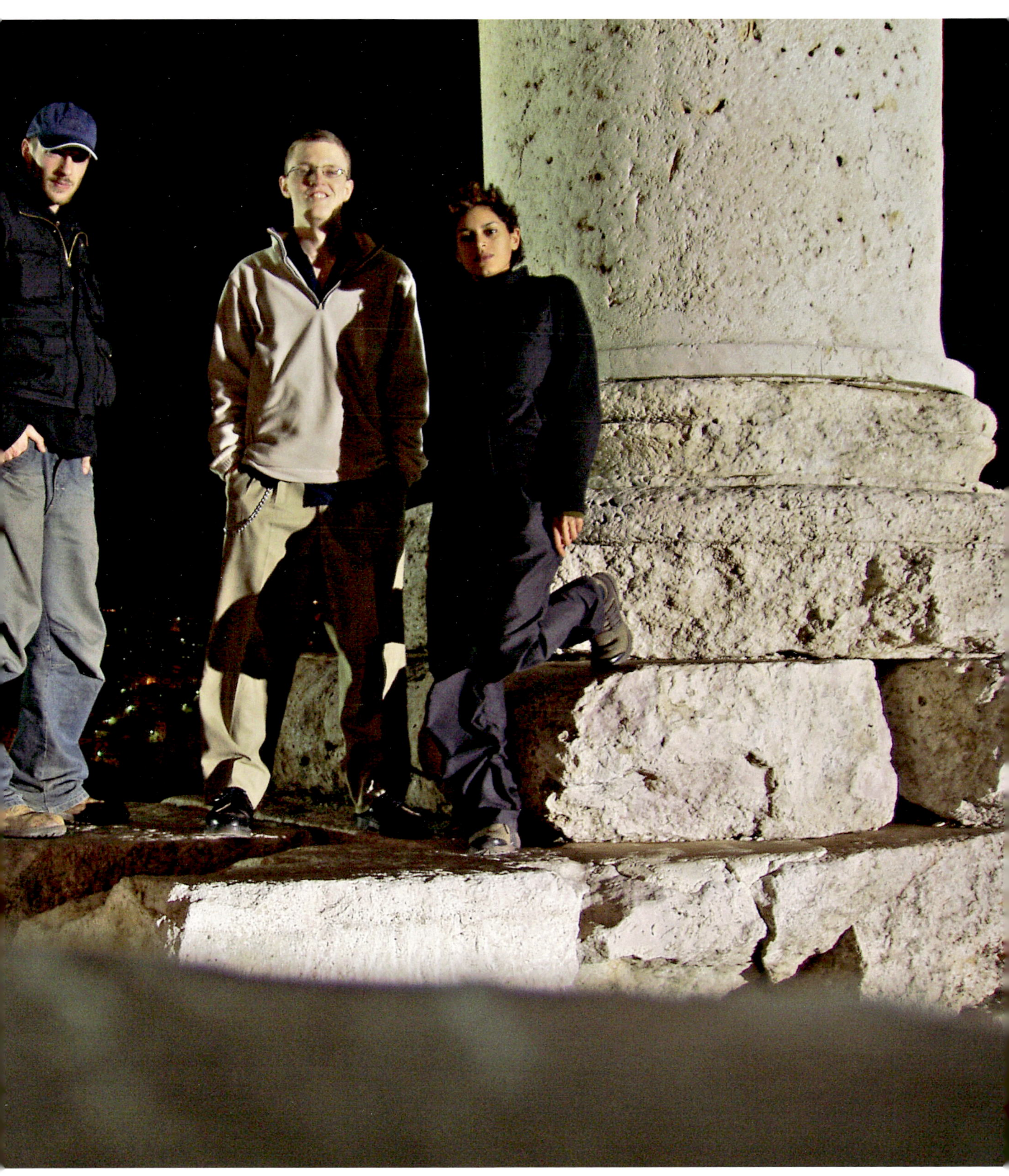

Anthony, this is just so that you can have my e-mail address. I probably won't be able to check my account for quite a while, as internet access in Iraq is constricted and hotmail and others aren't available. I talked to you last night, so you know that everything is ok. give my love to everyone, speak to you soon,

    Tom

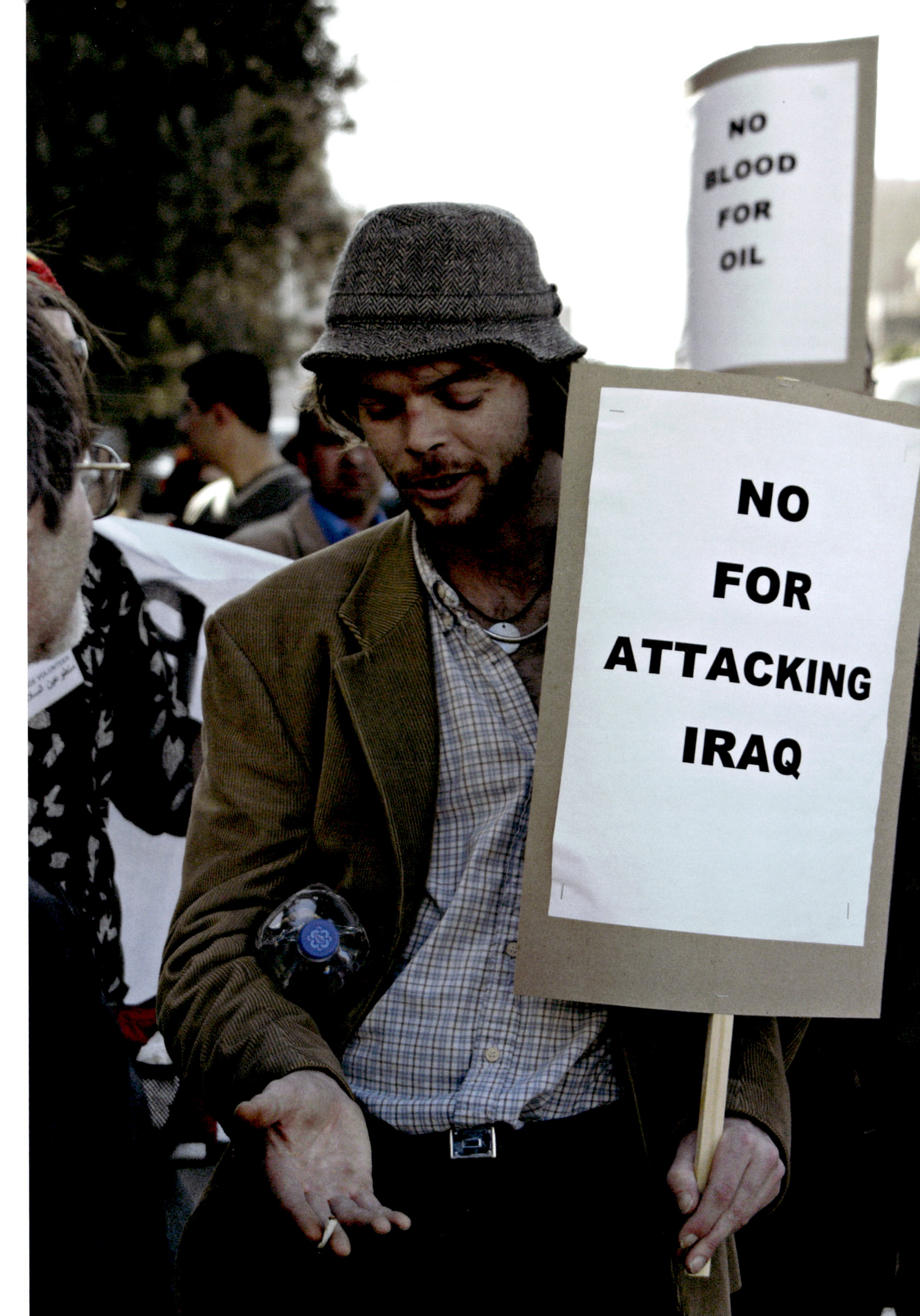

NO
BLOOD
FOR
OIL

NO
FOR
ATTACKING
IRAQ

14 MARCH

AMMAN

Walking through the streets of Amman this
afternoon I just felt at home.
On my own, I wouldn't pass as Jordanian/
Palestinian, but people don't notice me. I can
watch and learn new things without a charade
being played out for me everywhere I go. I just feel
like I'm home, and it feels right.

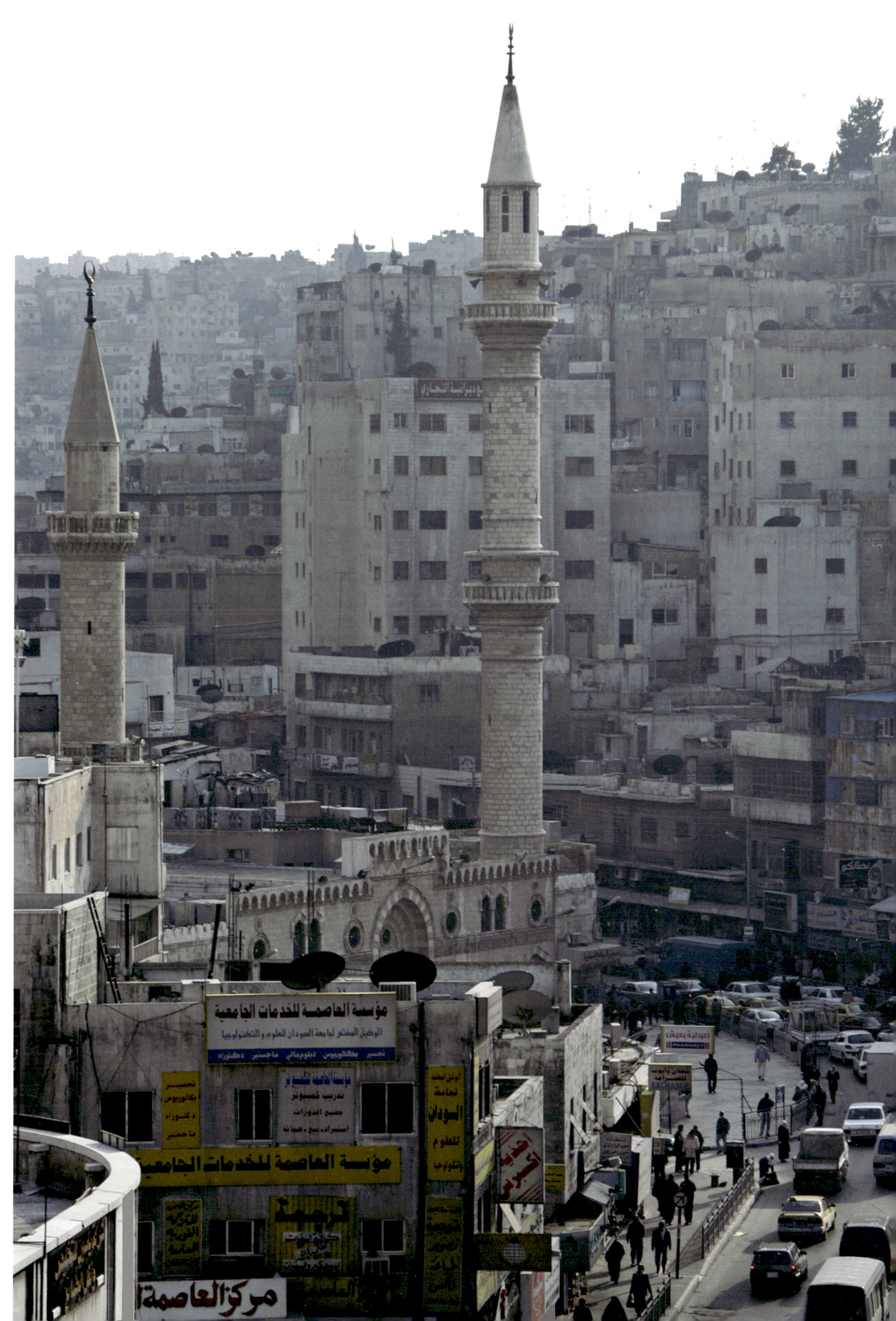

15 MARCH

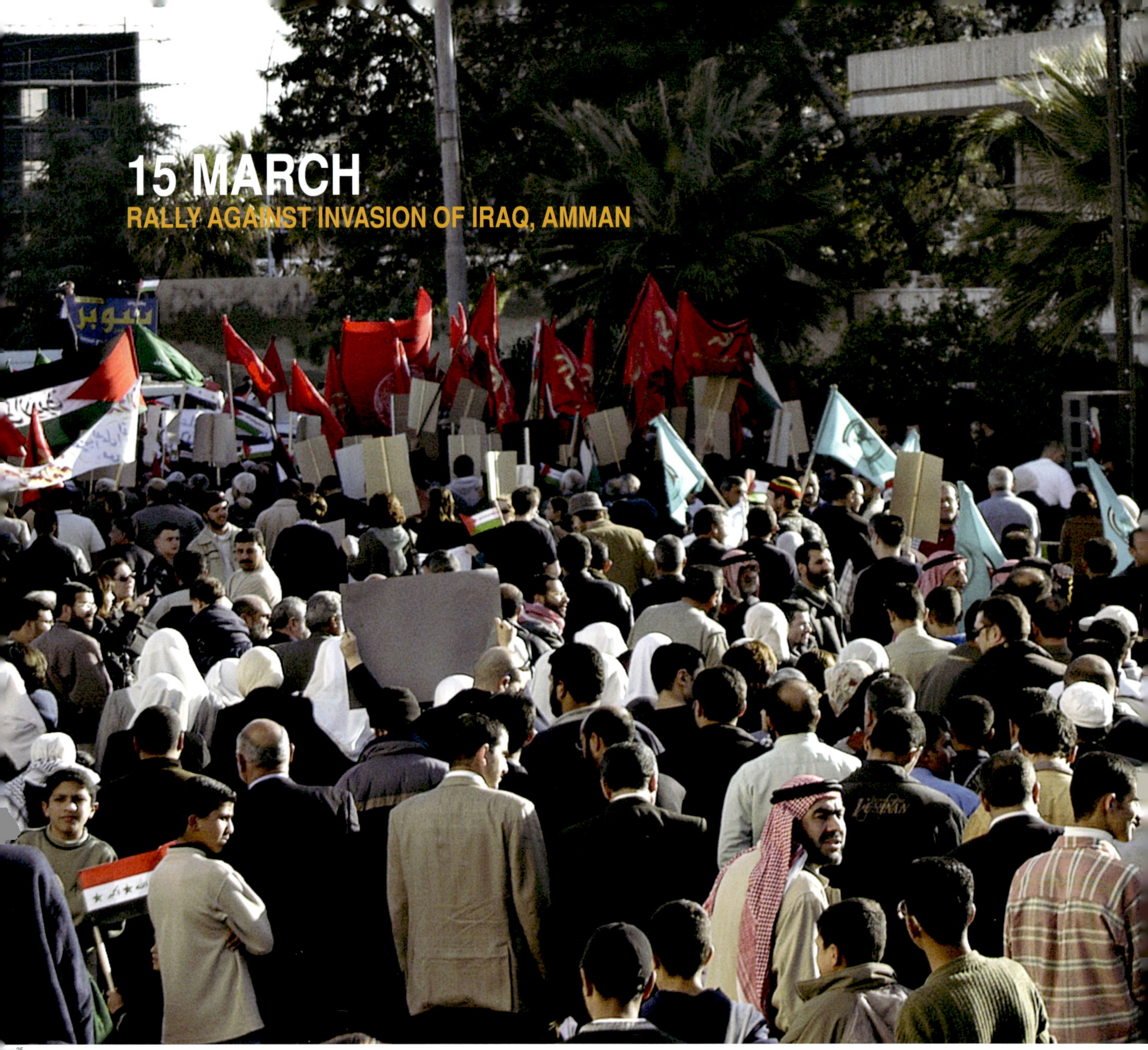

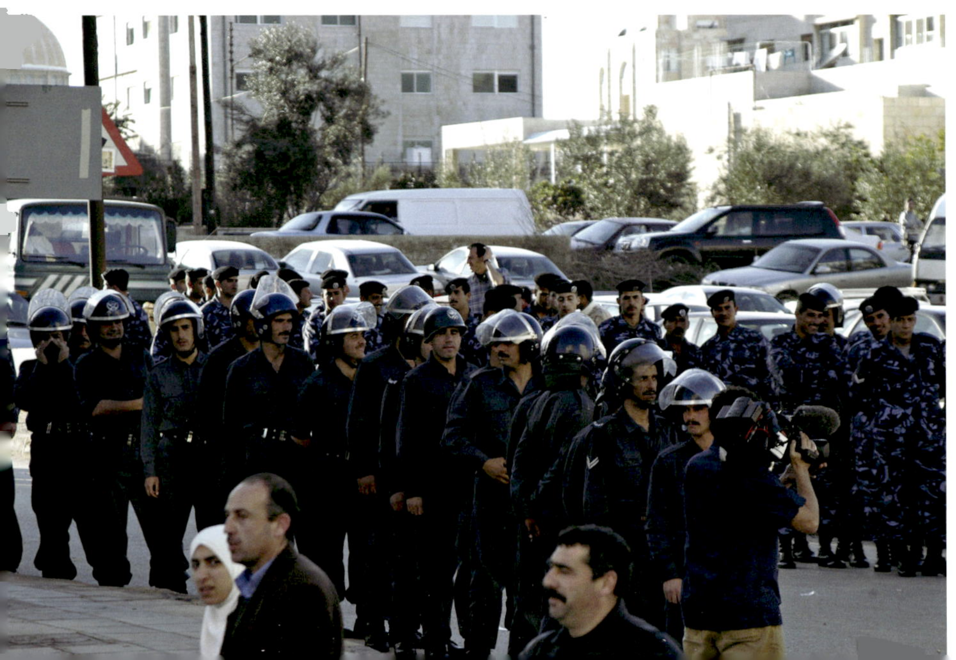

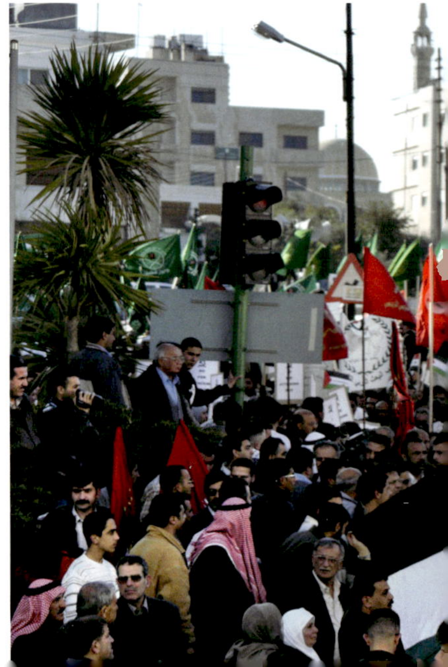

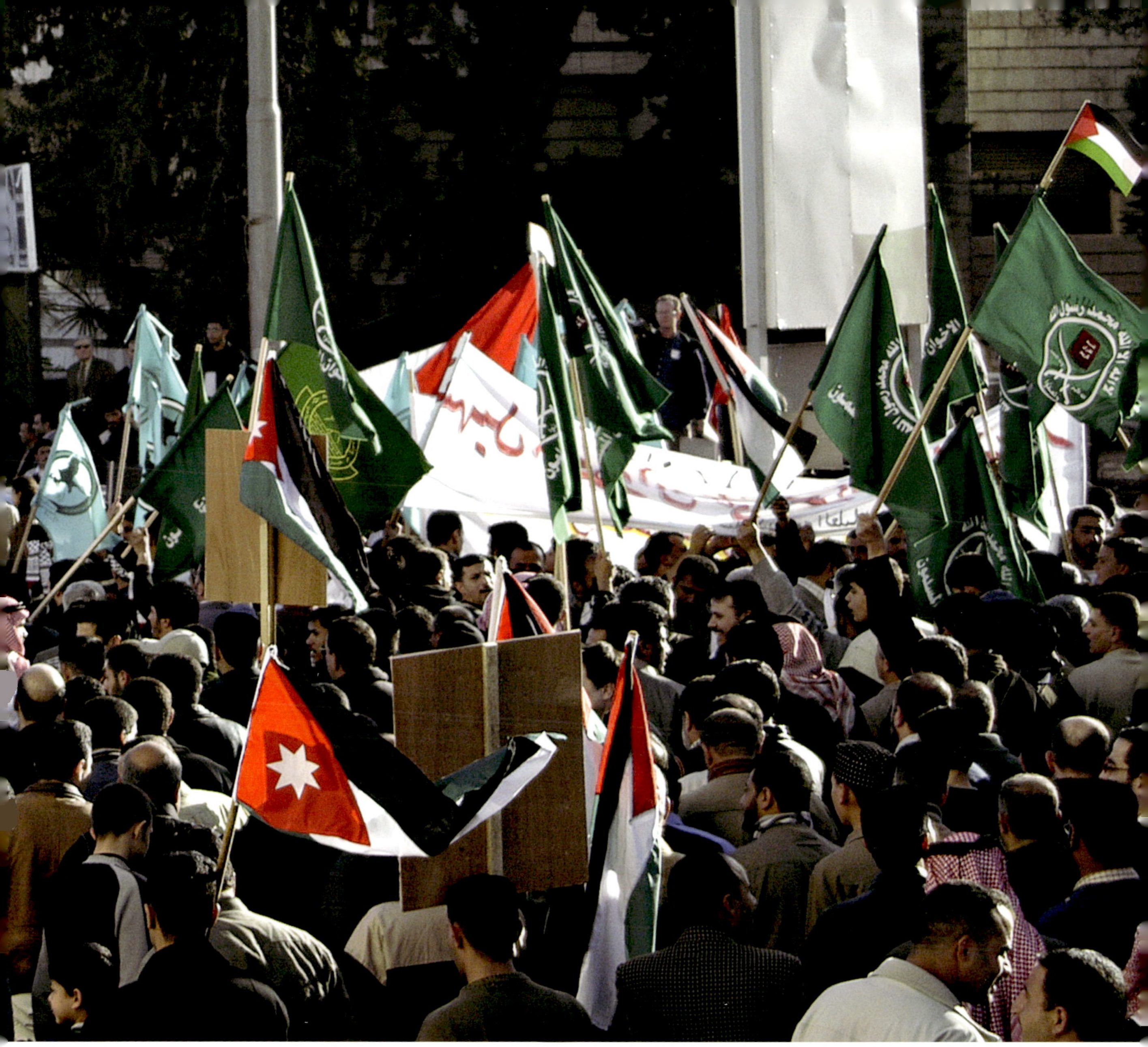

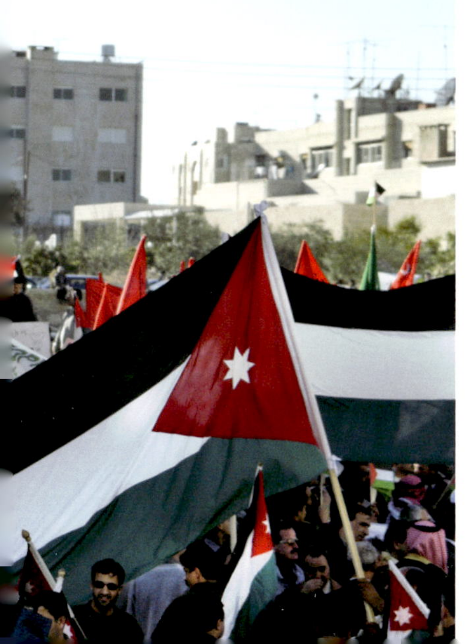

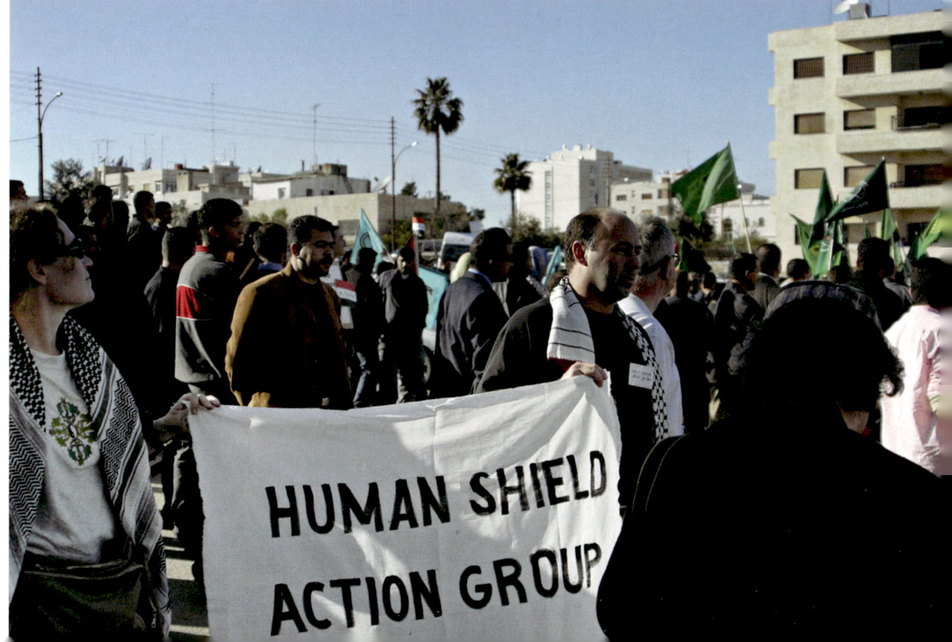
HUMAN SHIELD
ACTION GROUP

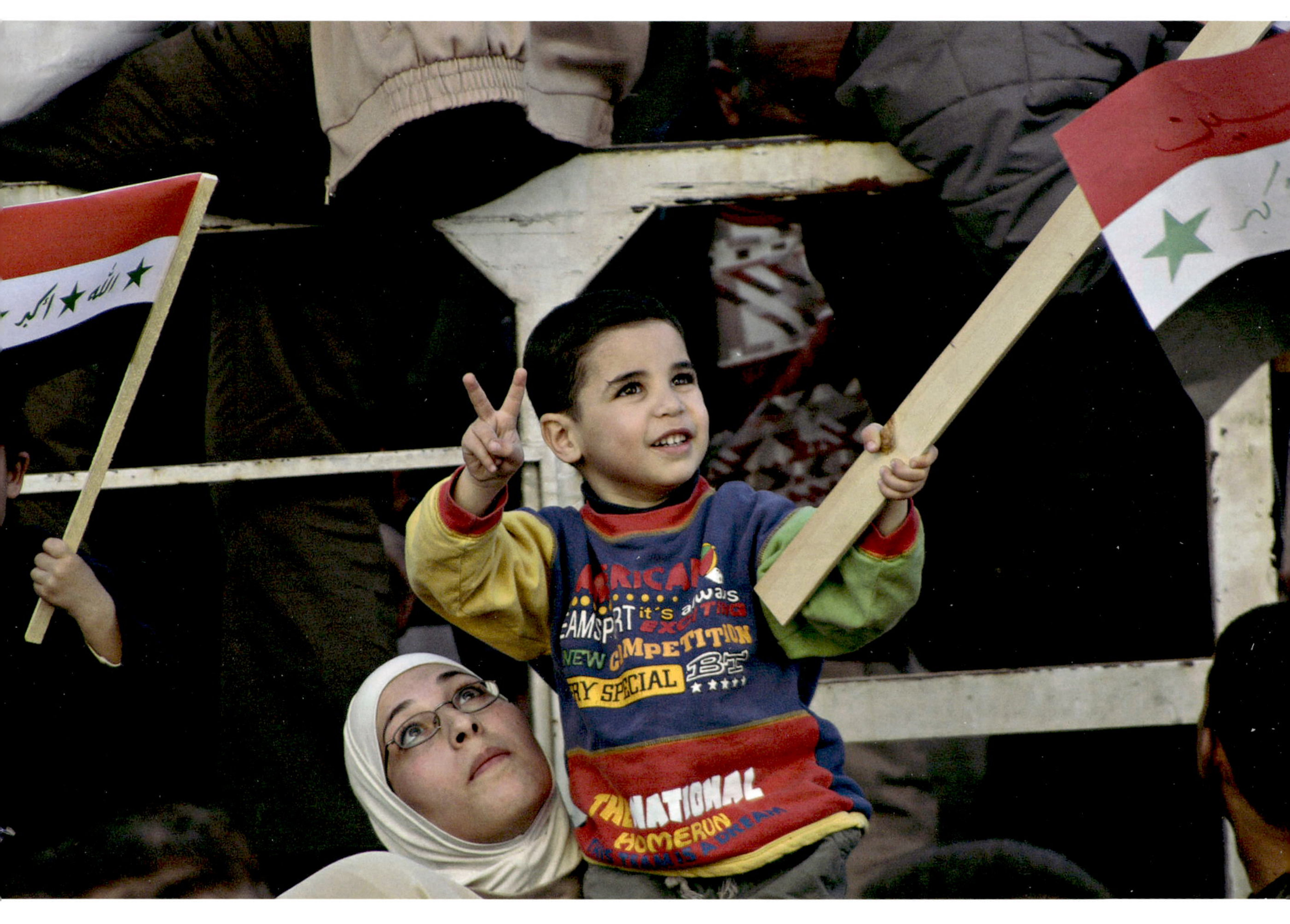

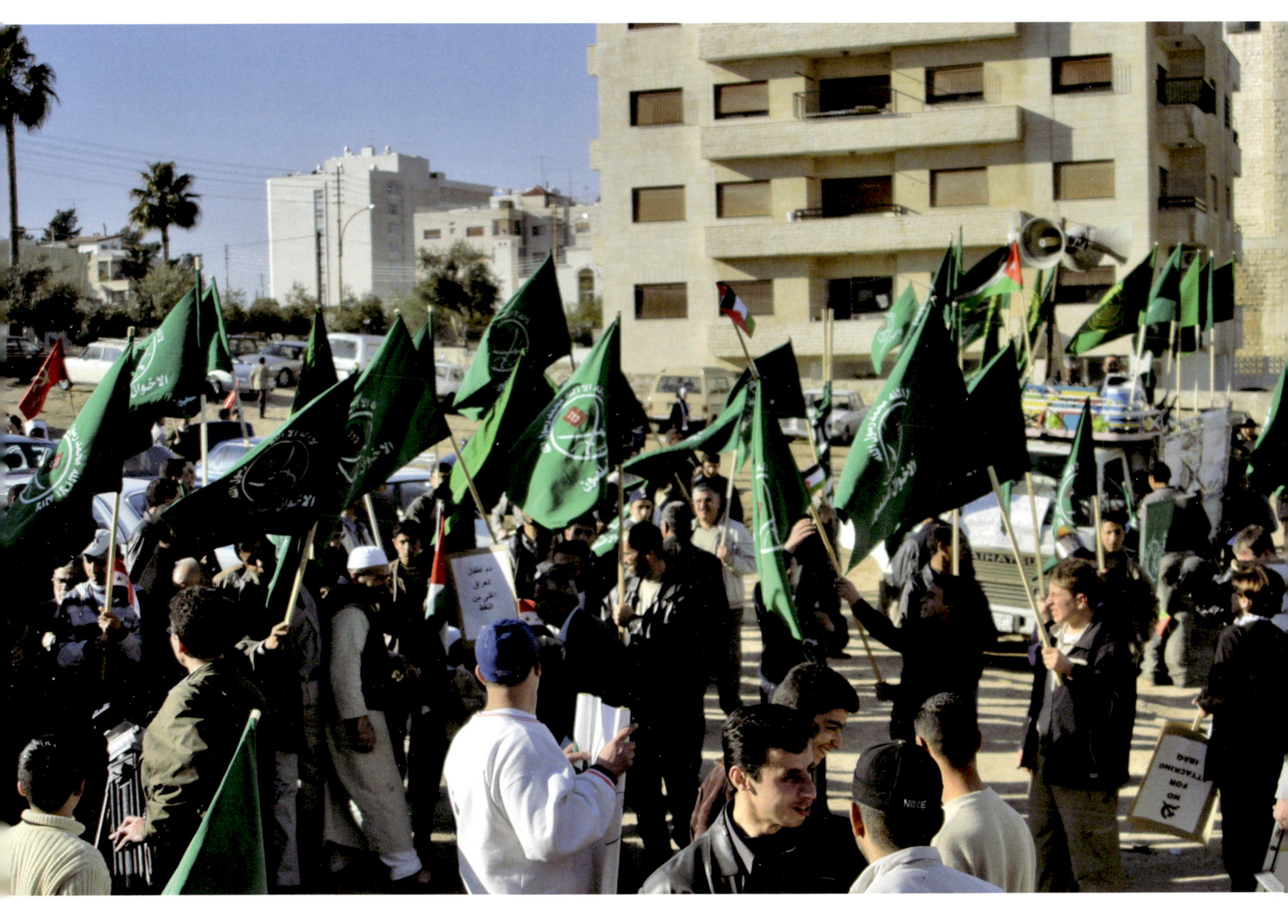

1026170303
   This is it. This is the countdown,
hour by hour until the bombs start to drop on the
city I was in last week.

17 MARCH

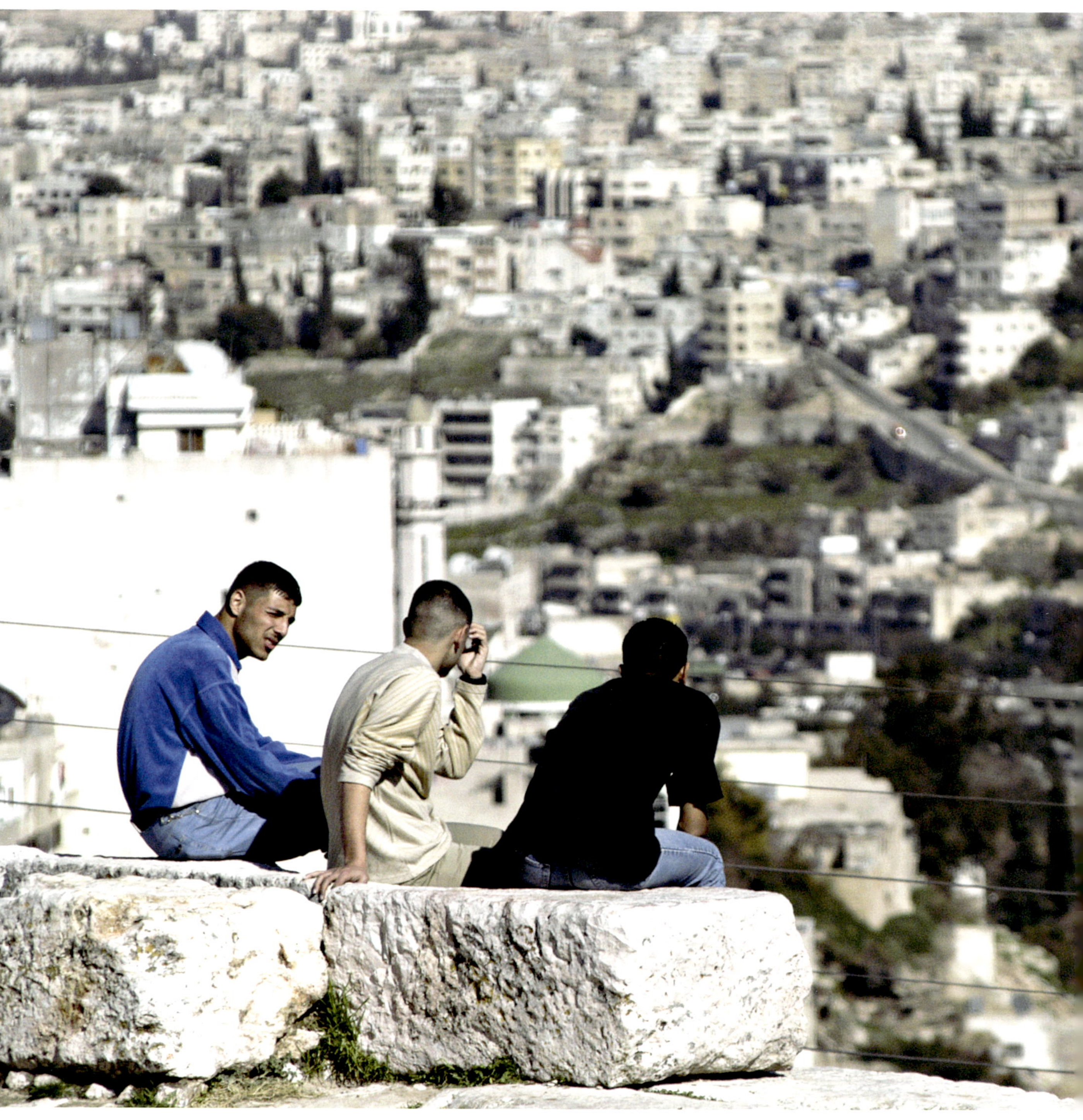

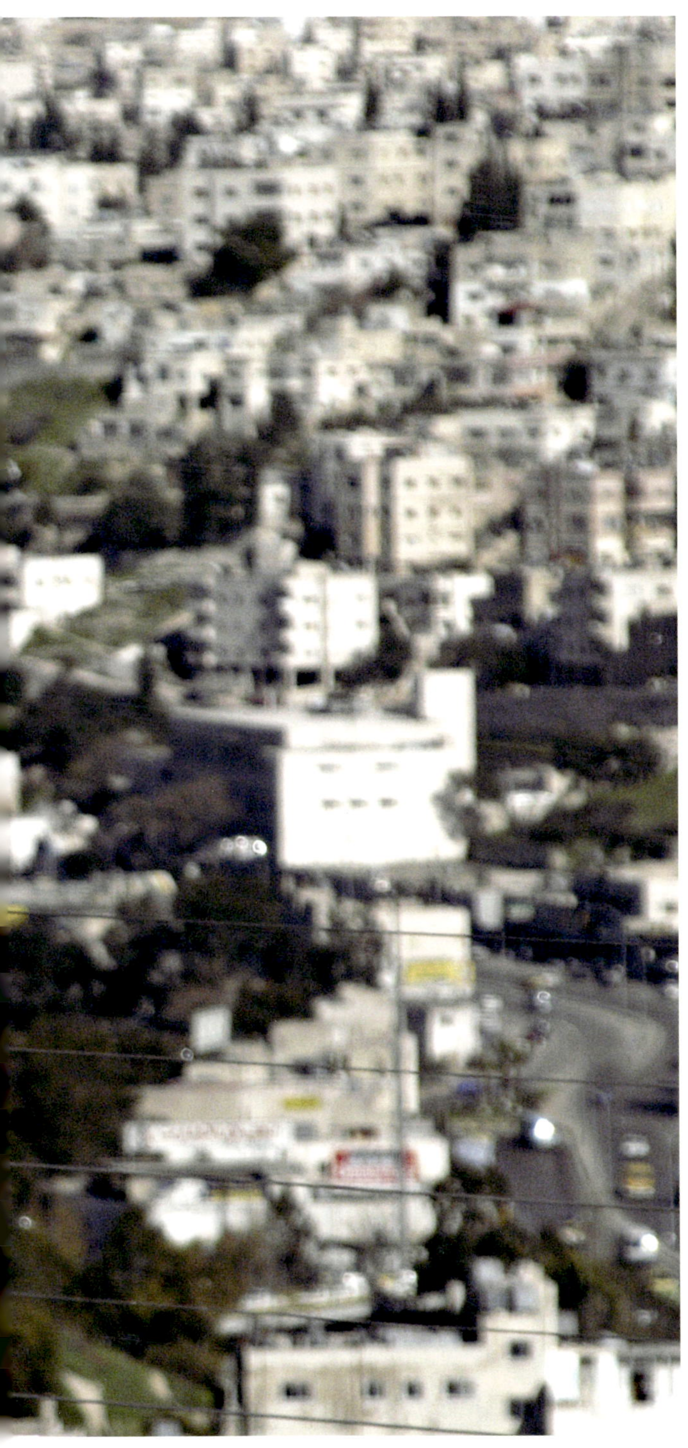

This is it. This is the countdown, hour by hour until the bombs start to drop on the city I was in last week. To the people I know, some of whom I've come to love, some who are the most amazing people I've ever met, and all who are innocent.

I feel so sick that I'm not there, so guilty though it would have achieved nothing.

I may not be a human shield, and I may not adhere to the beliefs of those I have travelled with, but the way Britain and America plan to take Iraq is unnecessary and puts soldiers' lives above those of Iraqi civilians. For that, I hope that Bush and Blair stand trial for war crimes. It's not so simple as war/no war, black and white. Things I've heard and seen over the last few weeks prove what I already knew - neither the Iraqi regime, nor the American nor British, are clean. Maybe Saddam needs to go and maybe an invasion is the only way, but people are so blinded by their stances on war/no war and the UN position that they have ignored the "how". The air war that's proposed is largely unnecessary and doesn't discriminate between civilians and armed soldiers. Tens of thousands will die, maybe hundreds of thousands, just to save thousands of American soldiers having to fight honestly, hand to hand.
It is wrong.

19 MARCH

Twenty-five hours left and counting until the deadline set by Bush.

We watched avidly at 3 am last night as Bush gave his ultimatum to Baghdad. It was one of those defining moments I will never forget… wondering if I would be on the receiving end of the ferocious might he said would come to bear on the region.

Though not entirely void of a sense of dishonesty, not entirely virtuous and persuasive, his speech was taken for what it was - a war cry - and not for its content. I felt as if I could hear all the collective screams of the wounded and dying as a result of those quiet, serene words he uttered with such intended deliberation. Though I know it was in my mind, it seemed so real, and for a moment all arguments and justification left my thoughts. Everything went quiet and all I could hear was the crying of thousands of people. Despair can be such a powerful word when you stop to think on it. I had to hold back the tears.

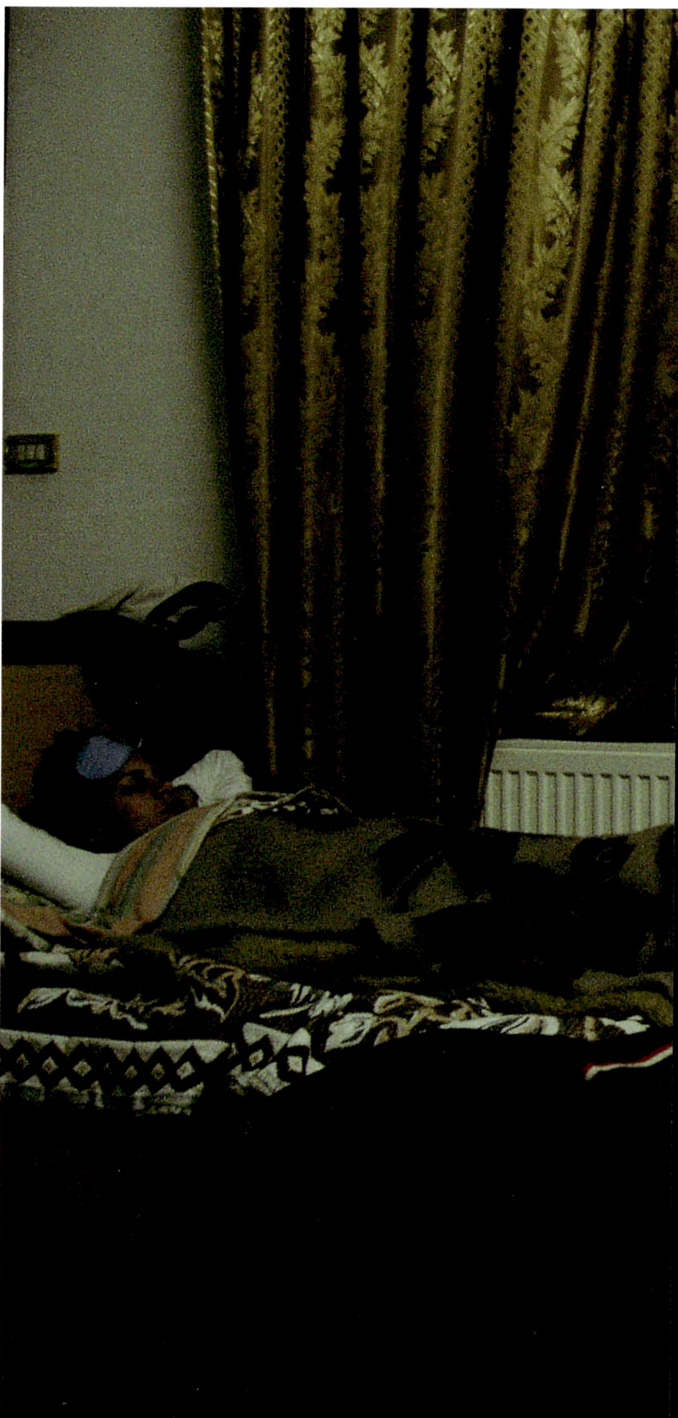

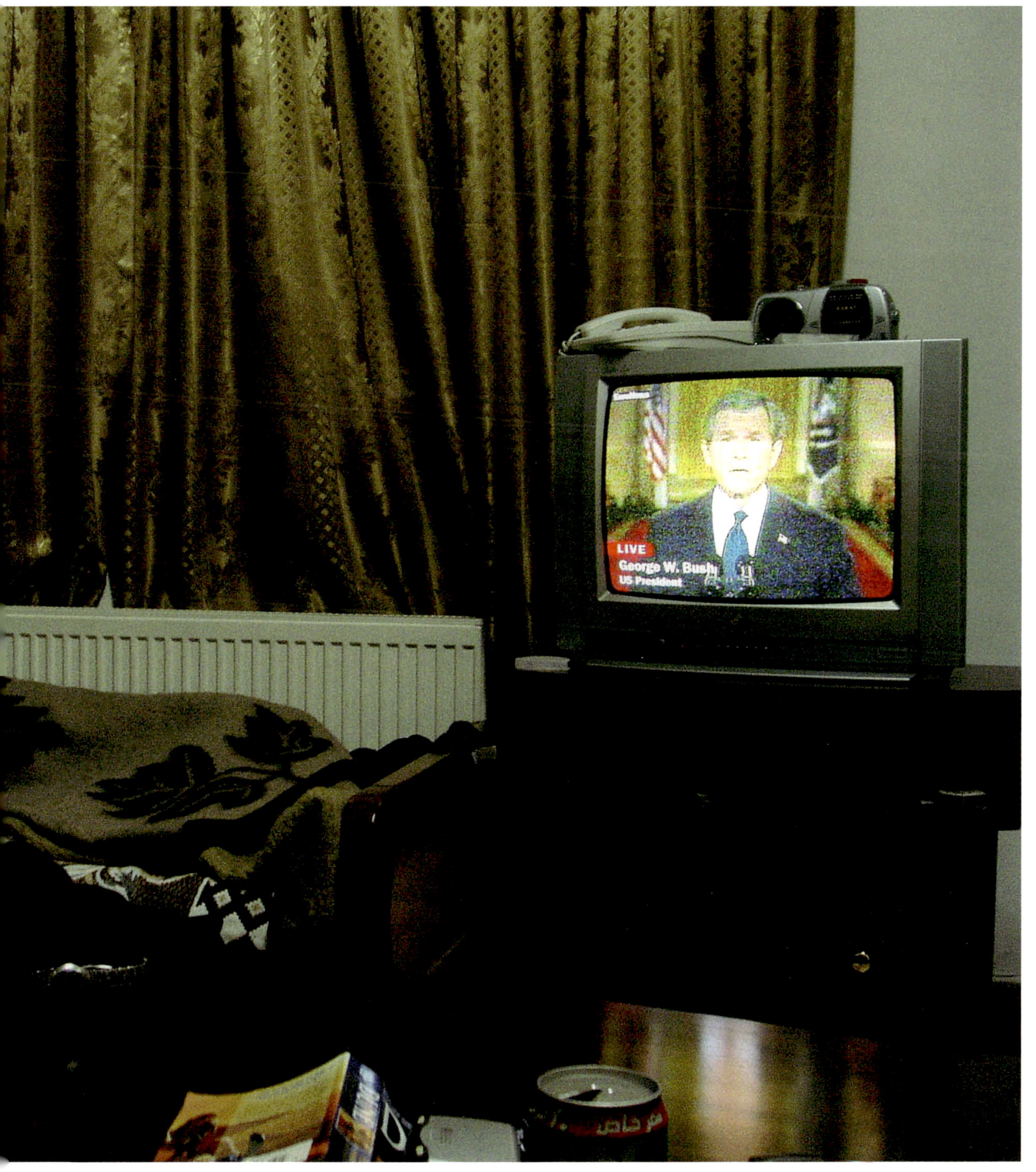LIVE
George W. Bush
US President

19 MARCH

As I sit here, in a hotel room in Amman, it occurs to me that over the next few days I may be about to embark on something the likes of which I have never attempted.

  I know the way I act suggests, to many people who don't know me to such great depths, that I am unrealistic in the face of risks I choose to take. Some would call it arrogance. But I assure you that I am under no illusions about what I am doing. I know that for the next month or so I will be giving up control over my life, surrendering it to people I have never met. And I know I could die. So I am writing this now, and will send it to someone I trust, to be read if anything happens to me. I want to set the record straight because my life until now has been a series of fractured elements, and there are many people who are under false impressions. I have lived, and do live so many different lives. And I couldn't leave without telling everyone who I really am.

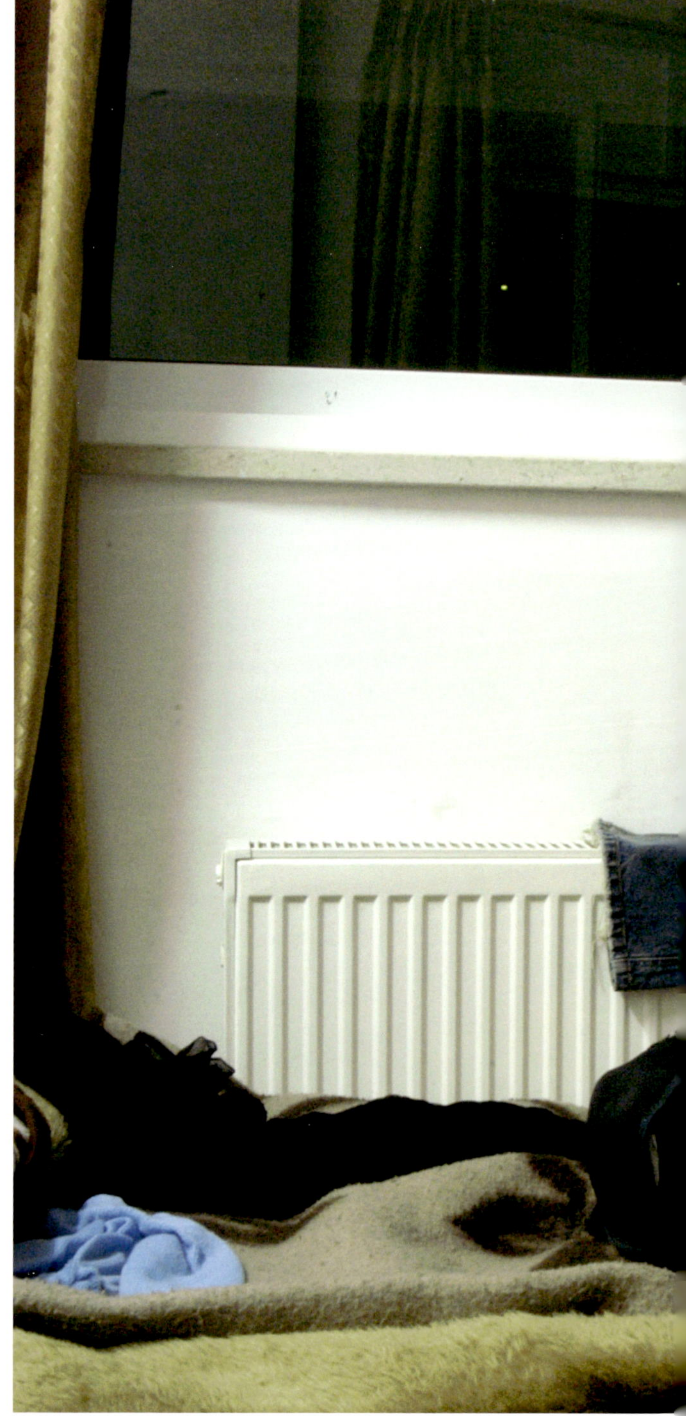

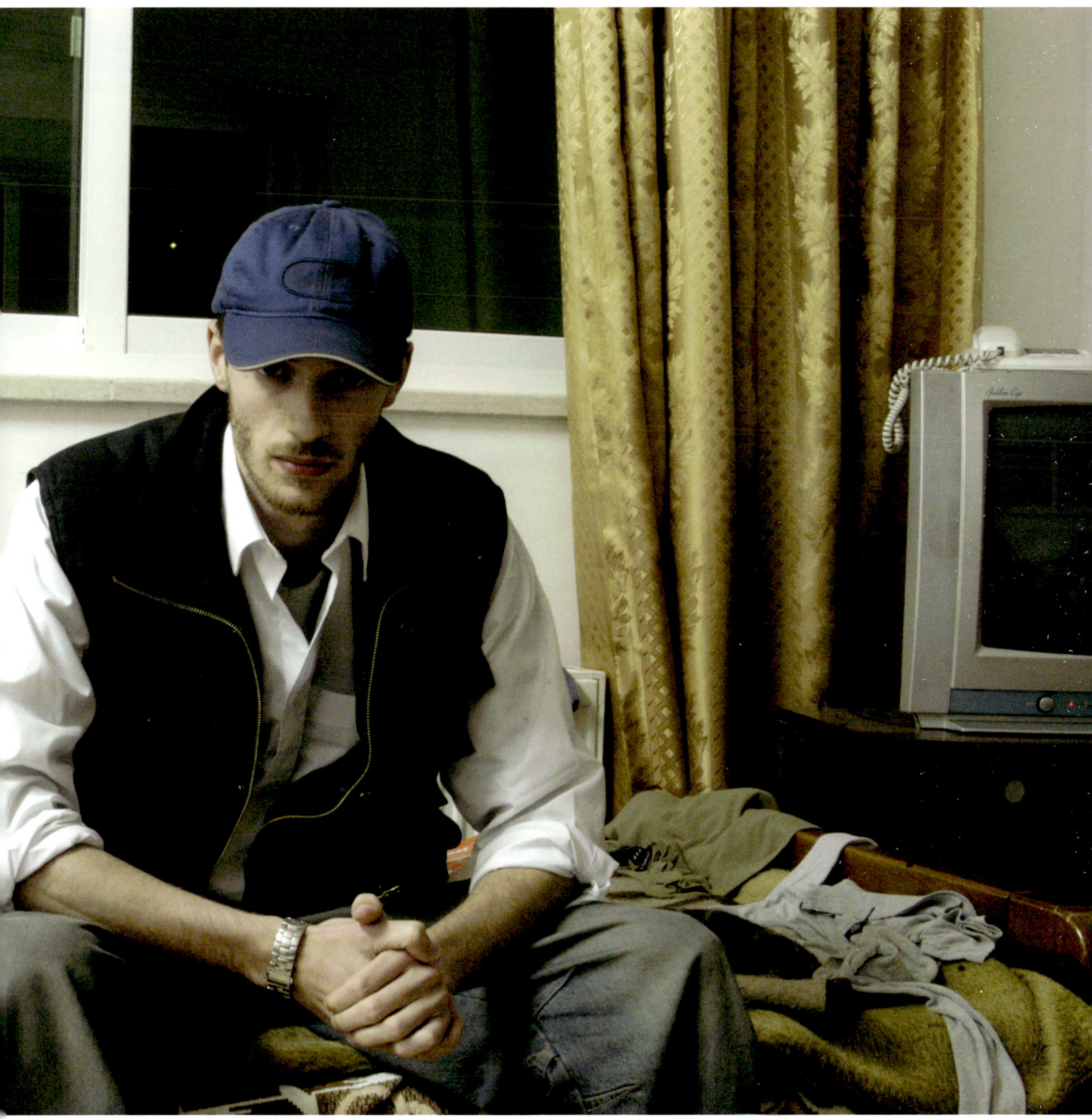

I love all of you, by name or not, everyone, you know who you are.   I am blessed to have known you. Thank you.

AL-RWEISHED REFUGEE CAMP

21 - 31 MARCH 2003

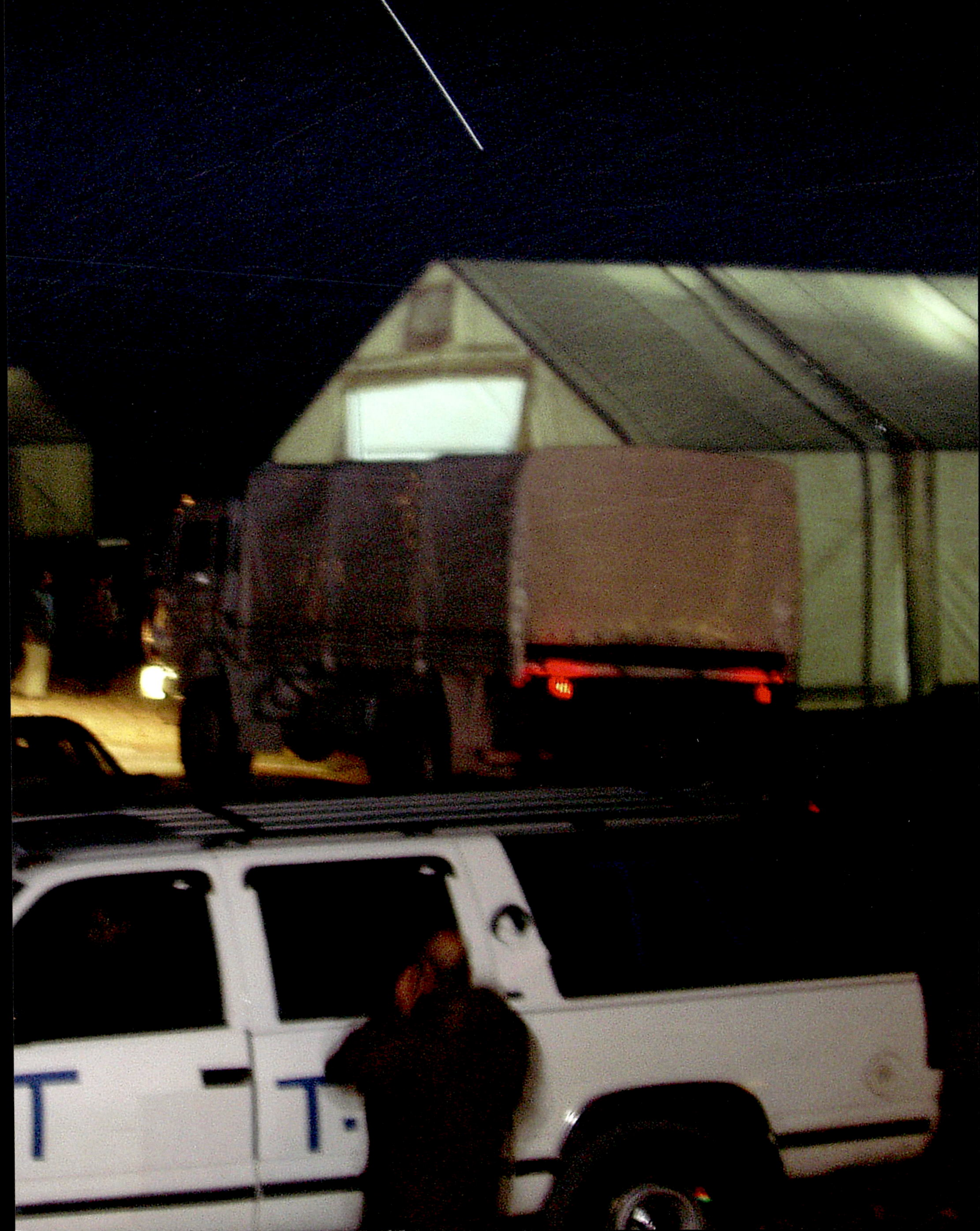

23 MARCH

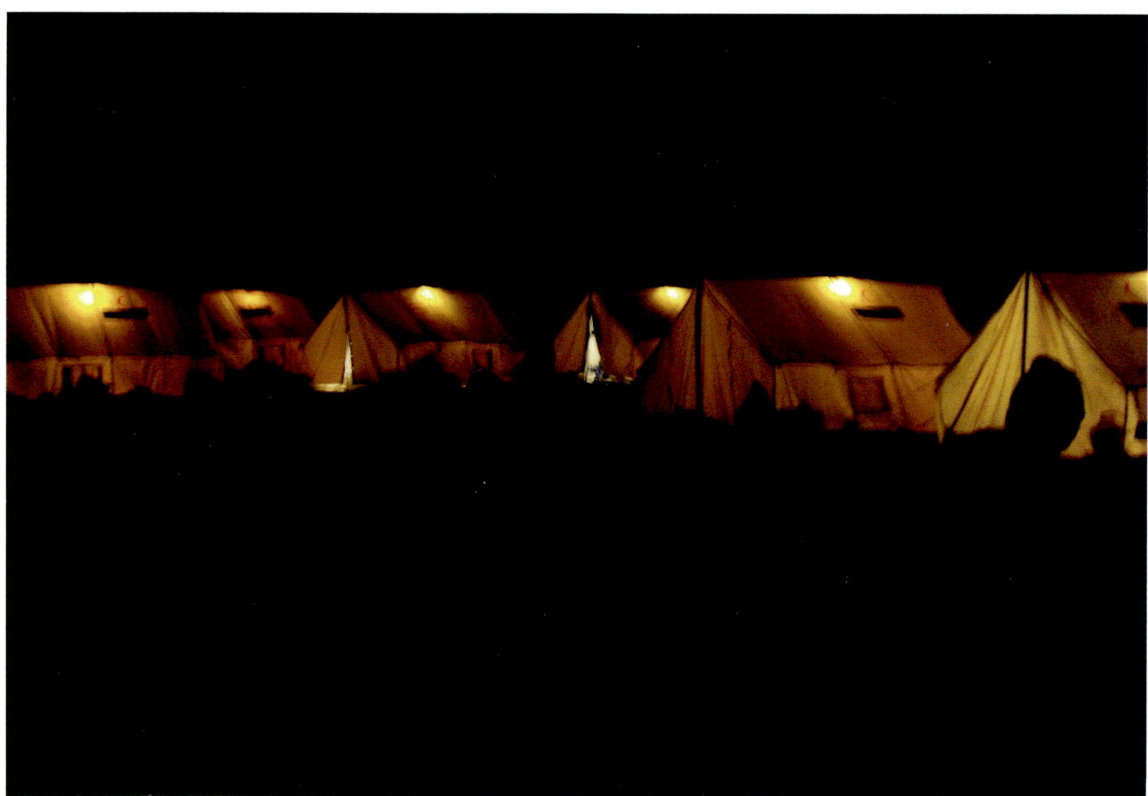

I'm sitting in my tent in the western desert 5 km from the Iraqi border, trying to stay warm by a kerosene heater.

It's crazy how out here it can be so cold at night that you couldn't survive without heat or protection, and yet during the day you can't work for more than 10 minutes without having to take a break in the shade.

The wind whips up across the plains and by the time it hits us, it is carrying fine sand that rips at your face. It is as if the desert is alive, rising up at you, attacking you.

Most of the workers in the refugee camp are wearing ski-goggles to protect their eyes. At the outskirts where we were working today it's a necessity. It gets everywhere, the sand, and you can't escape it. I've just about become used

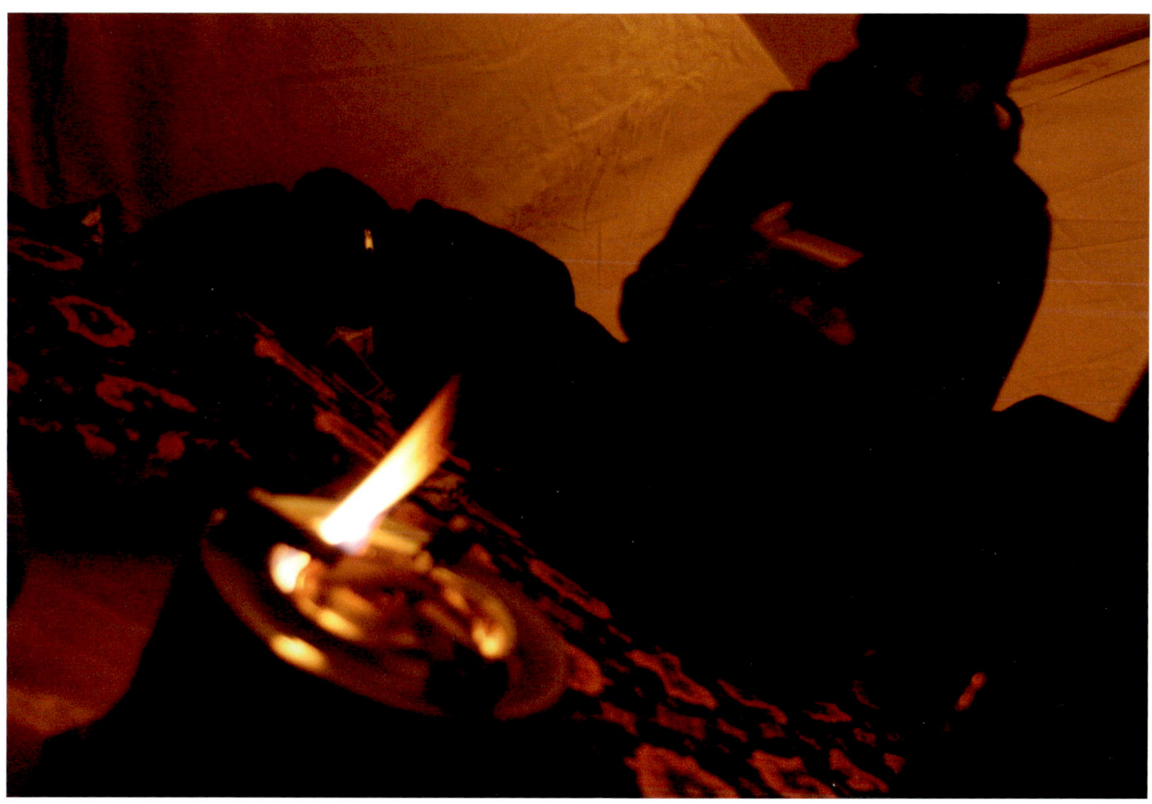

to the water, from the huge tanks we installed, tasting of iron and sand.

Each evening I empty my boots and clothes of grains of sand and enter a tent where it is inside my sleeping bag. Each new entry I write with a new pen because once used they become blocked from it.

That and the kerosene. My hands are stained from the carbon it produces. No one knows how to use the lamps and I keep having to take them apart. My clothes are saturated with the intoxicating alcohol smell, and the only way to stay warm is by using a kerosene heater that gives you a searing headache if you use it in your tent for long.

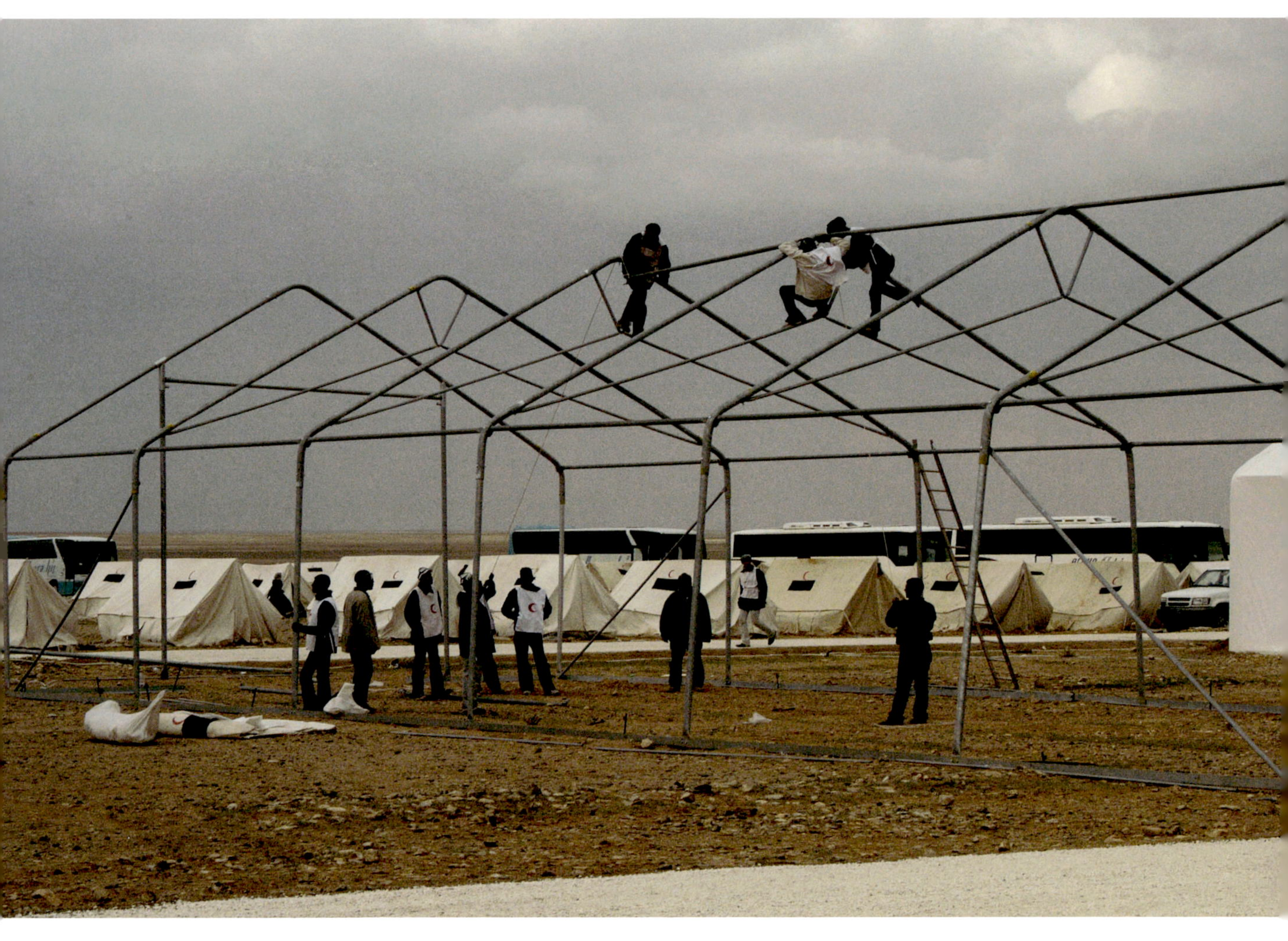

Today, our group started putting up more tents at 7 am. Maybe it sounds easy, until you try it.

Even after everything is erected you have to anchor the sides with a foot of rocks and earth, which must be brought by hand from 50 yards away, dug up and put in sacks. We started trying to dig it up around the tents, but the ground is rock solid and you need a pickaxe to break it, and then it is still just small boulders. Given my age, I'm a fit guy, but I've never worked so hard. We finished at 5, having eaten only bread and had lentil soup and more bread…

not particularly diverse. It's 7.30 now and I am fucked. My body aches.

I'm starving and have no more energy. But I'm enjoying it. Energy tablets are helping me keep going and for the first time in a long time I'm doing something that I'm proud of.

The bombs are still dropping only a few miles away, and will probably continue for weeks and I am helping in some small way to make the Iraqis, Sudanese etc. more comfortable. Some people reckon we are saving lives…I doubt that, not yet anyway, but we are making a small, but important difference.

I've had a premonition,
such that my life changes course,
colours are merged and defined,
and new thoughts breach the barriers of my ears.
I have a new sense lent to lift my life.

No God showed me the light
nor a woman the way,
but the total power of a mind in focus,
clarified in a moment overwhelmed.
Though before, I knew the pain, now I see the cause.

And not just the fear, of all those years possesed,
but the love or obsession, truth or want of it.
I have learnt to feel my thoughts.

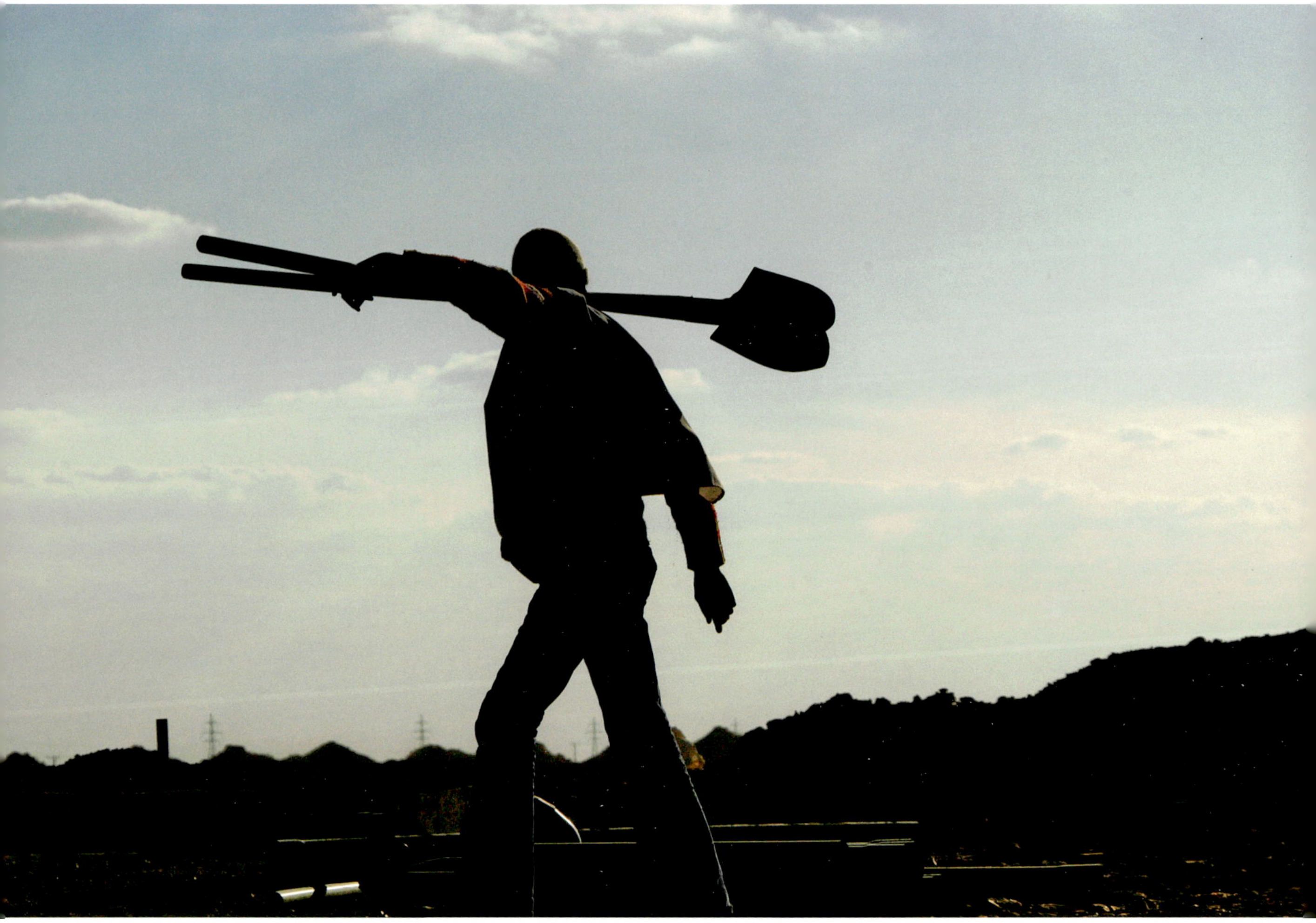

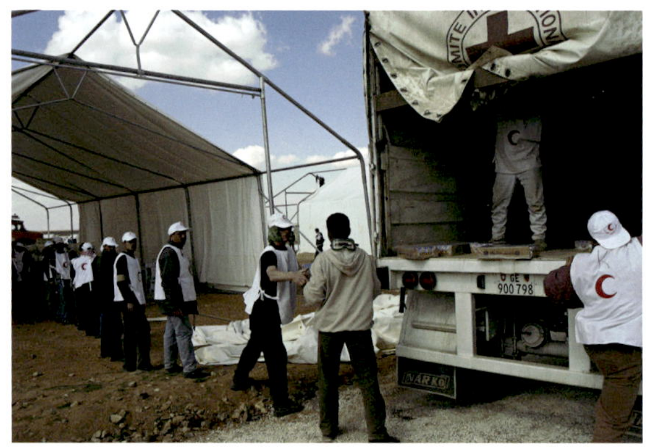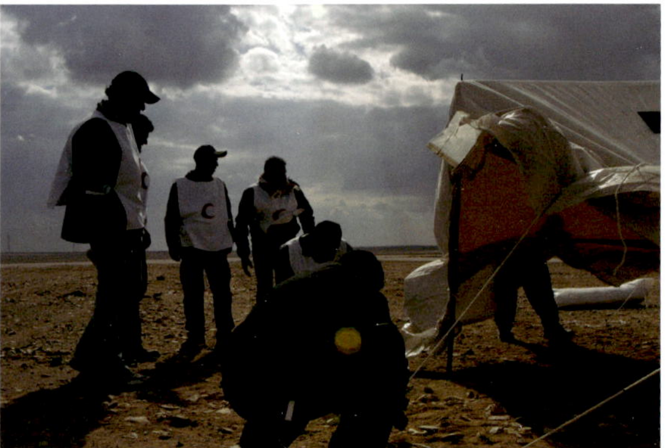

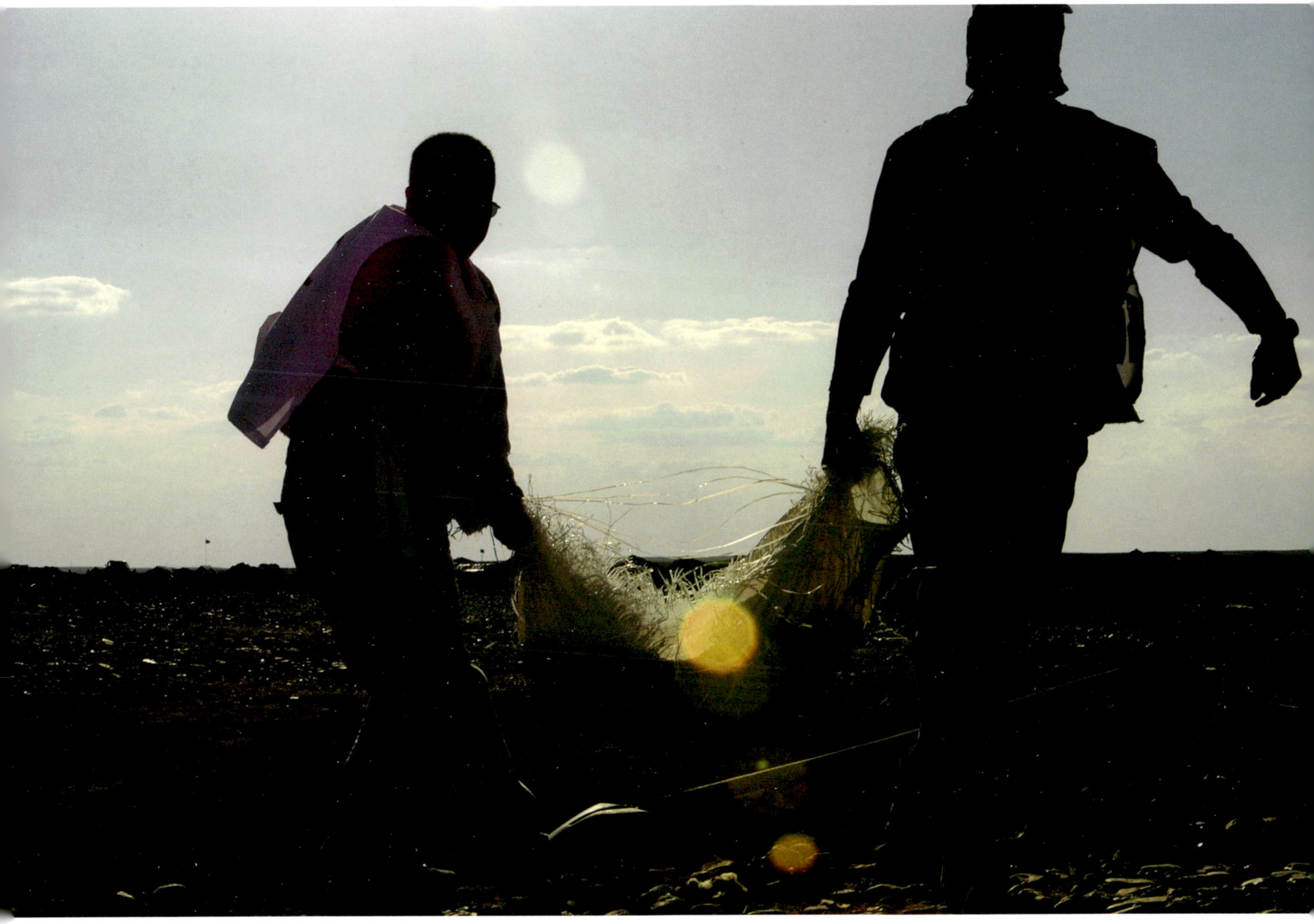

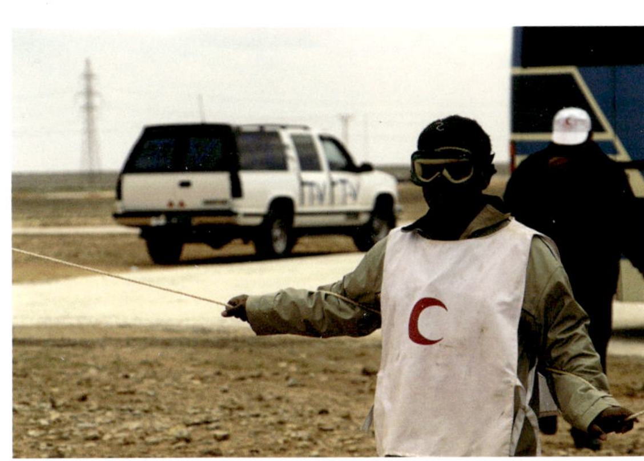

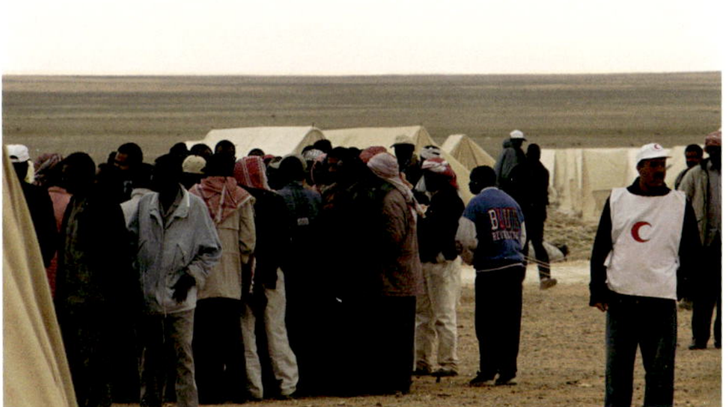

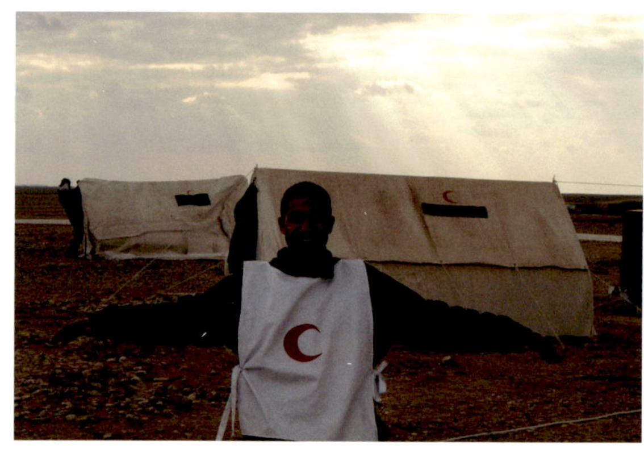
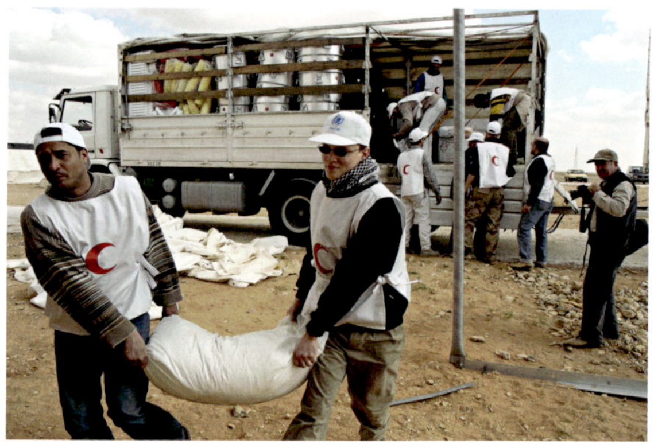
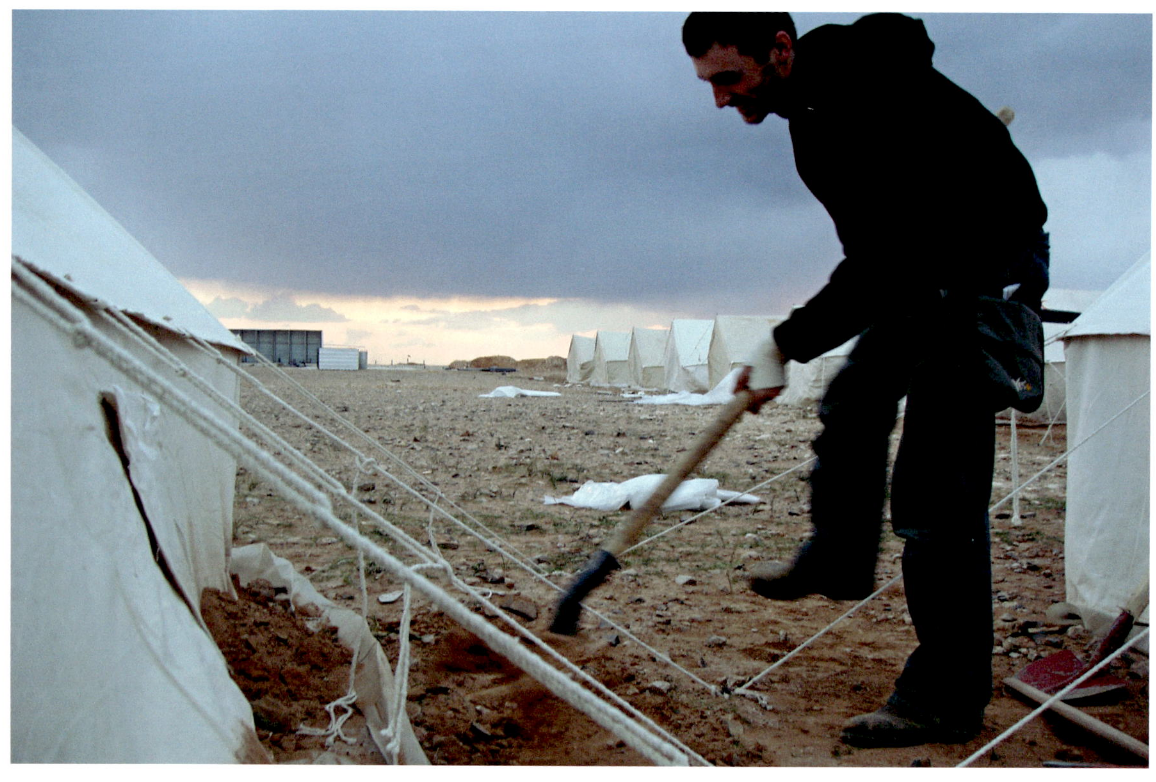

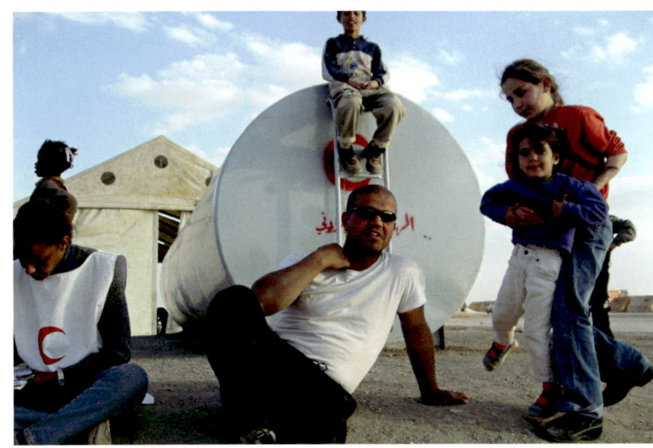
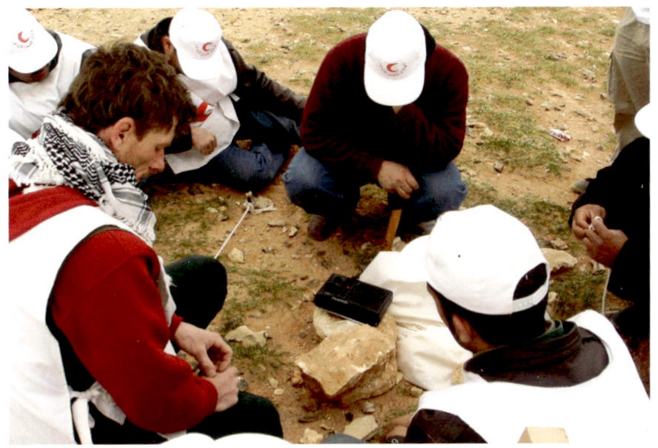

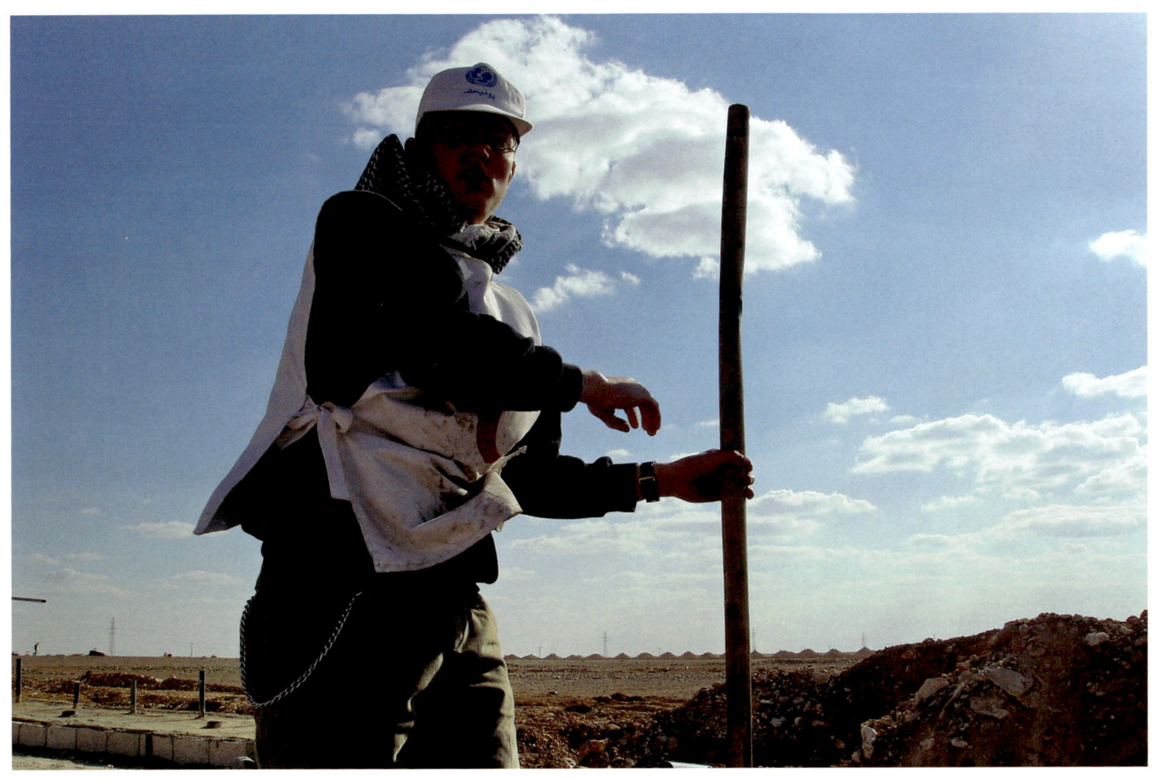

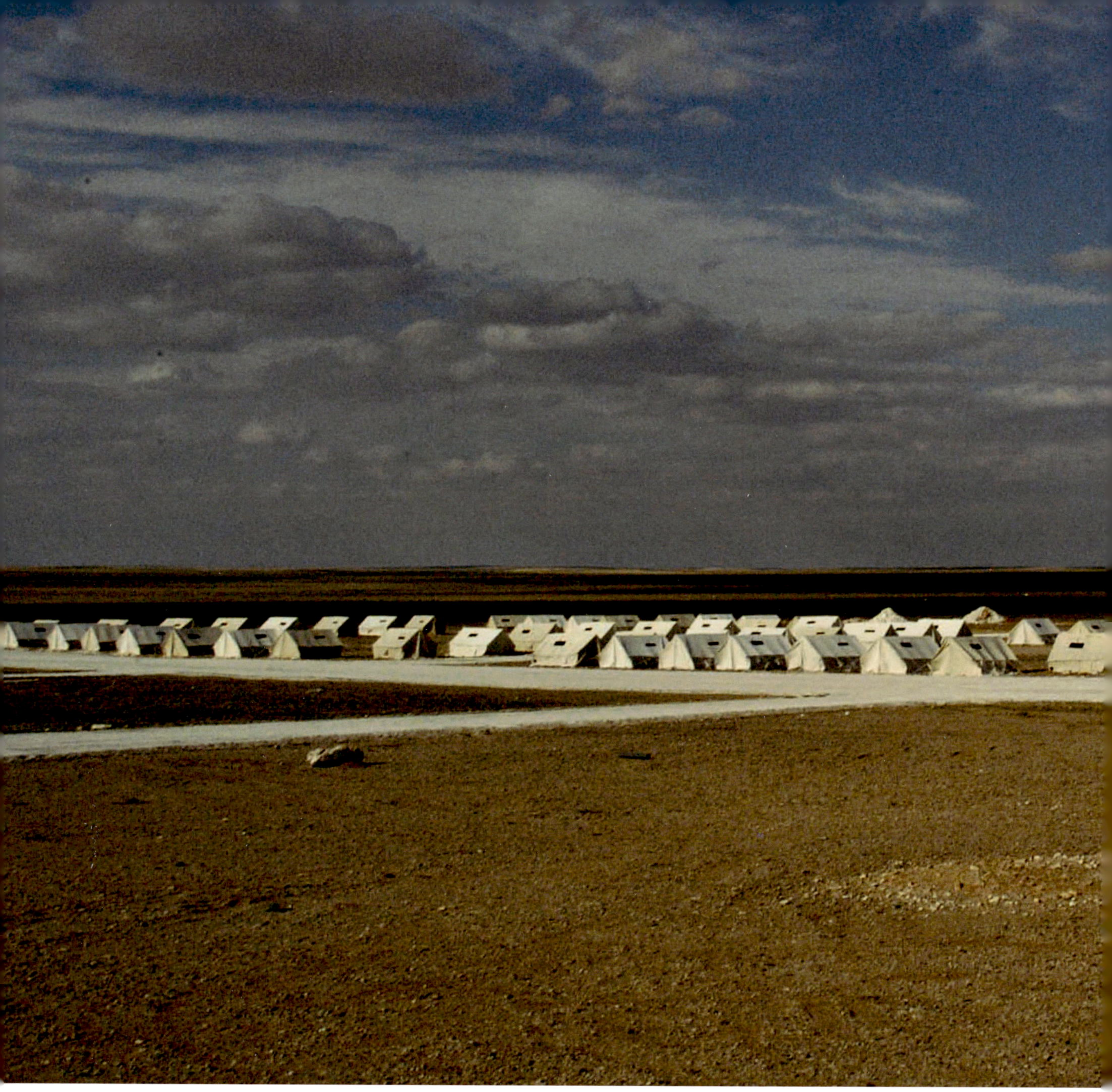

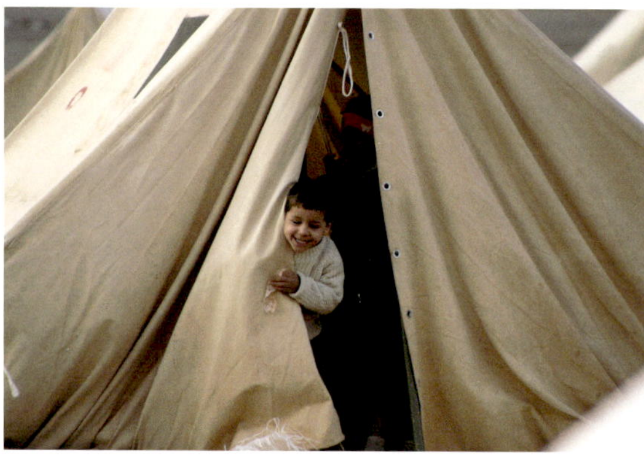
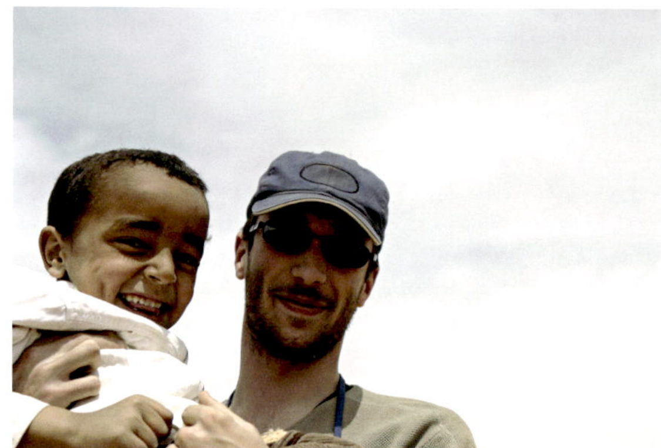

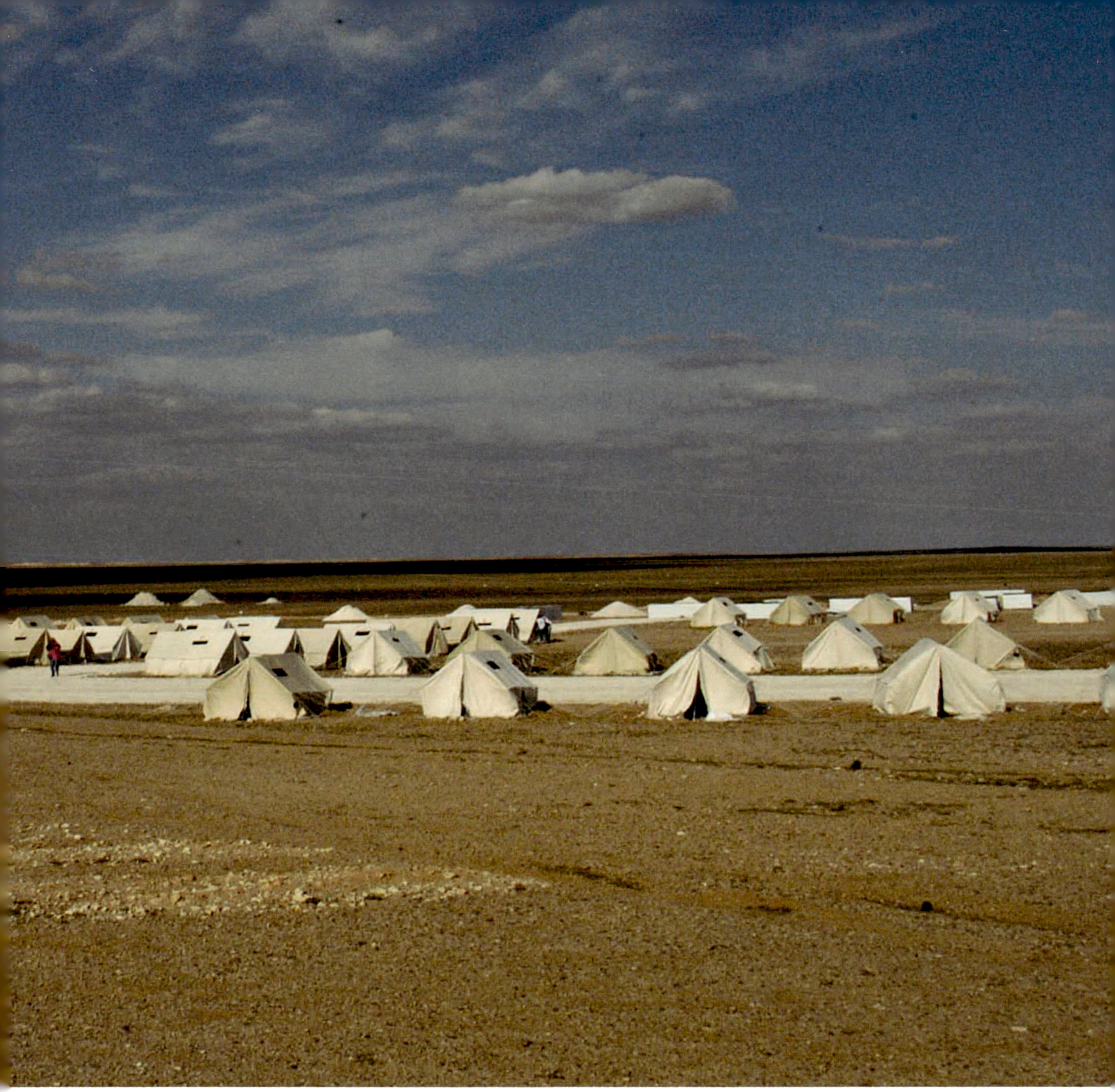

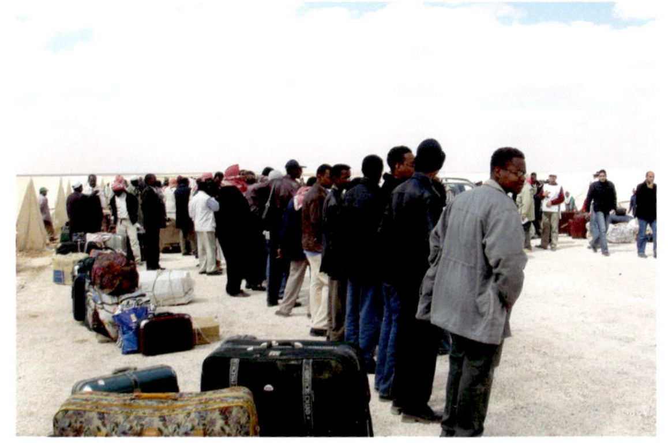

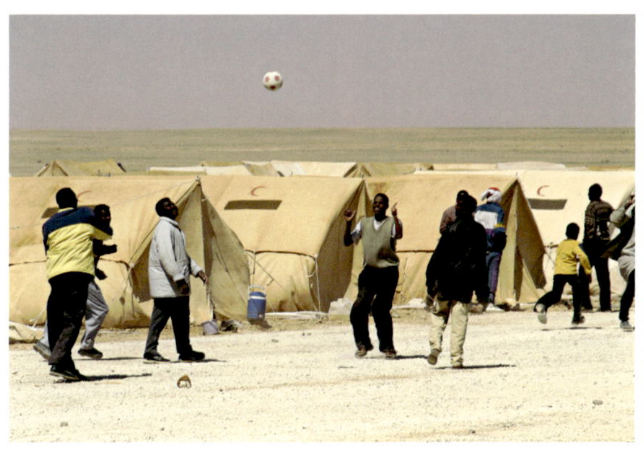

27 MARCH

AMMAN VISIT

So, sitting back indoors in an American franchise in Amman...air-conditioned, with a music channel showing on TV and cushioned chairs, not to mention clean, metal cutlery (actually cutlery is a blessing on its own) and actual china plates (or porcelain, or whatever). It feels like years since I was here last, and my muscles still ache from overworking. My hair is matted and my skin still covered in dust, etc...

All this and the remnants of my dream still hover at the back of my mind from last night.

It's a strange place I'm in, in my head - these circumstances and the way of life back in the refugee camp. I feel like I owe something to the people of Iraq who are suffering for me and the sake of my 'national security'. No, it's wrong to say that… I do owe them something. But no matter how hard I work here, it has become apparent that I'm not going to make a difference.

There are so many questions I'm having to ask myself that no one ever does in England. The world is clearly an unfair place. Someone intelligent can work their arse off in one part of the world and get paid half of what a student would with a weekend job in another. Actually, that's not true...it's more like 1/10th.

We have it so fucking good and the vast majority of us don't do anything at all, or even contemplate evening the score. There are good people in England, so why do they do nothing?

The answer is simple, but rarely given credence. Each of us at any one time has a hundred voices in our head. They are all of our thoughts, many of them from something inside us that wants to be quenched. On a basic level, they are physical needs and comforts, and on a more complex level, are psychological - almost pre-emptive. Some

say "obtain" and some say "avoid". The problem is that they almost always clash. Normally, the need to eat outweighs the effort of cooking and conflicts on the same "level" will have a fair fight. But some voices are from a deeper part of your soul than others, and can shout louder. You can be trained to plan for the future, or be given a set of morals, but you will always have your genes, and they are impossible to quieten. Unfortunately, the only way your mind can deal with such huge, conflicting demands from many voices is to focus on only one. And the loudest call is for self-preservation, and procreation. In the face of challenges to them, your mind uses tricks to avoid giving attention to morality.

People are born with instincts that are largely all selfish. It's what they learn that challenges, not replaces that.

And so it goes with what people know they should do to help other people. They want to look after themselves and without the sight of the suffering that exists elsewhere being forced on them, they don't even contemplate it. I myself am no different, I know, but when I try, I am not afraid to look, that is what I am doing over here now.

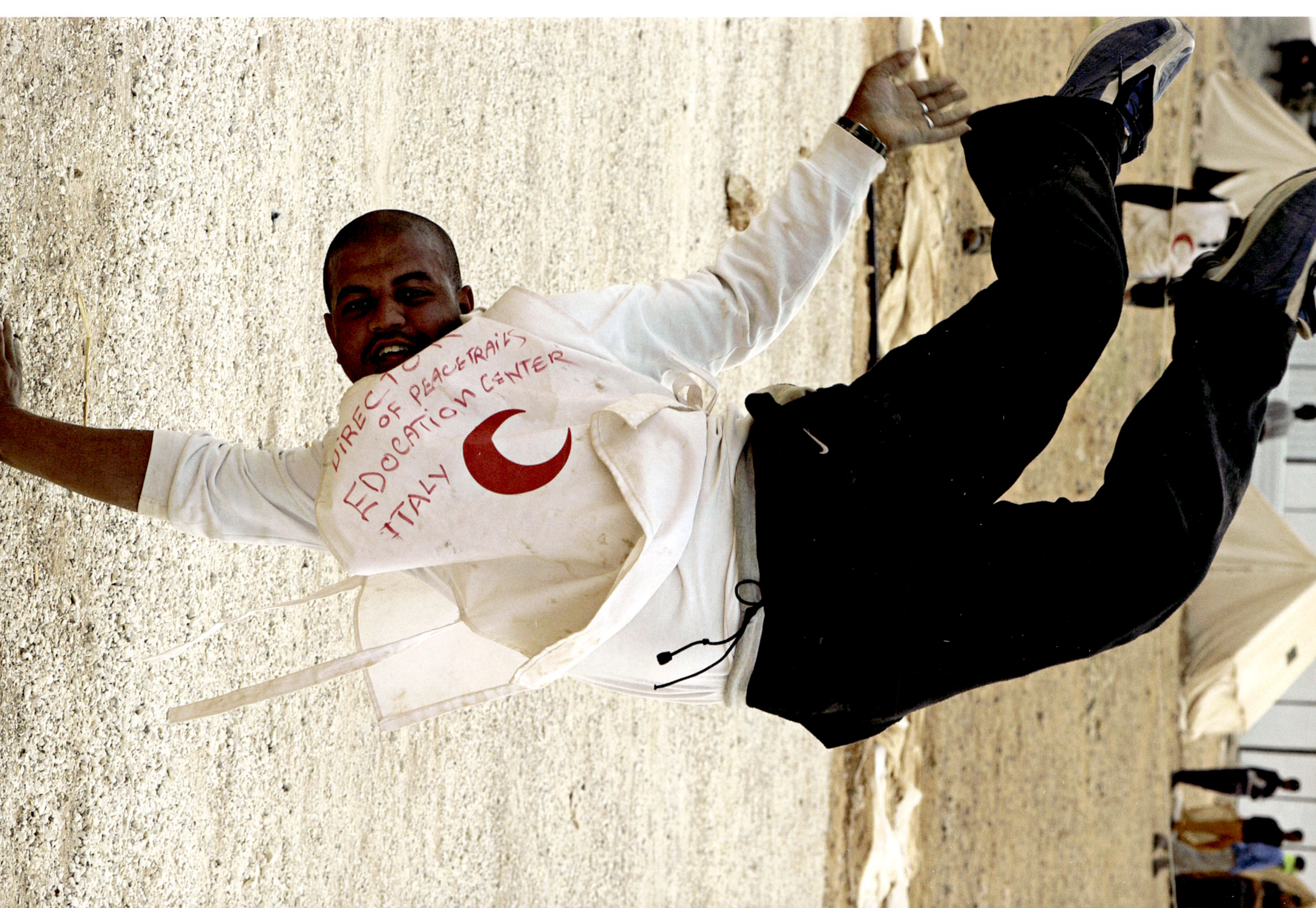

DIRECTOR
of PEACETRAILS
EDOCATION CENTER
ITALY

Hey,

I've met a whole load of Al-Jazeera journalists, and along with Reuters and AP representatives, (and a few of SABA's) they are the only reporters left in the city of Baghdad (not including the few BBC/CNN crew who are just staying in their hotel rooms the whole time, and were hand-picked by the coalition military so as not to reveal too much that might cast a bad light -no offence Mr Omar!!?!?!). Sorry I can't send any of my stuff, but I don't have the necessary cables, and I'll show everyone when I get back. Unfortunately I've already had a whole load 'confiscated' from me by security forces at the border a couple of weeks ago (ironically the whole point of leaving was to get images out to Amman to keep safe before going back in). It's a learning curve that's proving to be mildly expensive, what can I say?

Just so everyone knows what I'm doing, whenever I can get out, when everything is over, I am going to spend a couple of weeks (if money permits) probably in or around Hebron, covering the ISM (International Solidarity Movement) in the Palestinian Territories. This is because of a lot of reasons, not least that I want to see what is going on with my own eyes to disrupt the whole of the region. All in all, I should be back 2-3 weeks after the 'dust' settles in Iraq. (if I don't get shot by Iraqis, Israelis, Palestinians or Americans... I'm going to try to get a photo-essay published called 'in the middle')

Until then I probably won't be able to get anything out too easily, so I love you all loads, stay safe,

Tom

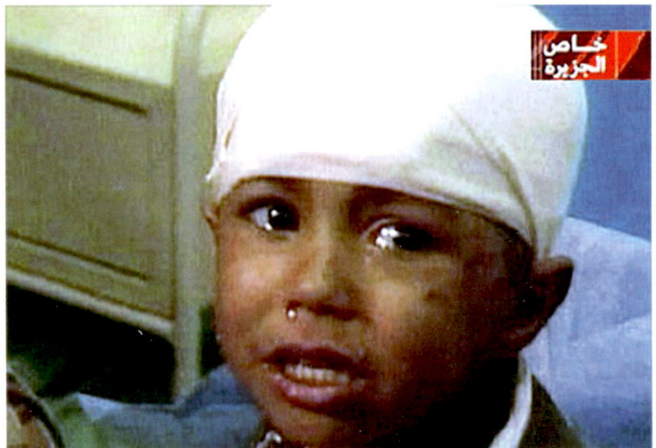

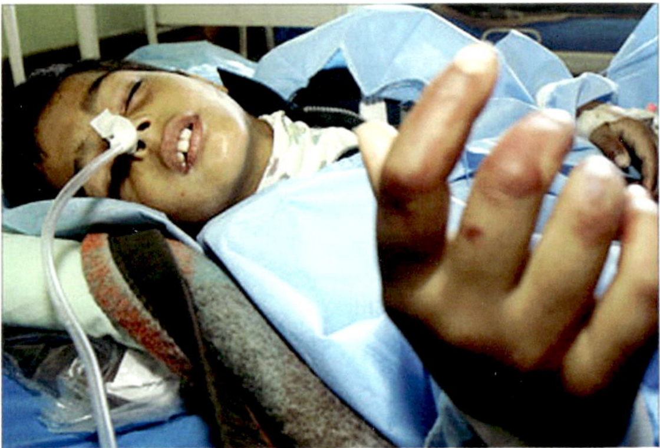

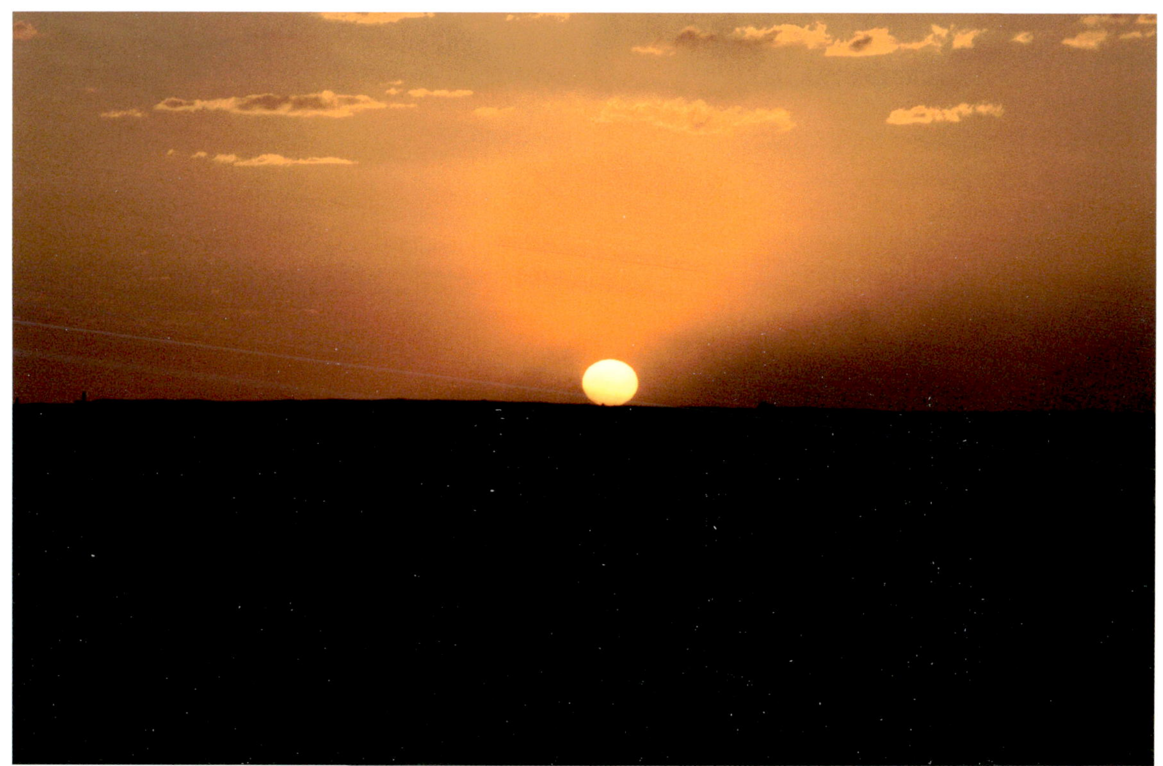

30 MARCH

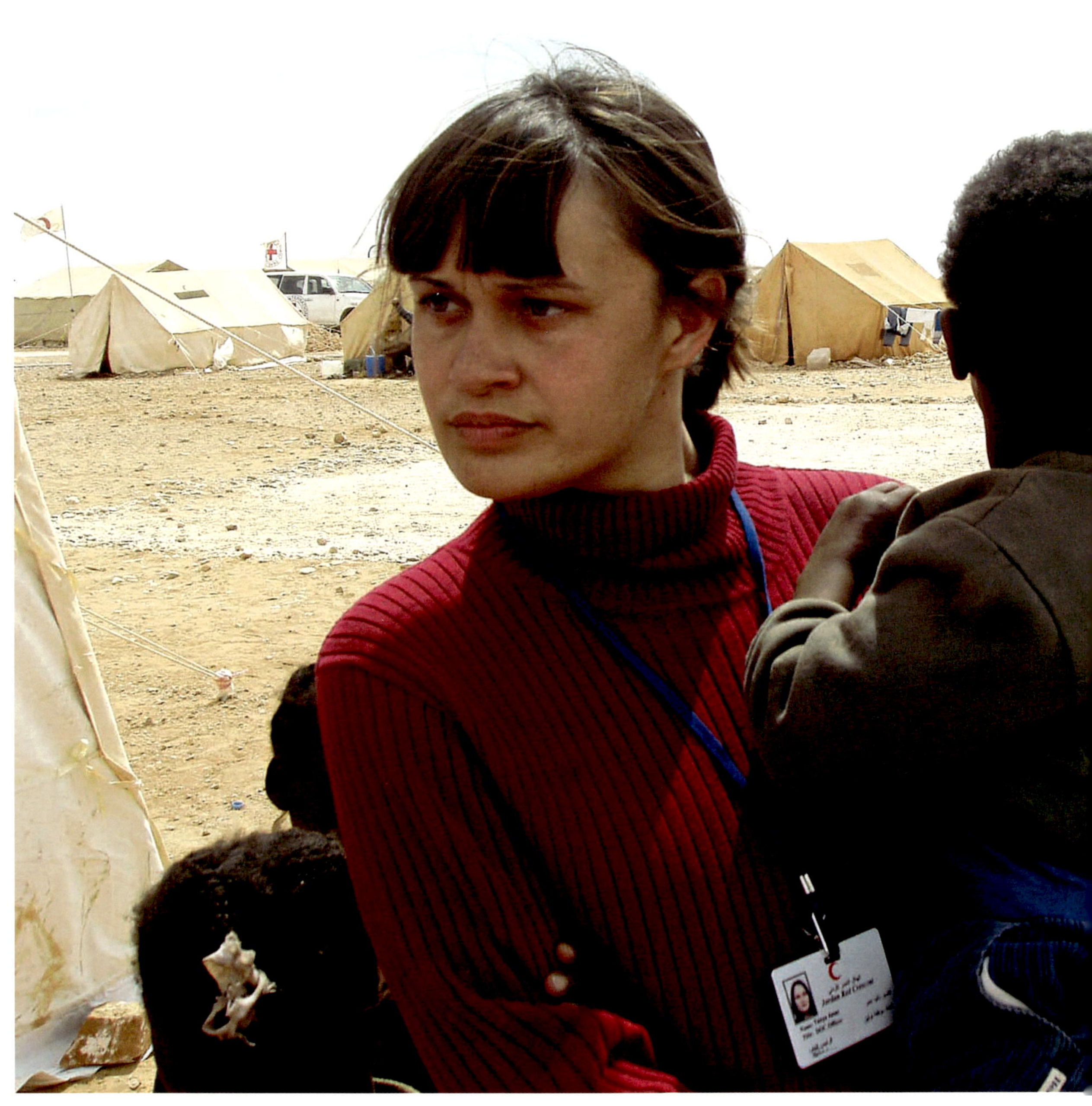

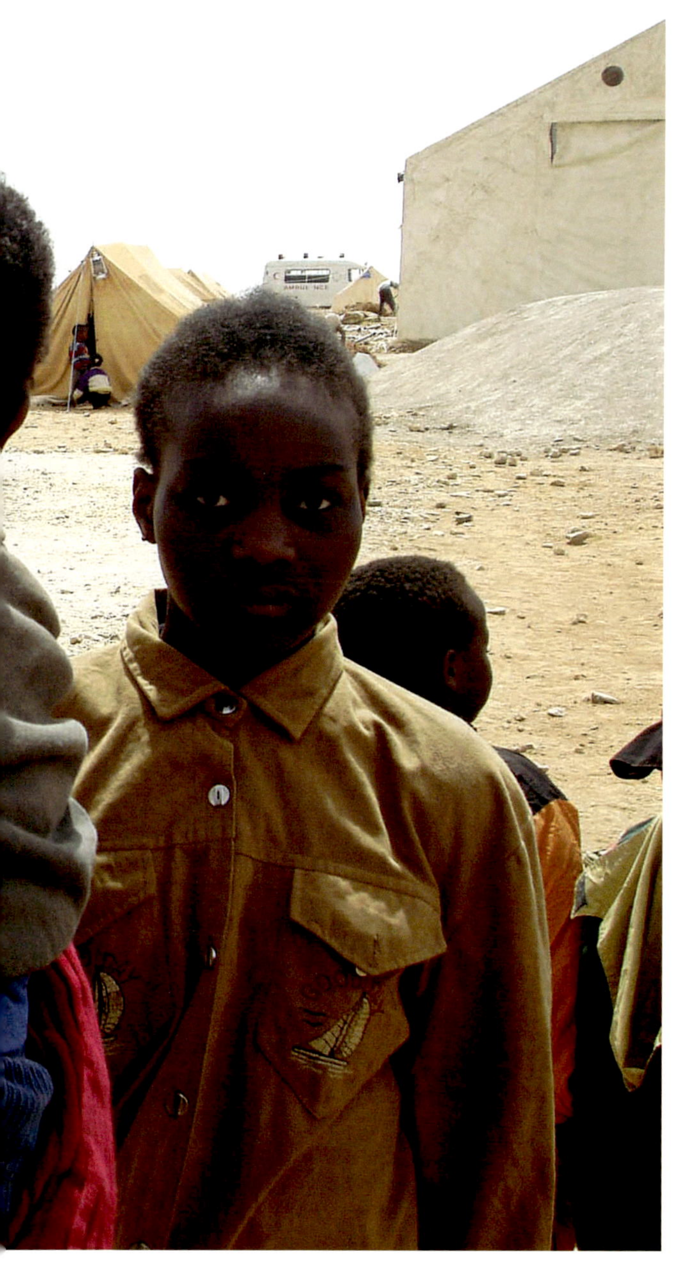

It's kind of calmed down in the camp.

There are just over 200 TCNs left, with some coming and going all the time. It's amazing to have seen it change into a small town with everything including a mosque, a church and a school. But it only takes so many people to run it and there is little to do.

Now is the time I have chosen to leave and go to Palestine. I feel guilty and I don't know why. Maybe it's because I don't feel anything else. I should be overwhelmed with everything, but I'm not, I just feel shit. I wanted some kind of release, but I haven't had it. Maybe I shouldn't leave Palestine until I feel it and if it takes forever then I'll know I am dead.

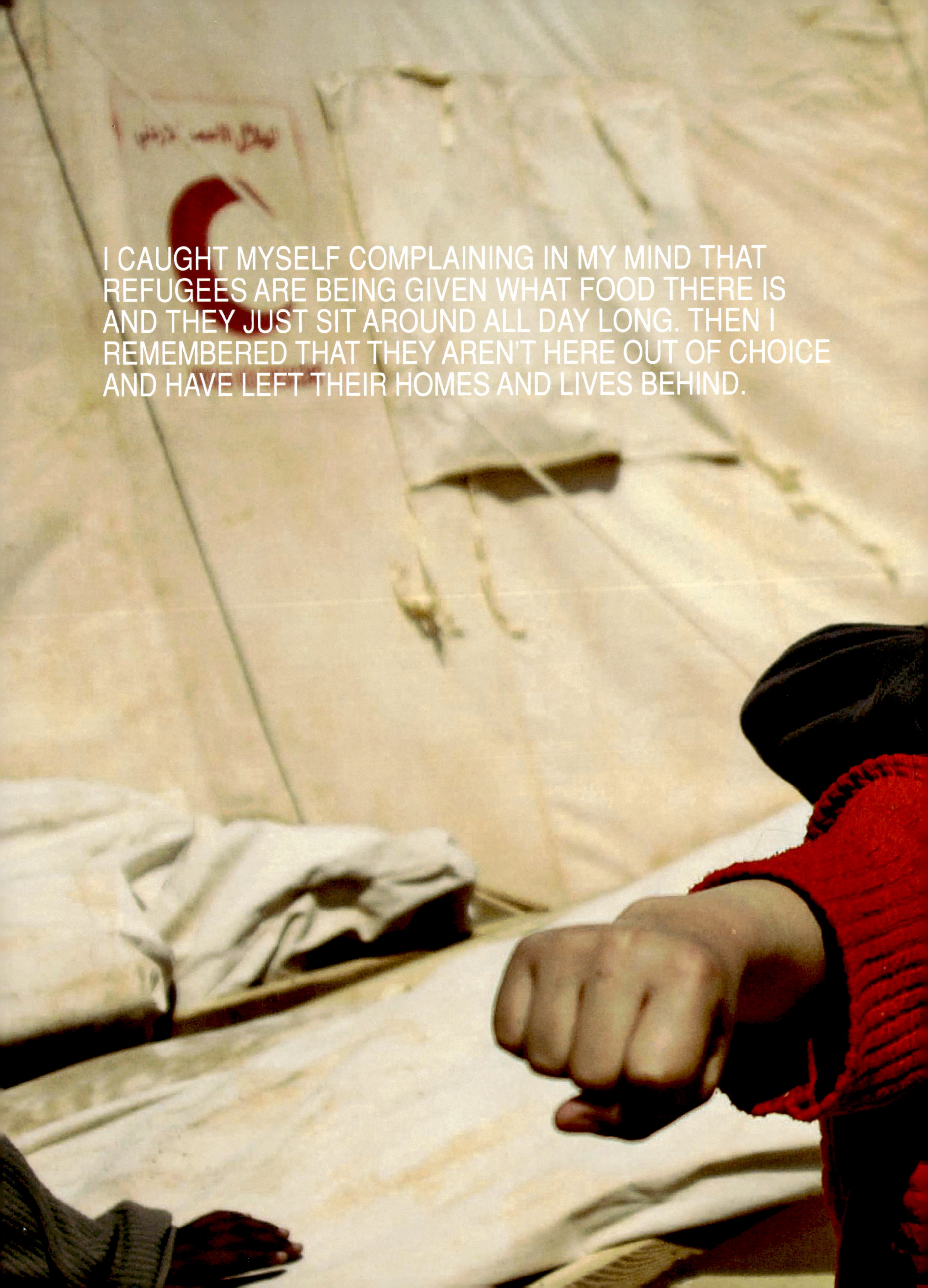
I CAUGHT MYSELF COMPLAINING IN MY MIND THAT REFUGEES ARE BEING GIVEN WHAT FOOD THERE IS AND THEY JUST SIT AROUND ALL DAY LONG. THEN I REMEMBERED THAT THEY AREN'T HERE OUT OF CHOICE AND HAVE LEFT THEIR HOMES AND LIVES BEHIND.

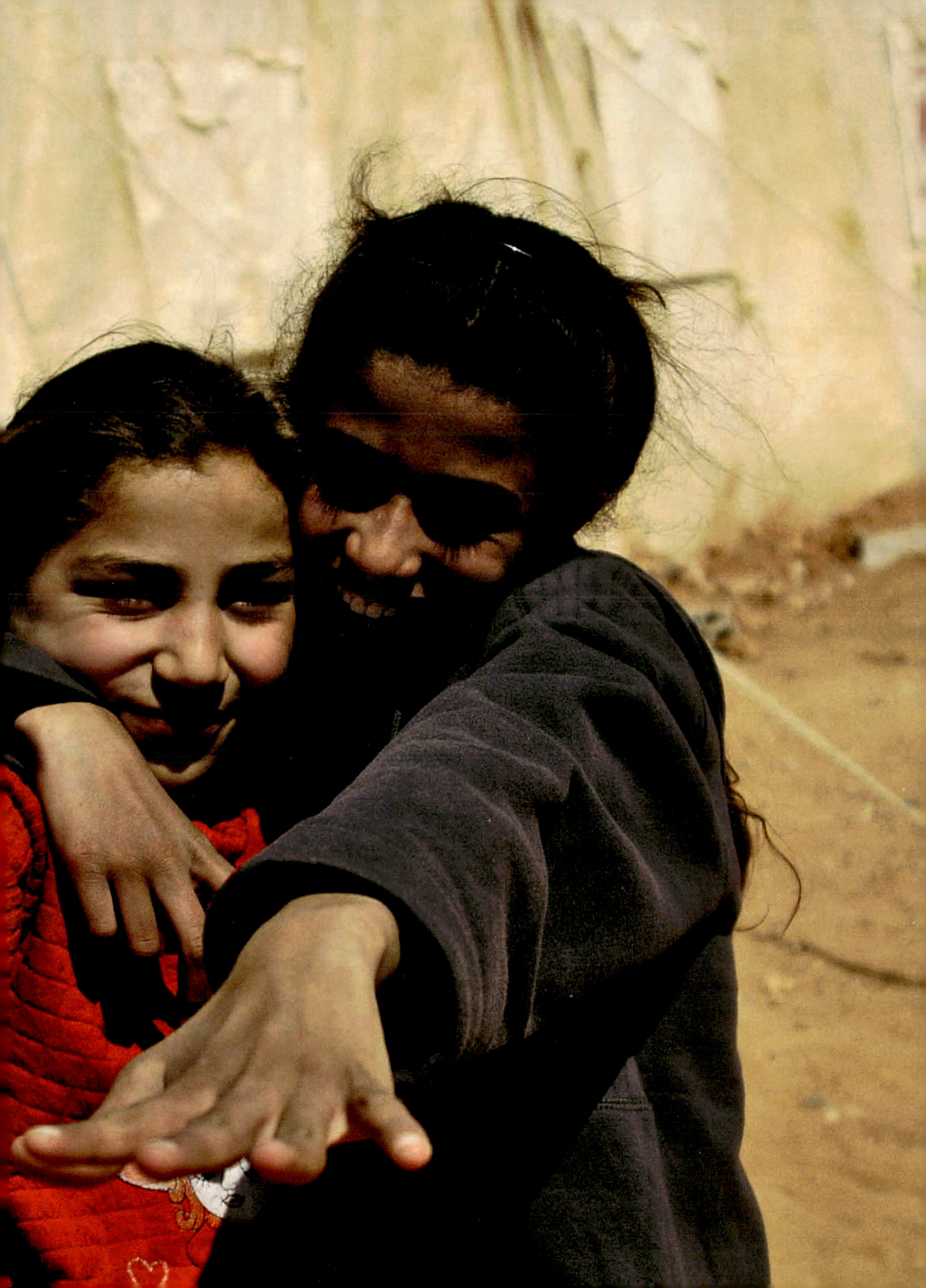

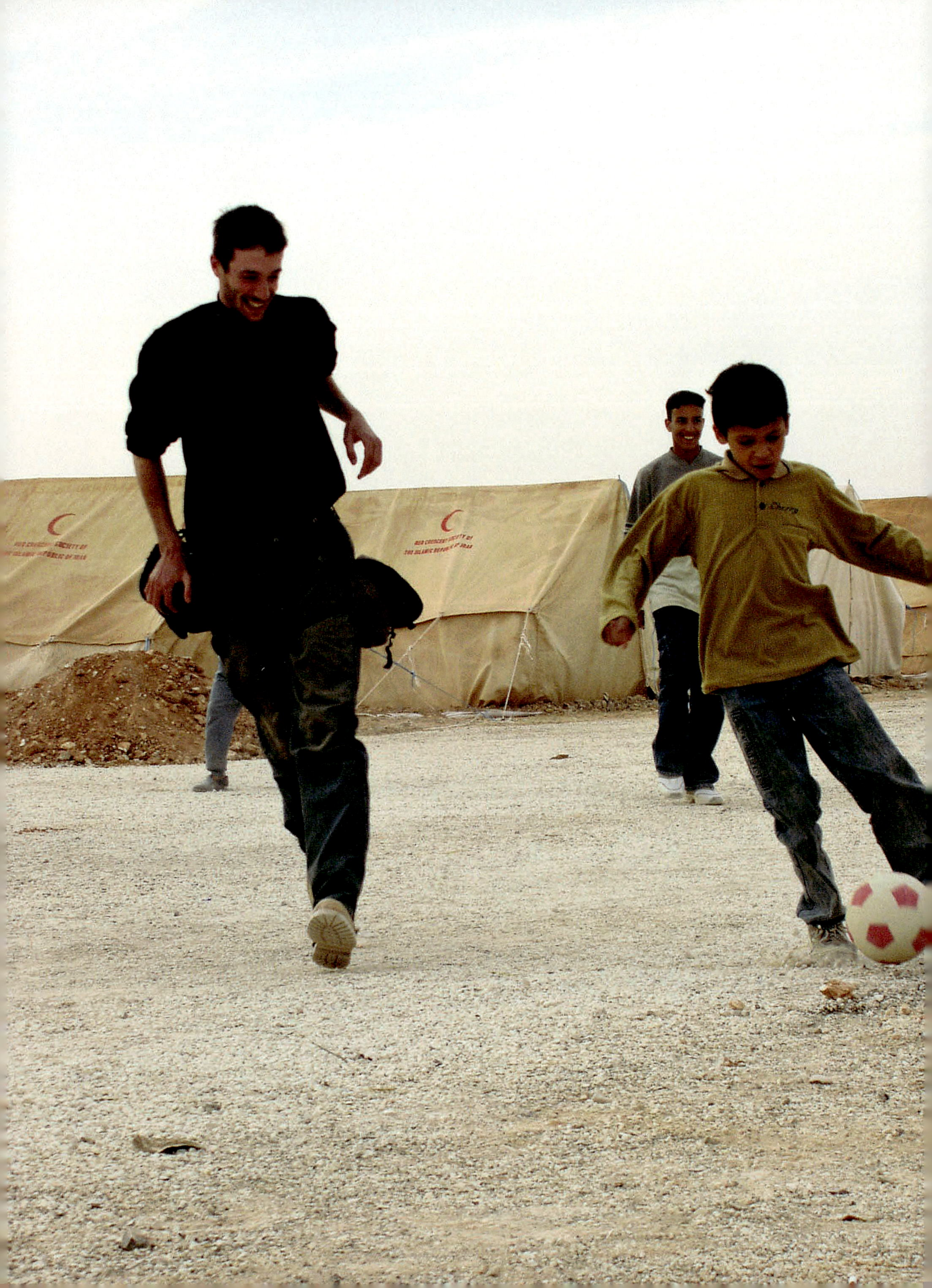

I wont give up on this life,
my only chance, no mistakes allowed;
it wont pass me by.
I would sooner end myself.

If one morning I should wake,
to find no change from the one before;
it wont rule me, it is mine,
and it wont pass me by.

Those before me, in their misery,
not seeing beyond their worth,
do they not know who they became?
Or have they let it pass them by?

It is not a life of madness,
born through pubescent dreams,
but a want, a need of mine,
to treasure each day, remembering as I pass them by

I will die with images of all the earthly
heavens in my eyes.

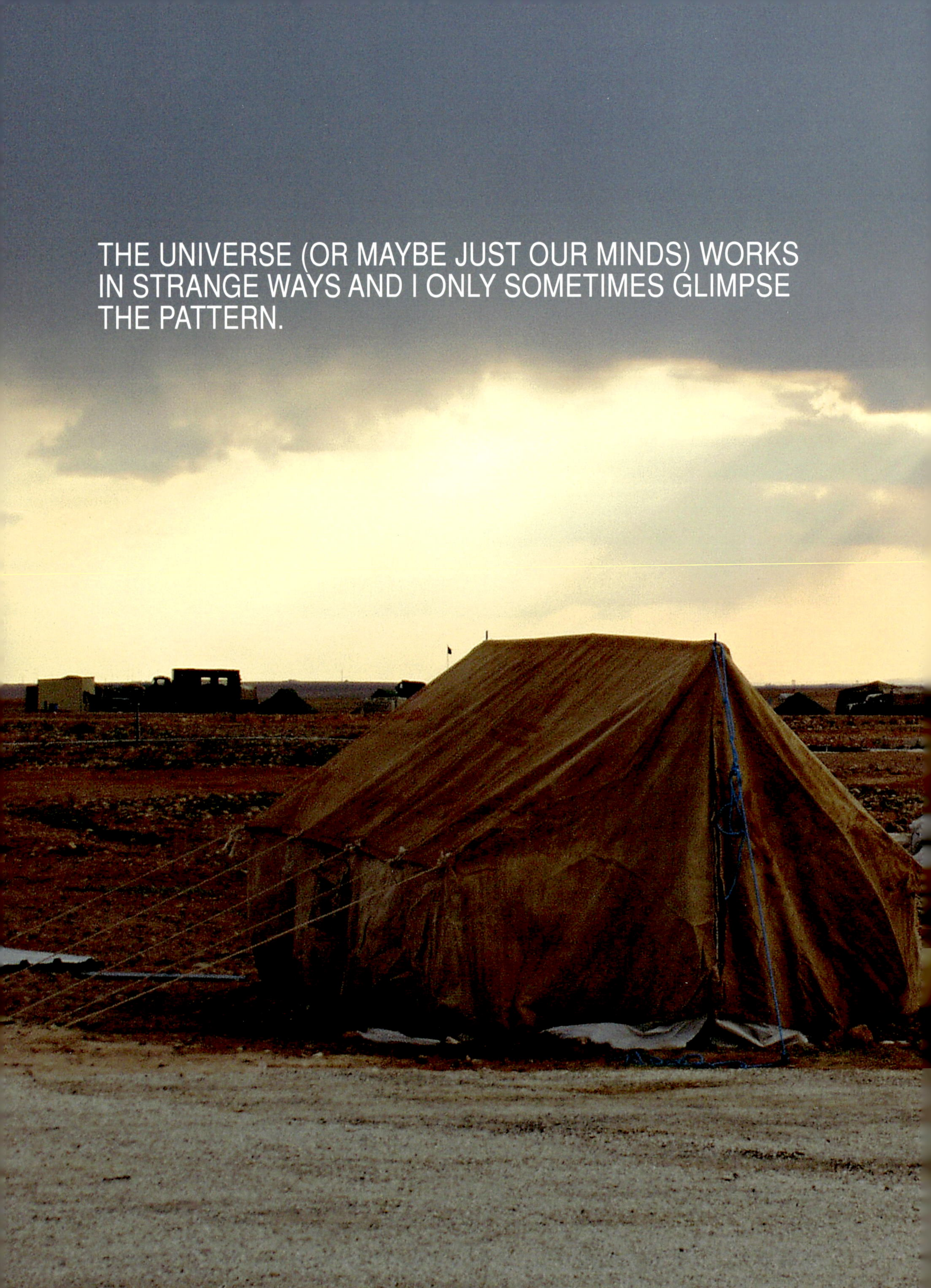

THE UNIVERSE (OR MAYBE JUST OUR MINDS) WORKS
IN STRANGE WAYS AND I ONLY SOMETIMES GLIMPSE
THE PATTERN.

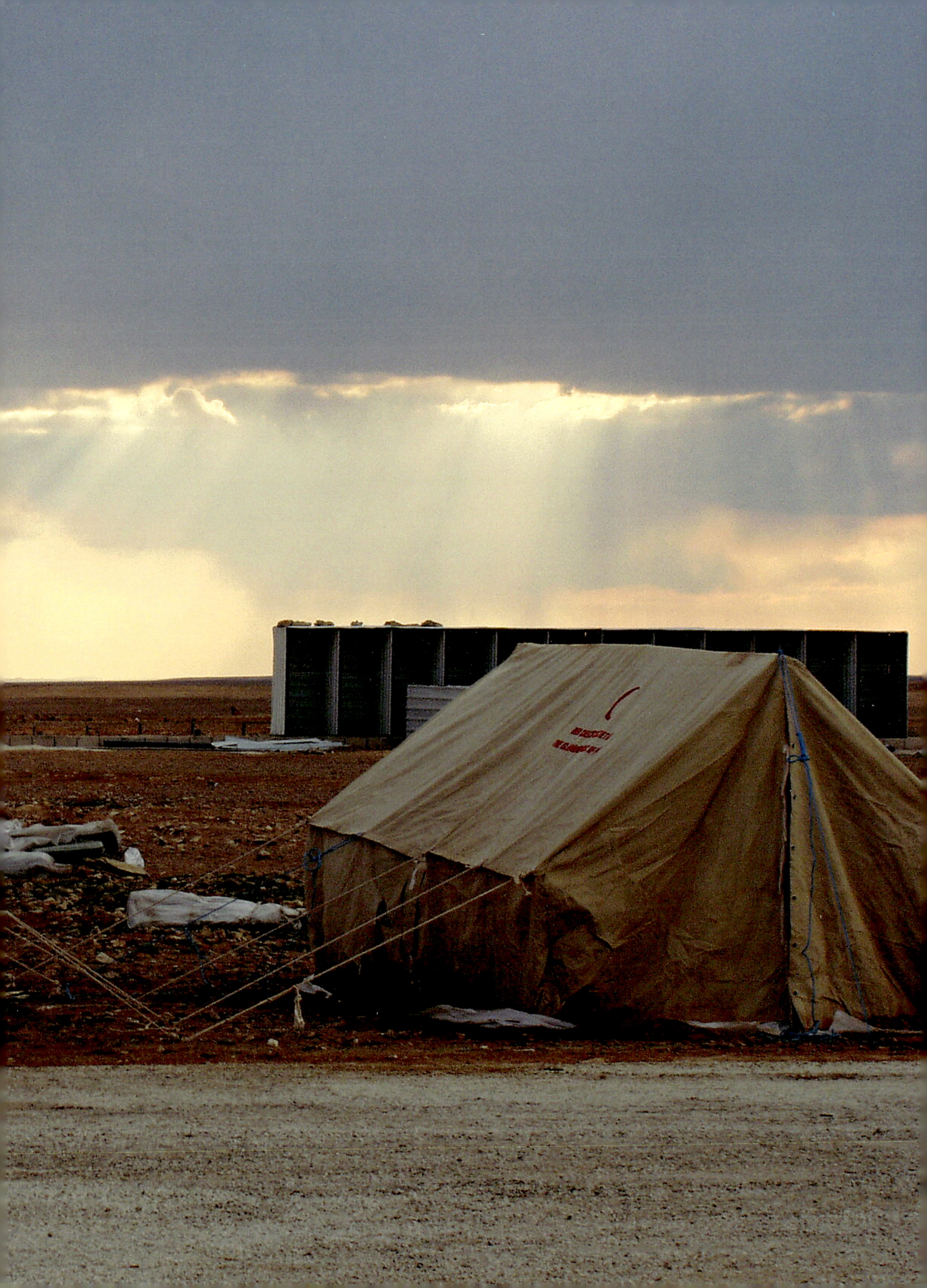

01 APRIL
AMMAN

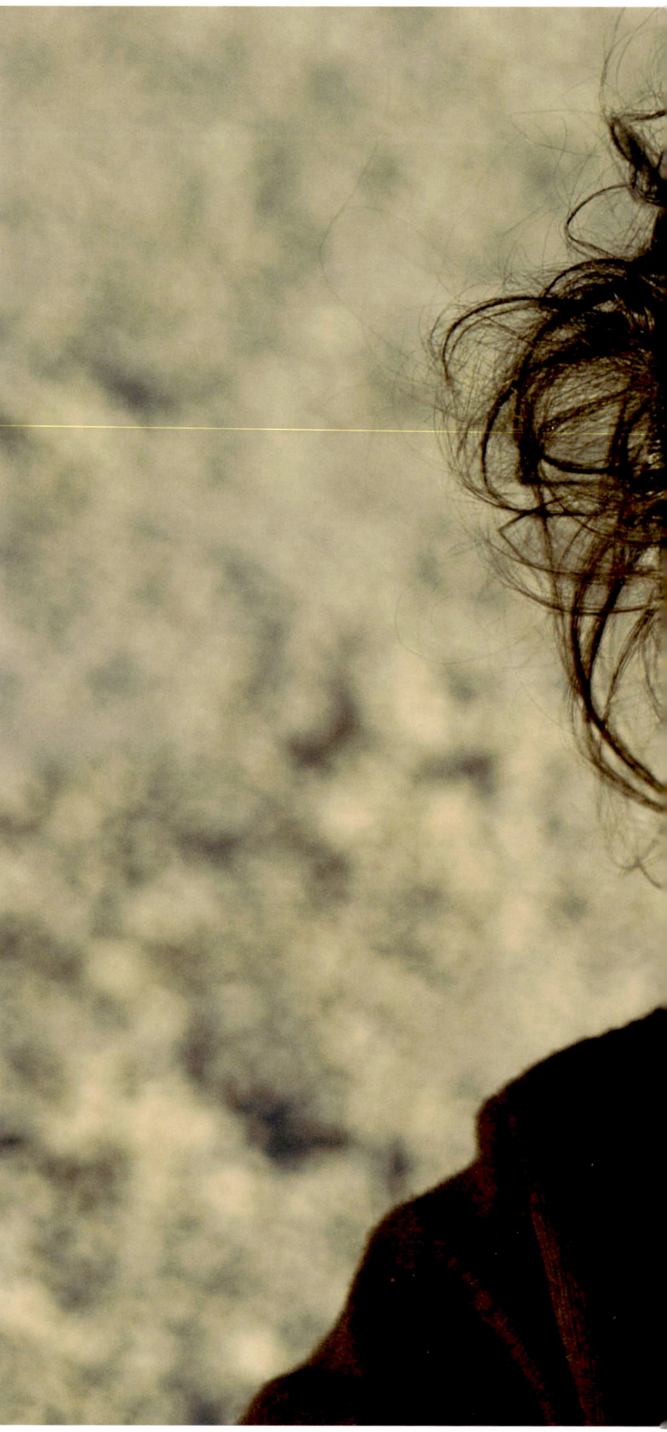

She had the most beautiful eyes. This 5-year old Iraqi girl at the refugee camp.

Something I saw in them stuck with me. Up until then, it had almost been surreally irrelevant, like a holiday camp. The children ran around and laughed, the men played football and the women sat around talking. It seemed so relaxed, so unlike what I expected. Living conditions were harsh, but they took it in their stride as if it were nothing and just made the best of it. The knowledge that they had left behind their homes and probably most of their belongings was a distant suggestion in my mind. You would never have known it. They were so proud.

But in this girl's 'stubborn' face was something I can't explain. It opened up a reality to me that I had only imagined and never experienced. Already she had gone through more than most of us in England would ever experience, and it showed in the steel and courage in her eyes and yet they were still innocent and curious, but refusing to cry.

Most of the children probably still think they will be going home soon. She won't be…her parents were Palestinian and technically don't have a country.

They probably won't be allowed back in, and when the Red Crescent packs up and goes home, they will be left with nothing but a very beautiful, young daughter.

They can't even go back to Palestine because Israel won't let them.

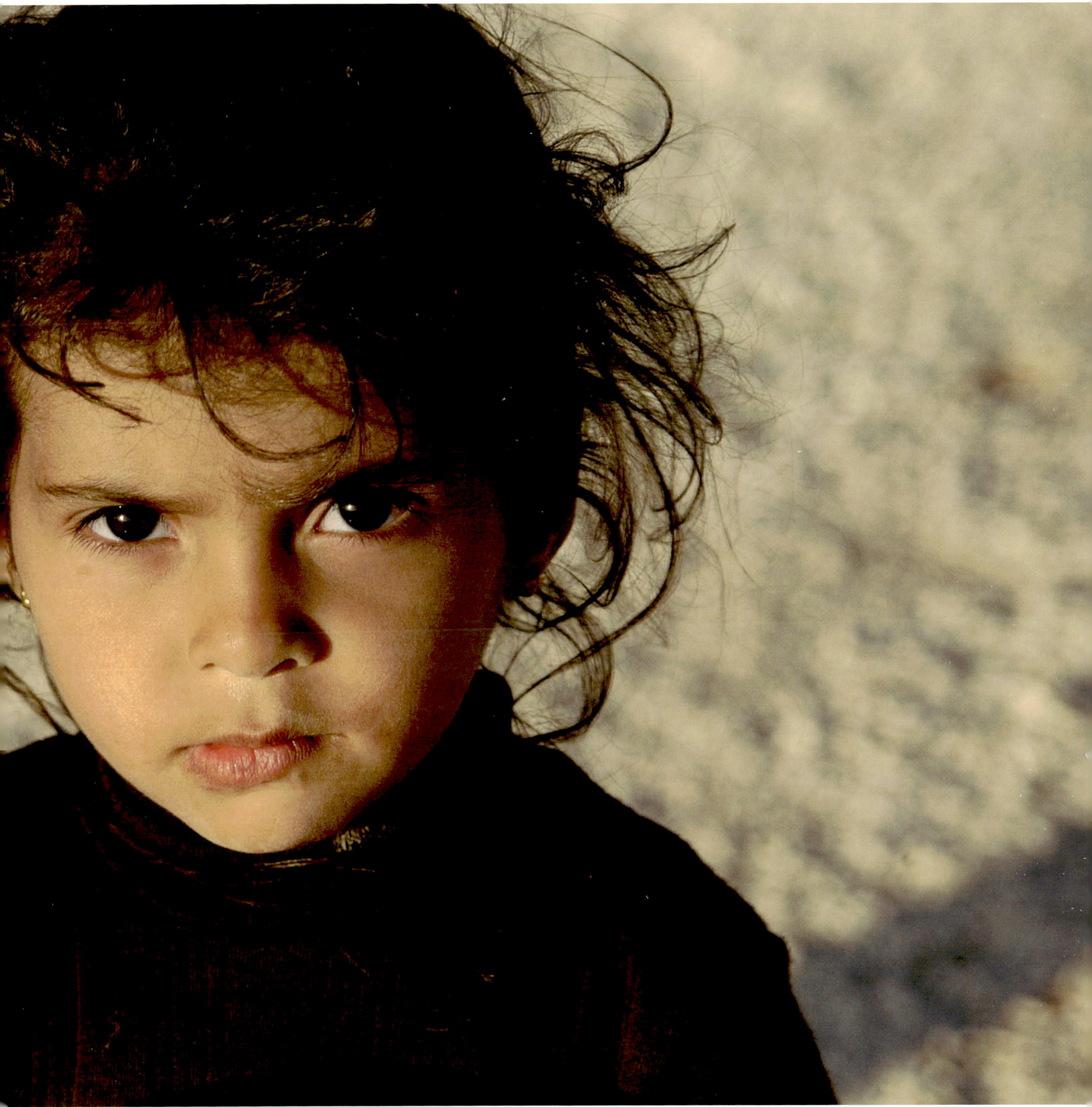

JERUSALEM

02 - 06 APRIL 2003

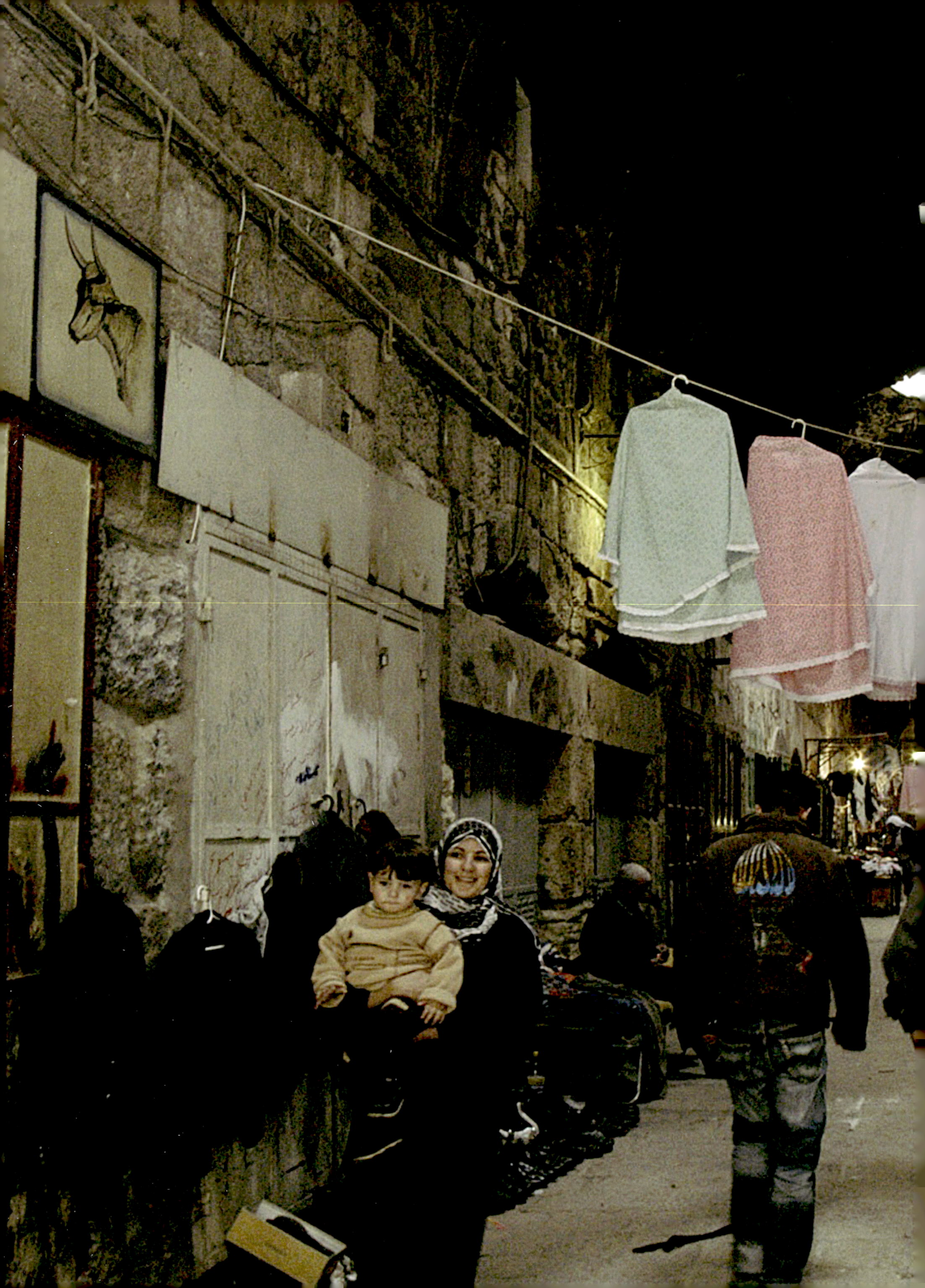

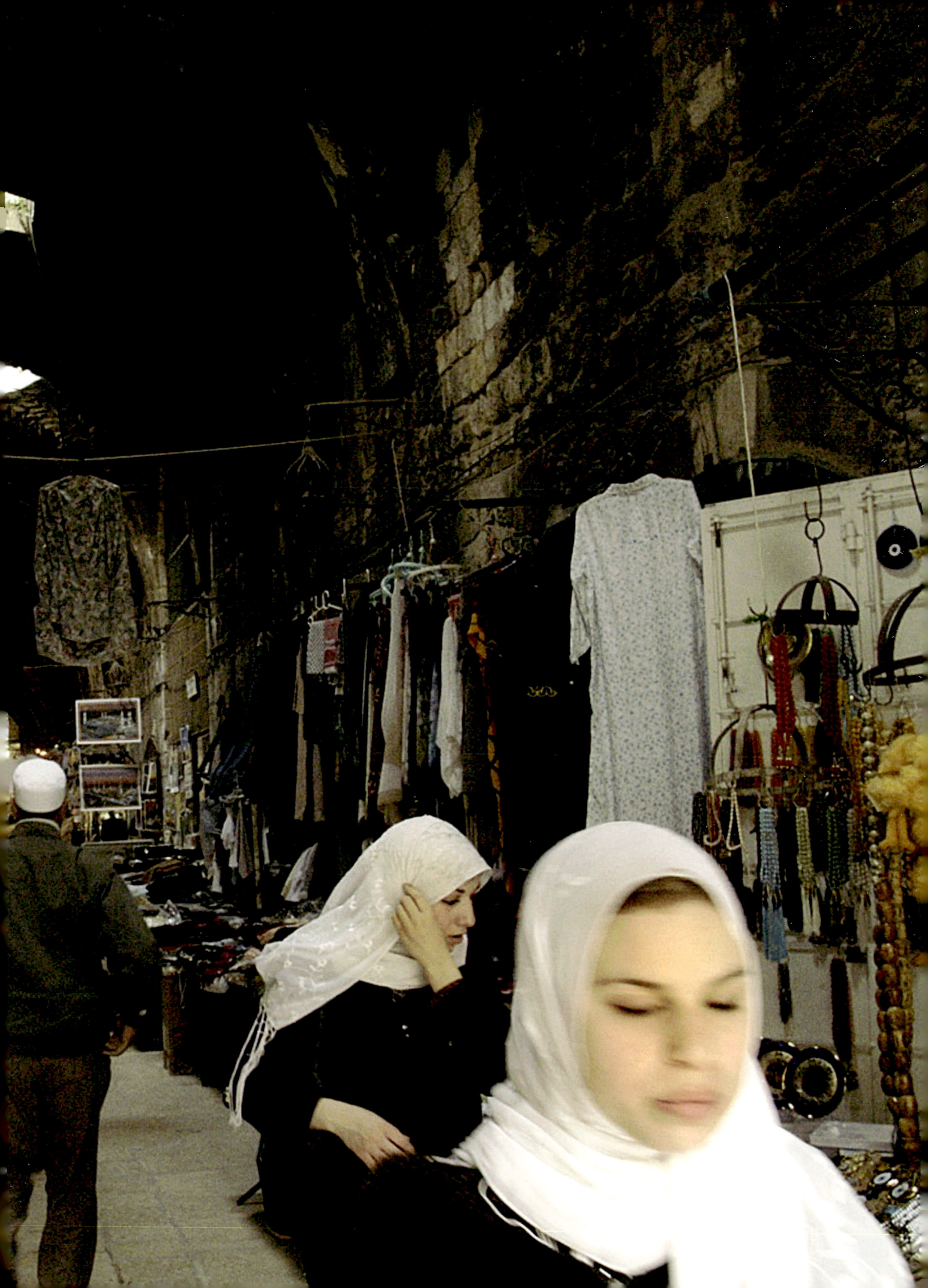

03 APRIL

I just had a very strange experience. I arrived in Jerusalem this afternoon only a few hours ago. It's already incredible… The place I read about so often and was taught about endlessly. The crucifixion, the resurrection and everything. It is the source of so many religions… Where Mohammed ascended to heaven. And now I'm here, in the place I equated with the religion that they tried to force upon me, that I didn't believe existed. And yet I'm here…Jerusalem. At the heart of the Holy Land and the reason I am here is because of war. Jerusalem is the centre of contention by so many factions and the epicentre of instability for this entire region of the world. Nations from thousands of miles away have been dragged into or opted to affect the conflict.

And throughout this afternoon I have felt it, walking aimlessly around the old city.

I saw children of ages between 5 and 15 fighting viciously, with sticks and shards of broken mirrors, throwing the sharpest rocks they could find at each other.

And it occurred to me; what would it do to the mind of a child growing up under these conditions? I can't imagine the number of tears they have cried and what they have thought they had to turn into just to survive. These children scared me, boys of only 7 years old and in them I saw no innocence, only hatred. It really fucking scared me but not physically, just that they could be moulded with such little conscience.

And then I came across a church and in it was the most serene atmosphere. In the centre of the Venetian-set slums and maze of alleys there was silence. The church of the Holy Sepulchre, the tomb of Jesus where he was crucified etc. It drew

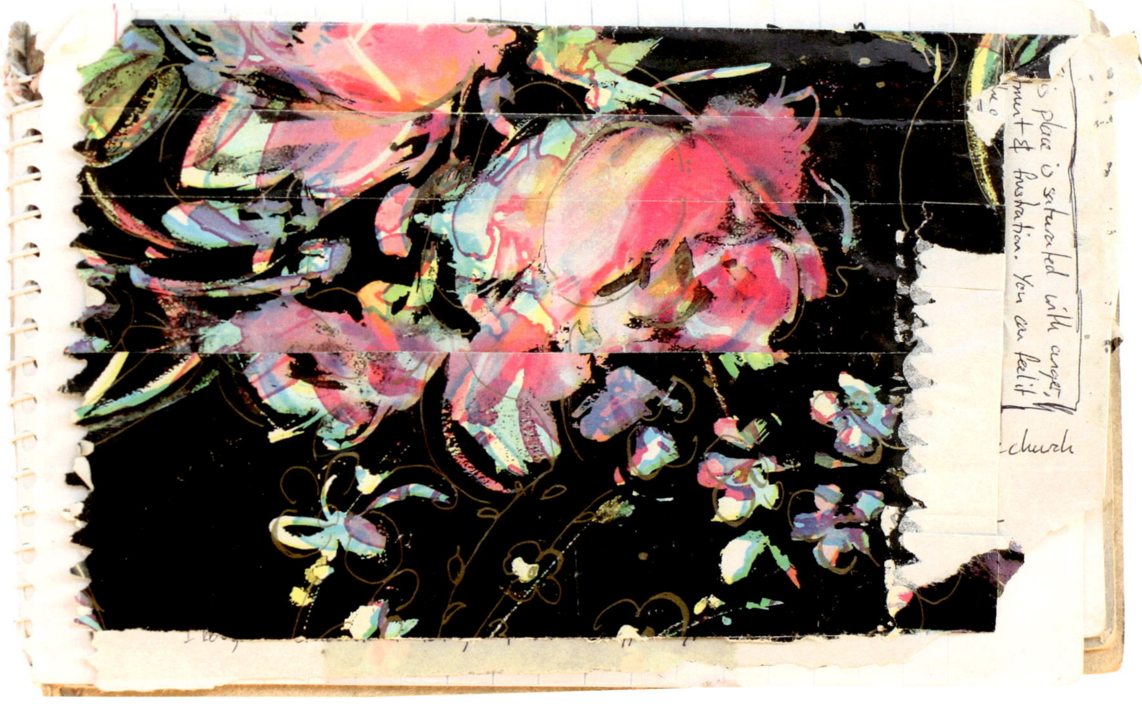

me in, an agnostic verging on atheism, and it touched me. I'm not saying I came out a believer but something really moved me. So much so that when I left I had to force myself to keep on walking.

I bought a crucifix and felt guilty for the hypocrisy, but I had to, I wanted to.

How can anyone find their way around this maze? One moment you are in the middle of a packed Arab market...the next surrounded by orthodox Jews. I'm now sitting on a rooftop looking out at the Dome of the Rock. It is peaceful. And you would never know that beneath the ground in the "hive" that is the real old city, so much is going on. This place is like no other I have ever seen, and in my short life I have seen many places.

This place is saturated with anger, resentment and frustration. You can feel it in the air.

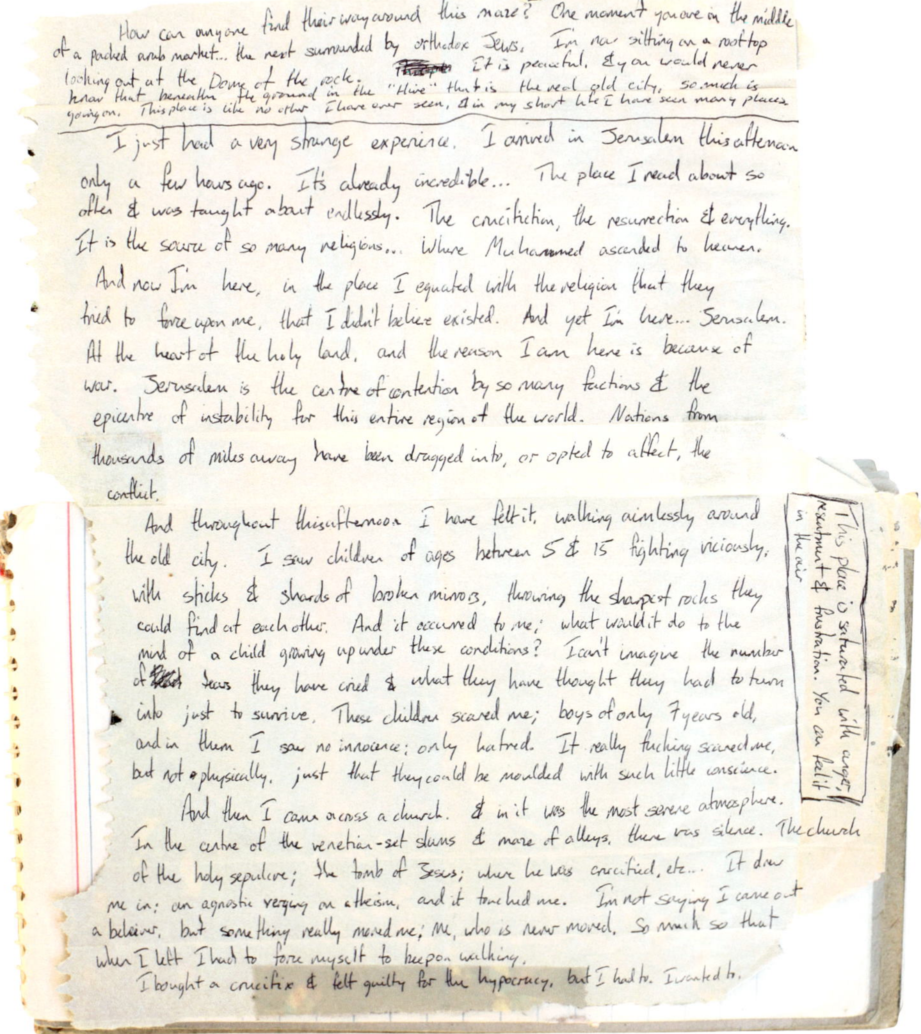

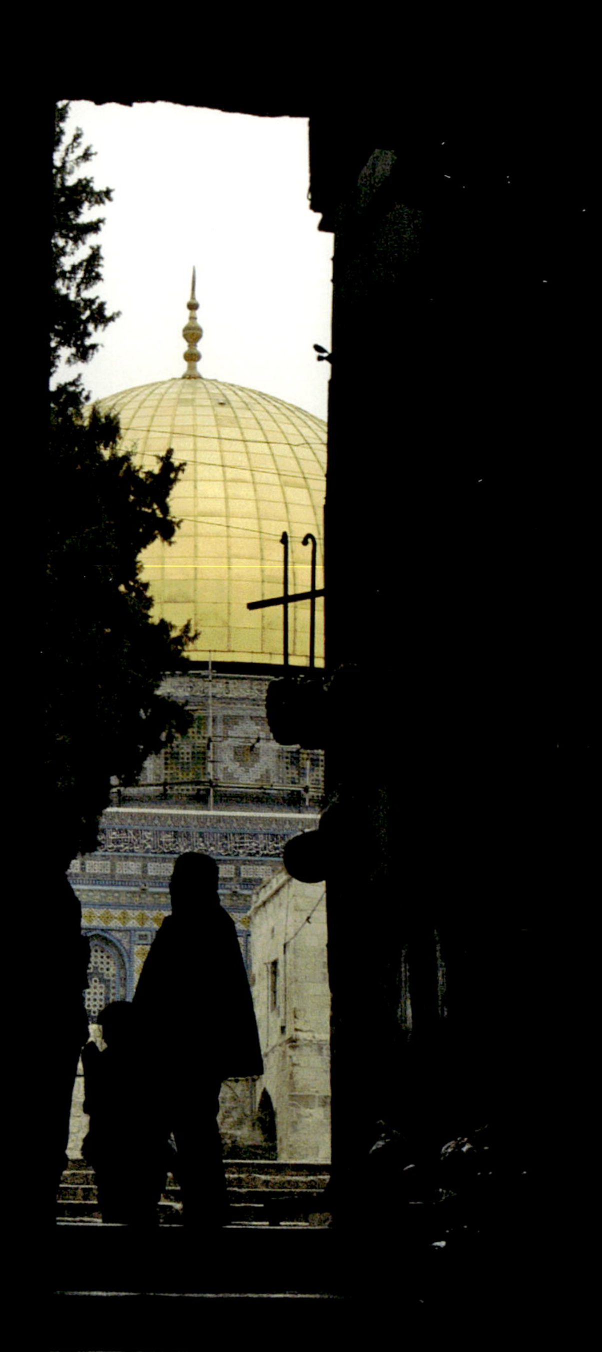

When you lie there on the floor
with nothing to hold to, your head empty,
but full with thoughts, and no hope.
You flatline, looking for something, not knowing what,
but needing it, to give a sense of worth.

There's nothing to look forward to; next week,
the same as last; boredom,
emblazened on a border of futility,
patterned with repetition,
the intricacies irrelevant.

You need someone to complete you,
show you the point.
Amplify the sound of silence,
realise your imagination,
and colour your spirit.

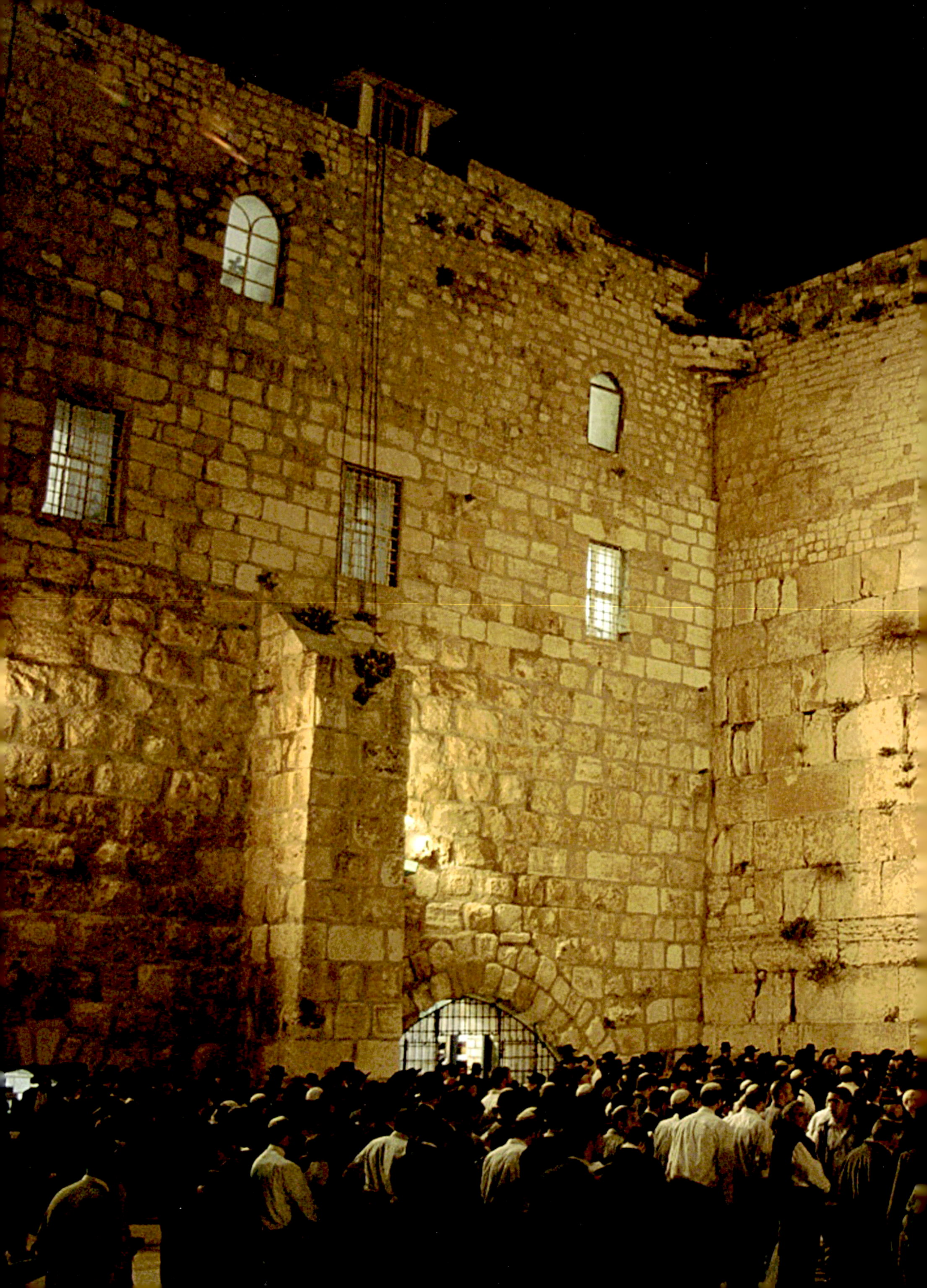

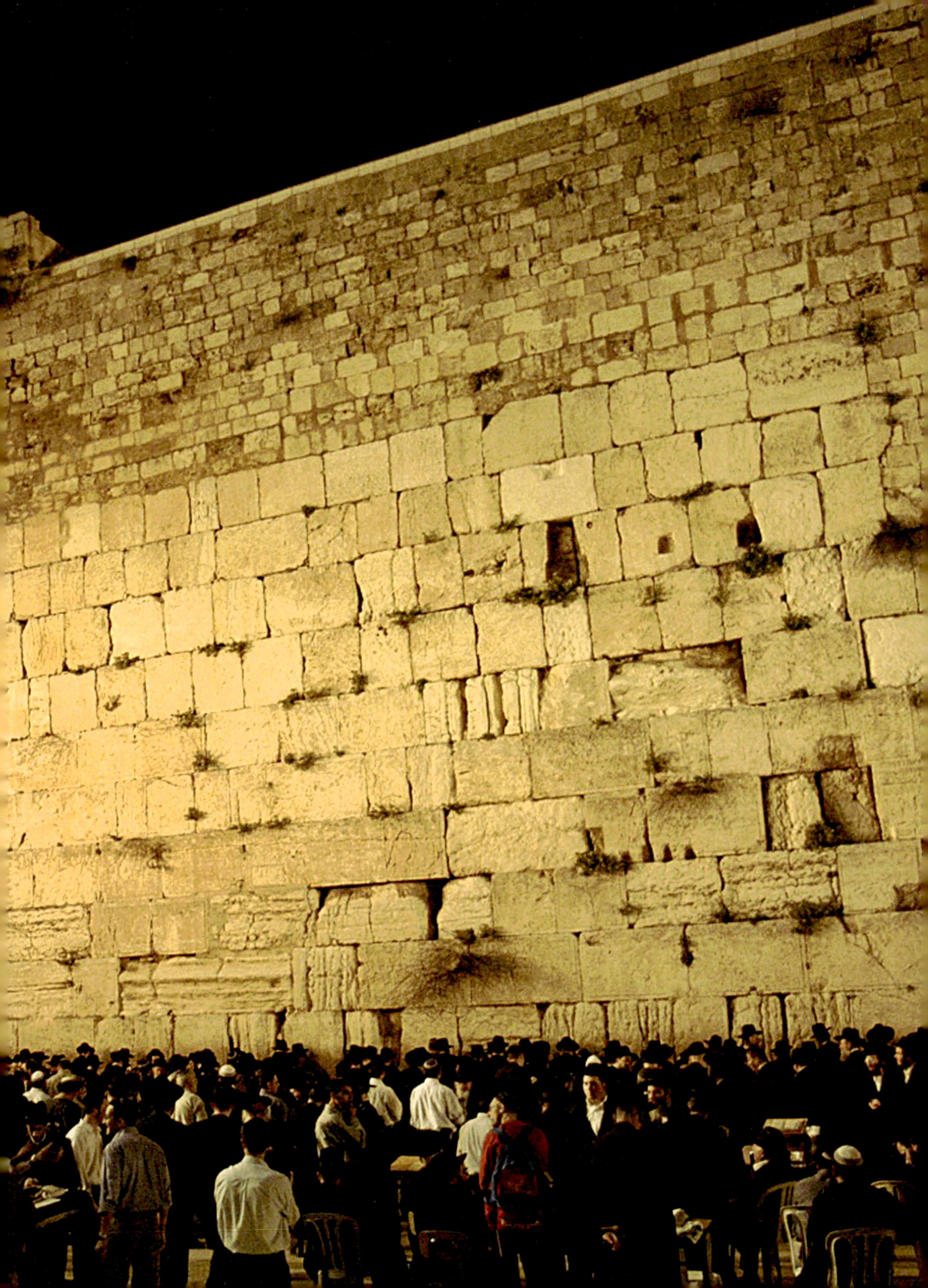

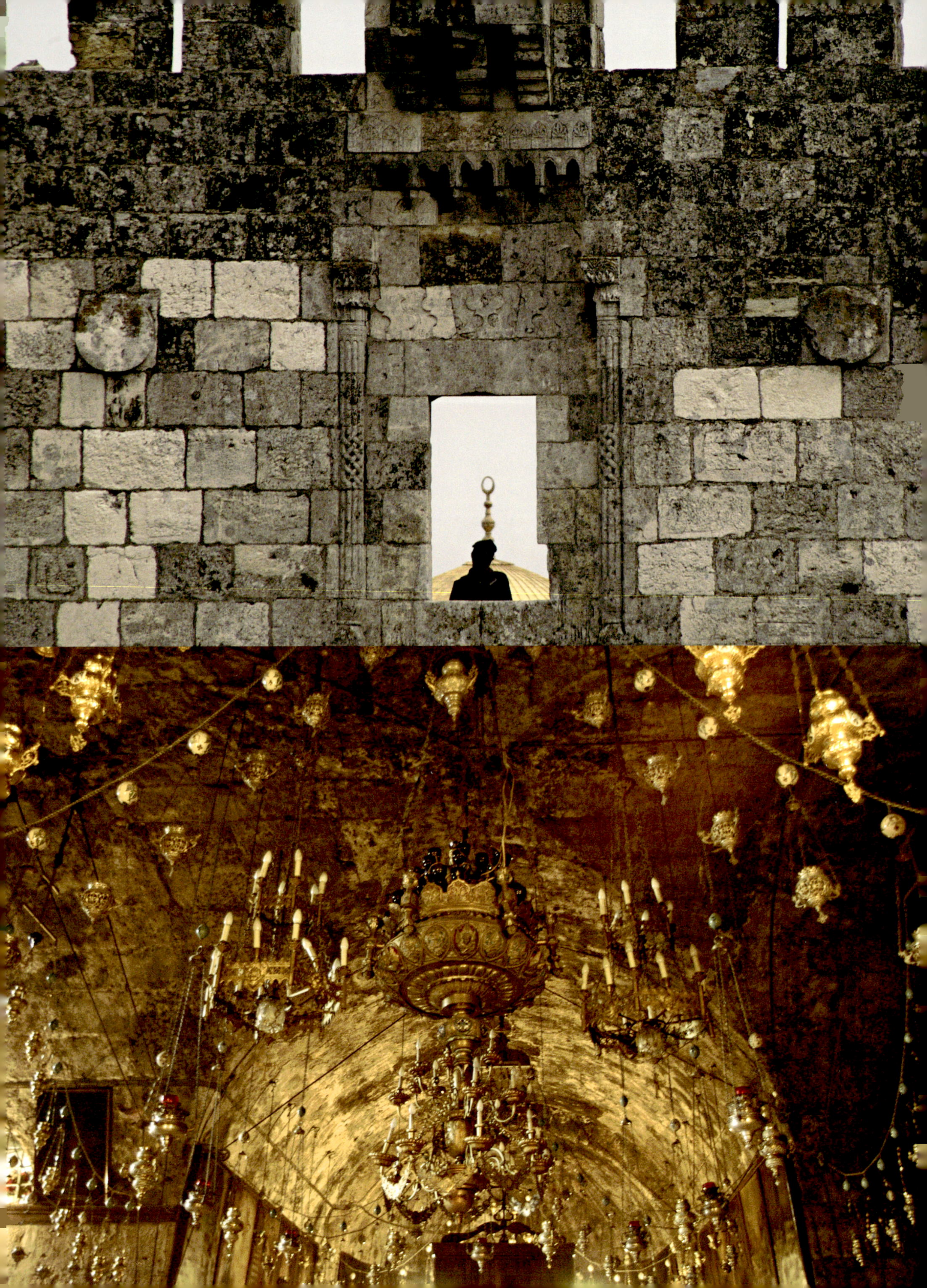

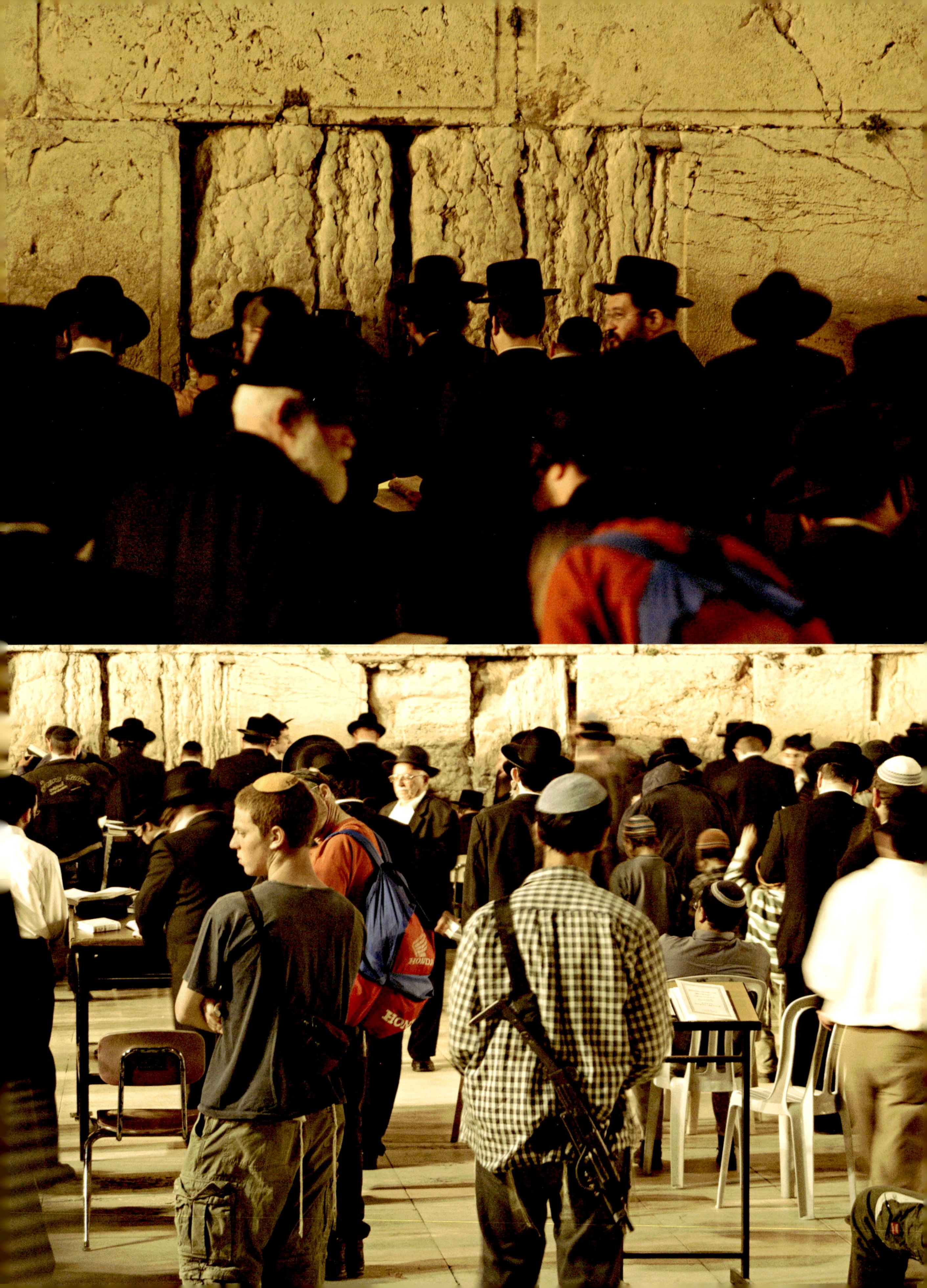

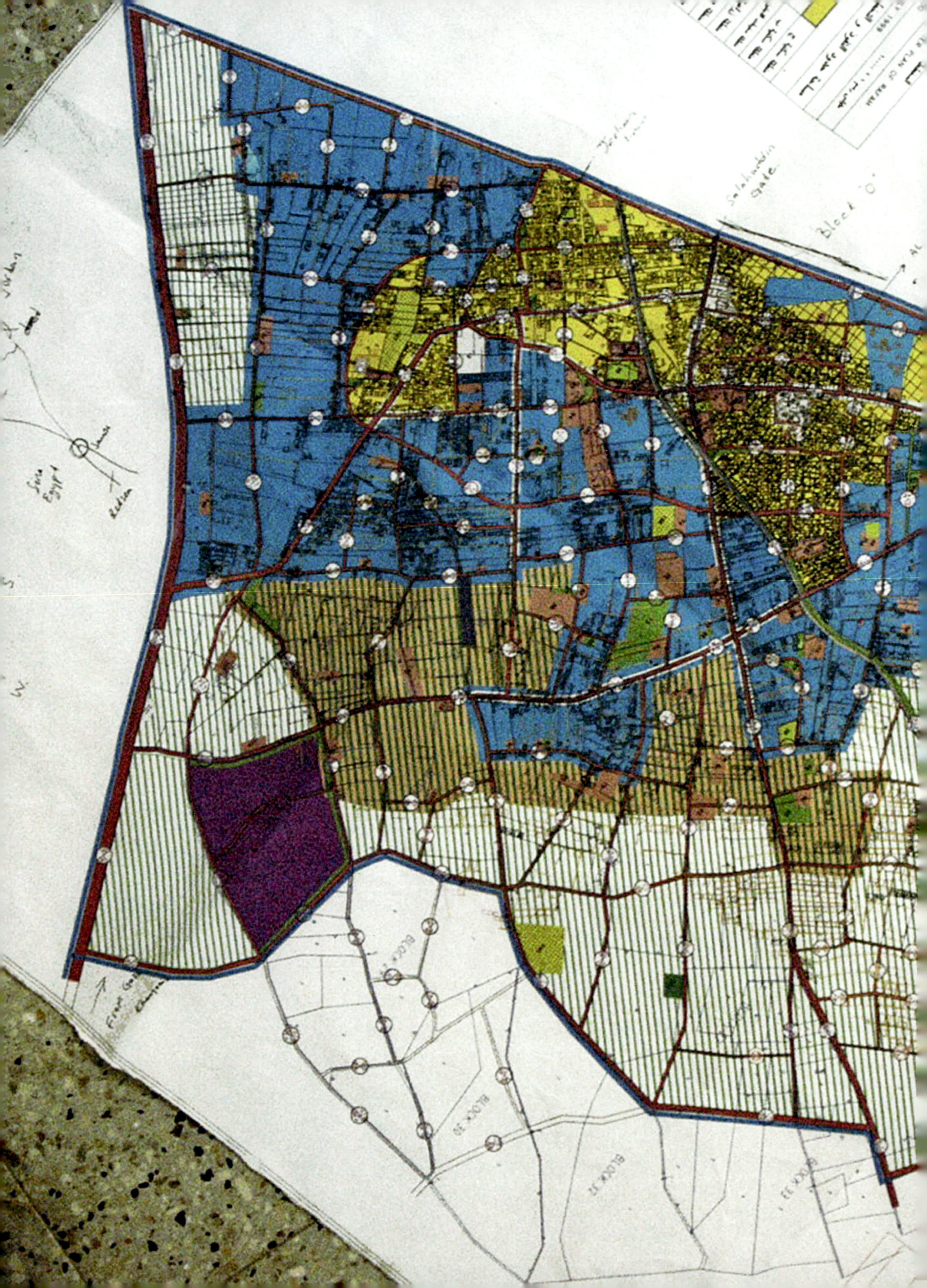

Salahaddin
Gate
Block O
First Gate
Canal
BLOCK 18
BLOCK 35
BLOCK 32
BLOCK 33

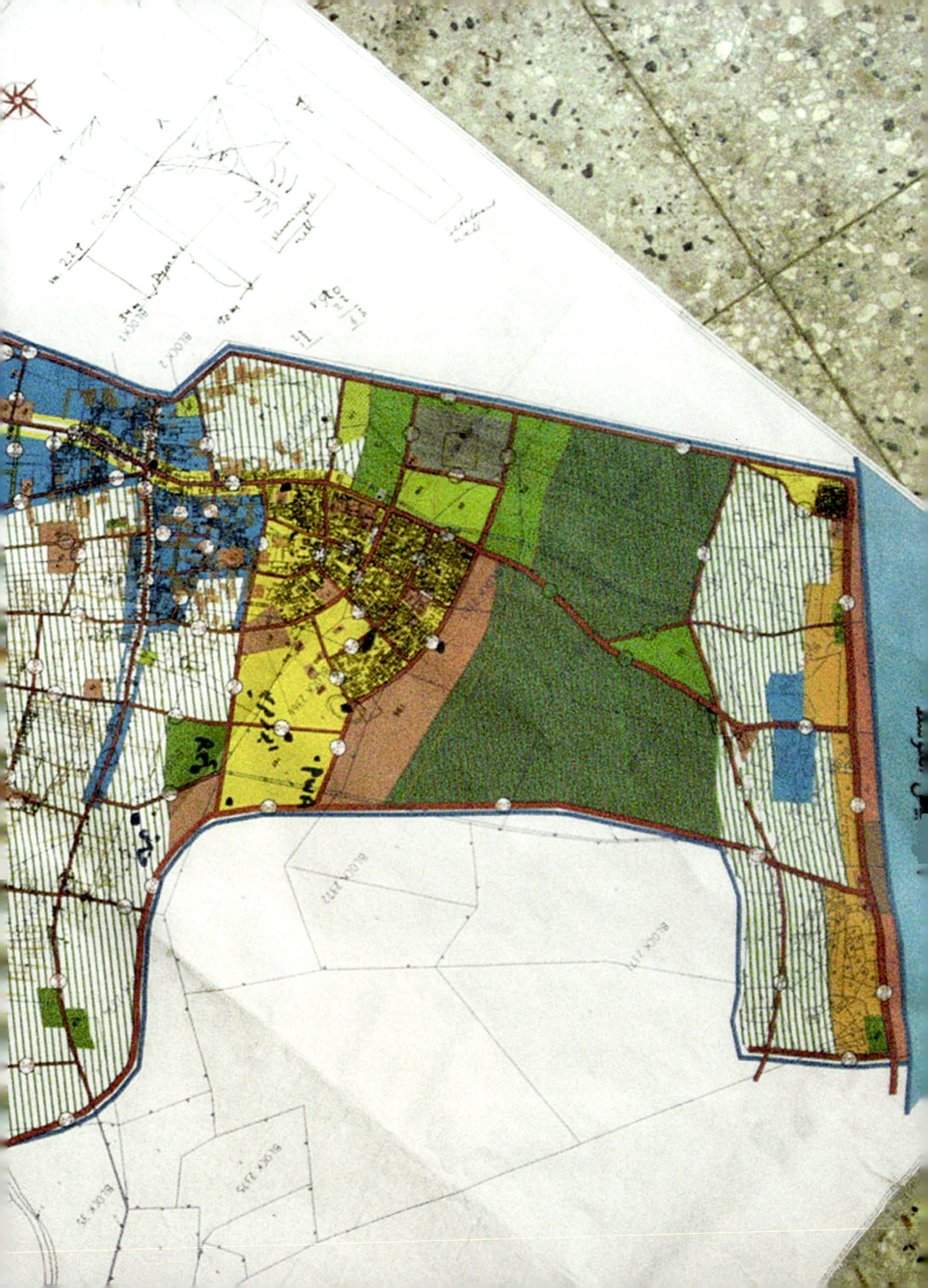

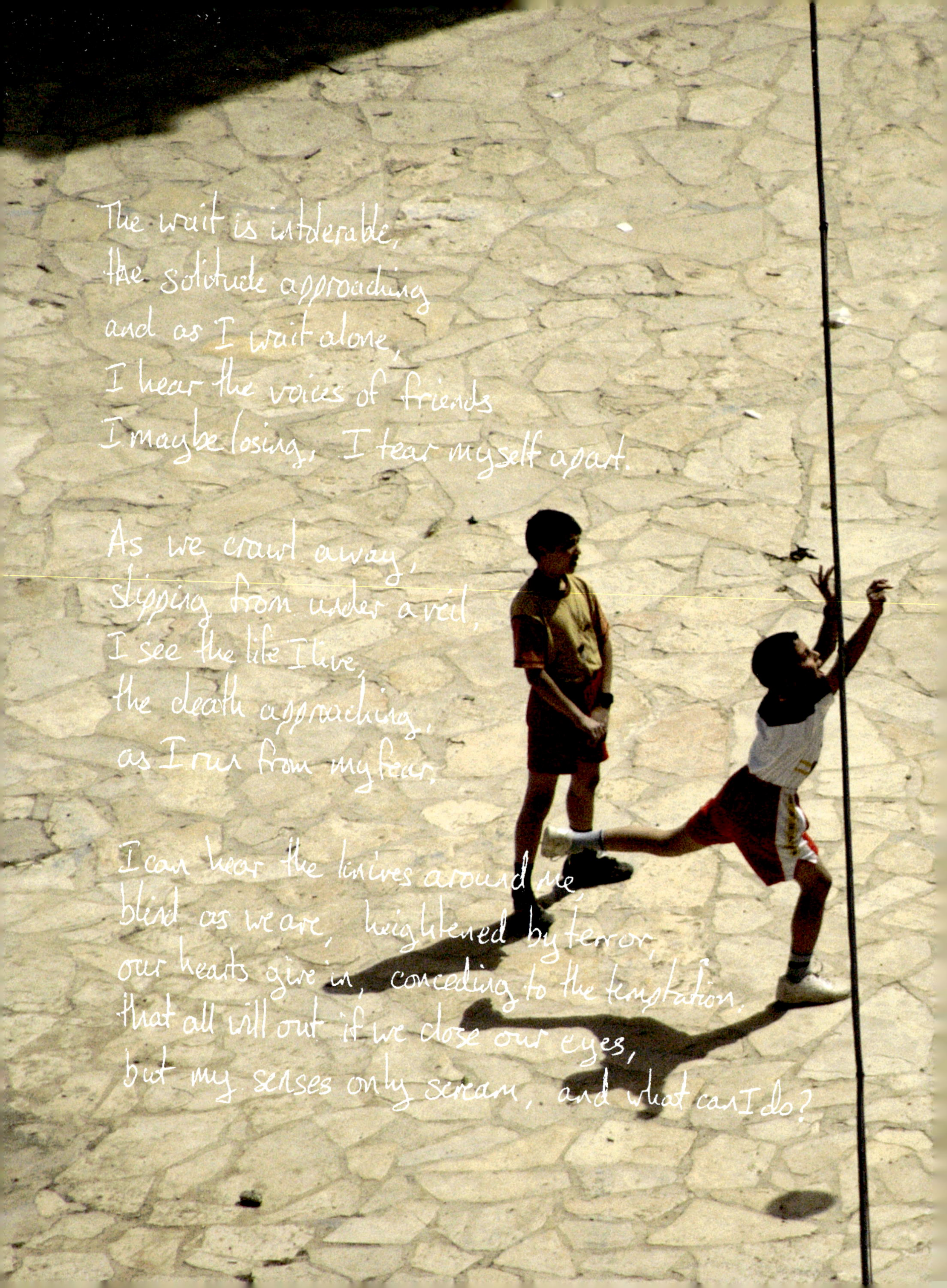

The wait is intolerable,
the solitude approaching
and as I wait alone,
I hear the voices of friends
I maybe losing, I tear myself apart.

As we crawl away,
slipping from under a veil,
I see the life I live,
the death approaching,
as I run from my fear.

I can hear the knives around me,
blind as we are, heightened by terror,
our hearts give in, conceding to the temptation,
that all will out if we close our eyes,
but my senses only scream, and what can I do?

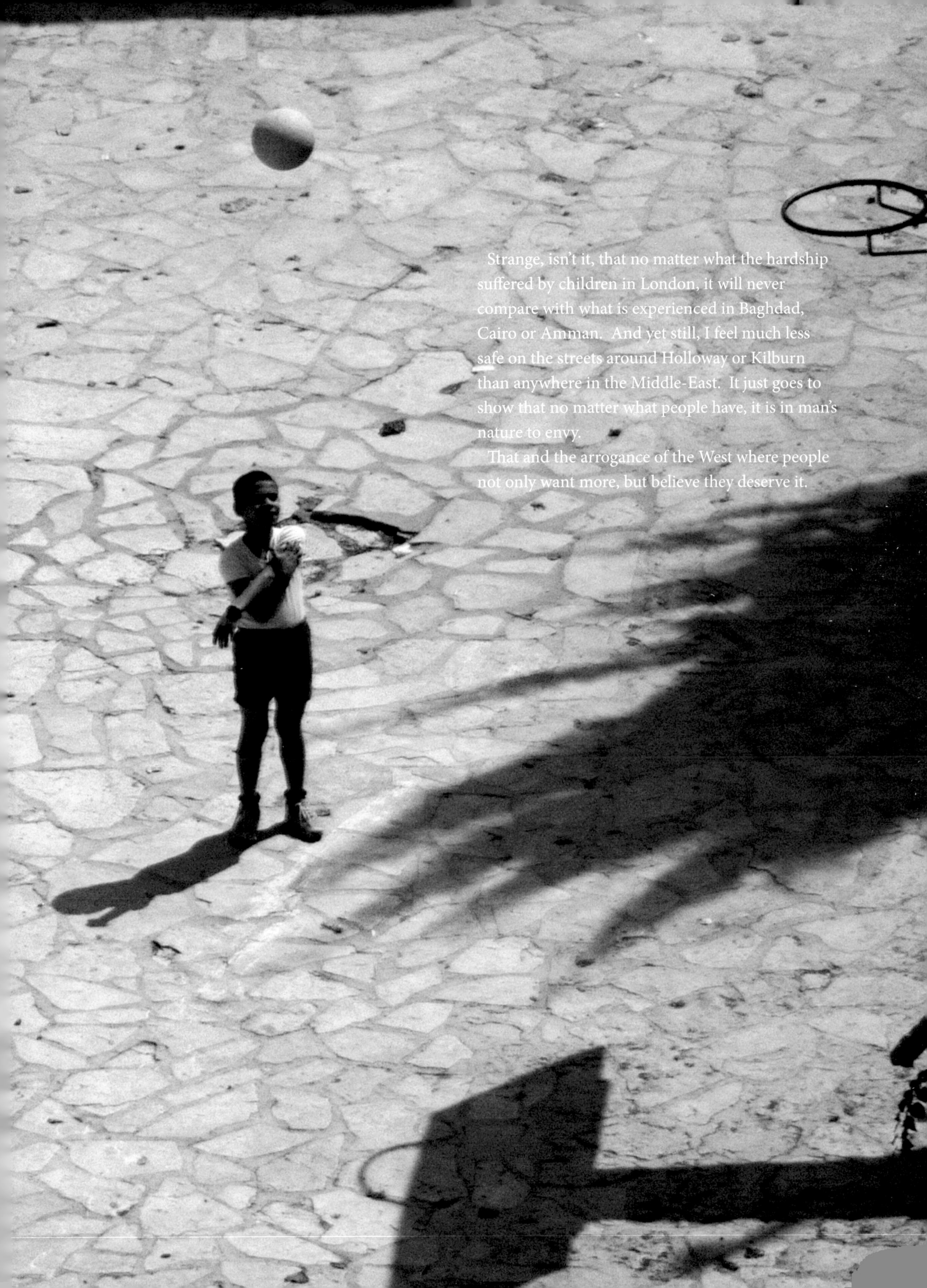

Strange, isn't it, that no matter what the hardship
suffered by children in London, it will never
compare with what is experienced in Baghdad,
Cairo or Amman. And yet still, I feel much less
safe on the streets around Holloway or Kilburn
than anywhere in the Middle-East. It just goes to
show that no matter what people have, it is in man's
nature to envy.
    That and the arrogance of the West where people
not only want more, but believe they deserve it.

03 APRIL
JERUSALEM

The girl, Rachel, who was killed in Rafah a few weeks ago.

It seems so unfair. Not just on the surface, but looking at the images. I wonder how few or many people heard of it on the news and just counted it as another death, just another number, maybe made slightly more personal by a realization that she was a person by her age and nationality. I doubt anyone imagined the details. Being crushed by a bulldozer is not just losing your life. It is your body being pulled apart as people stand and watch. Your arm may be dislocated by the tonnes of metal grinding it against some piece of rusted metal wire, while one side of your face is crushed in and the skin and flesh torn away on the edge of the metal sheet designed to clear boulders and huge amounts of rubble quickly. You don't die immediately. Maybe the weight instantly crushes your chest, deflating your lungs and splintering your ribs. If you're lucky it will crush, or send shards of bone, into your heart. Whatever, you will feel it for certain, and at best you are still conscious for several seconds. If not, you may feel your waist twisted, distorted, and if your spine isn't severed or dislocated you will feel your abdomen, hips and legs suffering fractures all the way through, outright snapping in places like matchsticks. I can only imagine the relief it would be when your skull implodes under the pressure.

I wonder if it would strike me…all the small things…biting my fingernails, shaving. All those little things you did that taught your every curve and detail of your body, all your life, and suddenly it is not your body any more. It is no longer the same shape, different to the touch. I wouldn't want to survive.

I wonder if I should be more scared than last time. At least there is some simplicity to these circumstances. You know where both sides stand and what they're capable of, and at least one side wants you there. Before, deception came from both sides and from within. The stakes were higher at any one instant and you could trust no one.

It doesn't help that I'm distracted. My mind isn't where it should be. Why do my thoughts seem to drift so easily these days to the same places in my head? Yet my thoughts are so strong and they won't relent. I don't want to be looking the wrong way when it matters.

It's like I'm conscious of every aspect of someone I pass; their accent, the way they dress, or smell, how they look at me.

The girl; Rachel, who was killed in
Rafah a few weeks ago. It seems so
unfair. Not just on the surface, but looking
at the images.

OK, this is the fourth time I've written this e-mail because the line keeps fucking up and I've had a long day... so sorry if it's brief...

Am in East Jerusalem...just finished training to go into Rafah, Southern Gaza, tomorrow, will be there for a few weeks until my money runs out or I'm shot... it's where a 23 yr old American girl was killed as part of the activist group ISM a couple of weeks ago... another ISM member was shot in the face tonight in Jenin, but you will hear about it on the news tomorrow if you look, and it's them that I will be covering... I chose Rafah because it is where the most activity is with an incursion every night on average... Ad F, you bastard, if I die because I didn't get that vest, I swear I'll come back as a poltergeist and throw shit around your house... Alex, could you possibly call people up, find out their e-mails cos I only have a few with me, forward this to them and ask them to mail me so I know how to add them to this list esp Caelia, cos you lot talk on a reg basis...Daniel, you and I need to sit down when I get back because being around activists 24/7 and being in Palestine is seriously fucking with my head and I need someone I trust who knows about the situation to help me sift through all the shit as this is my first time doing this and it's getting really hard to be objective, plus some of the stuff I've been seeing is pretty heavy and it's just making me lose it. It's like being under-cover and I'm watching myself slipping into a role when I wanted to be as detached as poss.
There we go... that wasn't so bad.
As always, love you all, stay safe,

Tom

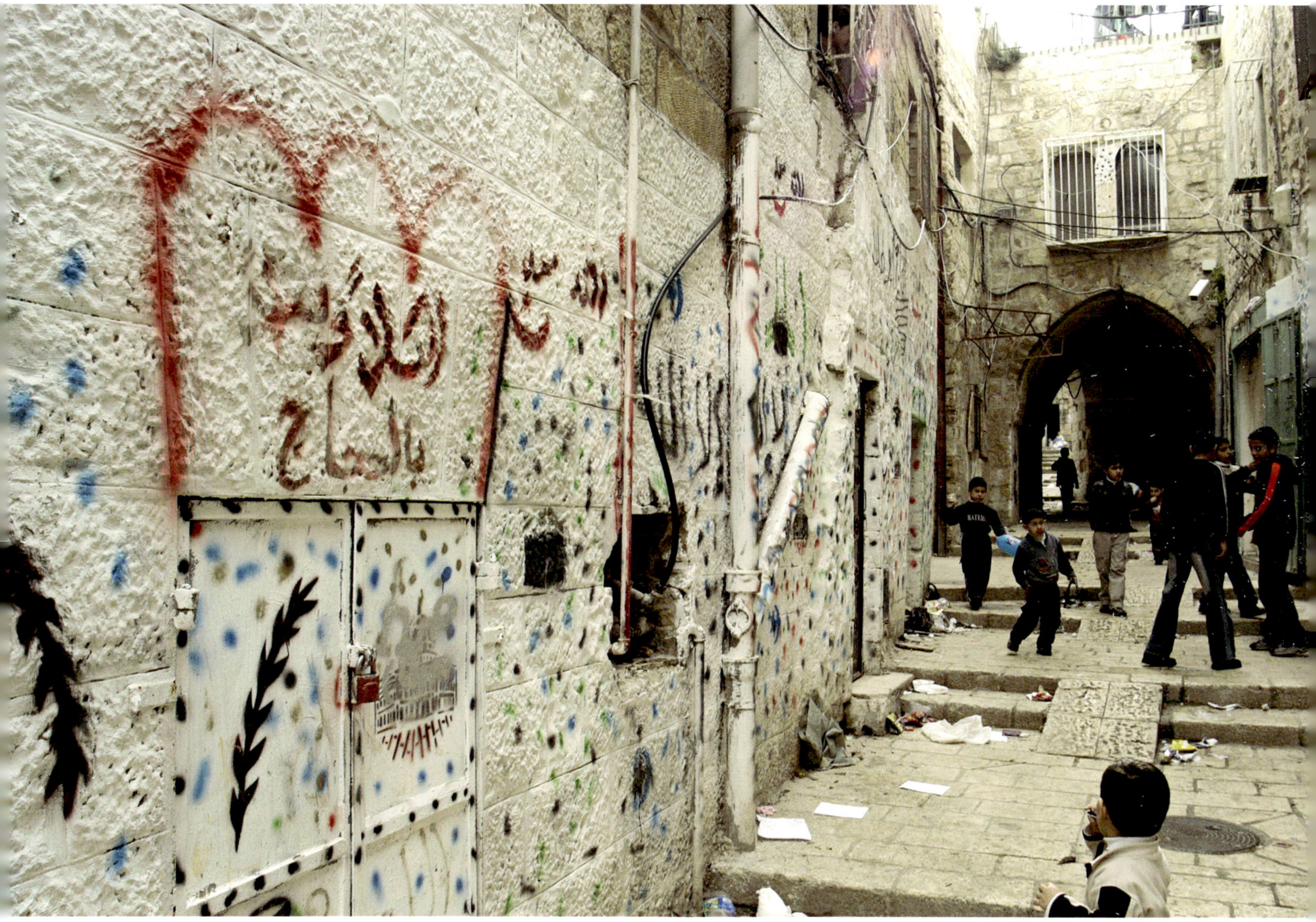

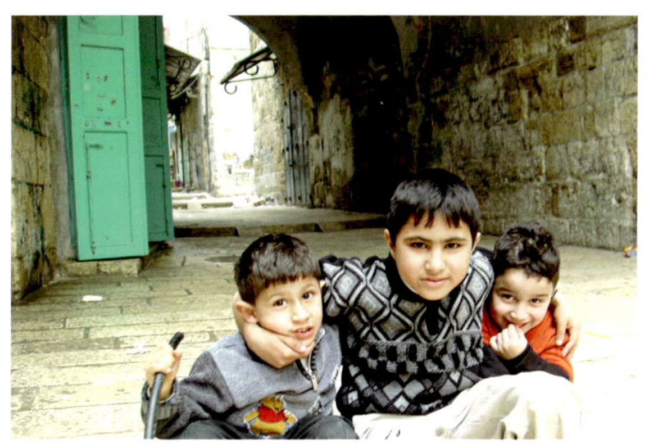

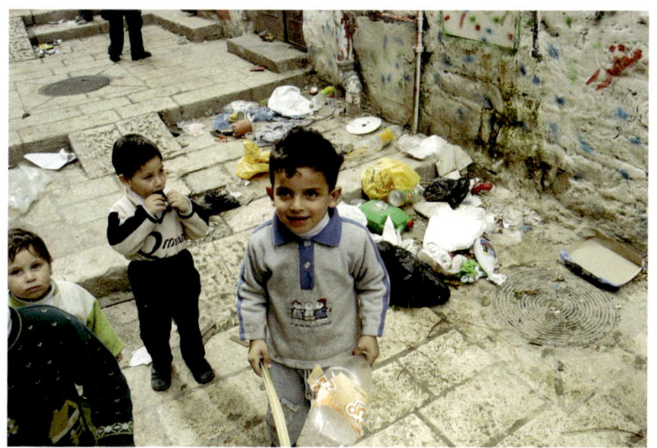

05 APRIL
JERUSALEM

One of the ISM volunteers who has been here for a while may have died tonight. He was shot in the face and taken to hospital in Jenin. I'm leaving tomorrow morning for Rafah, at the southern end of the Gaza Strip. It is supposed to be the centre of most 'action' at the moment. Maybe, it is stupid to do something like this, and throw myself in so deep…as deep as I can. But it's something I want to do. It isn't so much fear that I am feeling now, as a deep sense that things won't turn out so well this time. I just can't get a feeling that things could turn out well.

[later that day…]

"God bless you. From the bottom of my heart, may God bless you. God bless you."

I have rarely heard anyone say anything with as much conviction and desperate honesty as the elderly Moslem's words to us in the Islamic quarter of the Old City on realizing we were ISM, or the equivalent.

This shit really isn't fair.

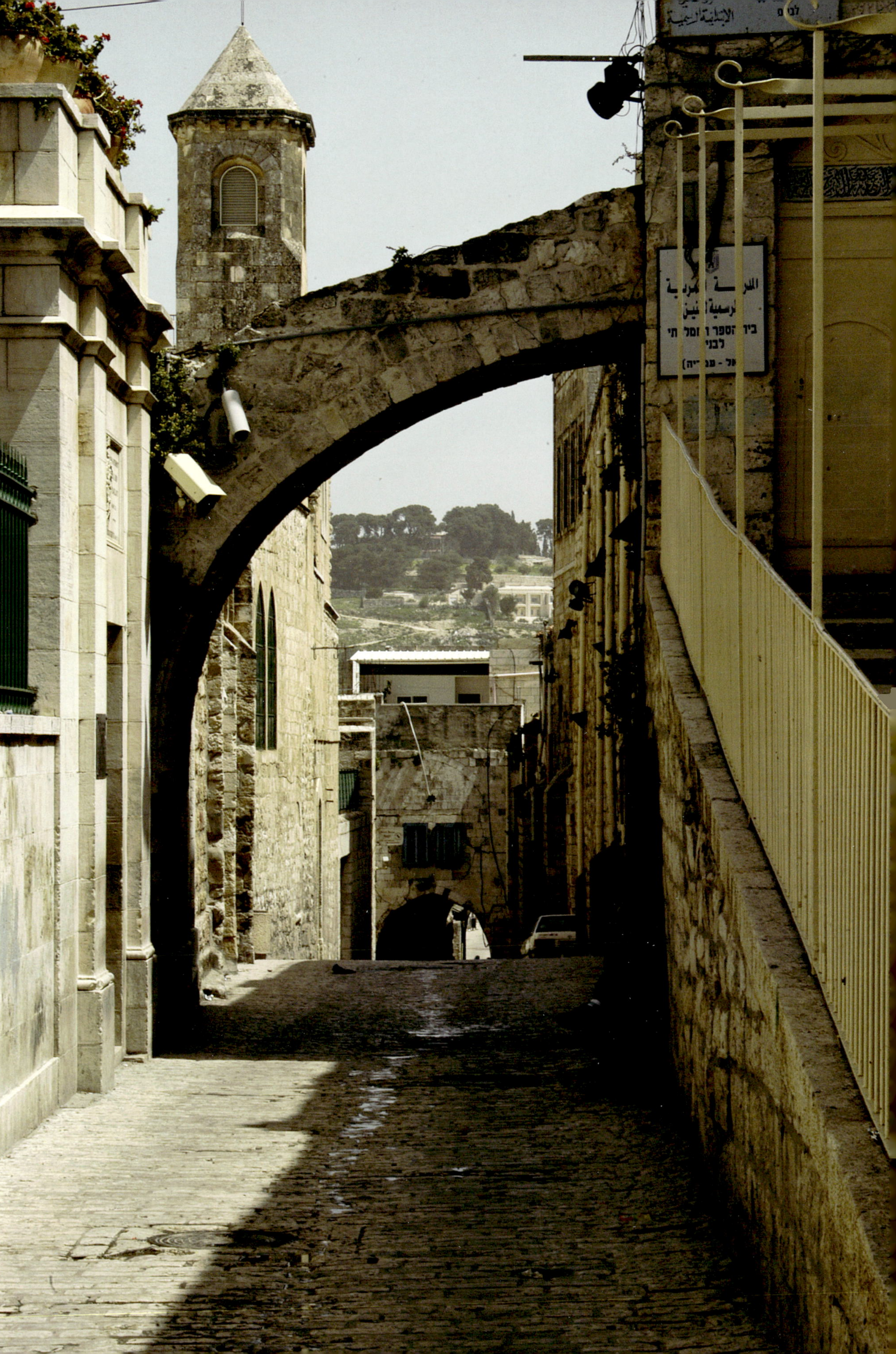
المدرسة العمرية
المدرسية العمرية
بית הספר ומסלולתי
לבני (אל - עמריה)
الإسلامية الرسمية

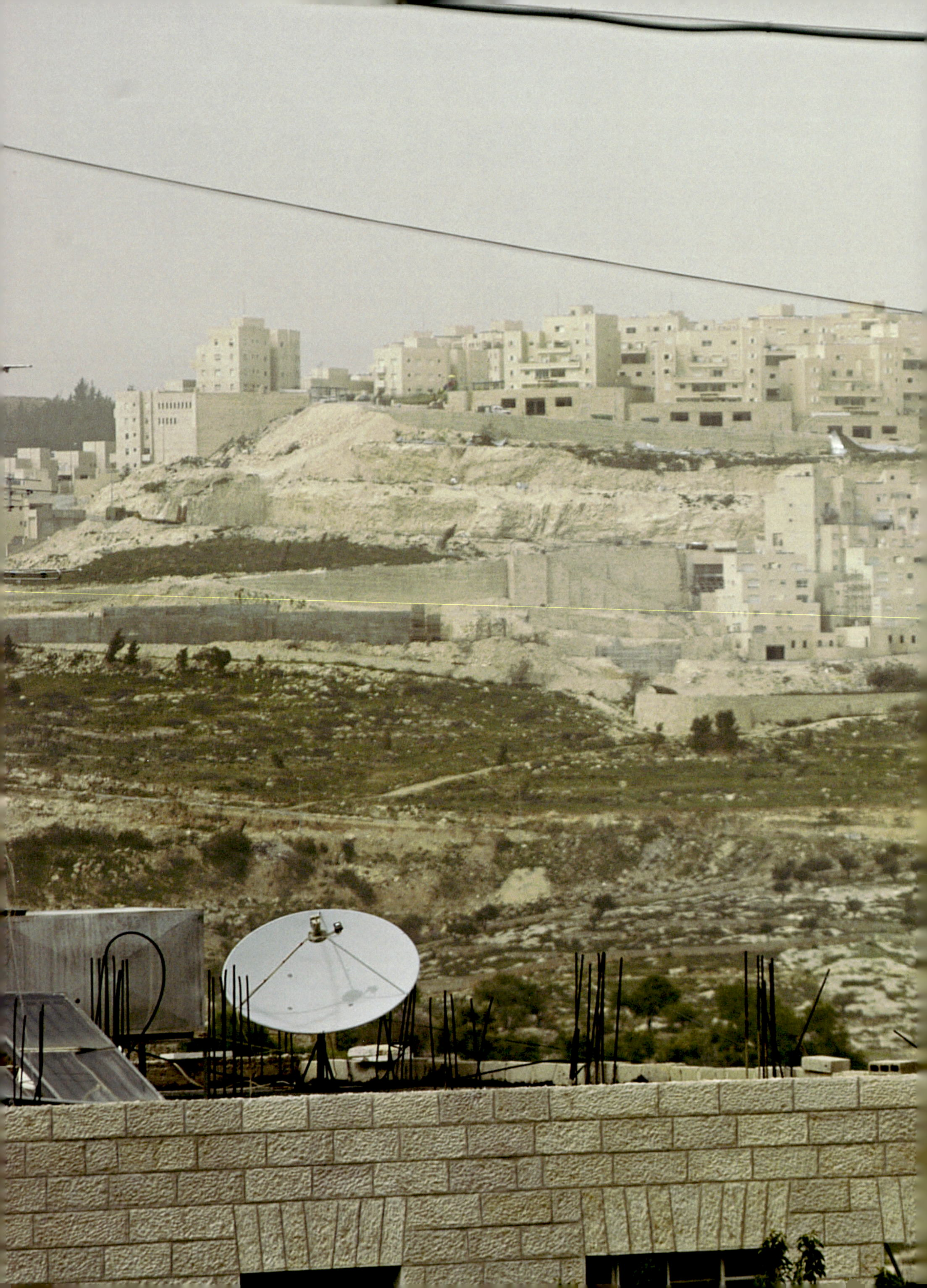

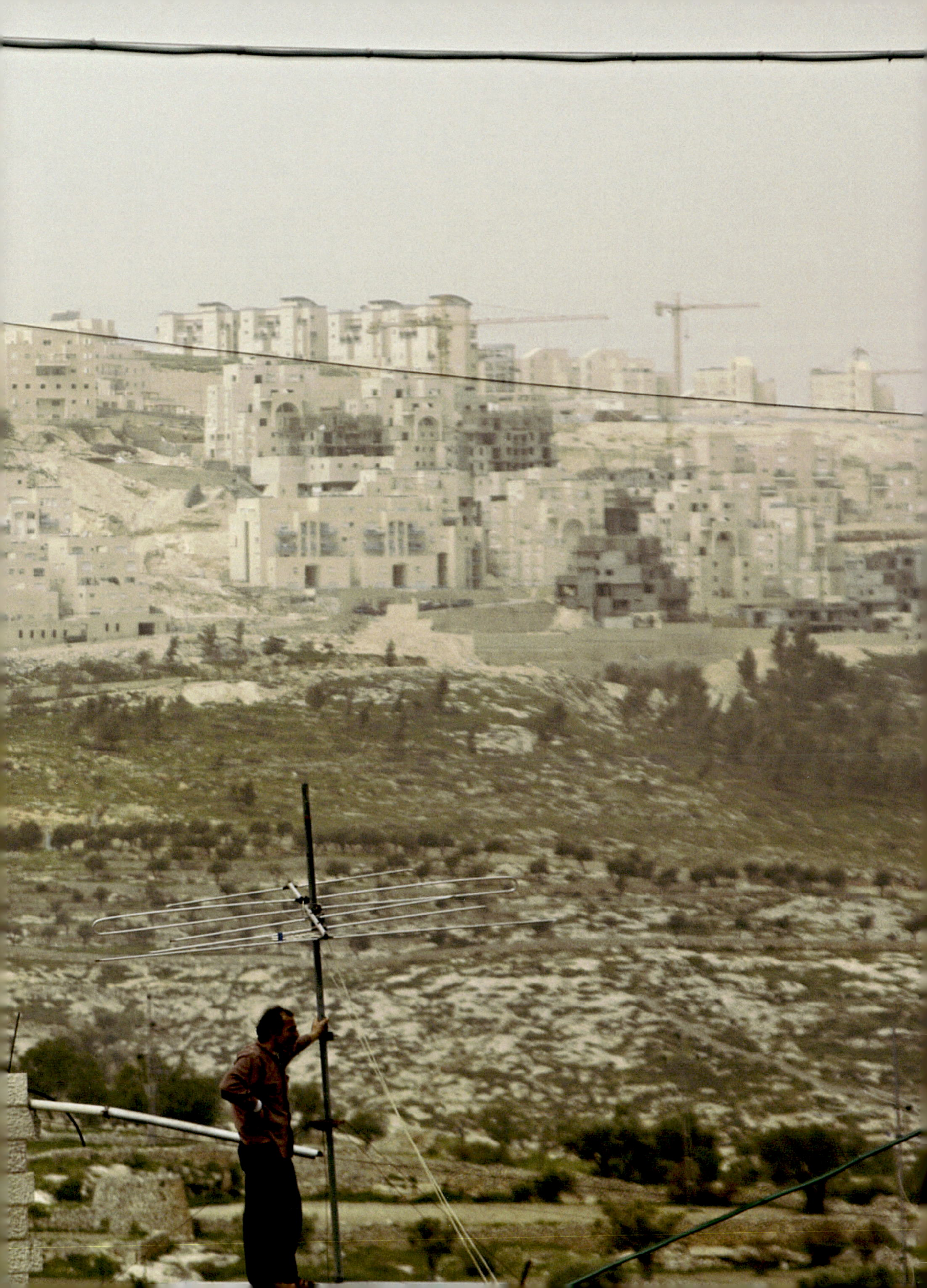

RAFAH, GAZA

06 - 11 APRIL 2003

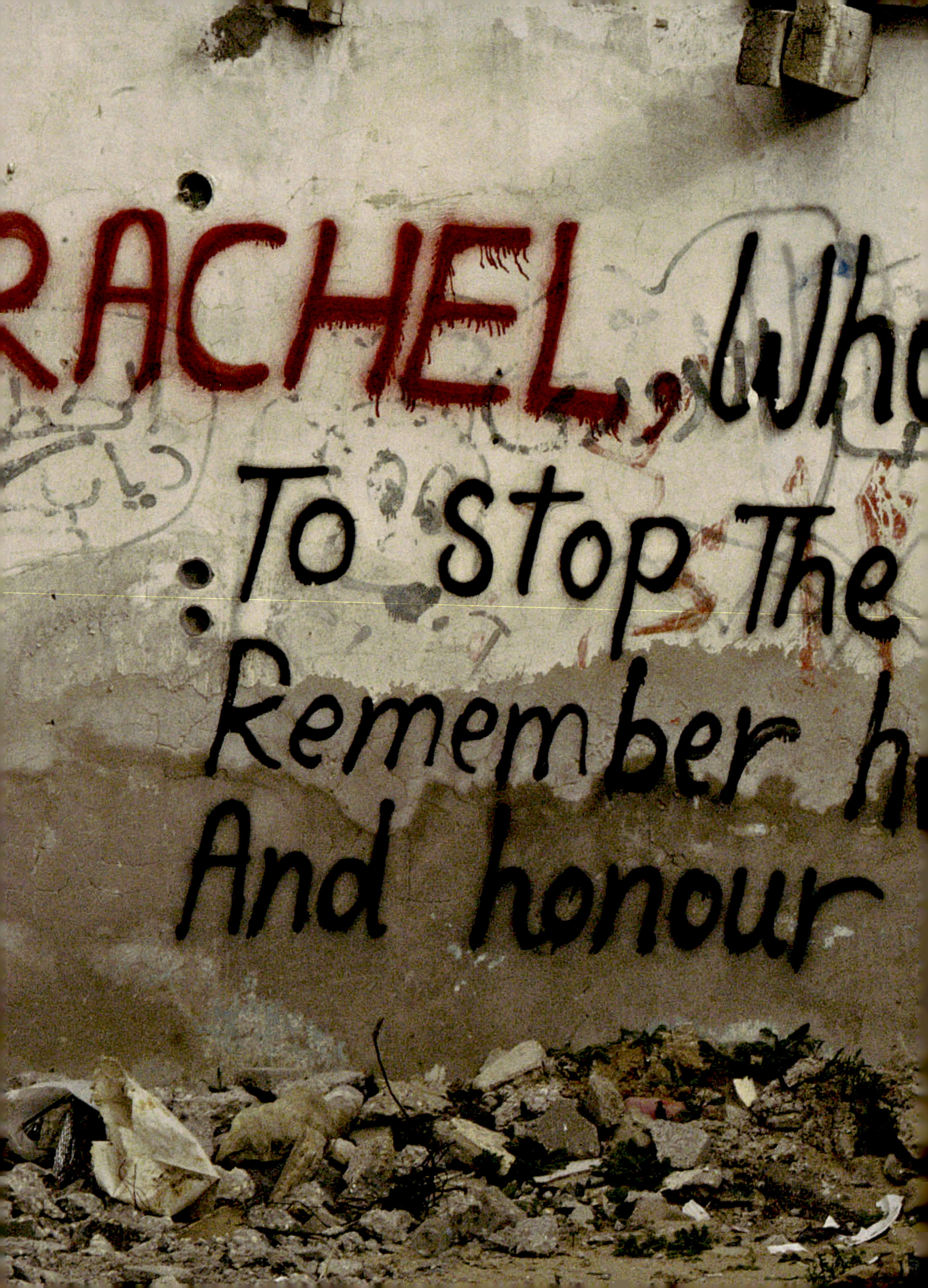

RACHEL, Who
: To stop The
Remember h
And honour

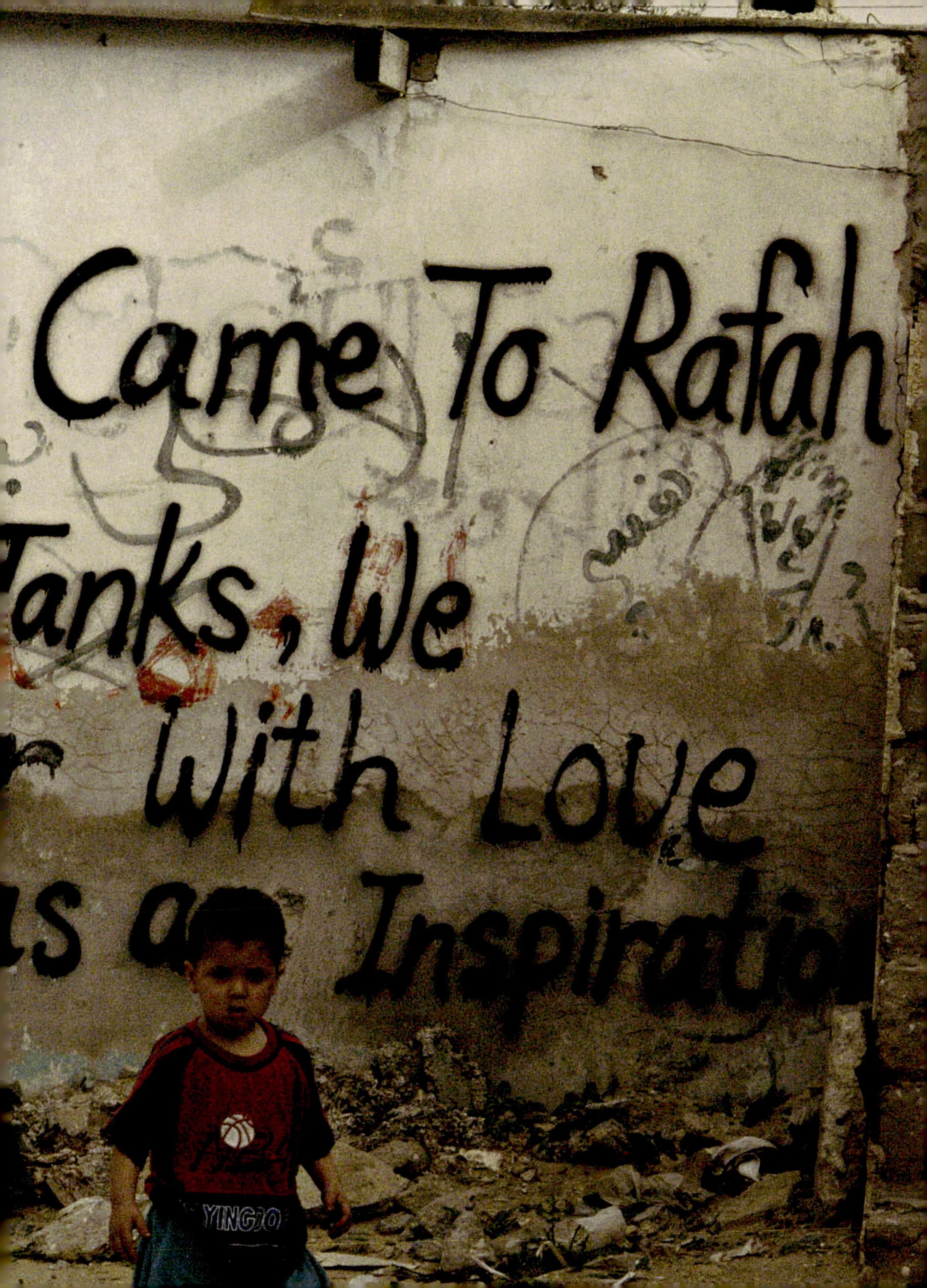

Came To Rafah
Tanks, We
With Love
is an Inspiration

MAP OF RAFAH, GAZA

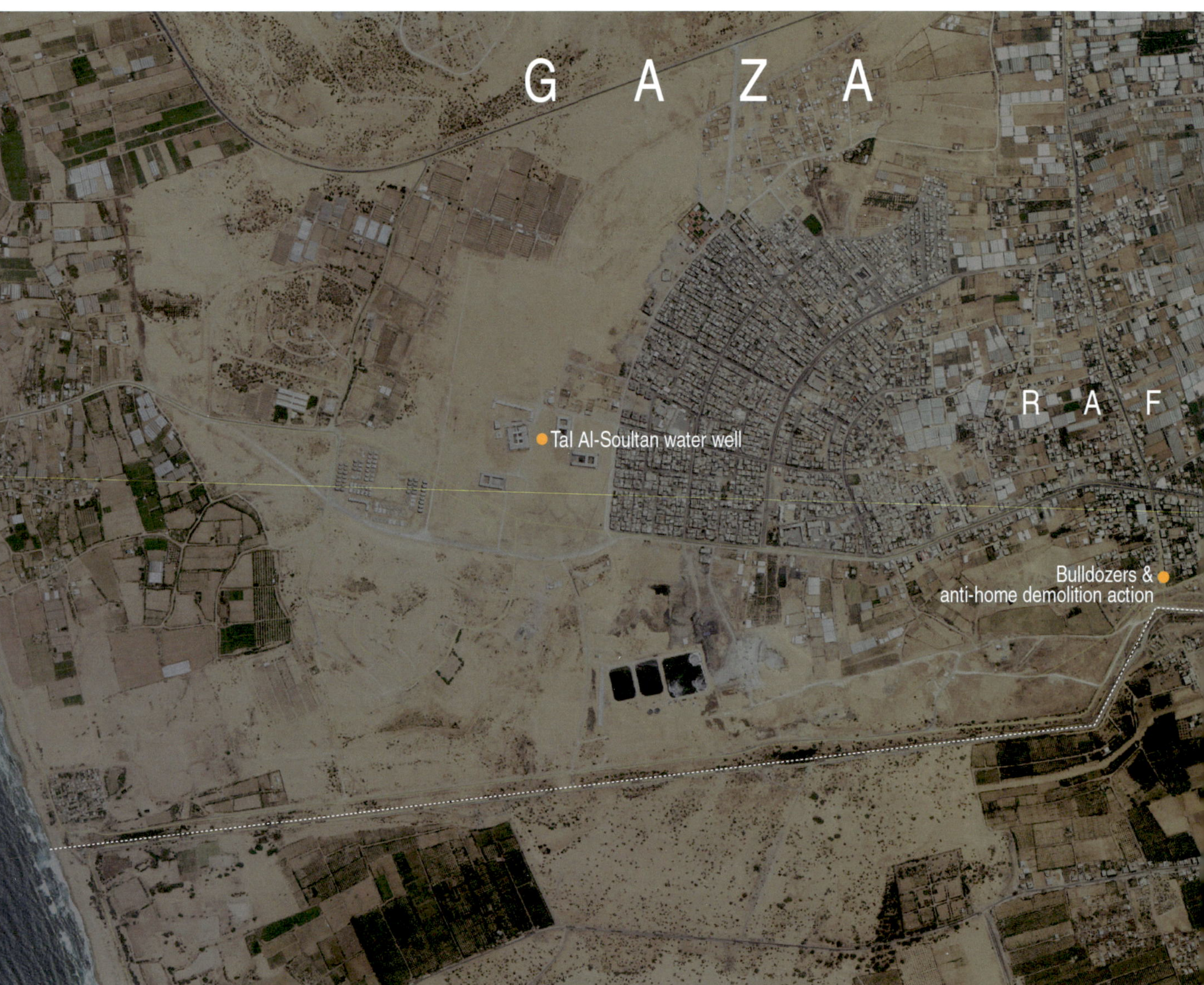

Map taken from 2011 Google Earth

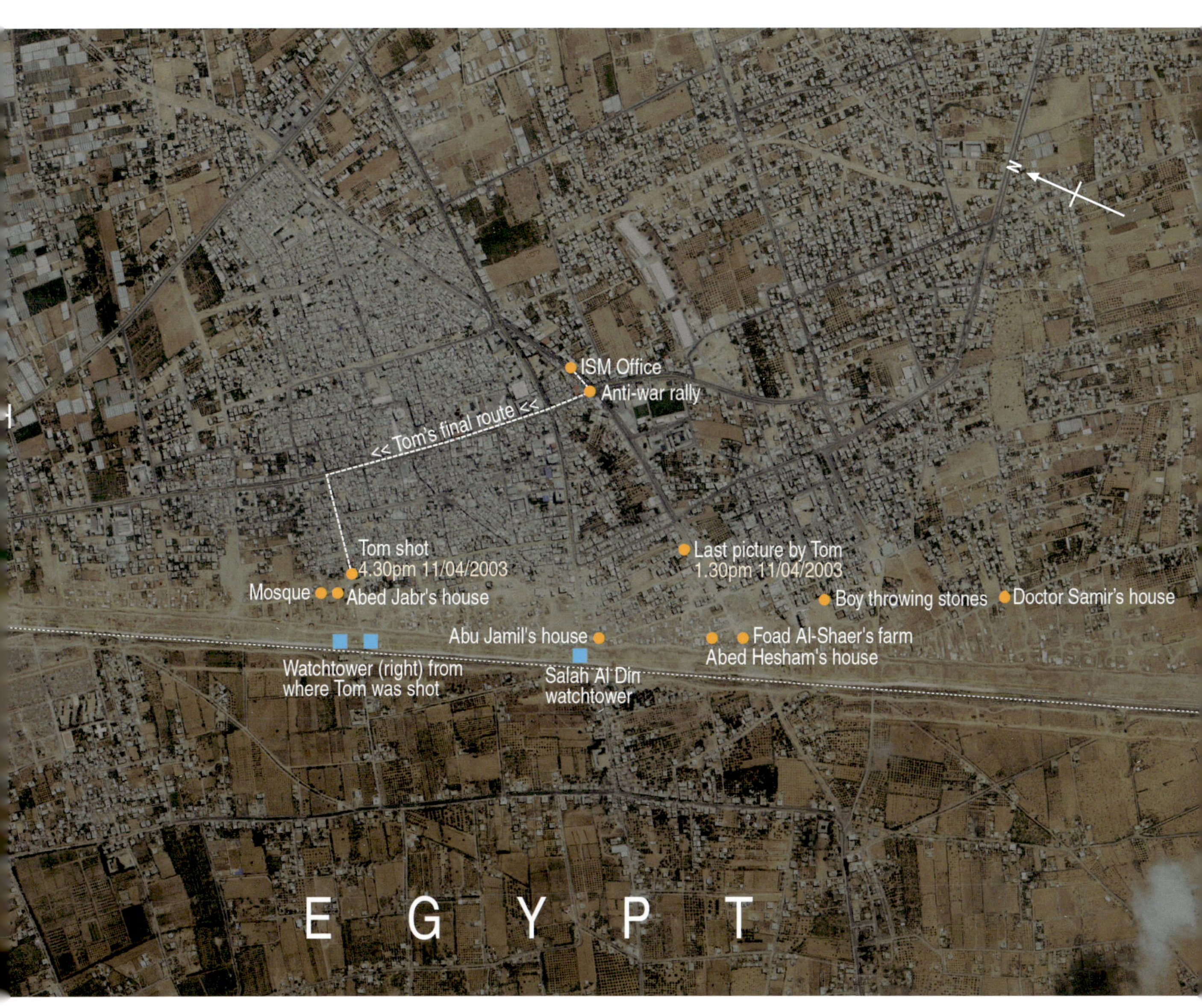

ISM Office
Anti-war rally
<< Tom's final route <<
Tom shot
4.30pm 11/04/2003
Last picture by Tom
1.30pm 11/04/2003
Mosque
Abed Jabr's house
Boy throwing stones
Doctor Samir's house
Abu Jamil's house
Foad Al-Shaer's farm
Abed Hesham's house
Watchtower (right) from
where Tom was shot
Salah Al Din
watchtower
EGYPT

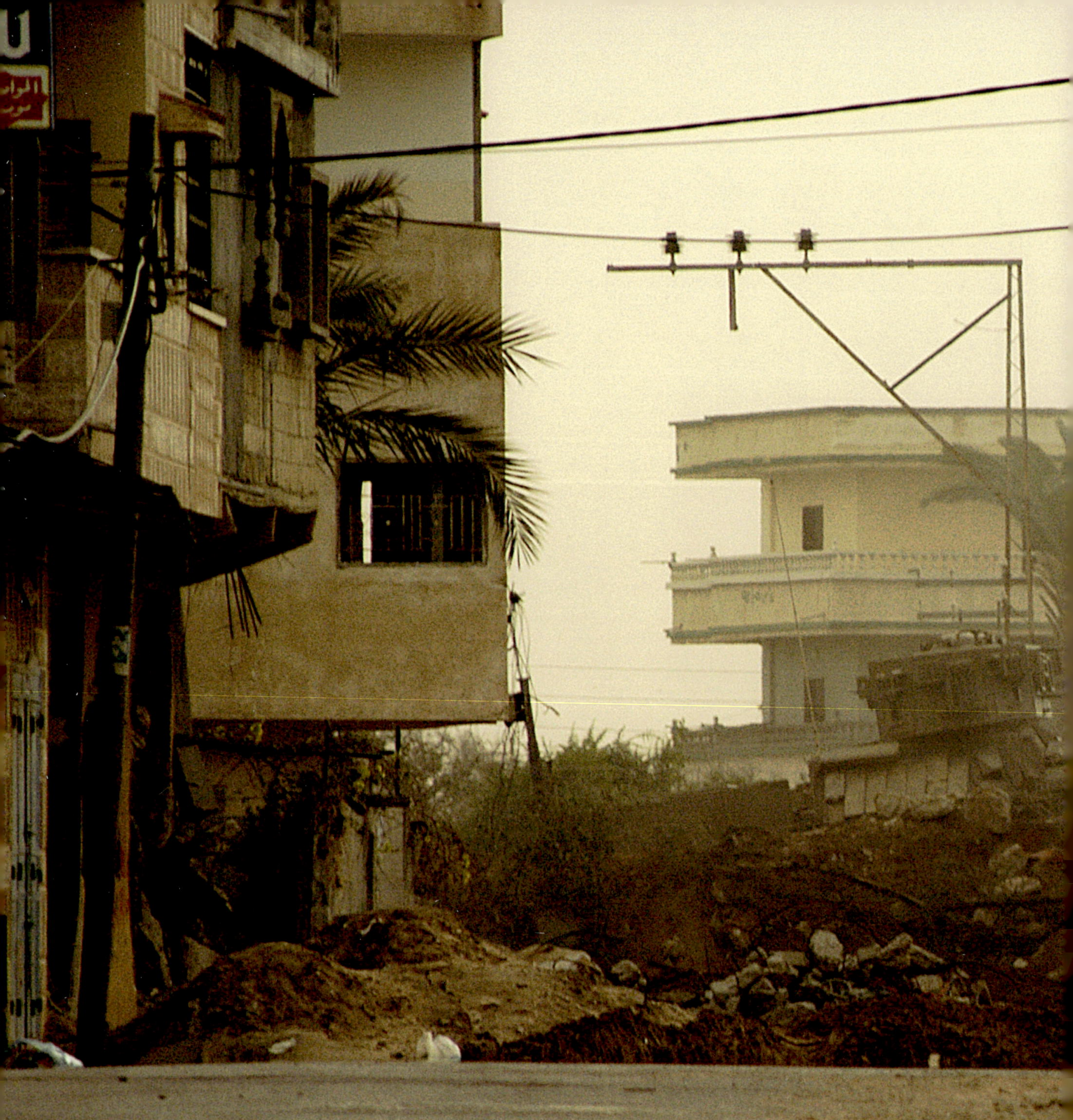
Welcome to Rafah.

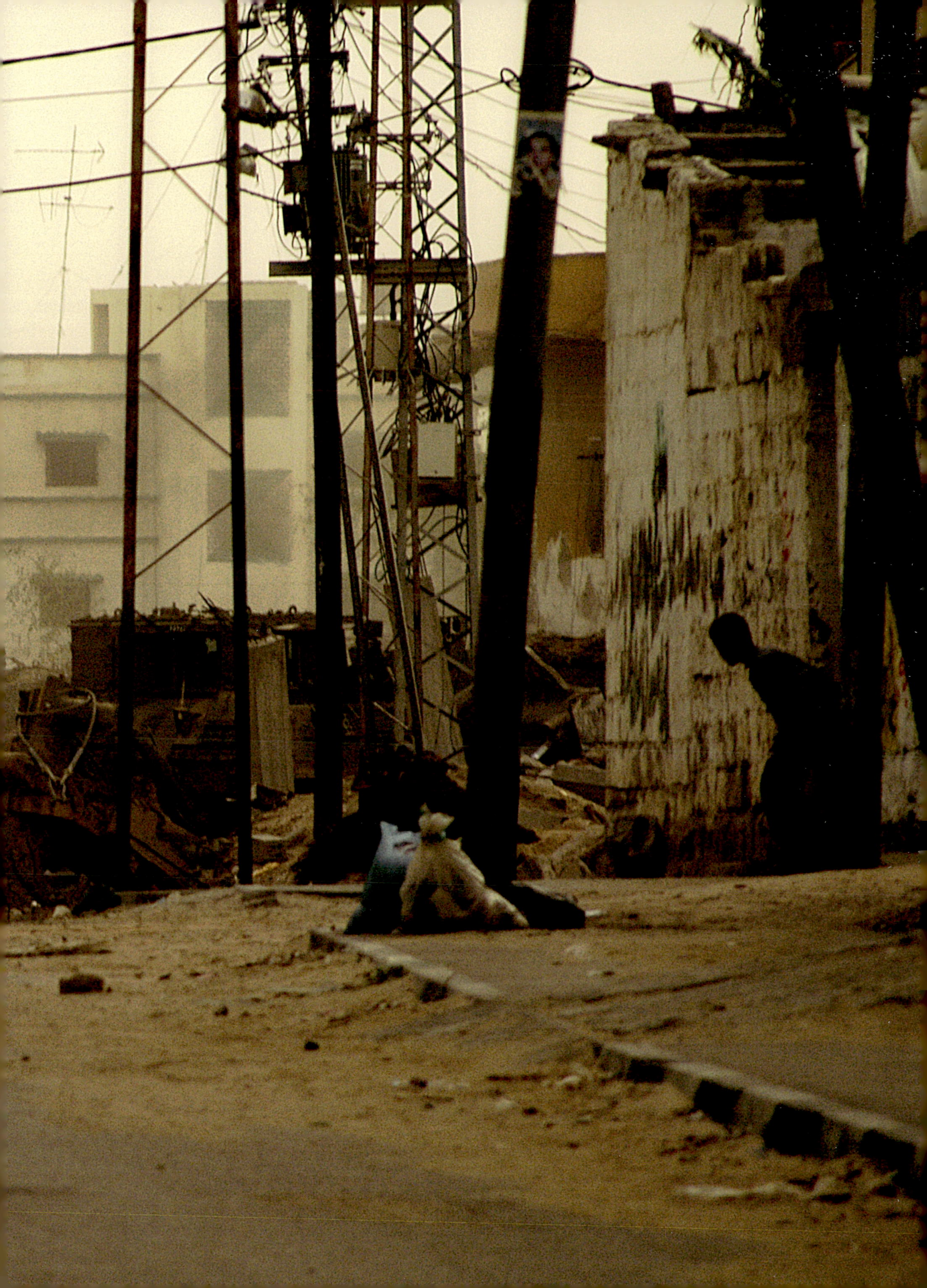

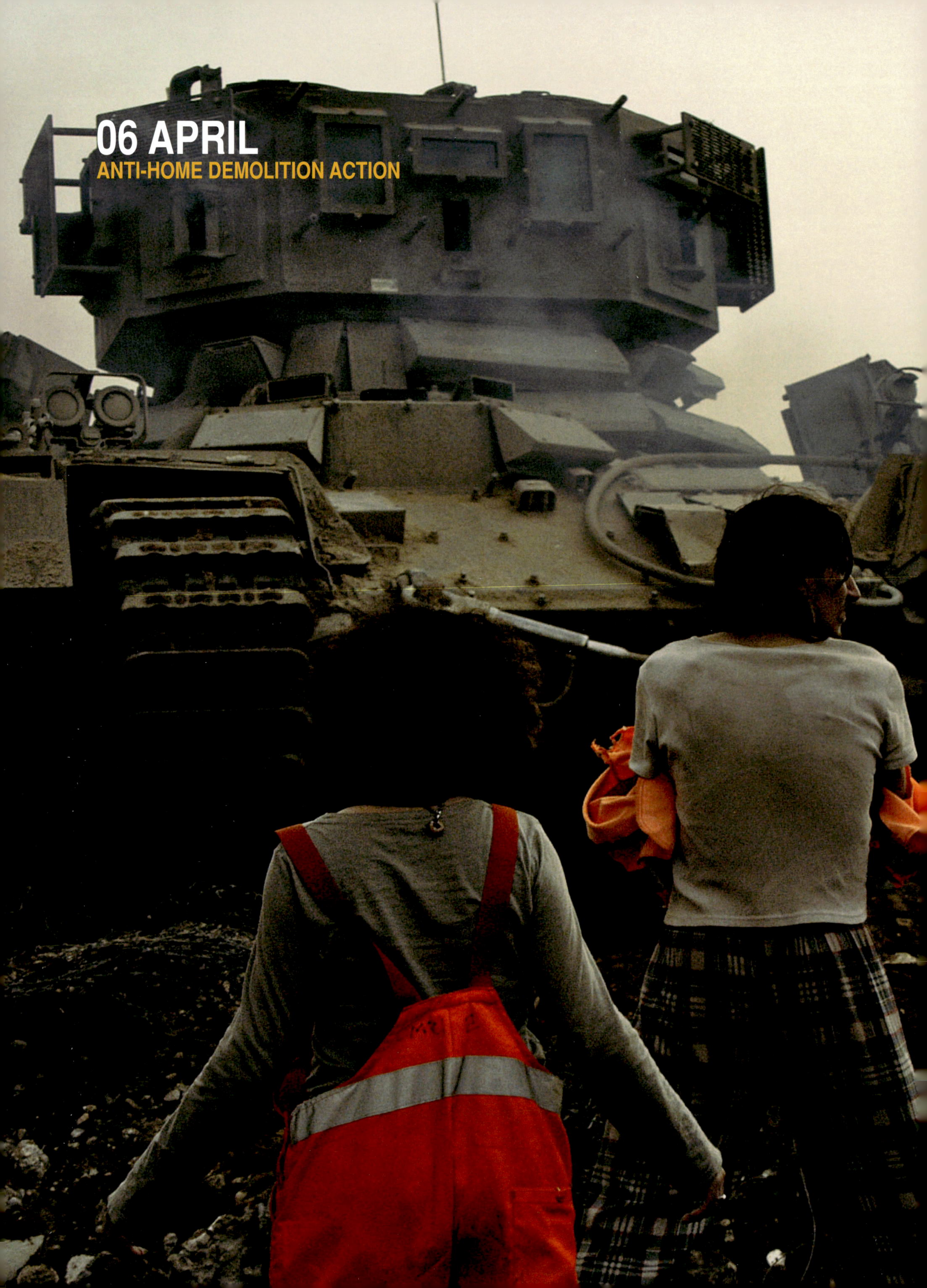

06 APRIL
ANTI-HOME DEMOLITION ACTION

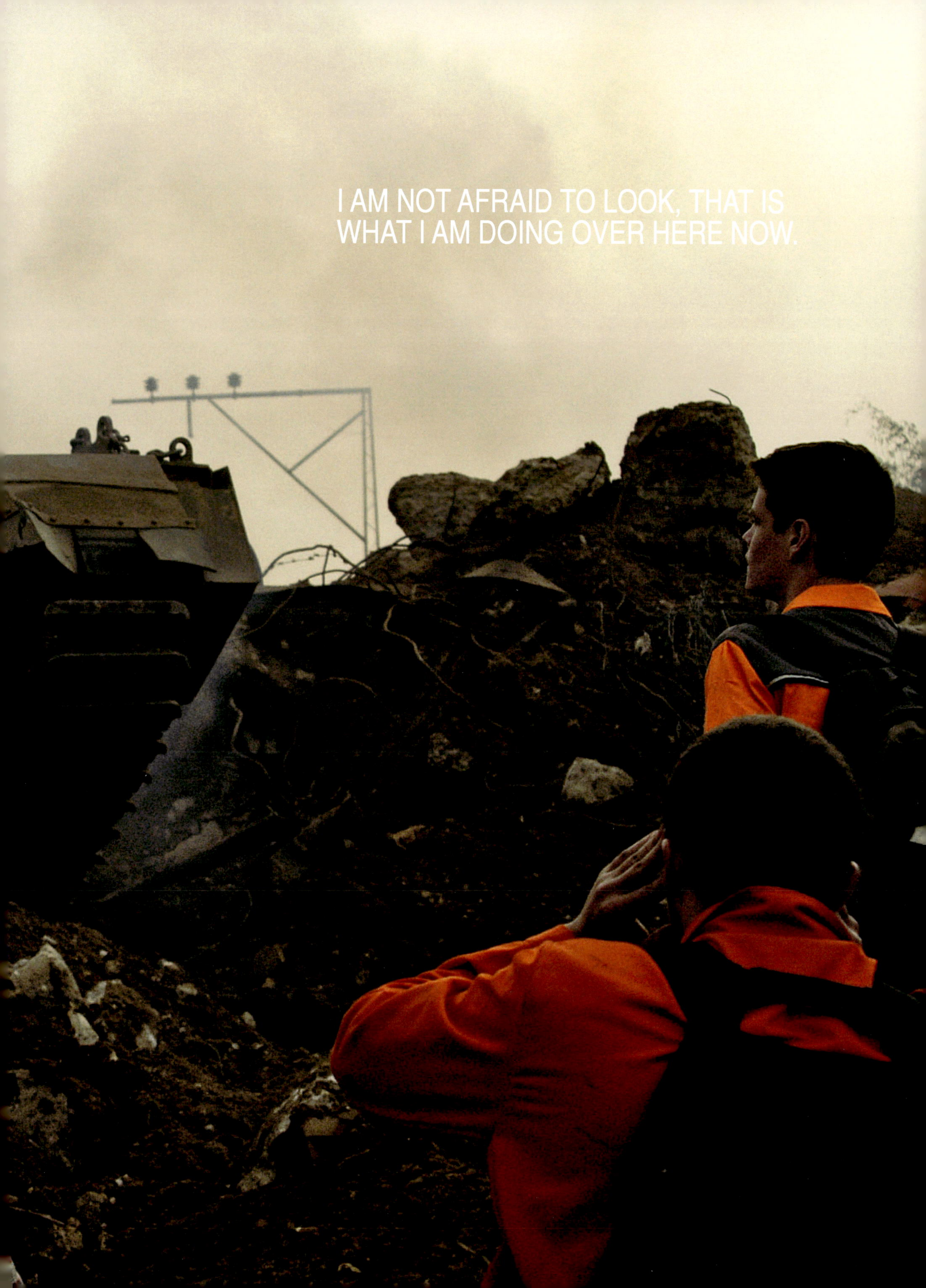
I AM NOT AFRAID TO LOOK, THAT IS
WHAT I AM DOING OVER HERE NOW.

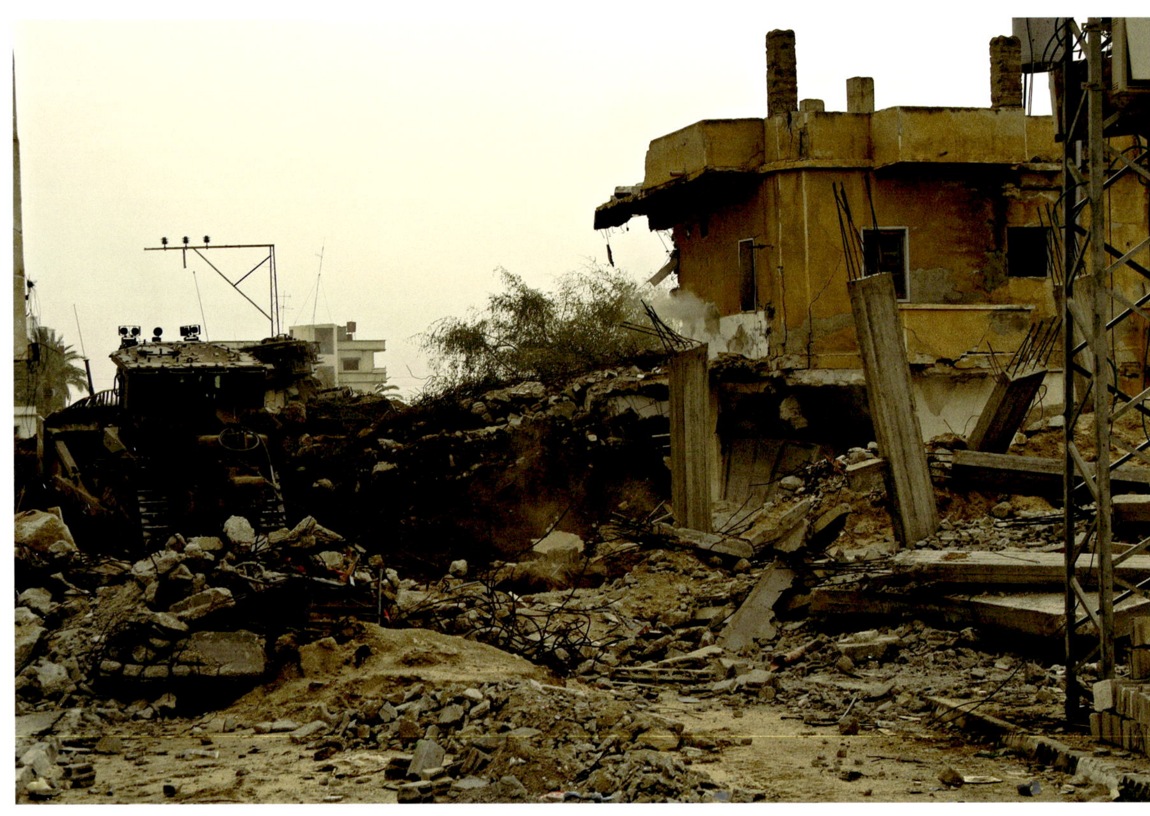

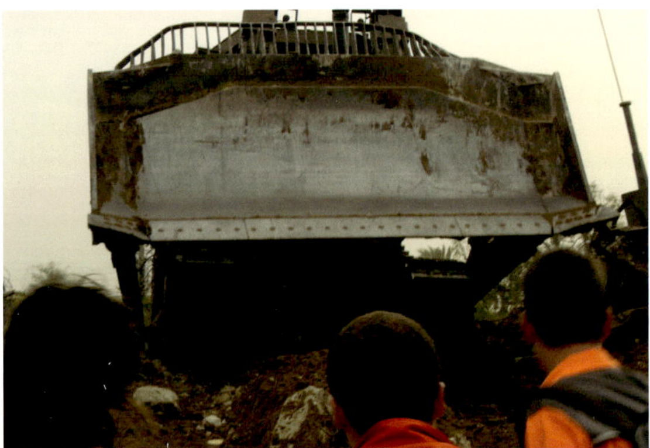

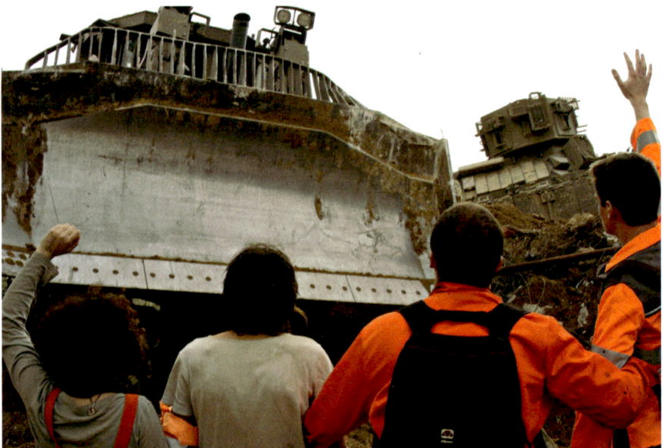

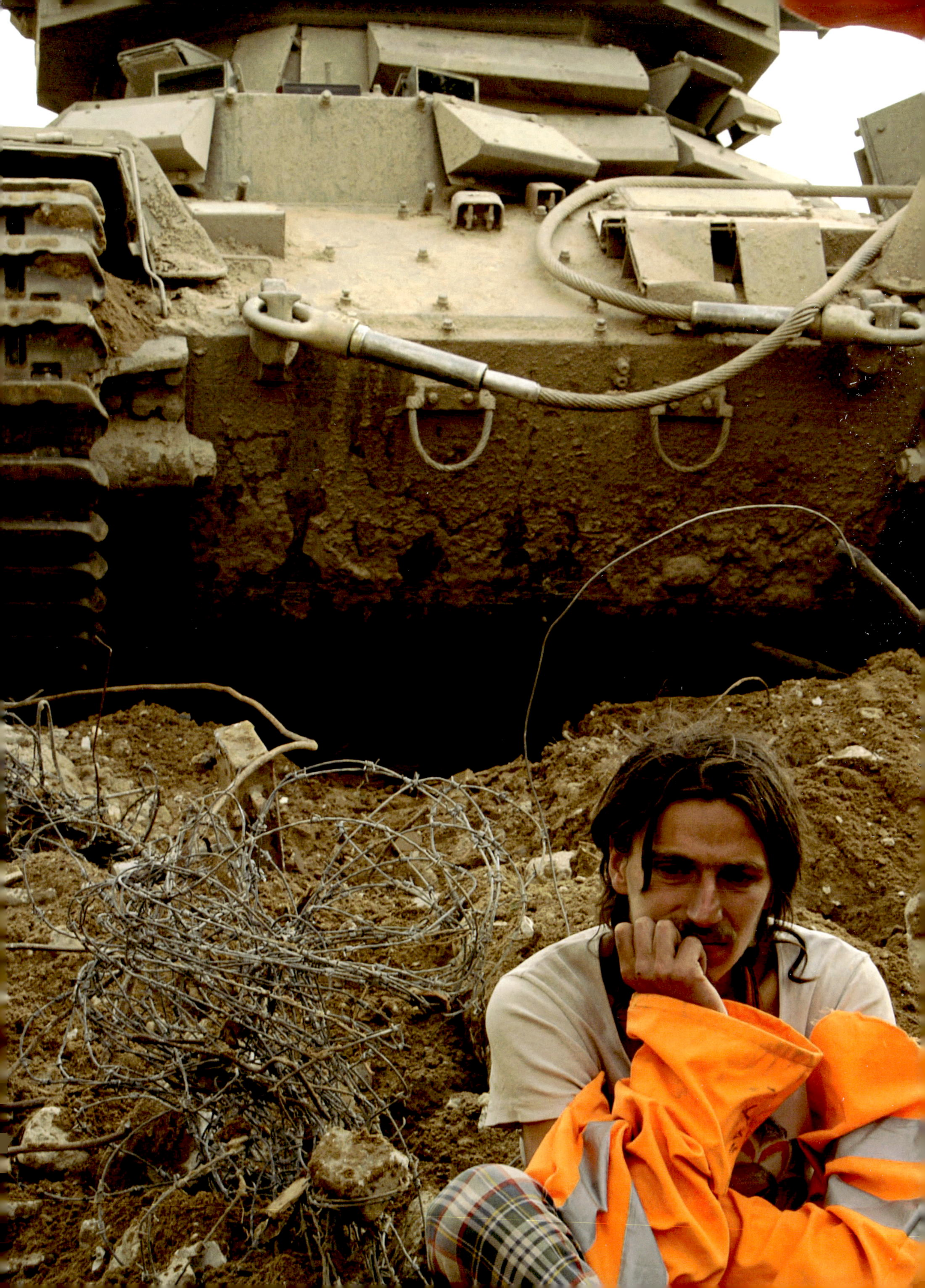

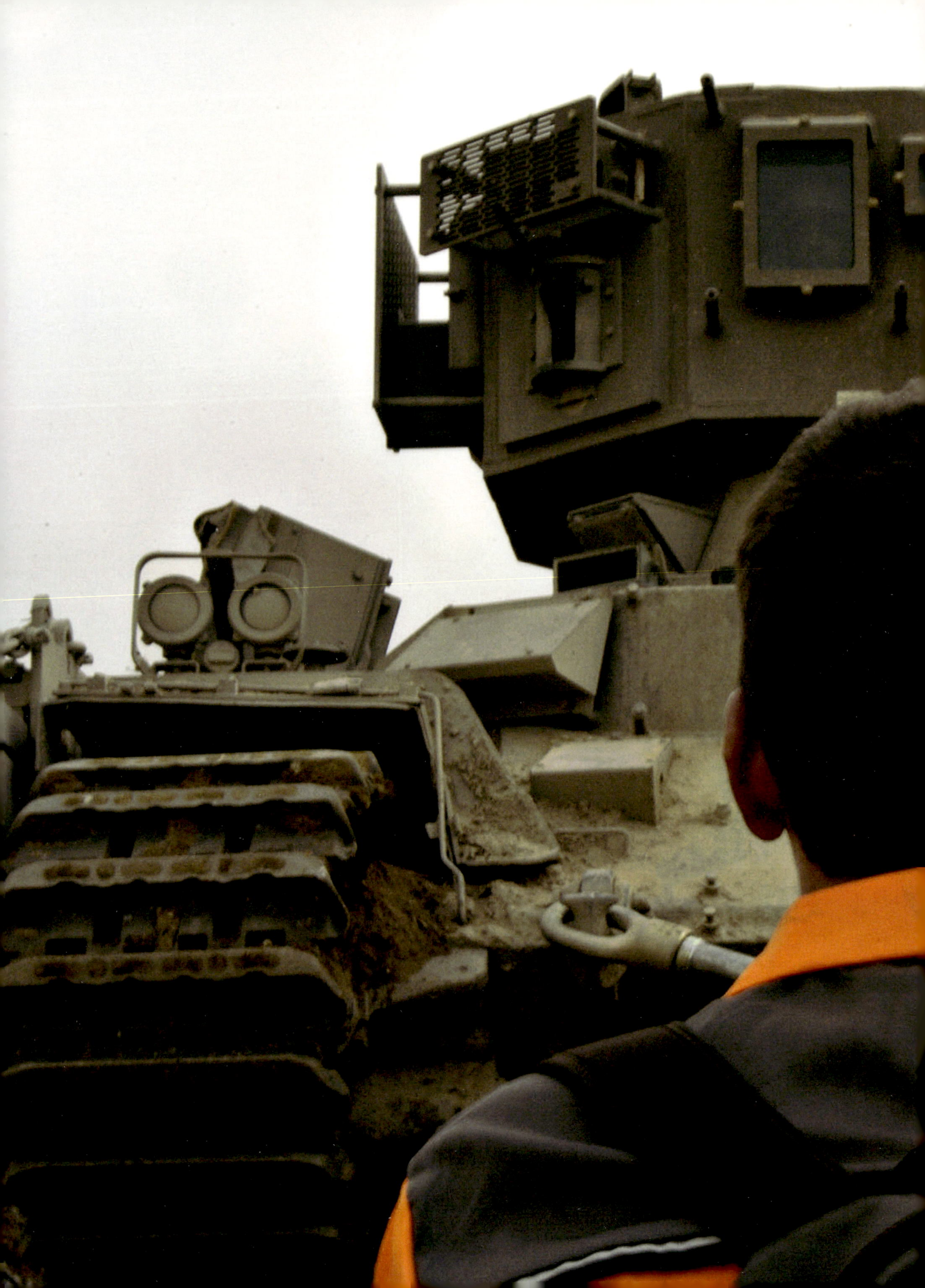

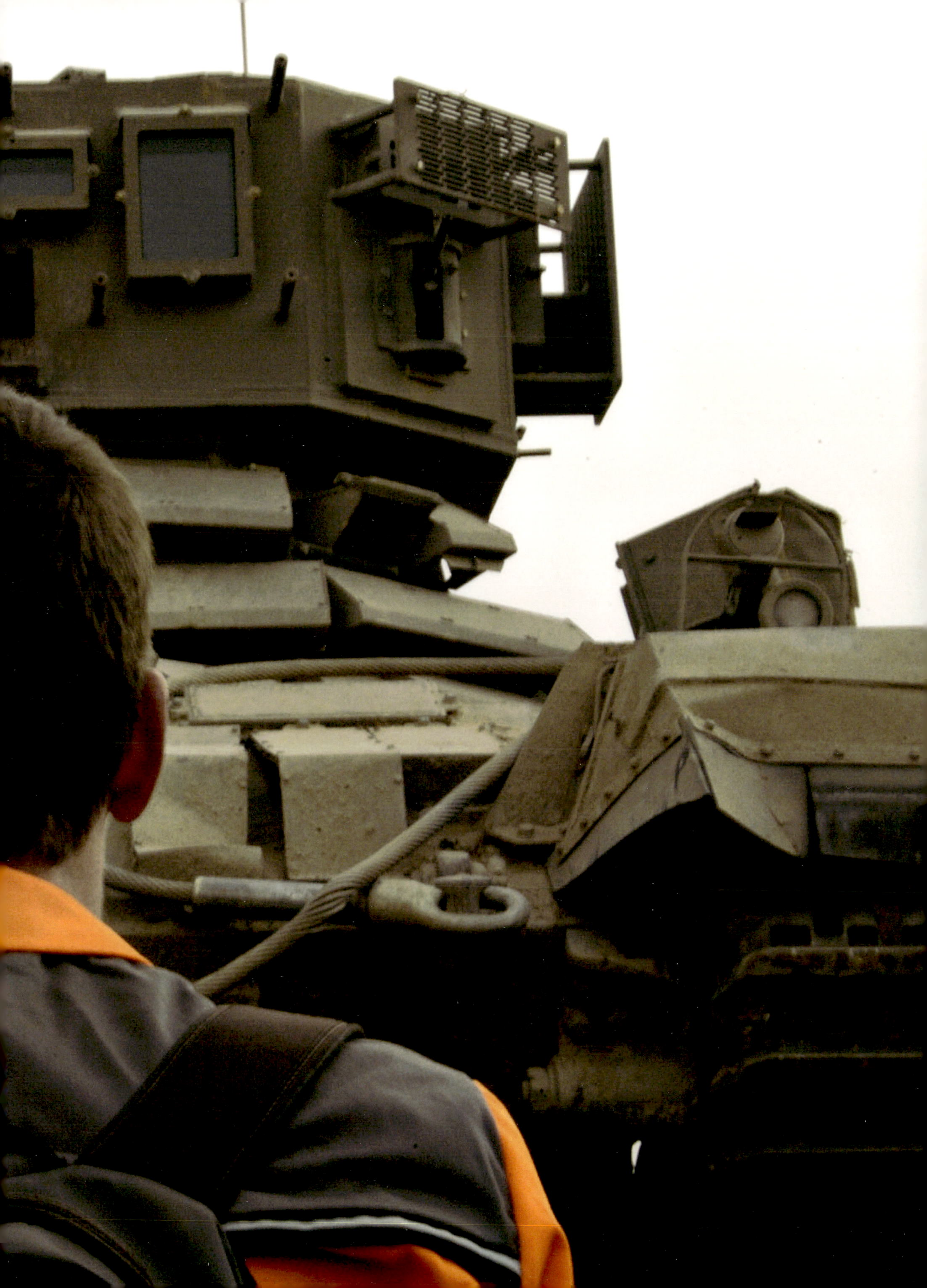

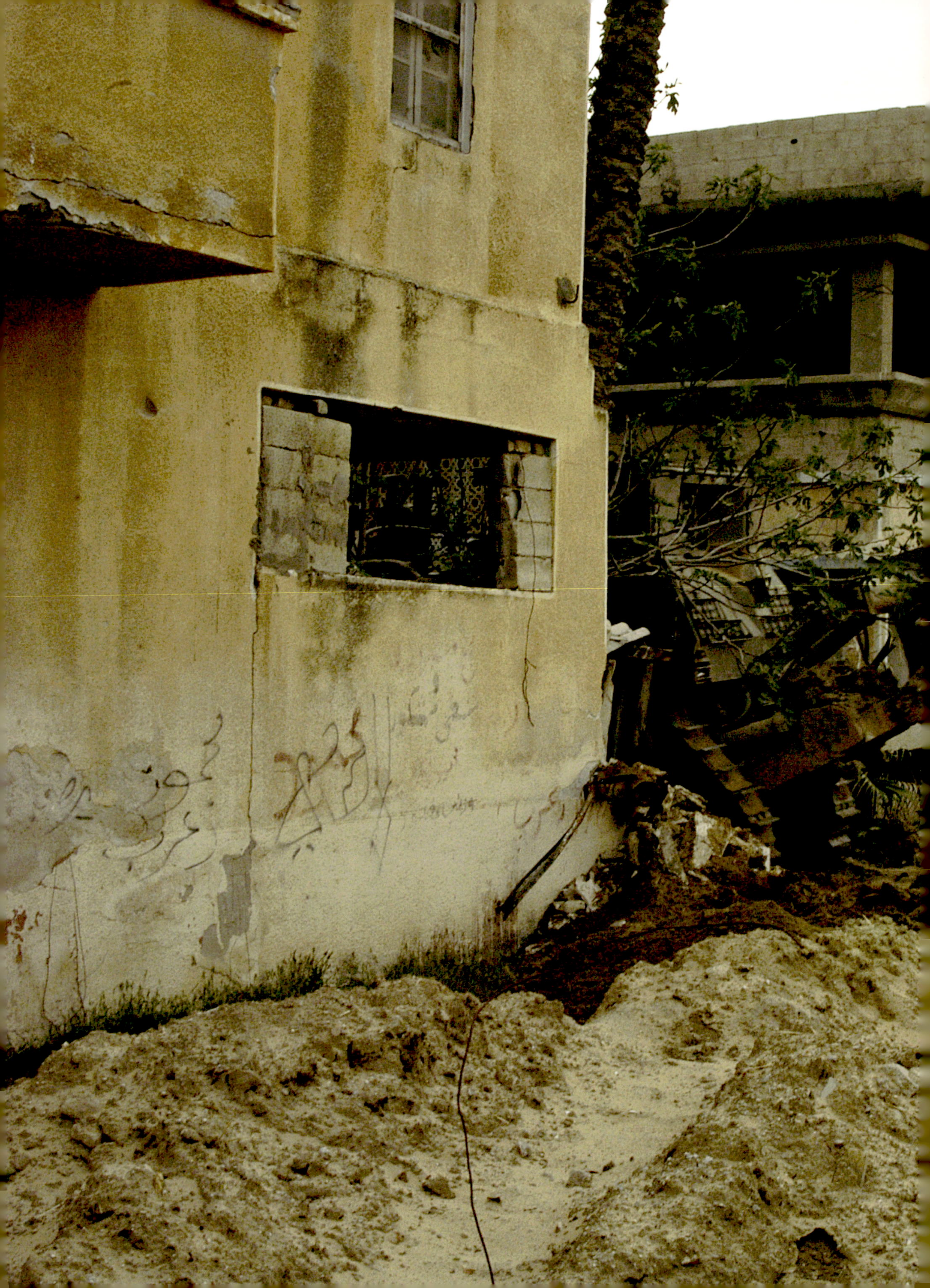

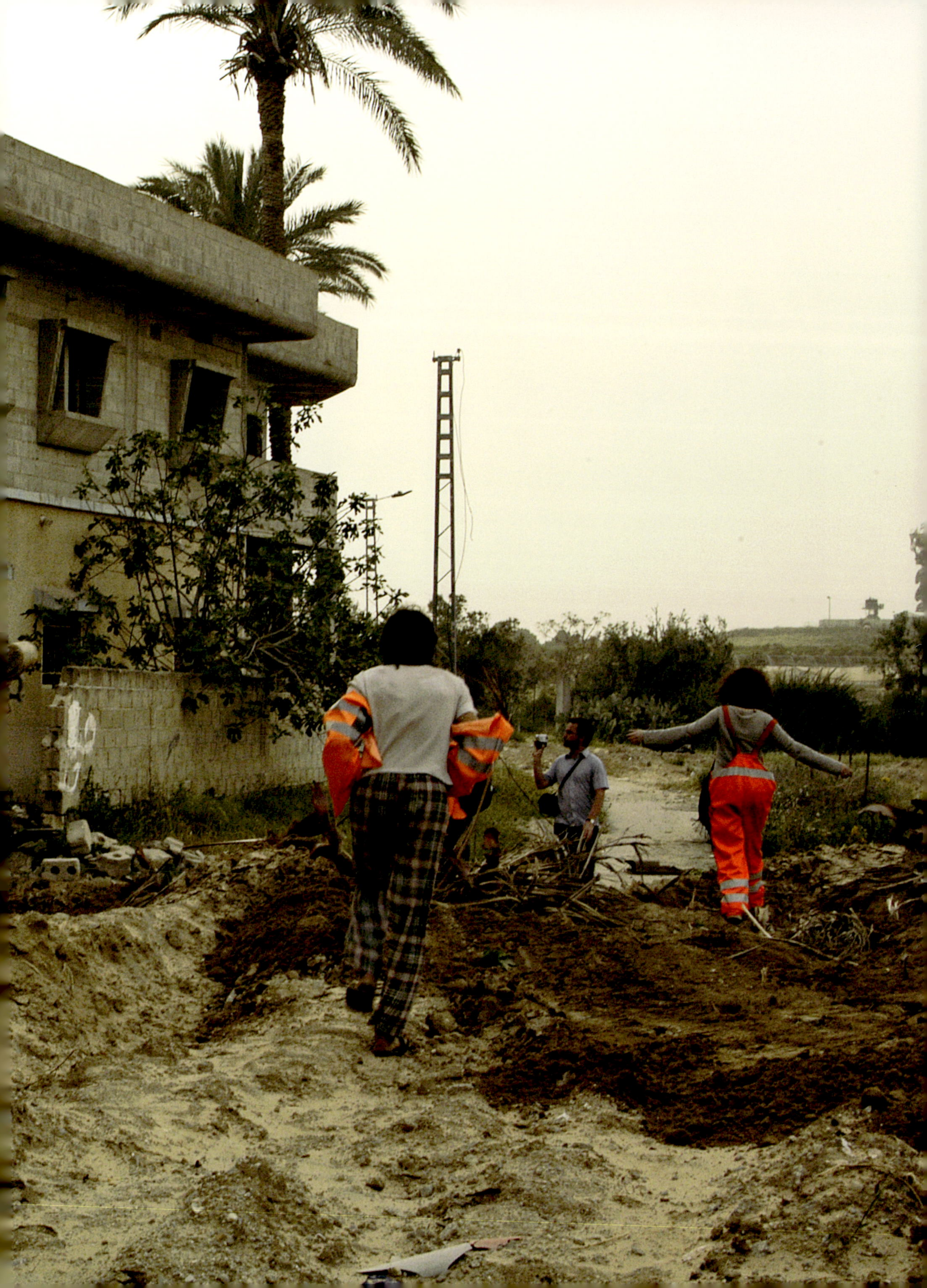

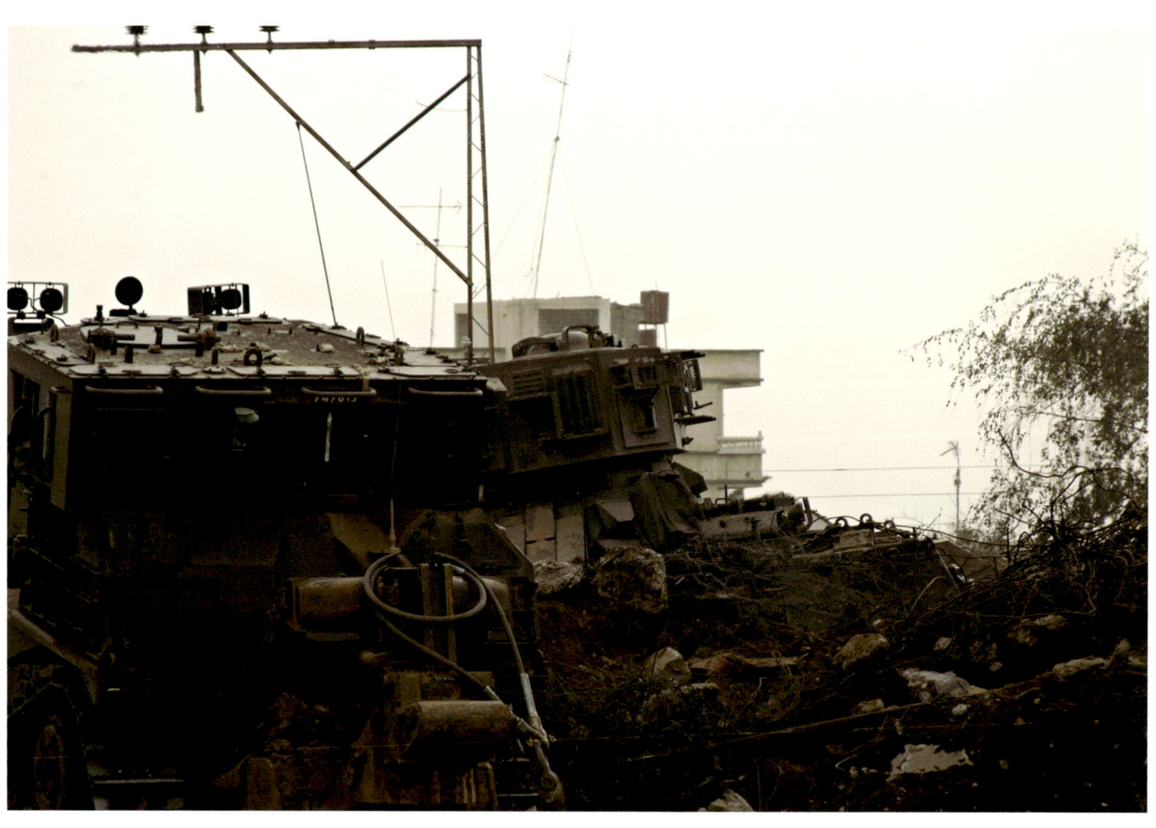

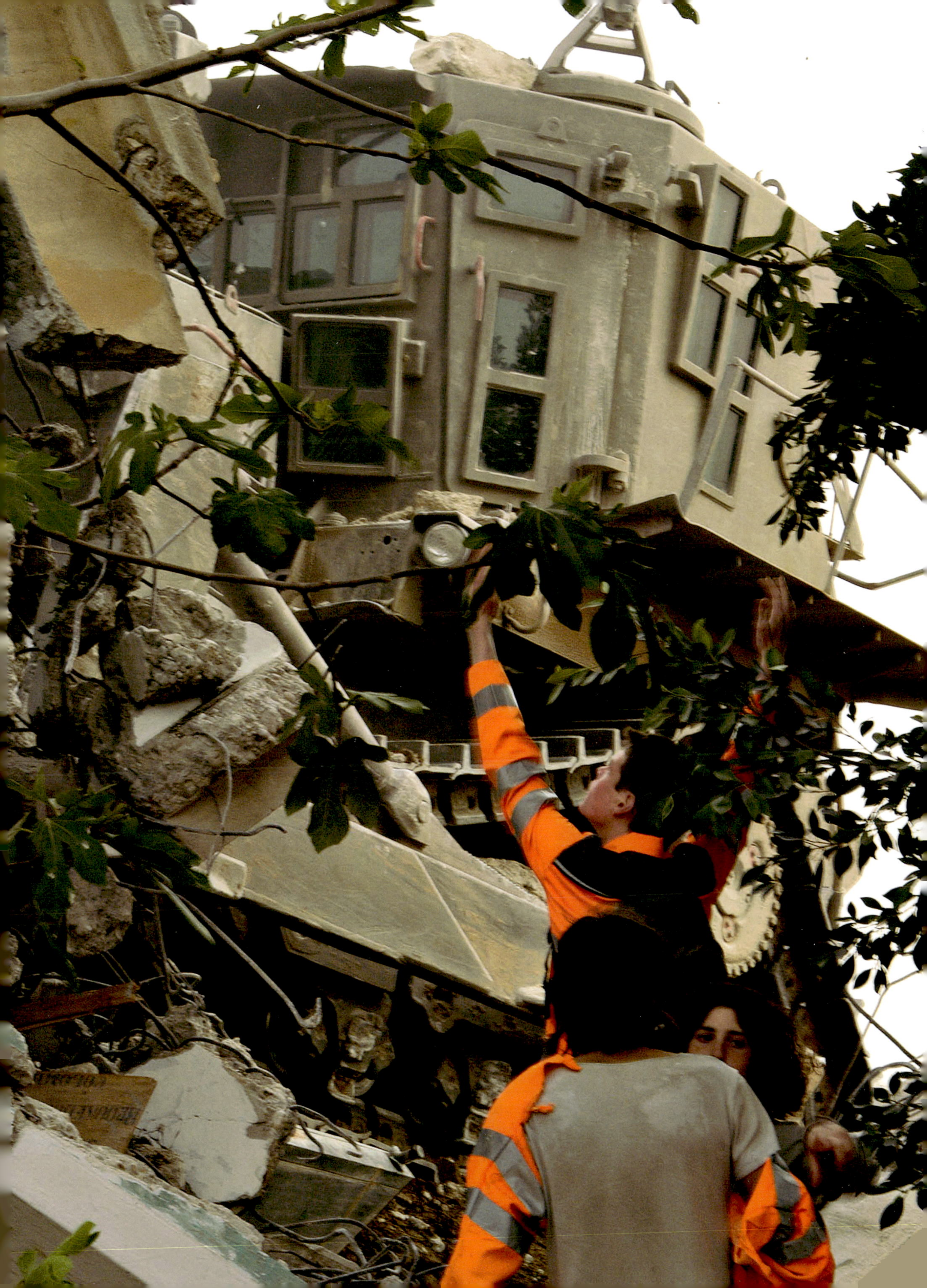

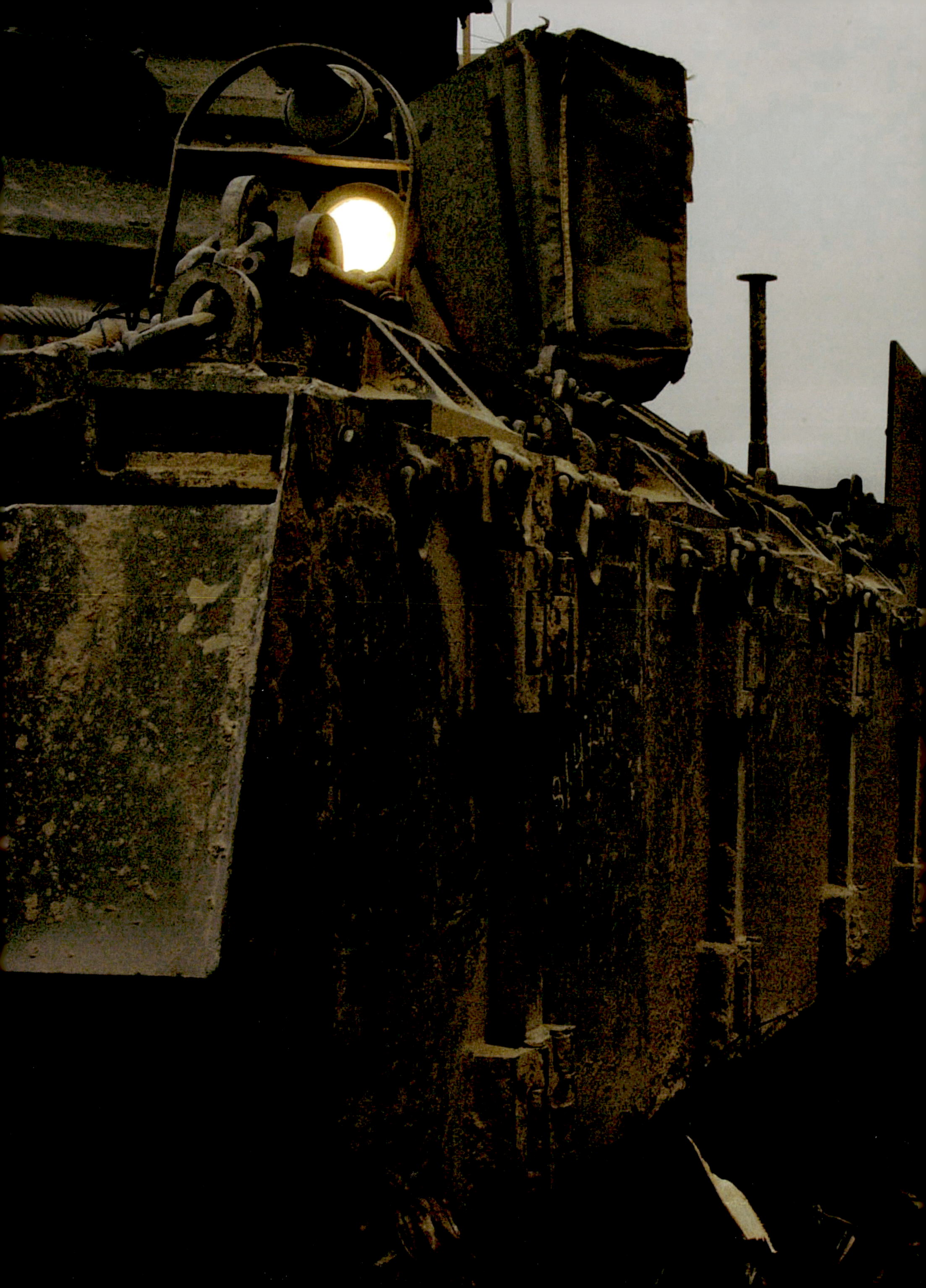

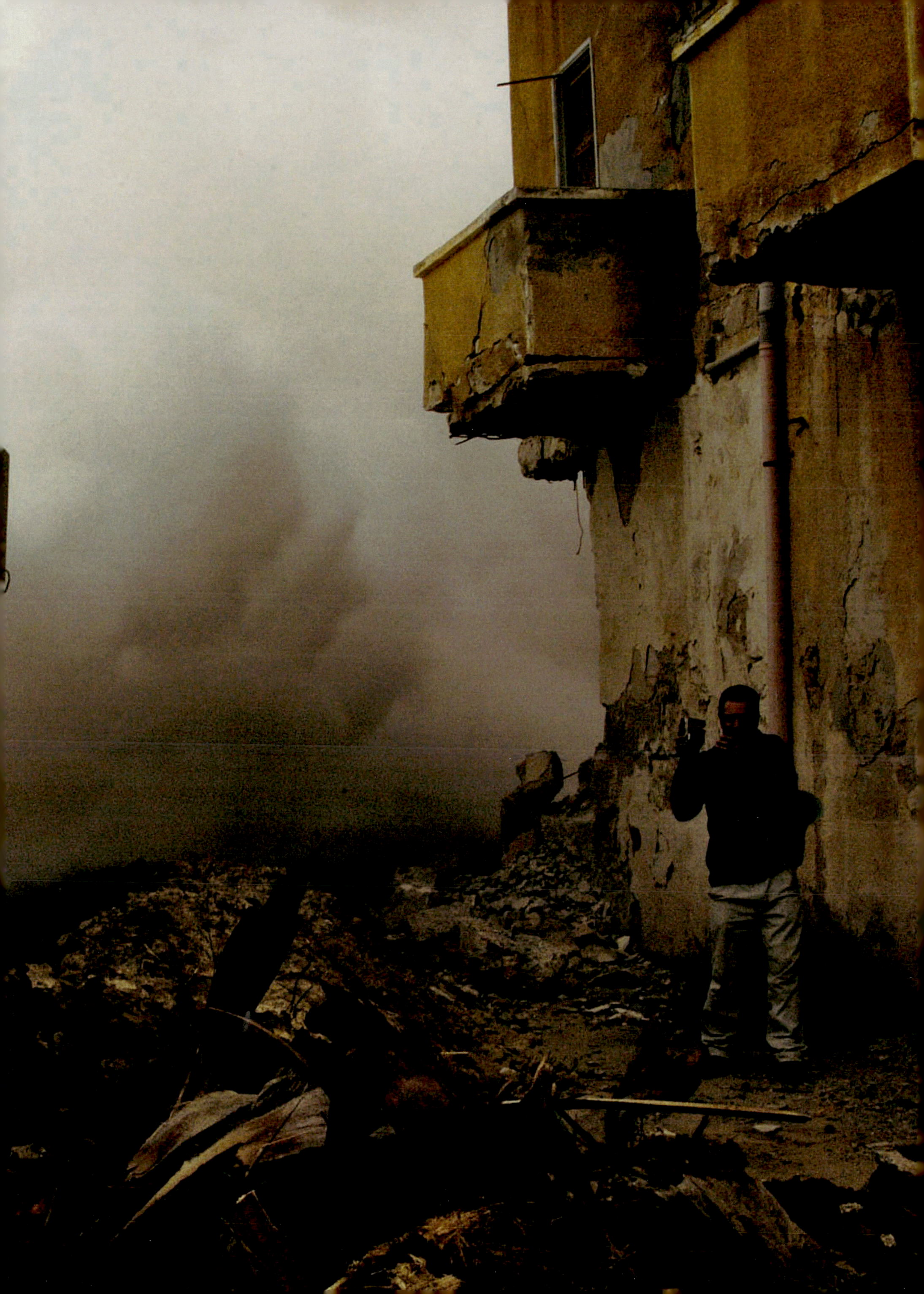

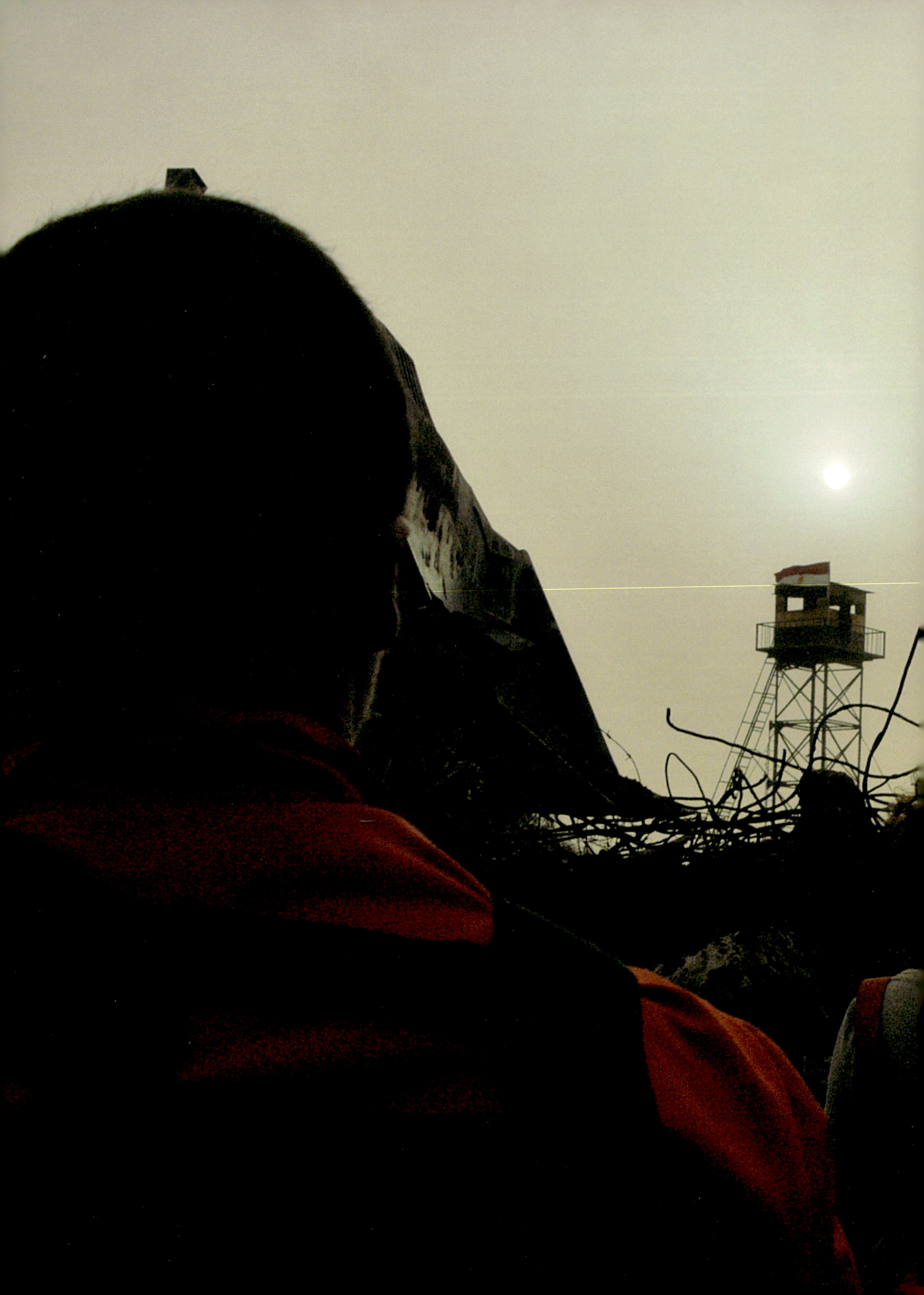

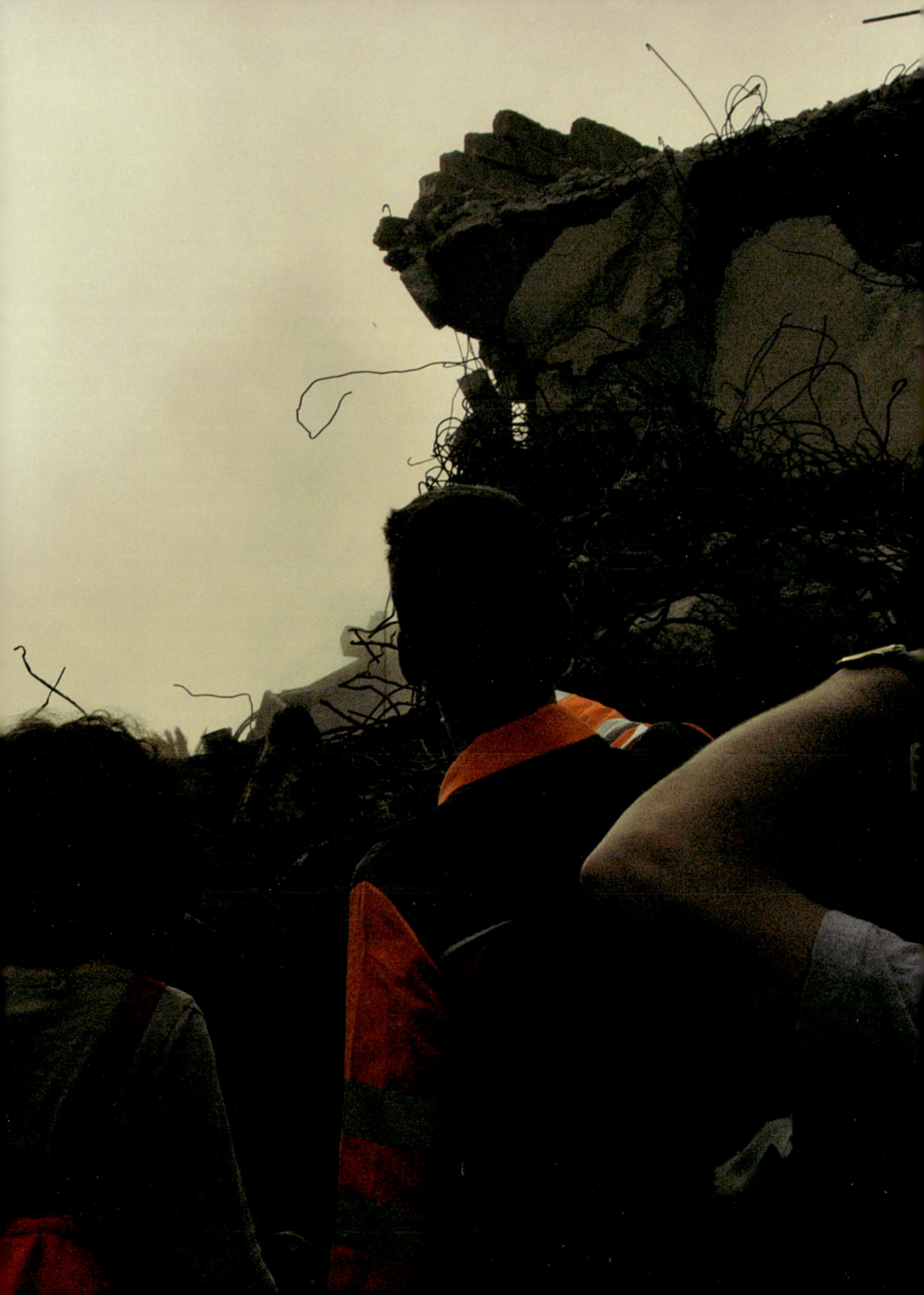

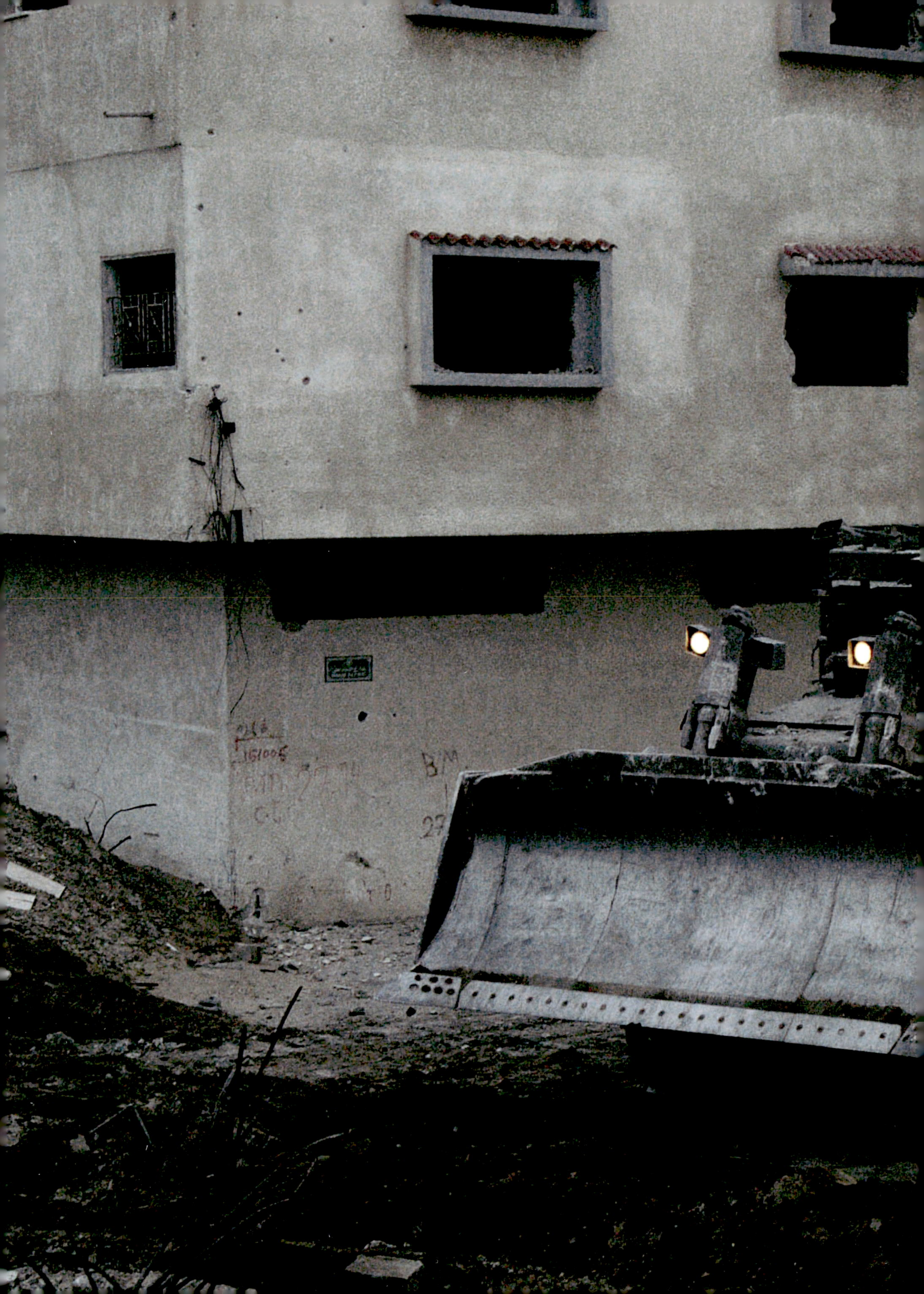

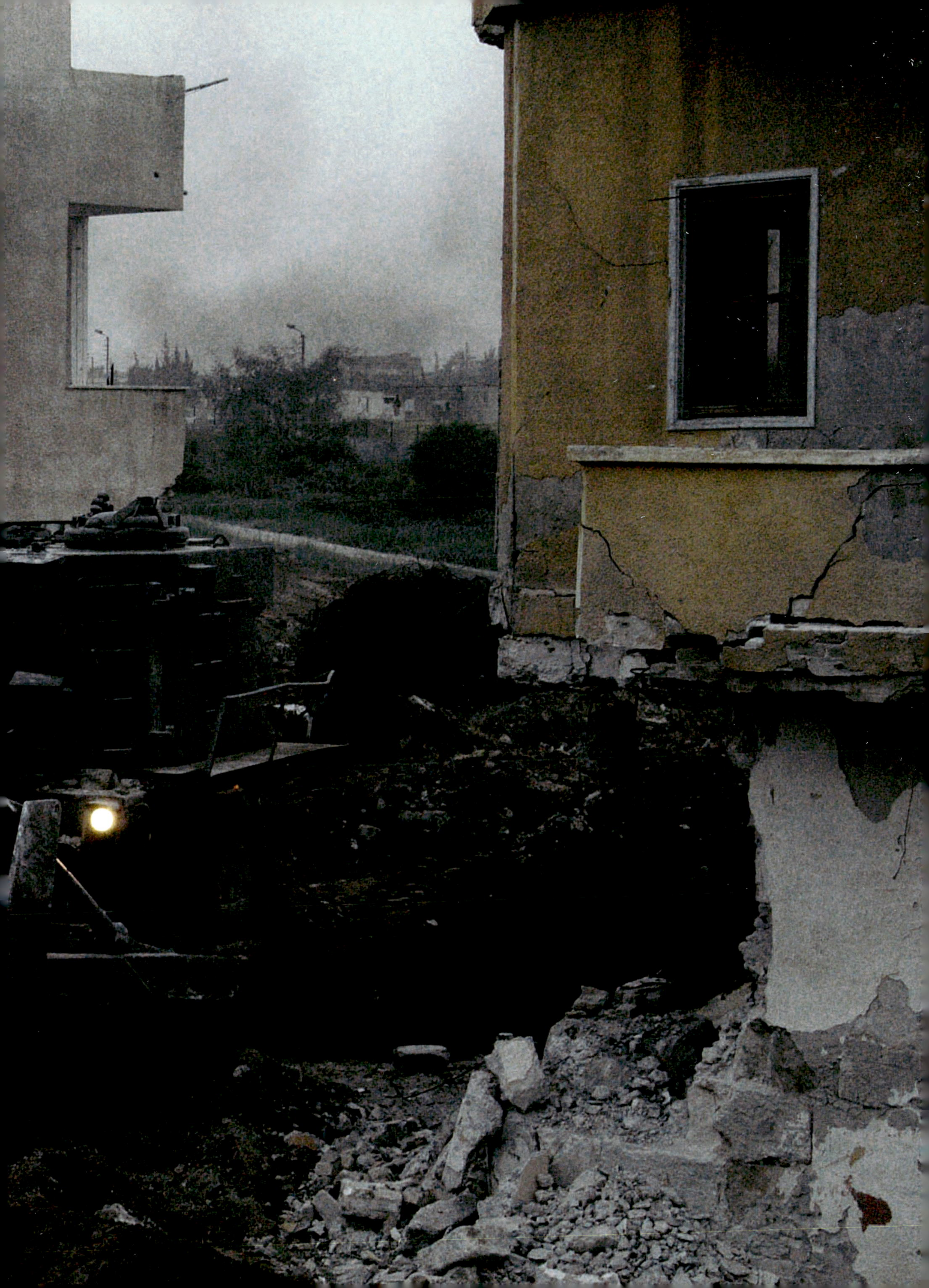

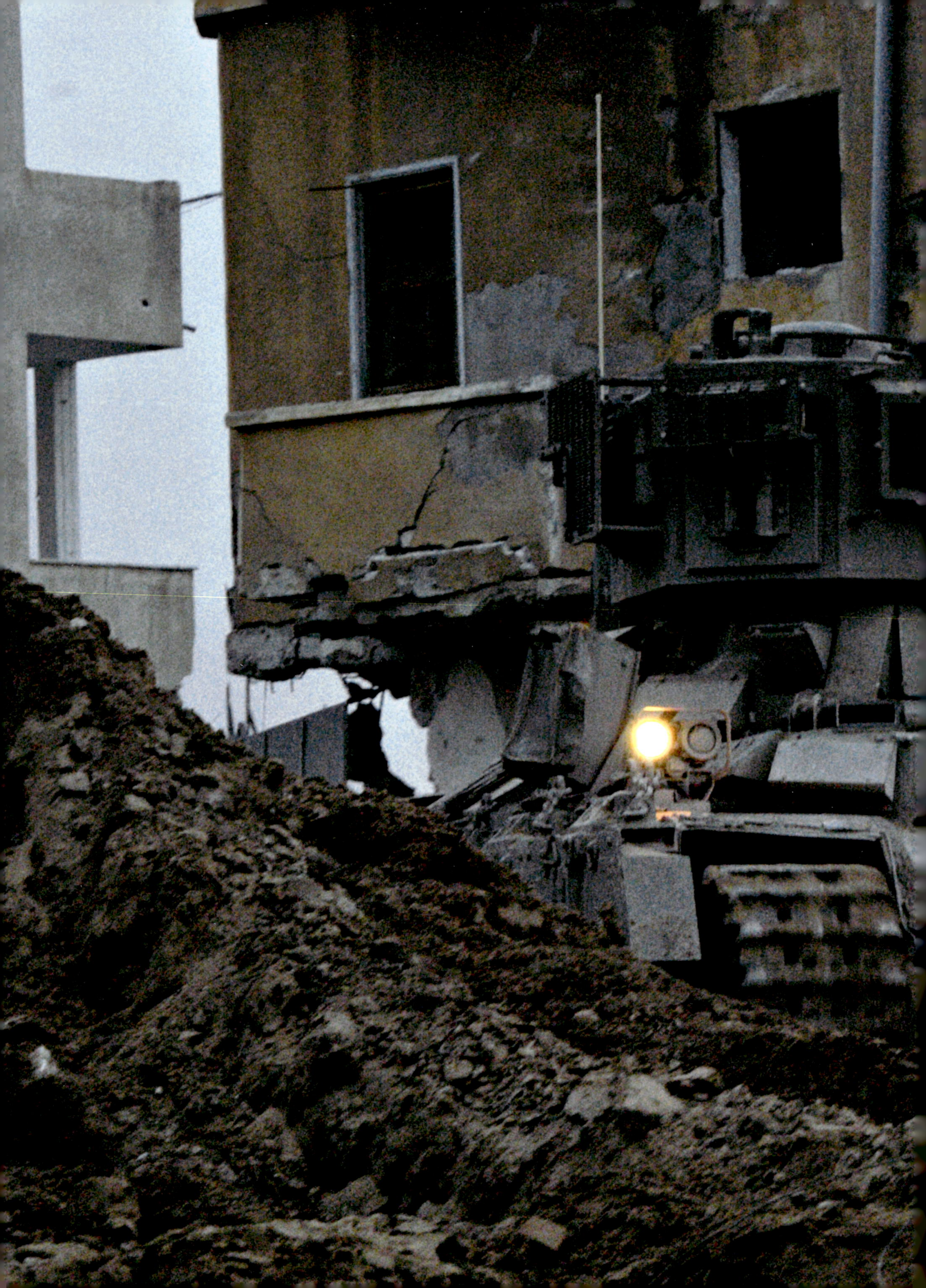

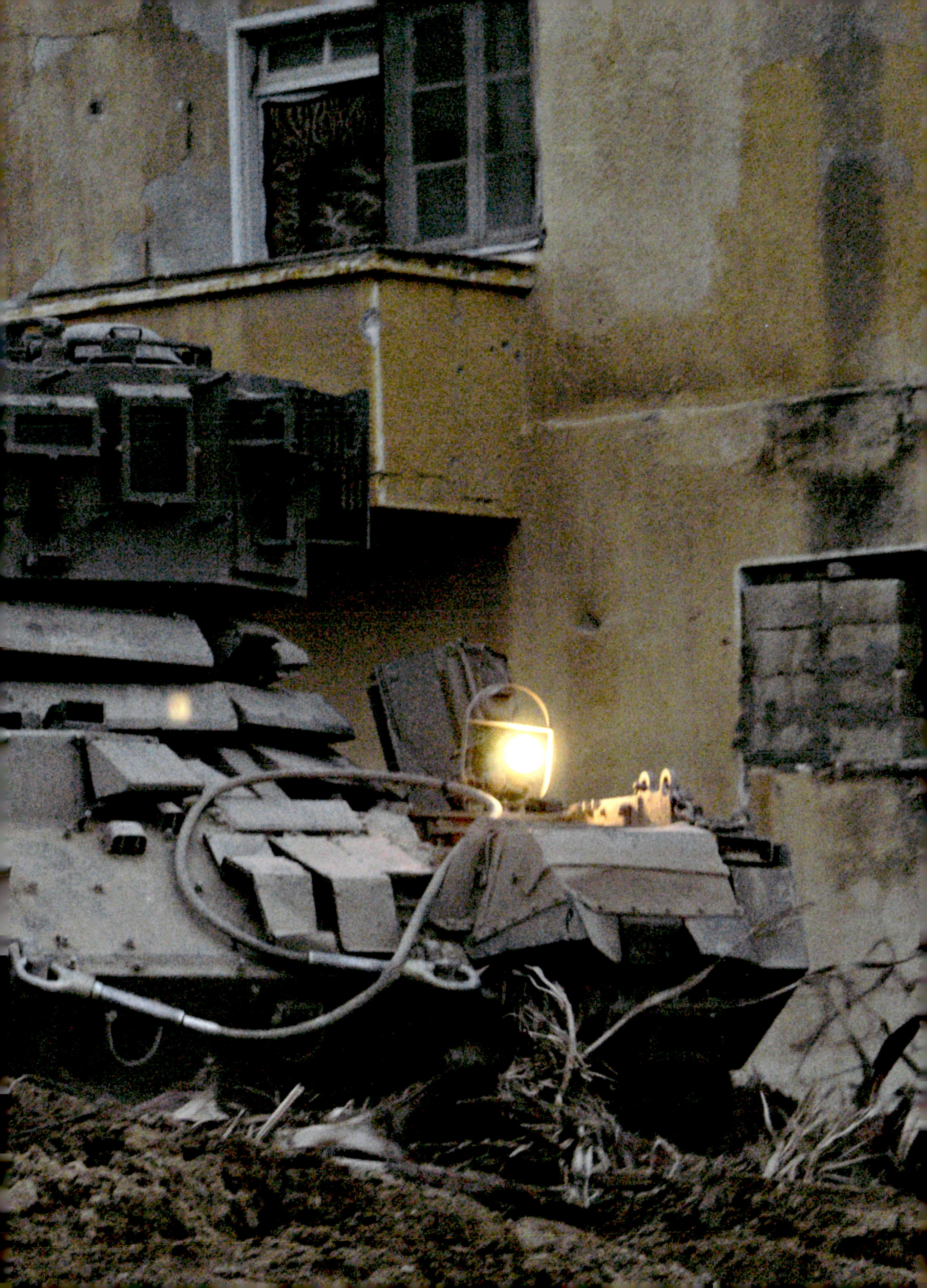

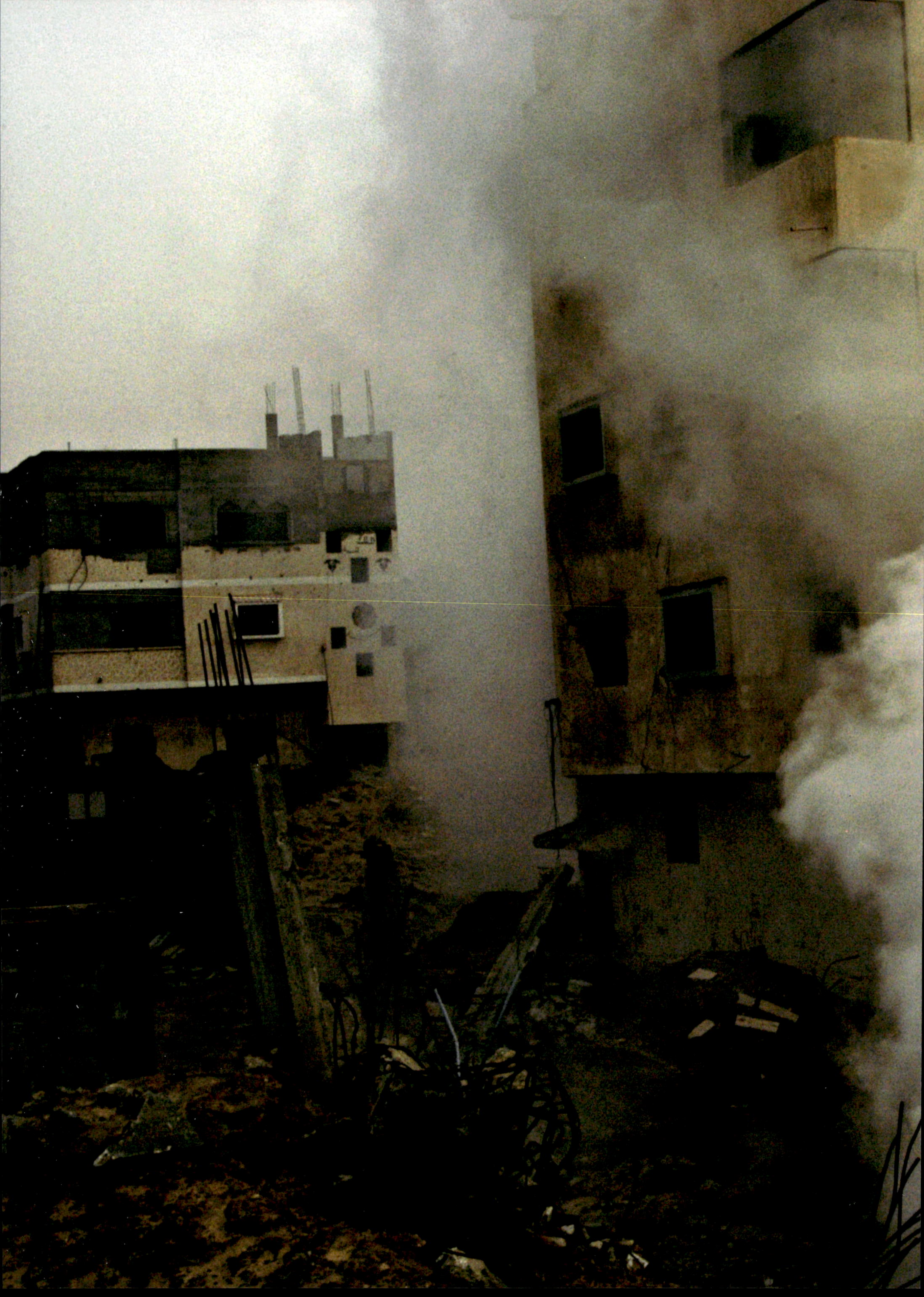

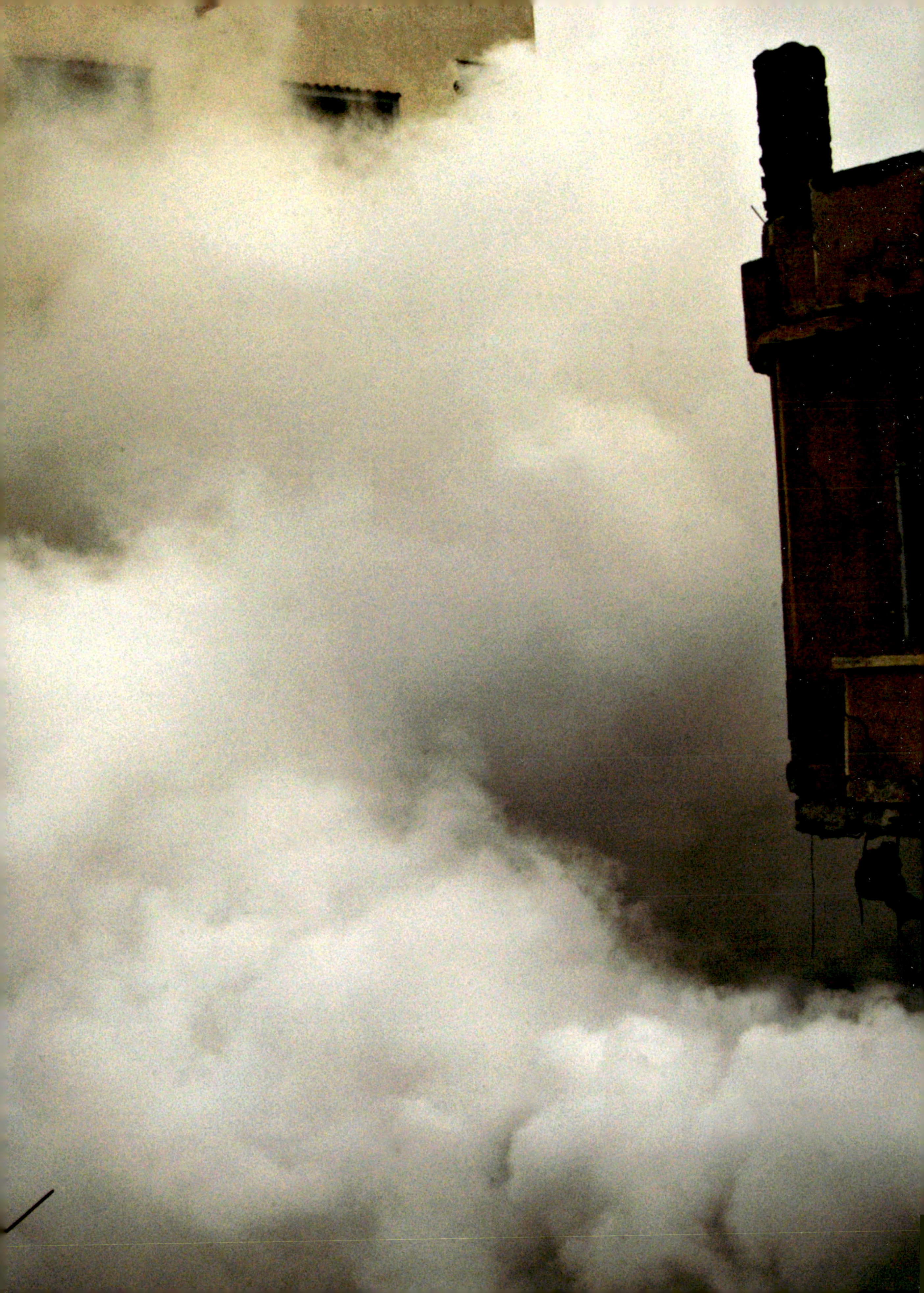

06 APRIL

It's been one of those days…
I woke up at about 8 in my bed in Jerusalem and lay in until 9.30. We left at 10.

In those hours since then, so much has changed. It seems like a world away - like someone else's life and memories. Since then I have been shot at, gassed, chased by soldiers, had sound grenades thrown within metres of me, been hit by falling debris and been in the way of a 10-tonne D-9 that didn't stop. As we approached, I kept expecting a part of my body to be hit by an 'invisible' force and shot of pain. It took a huge amount of will to continue. I wondered what it would be like to be shot, and strangely I wasn't too scared.

We got a call saying that the military was in the process of bulldozing some houses and got there within 20 minutes.

We were dropped around the corner.
I know where it was because I immediately saw people running around it with their heads down.

Then, as I approached the corner, I heard it…a single 'crack' of gunfire, followed by a burst from a machine-gun.

Welcome to Rafah.

On turning the corner, I saw a dead-end about 300m away and people hiding in doorways and peering out of alleys, but after a few seconds I realised it wasn't a dead-end because the end house moved. I'd heard that D-9 bulldozers were big, but this was fucking huge. It towered up like a lookout tower or airport control tower, with a thick sheet of metal in front of it that would reach up above my hand with a couple of feet to spare.

Over the last few days I had been 'worried' that I would be staying in people's houses every night as a symbolic message and doing nothing during the day, and would spend weeks here with nothing achieved. But within 5 minutes I had seen more than I could have imagined.

While approaching the area, over 300m, they continually fired 1-2 second bursts from what I could see was a Bradley fighting vehicle perched just above and behind the D-9.

It was strange. As we approached, and the guns were firing, it sent shivers down my spine, but nothing more than that. We walked down the middle of the street, wearing bright orange, and one of us shouted through a loudspeaker: "We are international volunteers. Don't shoot!" That was answered by another volley of fire, though I can't be sure where from.

I won't go through everything that happened, but they adopted intimidatory tactics such as shooting up the building beside us to shower us with bits of brick and plaster, or driving the tank or D-9 at us at speed and then stopping within a few feet.

At one point, the D-9 carried on coming as Nicolai tripped and stumbled in front of it. He was forced onto the top of a 10-foot mound, just as Rachel had been, and when the blade dropped in a 'cutting' action, he only just escaped getting his leg caught and being killed by a split second. At another, they brought in an APC, armoured personel carrier, and the soldiers ran at us to arrest us under the cover of the Bradley to shield from possible Hamas gunmen. They didn't show up this time, but it's obvious that the soldiers didn't want to be in the open.

Near the end, they began shelling a totally separate house at the back, just to continue the intimidation, creating a huge hole in the side of it. Their aim was perfect. It was obvious that they were all well-trained.

After it all finished, we were mobbed, and adrenaline was so high among the Palestinians that a fight even broke out between two of them. We got back to the apartment, and within moments I heard gunfire from a way off. It has continued since then, sporadically, but I barely even notice now, however close it is.

So now, I write this as I sit, visibly, outdoors, the hum of a generator in the background, in the 20m x 20m barbed wire compound of one of two remaining wells in Rafah. To one side, there is a street, empty. To the other is darkness. I only know that there is a curfew enforced at 6 pm throughout, and it is now 11.10. Our job is to keep water-pumping machinery on line during the curfew, because Palestinian technicians would be shot at if they came out to do it. We stand a better chance. Still, it is strange to know that each night people are shot and killed for breaking military curfew. And in the darkness, on the north-west side, there is an Israeli settlement a few hundred metres away with military snipers in between. Any one of us four could be being watched through a sniper's sights at this moment. The certainty is that they are watching, and it is on the decision of any one Israeli soldier or settler that my life depends. I know that I'd probably never know what hit me, but it's part of the job to be as visible as possible.

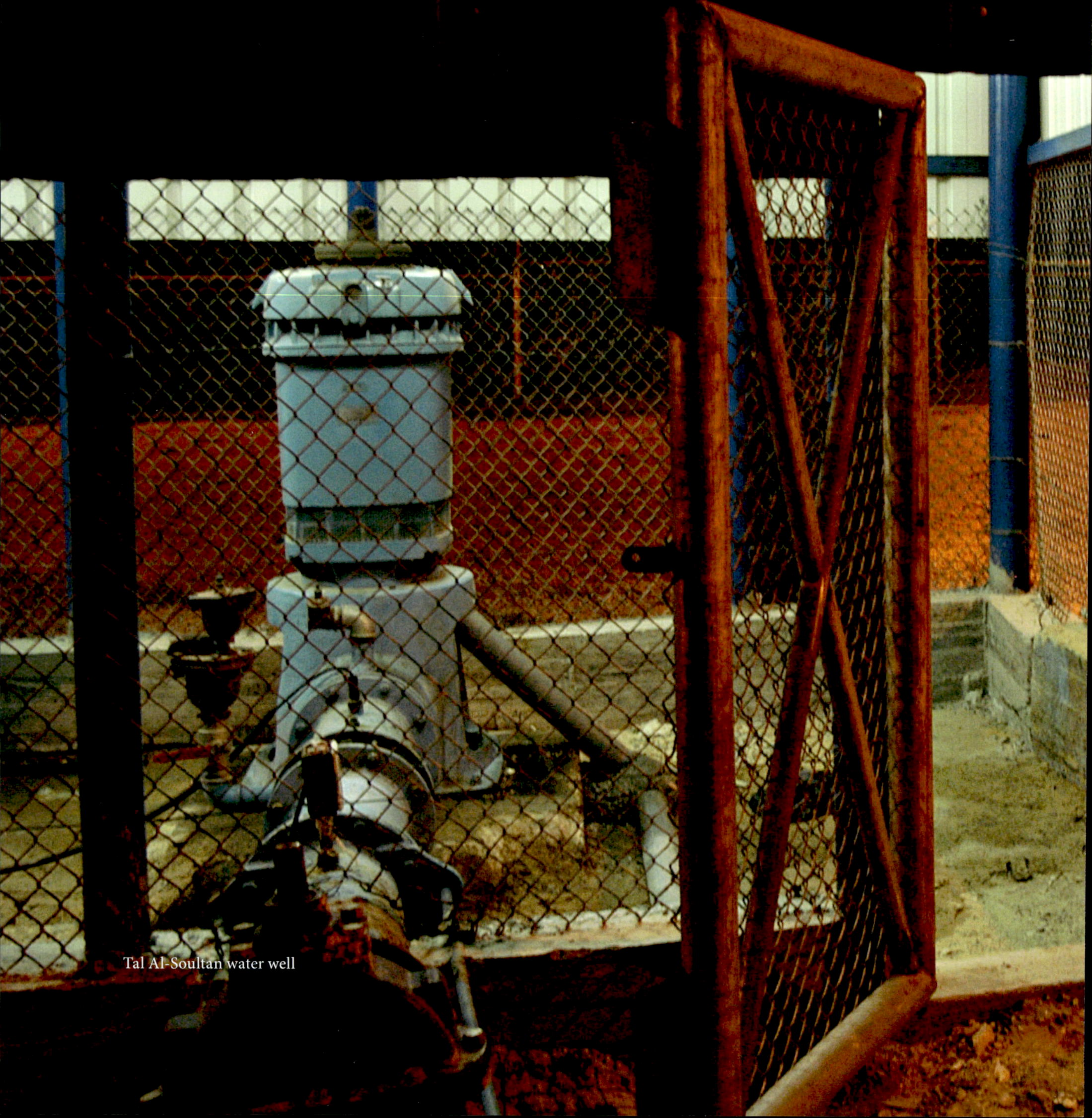

Tal Al-Soultan water well

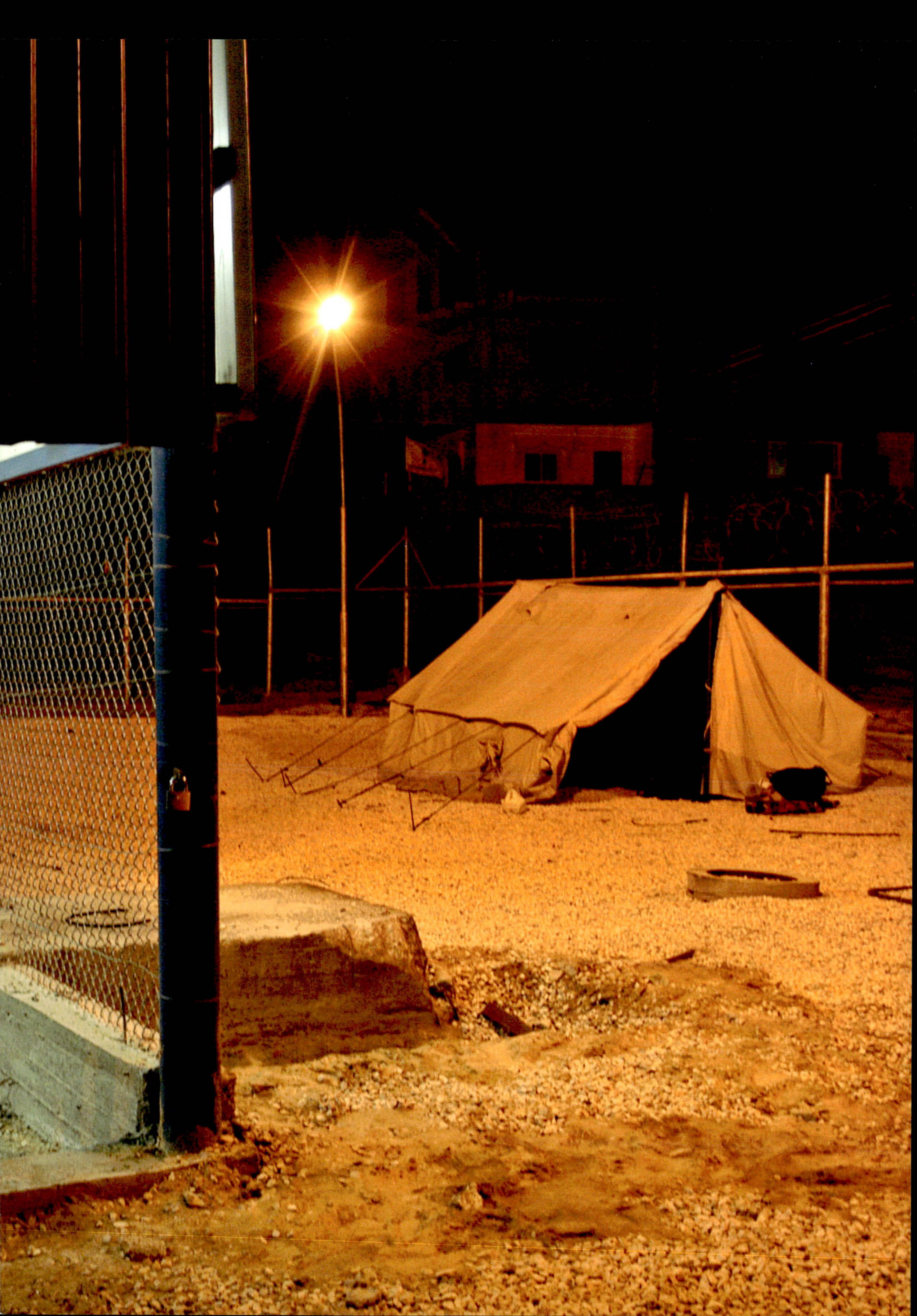

07 APRIL

From: Thomas Hurndall <aqimaging@hotmail.com>
Subject: Rather different from Baghdad! A welcome to Rafah.
Date: 7 April 2003 11:31
To: ah@hurndalls.com, 8 others..
▶ 🖉 1 Attachments, 143 KB (Save ▾) (Quick Look)

Just another update. I know it's only been 48 hrs since the last one, but a lot has happened since then. I'm now in Rafah, a few hundred metres from the Egyptian border, and it's around 23 hrs since I arrived. Within a couple of hours from our ride getting in, I had been shot at, shelled, tear-gassed, hit by falling brick/plaster, 'sound-bombed', almost run-over by the moving house called a D10 bulldozer, chased by soldiers and a lot else besides... on the downside: I didn't get a good night's sleep because I kept getting woken by the machine-gun fire that echos around the area at night. (and it didn't help that I was in a tent with 3 ISM volunteers 'protecting' one of the rare water wells in the open road in an area where the military 'lethally' enforce a curfew from sniper positions in plain sight). All in all, it has made for a rather fun excursion... I have already seen as much as I thought I possibly could, and to think that I was worried I would spend a few weeks here without getting the opportunity to do what I came over here to do.

The volunteers I'm spending my time with are really safe (London slang as opposed to 'without danger'..they're psychotic like that) and, although really young, and very idealistic, I think they know the situation, and what they can get away with. They are at present trying to build up ties with the Palestinians in Rafah (known as ruffians!), but they aren't too trusting for the obvious reasons. ISM's effectiveness relies largely on their ties with the community, for example, yesterday they were called to the scene by someone in the area where several civilian houses were being flattened. Because of that need, they were at an anti-war march this morning, showing solidarity, as it were. I've got a lot of respect for them, especially as most of them watched Rachel Corrie die a few weeks ago doing exactly the same things in exactly the same way. Just wait until you see the photos and you may understand a little better.

As for the Israeli soldiers, they are all jokers until you realise they they don't care much if they kill you. Maybe I'd get on with them a bit better if I'd met them somewhere else, and they weren't so afraid of taking fire from the Hamas and Fatah gunmen around.

Still, got to go and do some stuff before I go back to my lovely warm tent for the night. (when I left the Rweished refugee camp I swore I'd never step foot in another tent again, oh well!)

Hope you're all well,
Love Tom

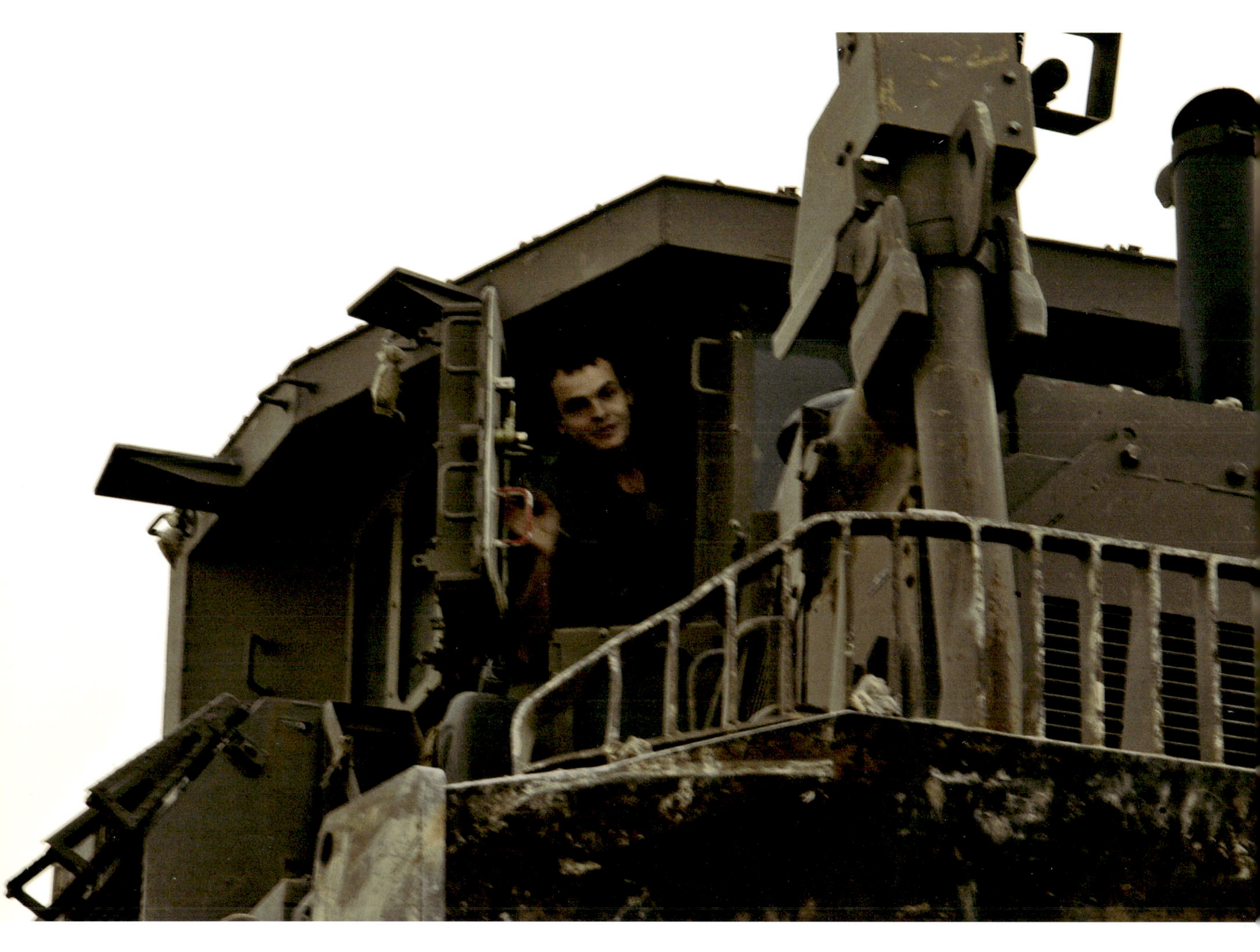

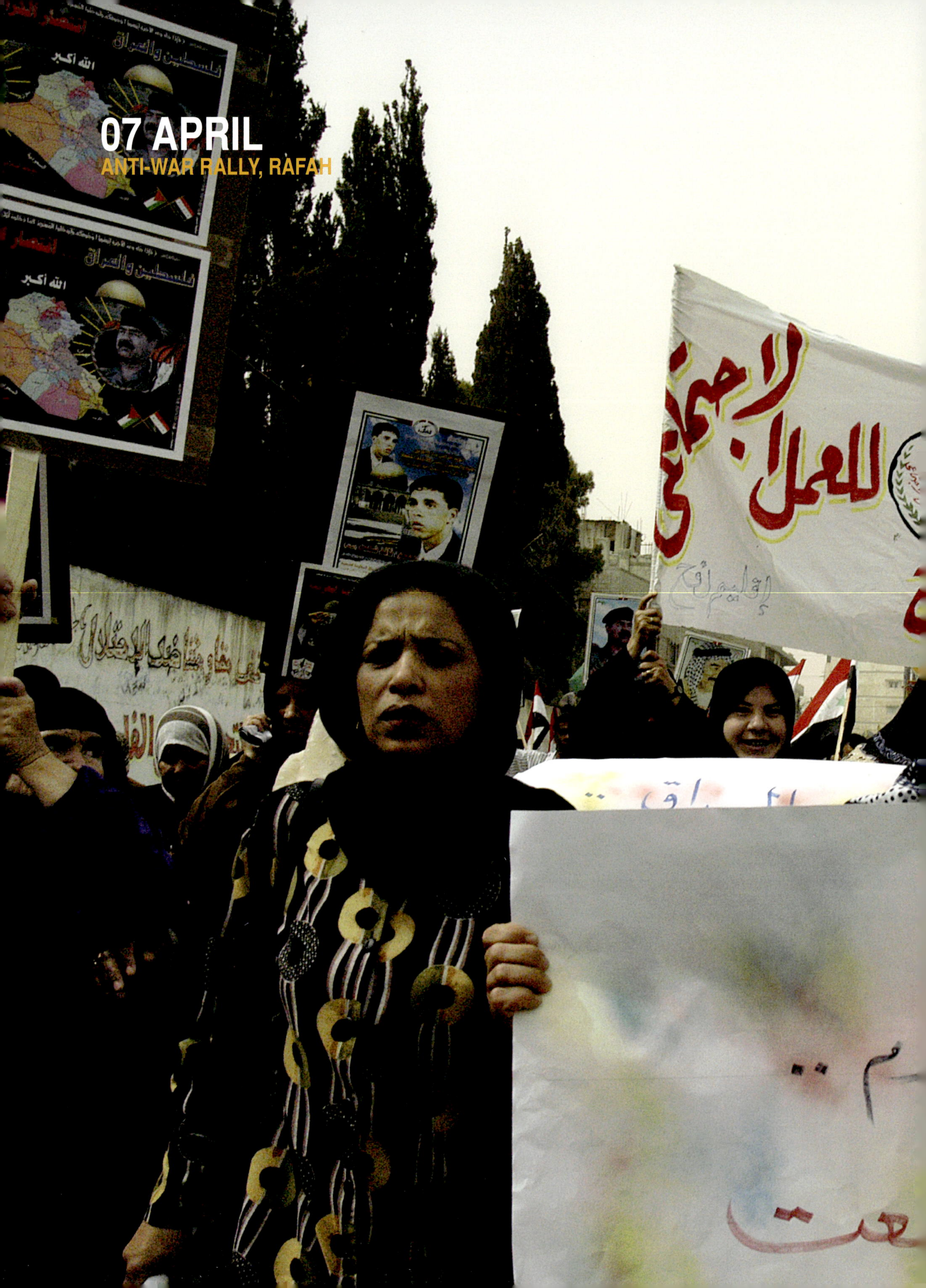

07 APRIL
ANTI-WAR RALLY, RAFAH

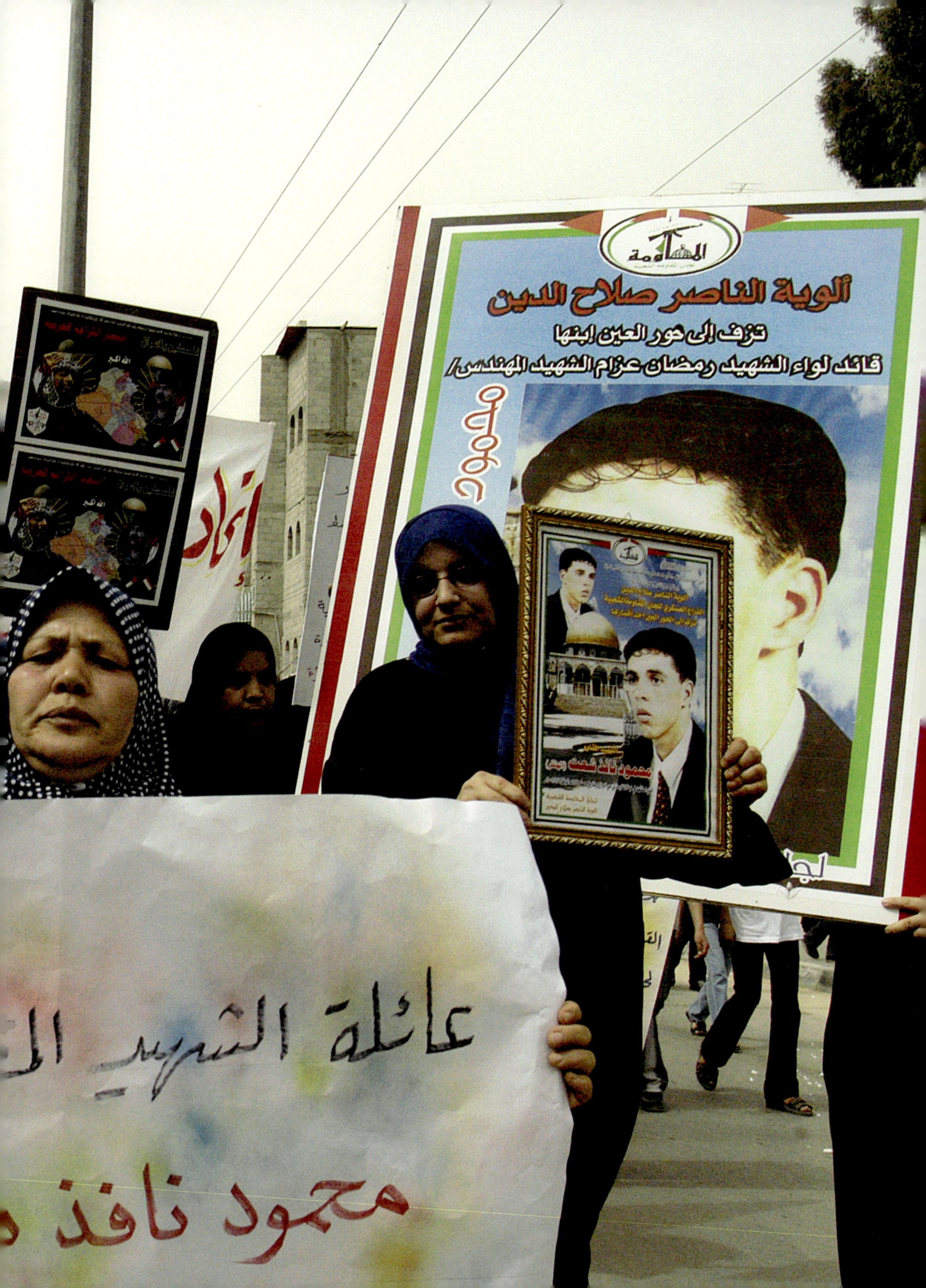
المقاومة
ألوية الناصر صلاح الدين
تزف إلى حور العين إبنها
قائد لواء الشهيد رمضان عزام الشهيد المهندس/
٥٥٥٥
عائلة الشهيد
محمود نافذ
اتحاد
الله أكبر

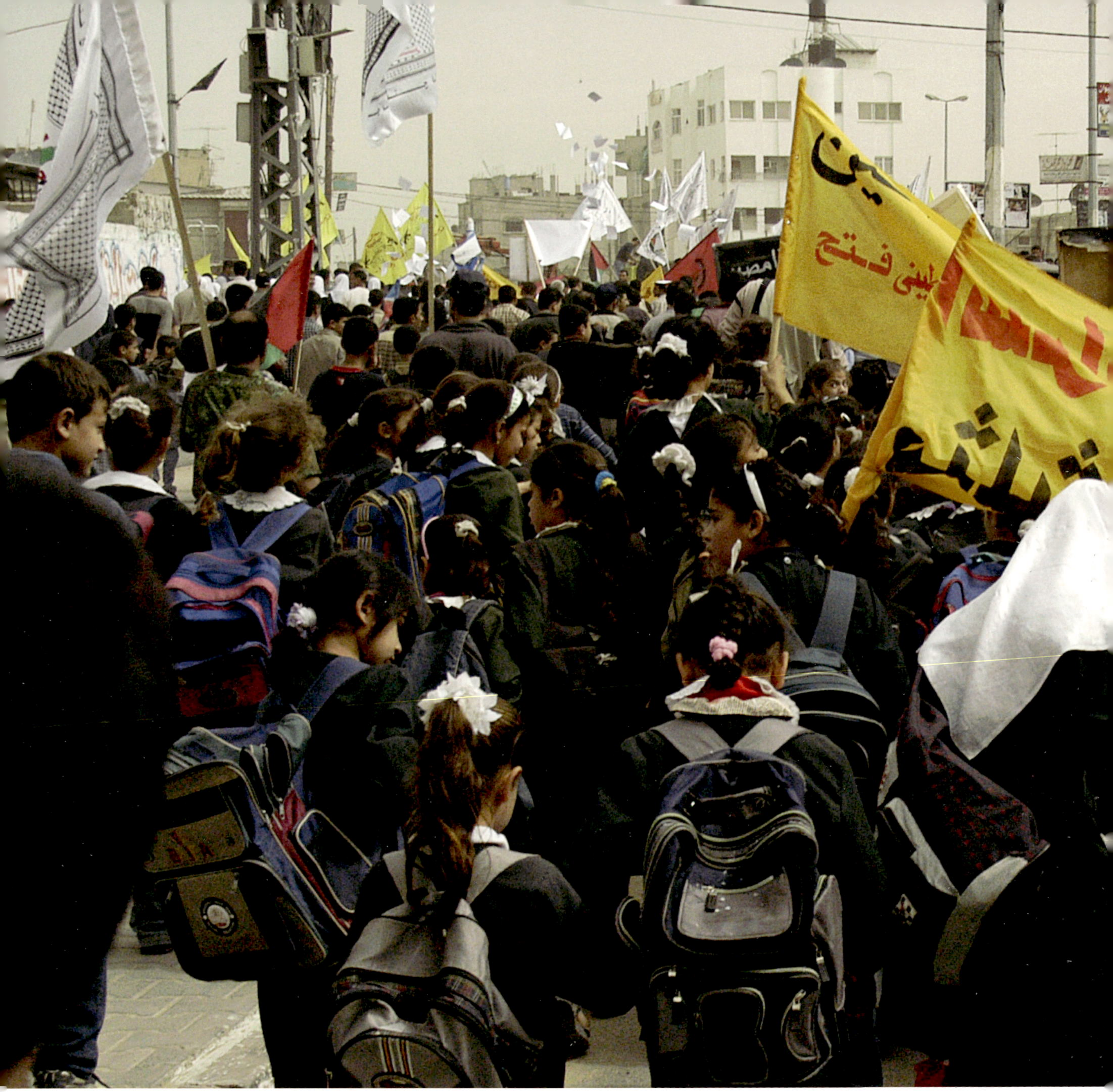

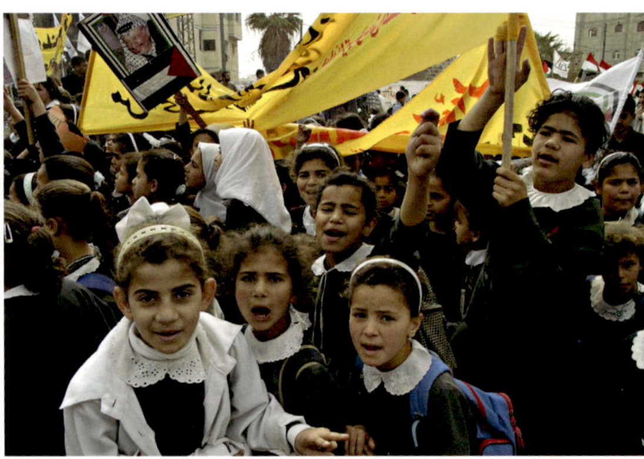

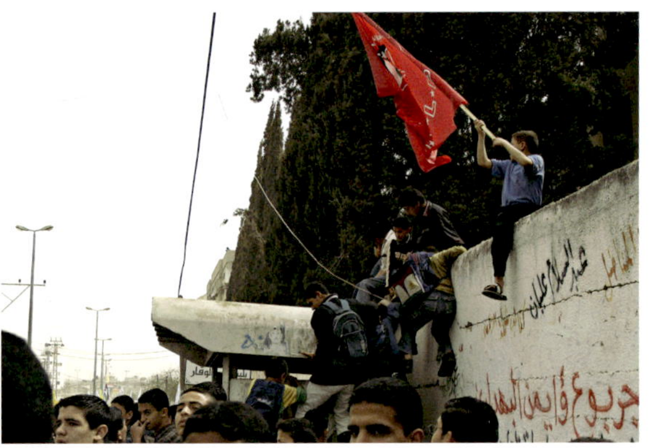

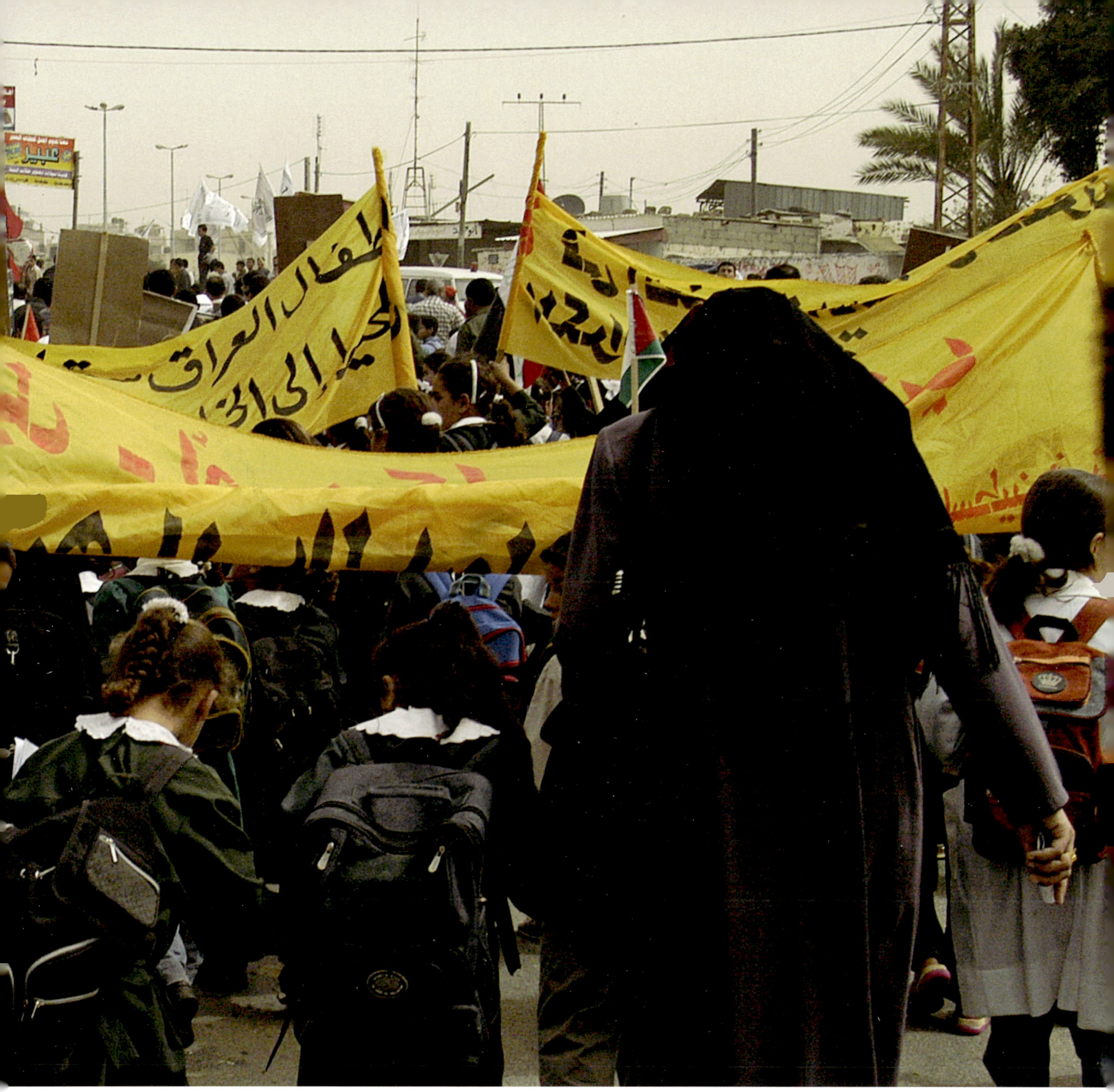

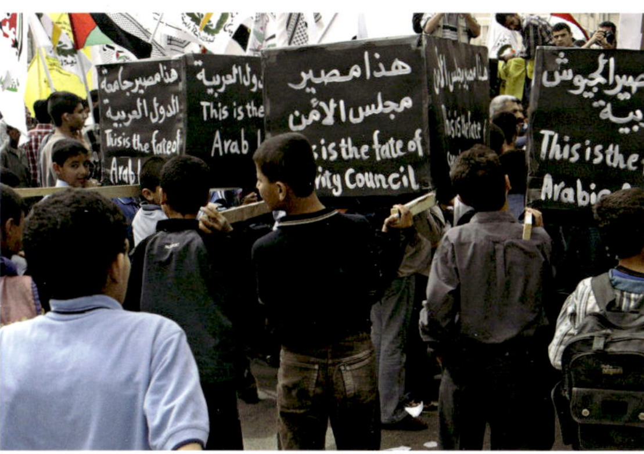

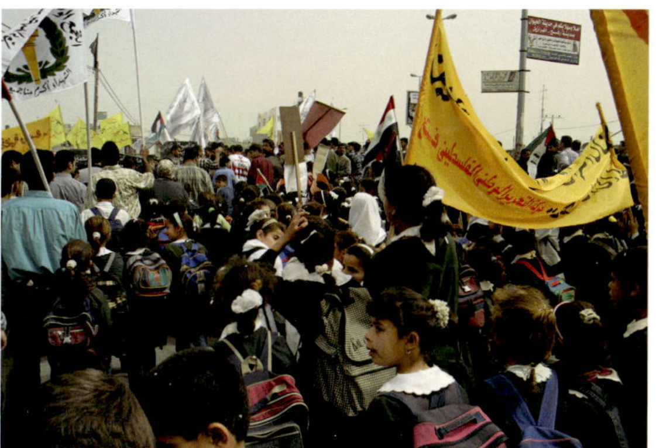

From: ism rafah <ismrafah@yahoo.co.uk>
Subject: **tom's images**
Date: 7 April 2003 16:25:42 GMT+01:00
To: ah@hurndalls.com, 8 others...
▶ 🔗 3 Attachments, 552 KB (Save ▾) (Quick Look)

ak47.jpg- a boy at the anti-war march on the 7th April

dirt.jpg- an israeli tower watches over a building that was just demolished in rafah, 6th April

flags.jpg- palestinians burn american and israeli flags at the march
images from tom hurndall

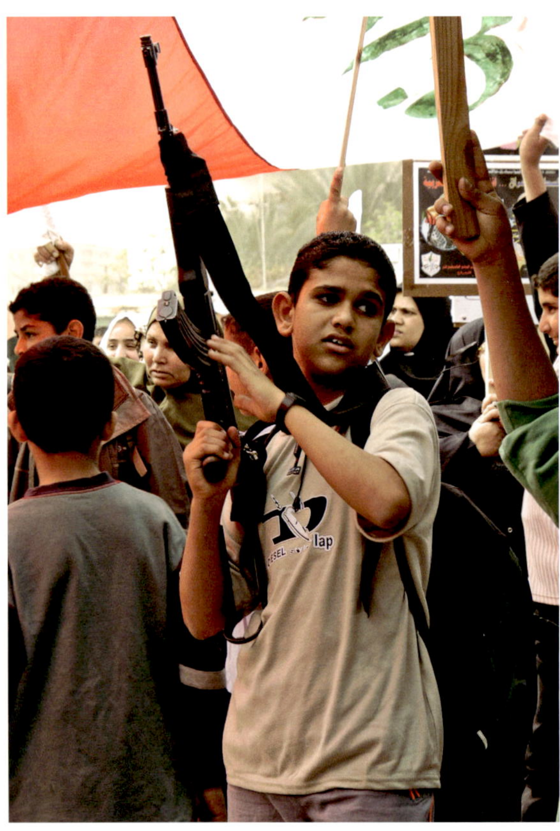

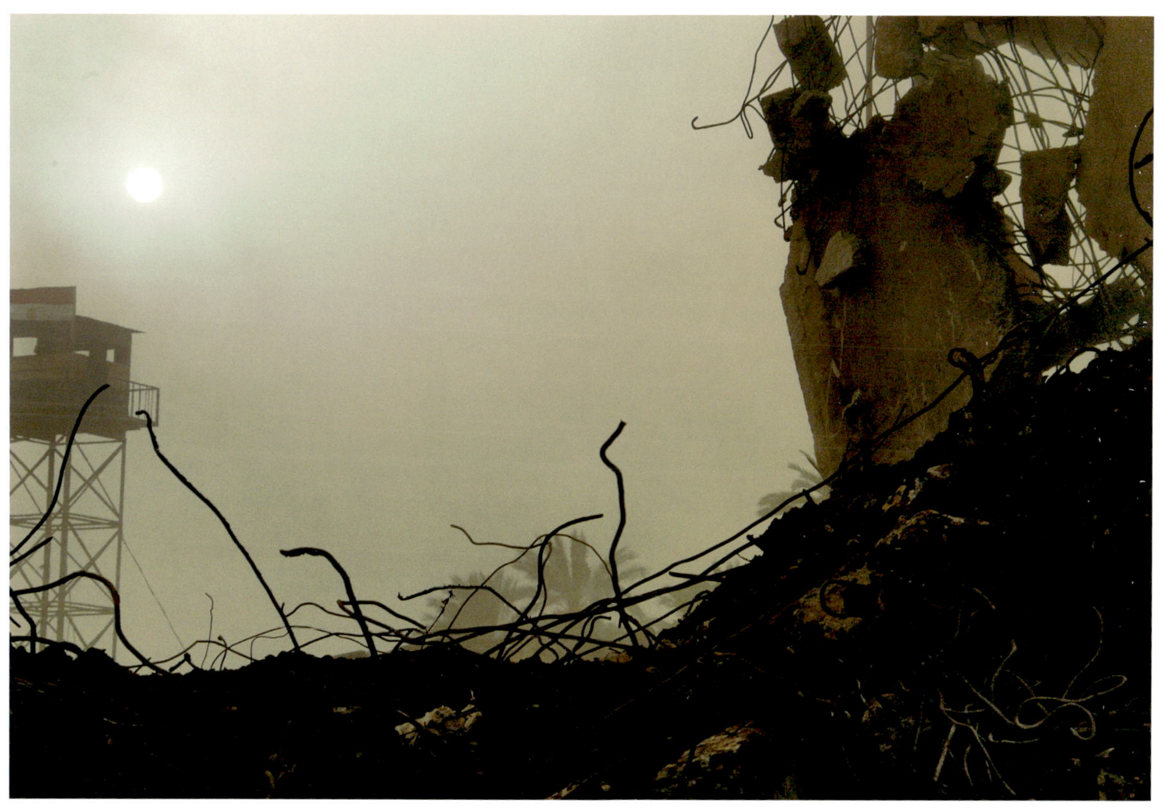

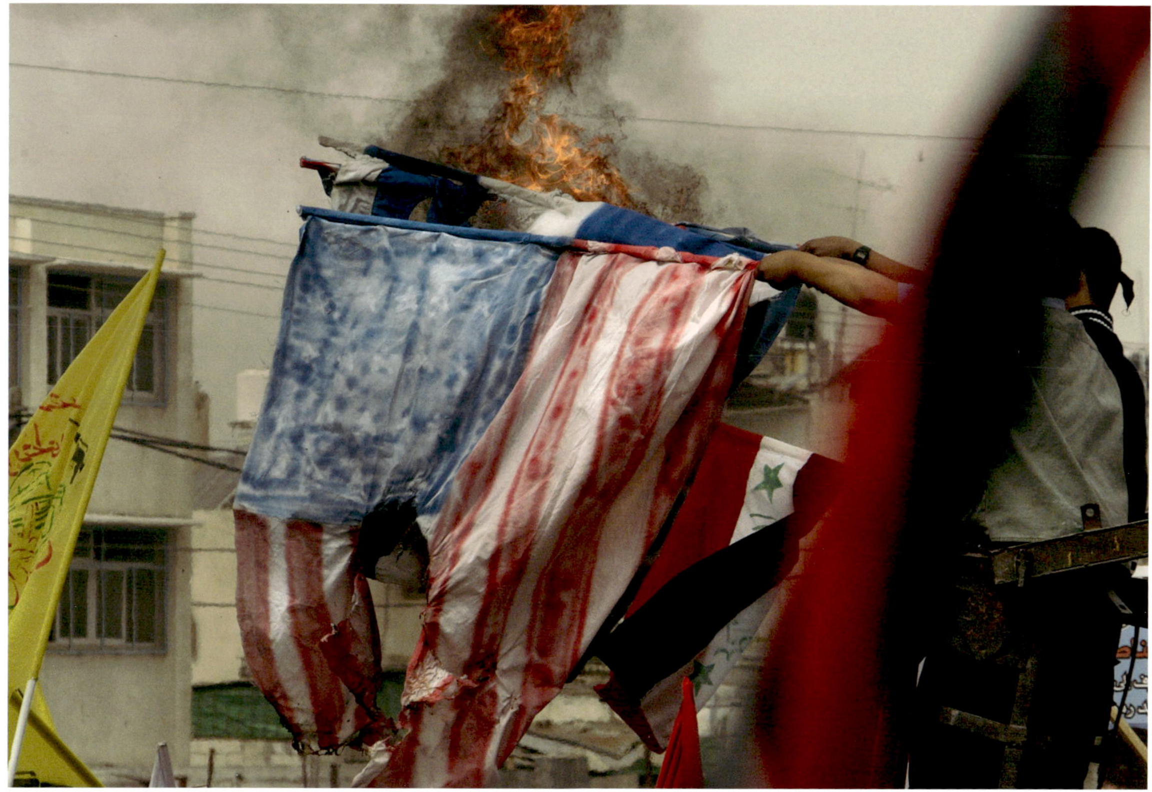

My second night…and things are no 'easier.' Indoors now, but no further from danger. To begin with, there is an Israeli tank less than 20 metres from my bed that was posted there two weeks ago, and has only left to be replaced each morning.

The room next to mine has several large calibre bullet-holes in each wall, many of them having travelled through the brick. This is the house Rachel was protecting, and outside which she died. I know now what motivated her to take such a risk. The house is owned by Dr. Samir and his family.

I have spent only a couple of hours here now, but I have never met a family that loves each other so much. There are three children: Harec, Rhue and Iman. They love their father, and he obviously loves them so much. They are the kind of children who never scream and always know what to do before they are even told. I watched him play with them. He is a good man, I could tell so easily.

So, why, aside from that, are we here? Well it is the same reason that Rachel was. It is the only house left standing where there used to be over 20. It seems to be in order to create a 'security' zone of 100m in front of the border with Egypt. The only reason I'm inside this house now, and not on top of a pile of rubble, is thanks to Rachel Corrie.

I asked Dr. Samir if his children slept ok with the tank so close. He said, "For the first few nights, they cried. Now it is ok. They are more used to it."

Then we started talking about how long he had lived here (1999) and got on to Alison's home in the Highlands of Scotland. He said, "It is in our dreams. That is our dream home. I wish I could take my children away for just one week. Just one week, so I could hear them laughing like children everywhere are laughing all over the rest of the world. But I can't. My children are brave in front of the Israelis. They don't show tears. I play with them because I love them and I laugh. But in my heart I am crying."

You want to know why as much as [shell drops] 50% of kills by the Israelis are Palestinian militants? It is because the tanks and APCs roll into an area, and shoot bullets and explosives in every direction, and the civilians run [shell drops]. The only people who are left are the ones who fight. It is not out of care and diligence that Israel's rate is only 50% civilians, but because the Palestinians know to run. If they stayed in their homes and hid under their beds as the English would do, there would be 95% civilians. That is not how to fight a war, expecting them to run. It seems there is no 'intention'. Just 'sifting' by taking out anyone who stays, assuming they're militant.

It seems to me that all over Palestine the strategy is the same. So much is done that could fit in no battle-plan of defence.
They [Israeli machine gun – 3 shells drop] shoot at water tanks on top of houses for fun. They demolish areas for security zones, walls, settlements or anything to push the Palestinians into a more compact area.
They destroy major roads, set up check-points through which Palestinians can't go, place settlements strategically to segregate villagers. They destroy wells, give all the water supply to the settlements and place the off-switch in settlers' hands to use as a weapon. Everything is deliberately designed to lower the standards of life for Palestinians so that they just get up and leave. I am certain that that is their motivation. Too much has no other explanation.

Gaza is the most densely populated place on earth. 1.2 million people in an area 10 km by 40 km. With 40% of the 'Palestinian Land' owned by settlers.

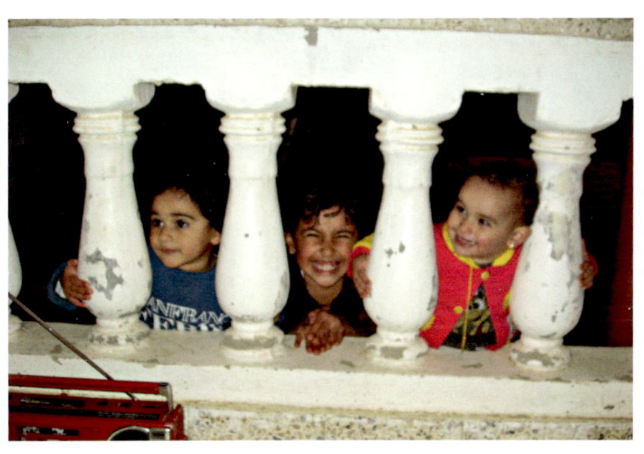

The average settler in the Gaza Strip owns 115 times as much land as the average Palestinian.

The plan is to make life so bad that they all just get up and leave and they are using every trick in the book that is below the belt. They are creating their own holocaust, but using bureaucracy to cover it. The PA has no power and is kept alive by Israel only in name so that the holocaust doesn't seem to be on their land, so they can say,

"It's not our problem."

What is going on is far beyond what is necessary or even relative to national security, and it is all underhand.

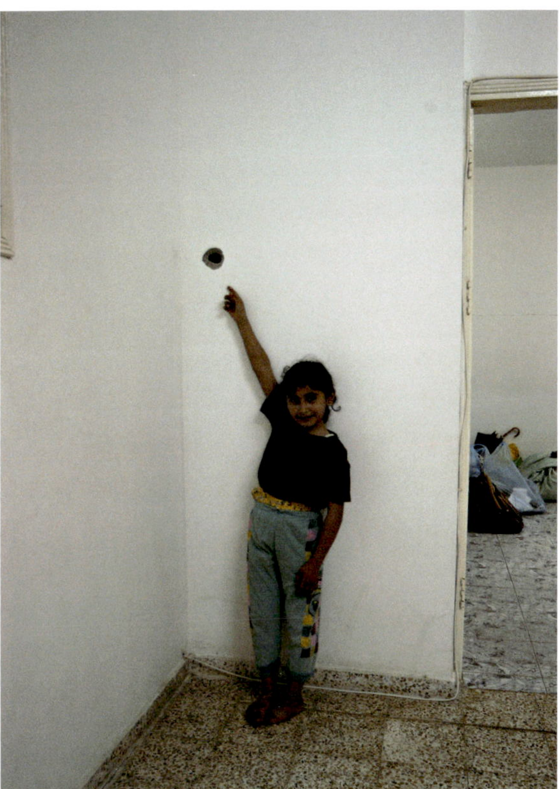

the only house left standing

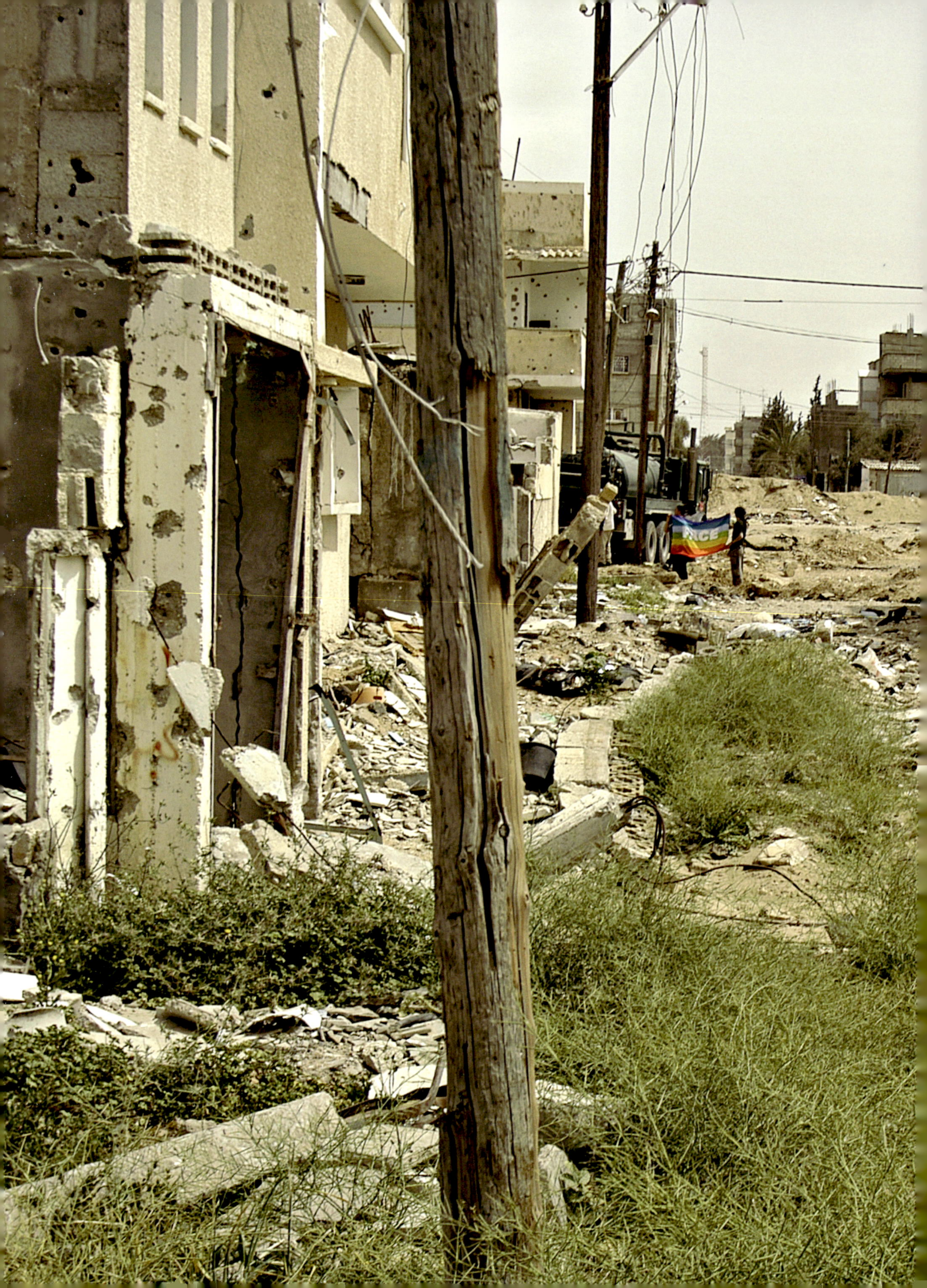
PACE

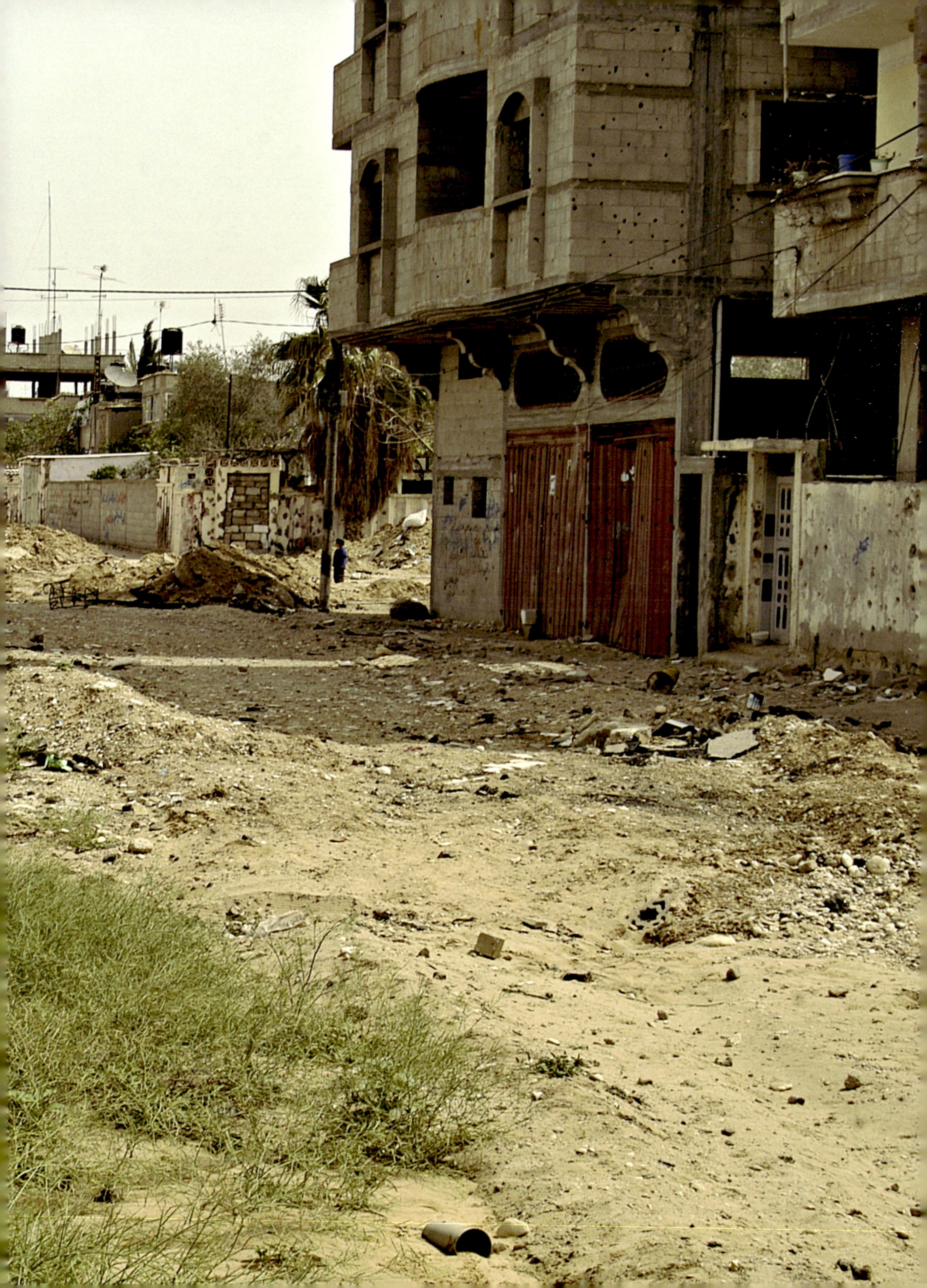

Every now and then comes a deep rumble from the other room as the tank chokes its engine for a minute or two. Then it returns to the monotonous thumping, supposedly at rest.

In the room on my other side, I can hear the noises children make in their sleep, the restless fidgeting, often prompted by the sporadic gunfire, occasionally in the distance, more often within a few hundred metres.

Dr. Samir, whose house we are in, told me earlier that his three children had become accustomed to life in a home listed for demolition by the Israeli Defence Forces. Weeks ago, when they were first threatened, they didn't stop crying. Now you would never have known. As Dr Samir put it, "They try to be brave in front of the tanks."

Their house is situated on the outskirts of Rafah; a city made up of long-term refugee camps that long ago spilled over their limits, at the southern end of the Gaza Strip.

Now it is the most densely populated area in the world, with little distinct area where one city starts and another begins. 1.2 million people live in Gaza, where 40% of the land has been confiscated for Israeli settlements and security areas around them (roughly 7000 people).

Water is scarce and, in the summer, can really be a problem. Especially because most of the water supply has been put under the control of the settlers, who have been known to withhold it as a weapon.

Simply, life in Gaza is tough, and you would know it, walking through the streets. It differs from the rest of Palestine (the West Bank) in one aesthetic way – you will never see a single Israeli soldier in the street. When they come, they come in tanks and APCs. Hamas and Fatah are too strong and too well-armed and the people are backed into a corner. Rafah in particular has one of the strongest 'resistance' movements around.

That is not, however, the reason I am here. I am here because, of a neighbourhood that used to consist of two dozen buildings, this is the only one left standing. And only that because a girl who came from thousands of miles away gave her life for it.

Her name was Rachel Corrie; a 23-year-old from Olympus in America. She died when an IDF D-9 bulldozer drove over her, twice, as she protested the demolition.

Perhaps the situation is more complex than is apparent and warrants some explanation.

The 'accident' can be attributed to three major factors. Firstly, there was the suggestion by many 'outsiders' that Rachel was naïve and unaware that the D-9 wouldn't stop. Simply, that is something no one but Rachel could have answered. The sentiment here is that she was totally aware, and gave herself as a full-fledged martyr to 'the cause'.

Secondly, was the inability of the IDF to simply remove her. This is Rafah, remember? The IDF never leave their tanks unless under total cover, which the area doesn't allow for tactically. If she stood her ground they could only leave or drive into her.

That leads to the final reason - frustration amongst the IDF present. This was not something that just happened one afternoon. The Samir family is an exception to the norm in that they refused to leave their house. The IDF rely heavily on people just walking away from their homes out of fear, and there are many ways that can be inflicted. In the last few weeks, their house has been 'raided' four times, with soldiers

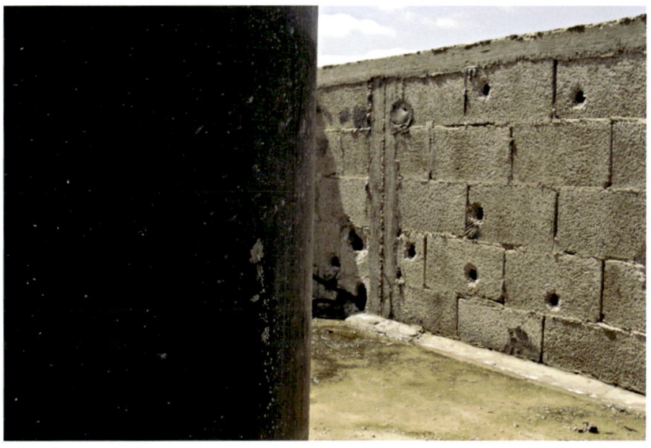

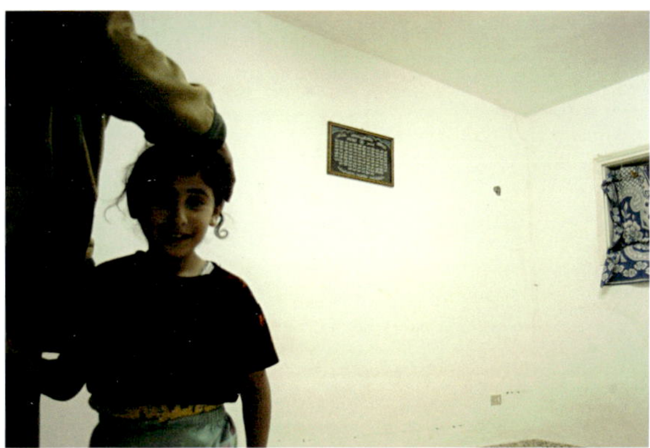

searching the premises without charges or legal authority from anyone. They have peppered the house with bullets, shot at the water-tanks all Palestinian homes have on their roofs and much more. On one of the house searches, they kept the men downstairs, made Reem, the 7-year-old daughter, show them around the house at gunpoint, knocked out a window on the second floor from which to fire a heavy duty machine gun out of, and left the family's prayer mats in the toilet.

Simply, after all this, Dr. Samir is still unflinching, and the IDF is getting impatient. Outside, the scene is almost comic. In every direction lies an uneven surface of rubble, all the way to the border, and only the one house remains. It must be a source of constant embarrassment to the IDF.

I have been on a fucking adrenaline high since I got here. It's affecting my judgement. I don't contemplate the risks as much any more. It doesn't seem as important.

Her name was Rachel Corrie;

07 APRIL

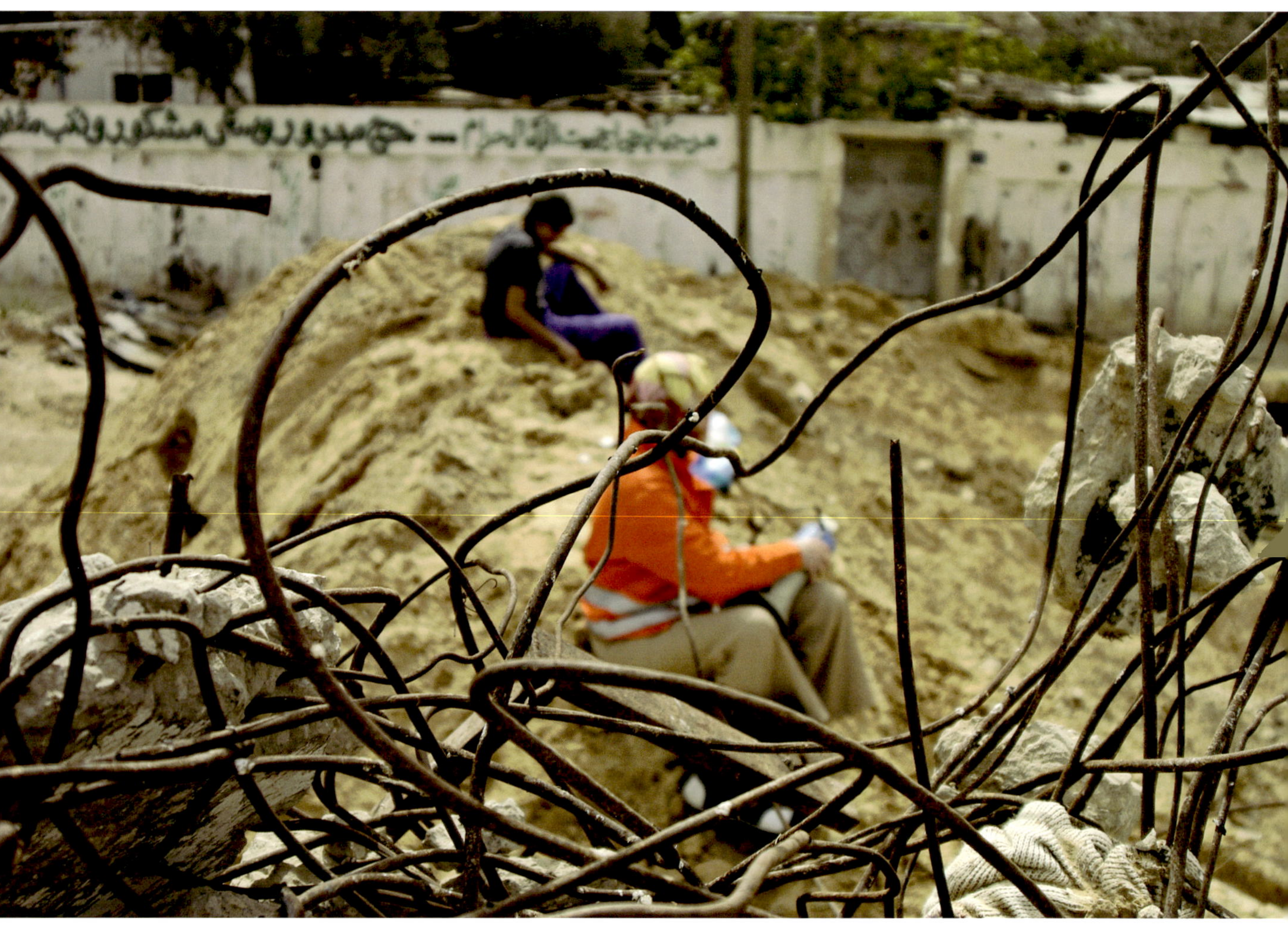

I've been here a couple of days now, and there is some comedy among the atrocity. Instead of asking whether you slept well each morning when they meet, the volunteers simply ask if they had a quiet night. The humour is in the fact that the nights are never quiet and there is always gunfire. It is what is meant by quiet - that no one woke you at gunpoint or tried to knock your house down with you in it. The humour is that it is a serious question asked each morning.

Today, Alison, Francesco, Nicolai and I sat on a 12-foot dirt roadblock looking out over the flat land in front of the border with Egypt. We stayed for a couple of hours to protect workers from being shot at, enabling them to fix the sewerage system dug up by Israelis.

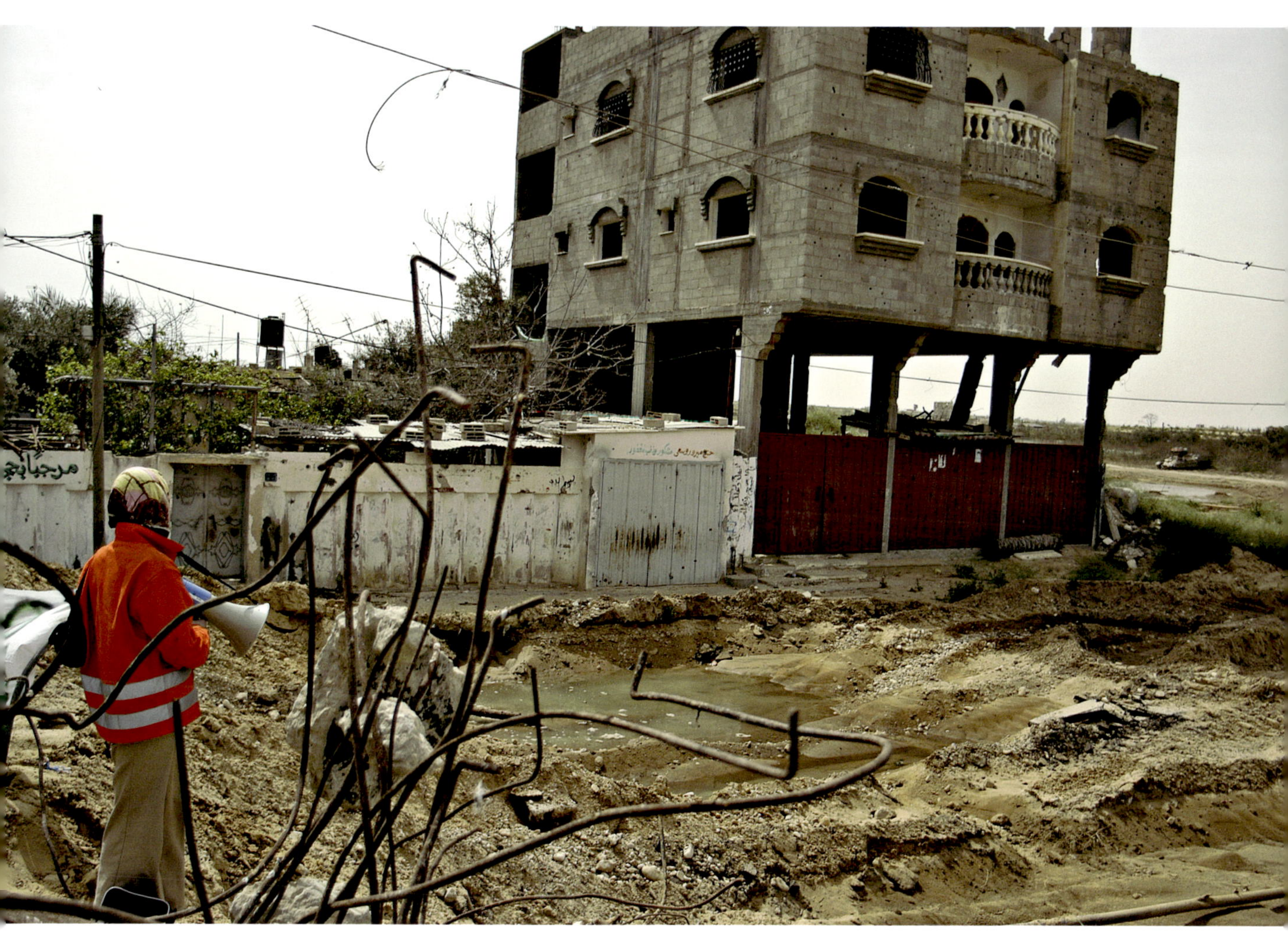

From: Thomas Hurndall <aqimaging@hotmail.com>
Date: 8 April 2003 12:46:37 GMT+01:00
To: af601@soton.ac.uk, 8 others...

▶ 🖉 2 Attachments, 53.1 KB (Save ▾) (Quick Look)

These are images of a boy who was shot in the shoulder this morning while throwing rocks at a tank in the Brazil area south of Rafah central, Gaza strip. I took the first before the shooting started, and the second, when he was hit, only a few moments after. The tank wasn't under fire at the time, but Hamas gunmen arrived soon. The tank's fire was indiscriminate to the extent that I was almost hit in the aftermath despite clearly wearing an internationally-recognised jumper with 'TV' written on it (representing all journalists), and having distanced myself from all the 'resistance' by around 50m (the tank at that time was around 35m away from both of us).
Shells were also fired at the surrounding houses from an IDF tower almost 1.5KM away, when Hamas returned fire.

This is how pointless this whole thing is! I haven't been able to find out how the boy is now because we were pinned down behind a wall while he was taken away by friends. Ambulances couldn't reach the area because the IDF had mowed up the surrounding roads weeks ago with bulldozers and put in 'makeshift' road-blocks with the rubble.

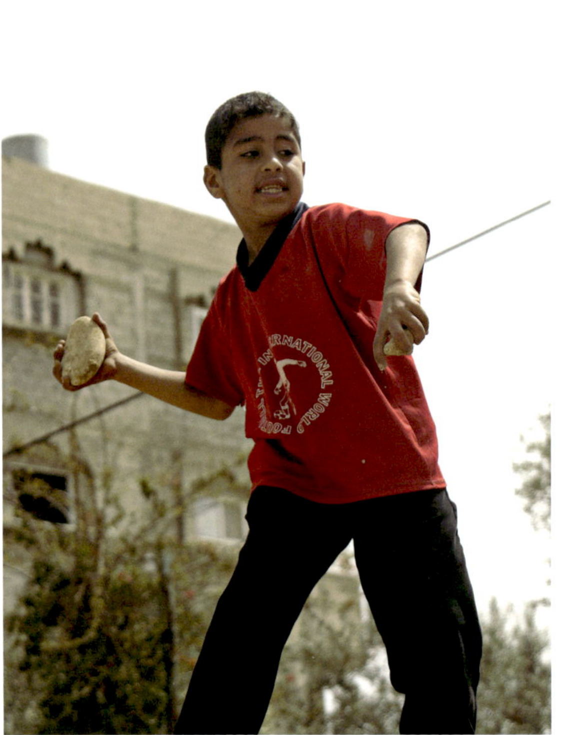
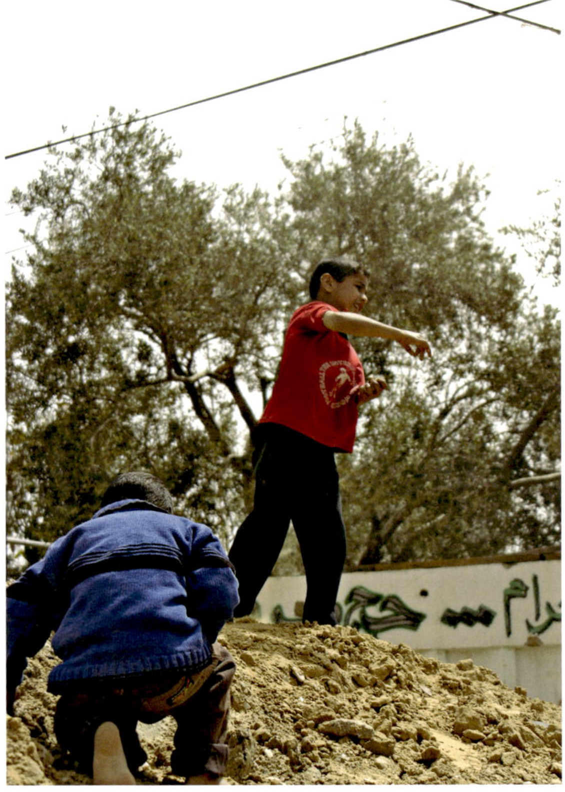

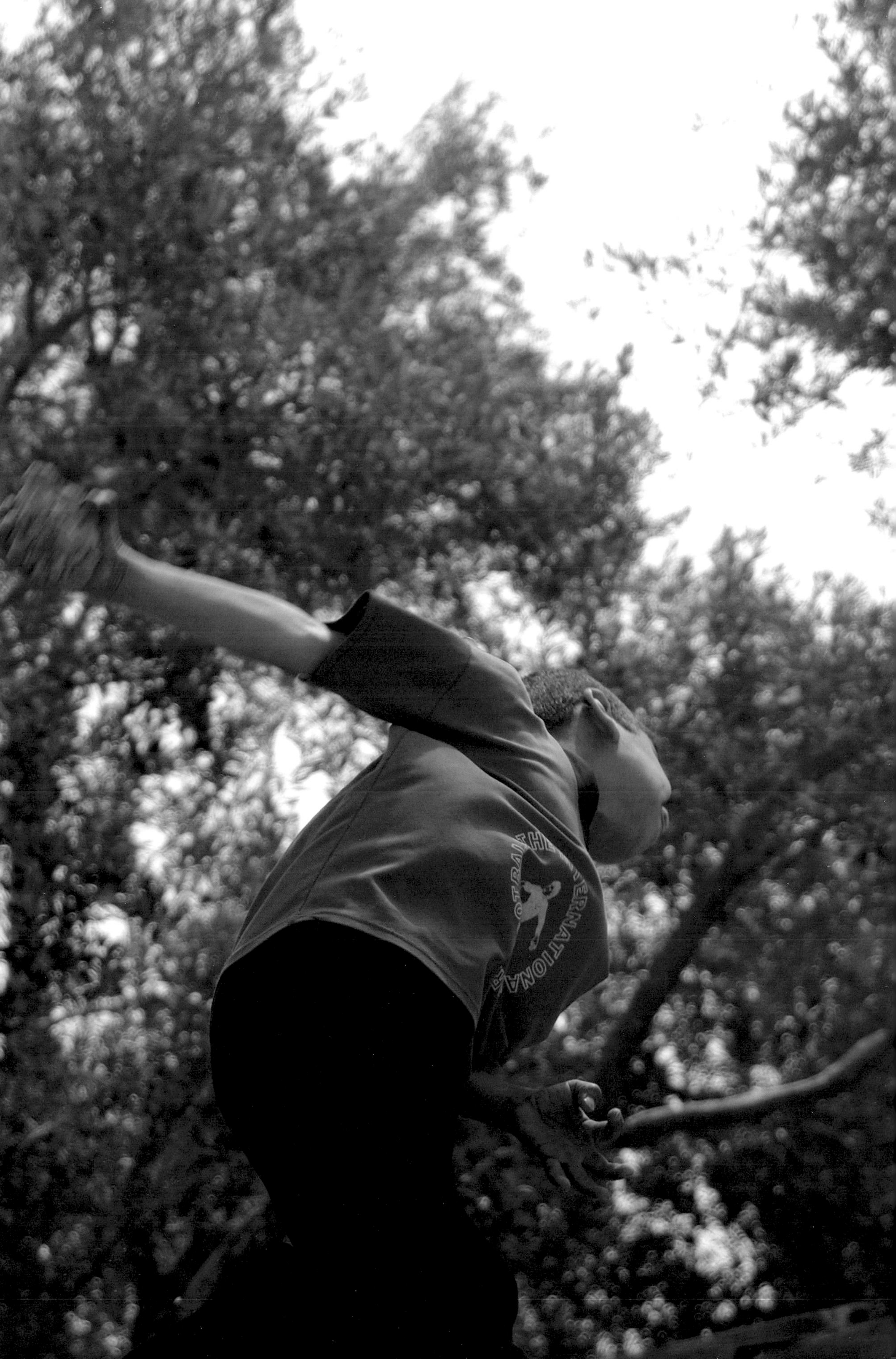

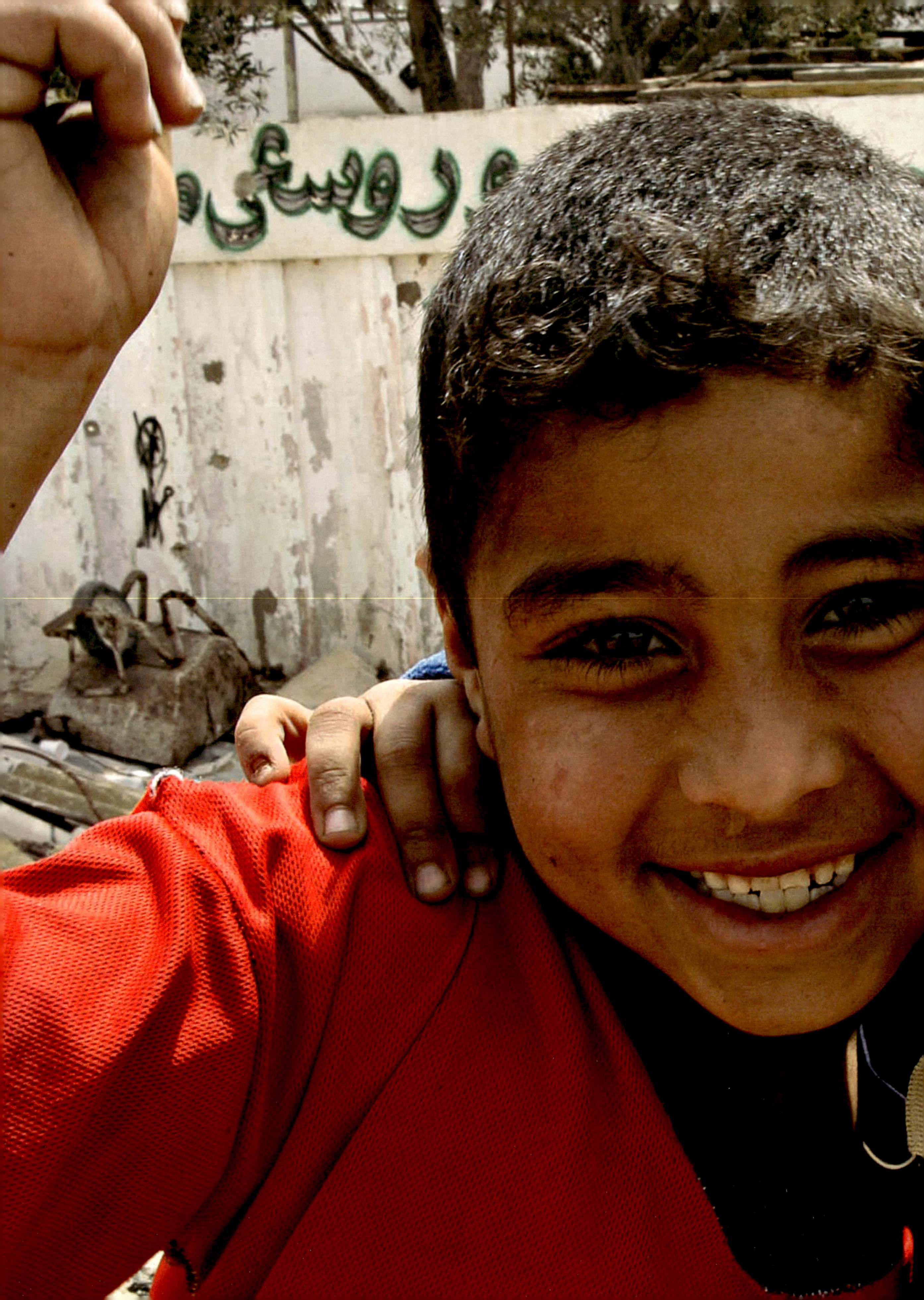
وسعى و

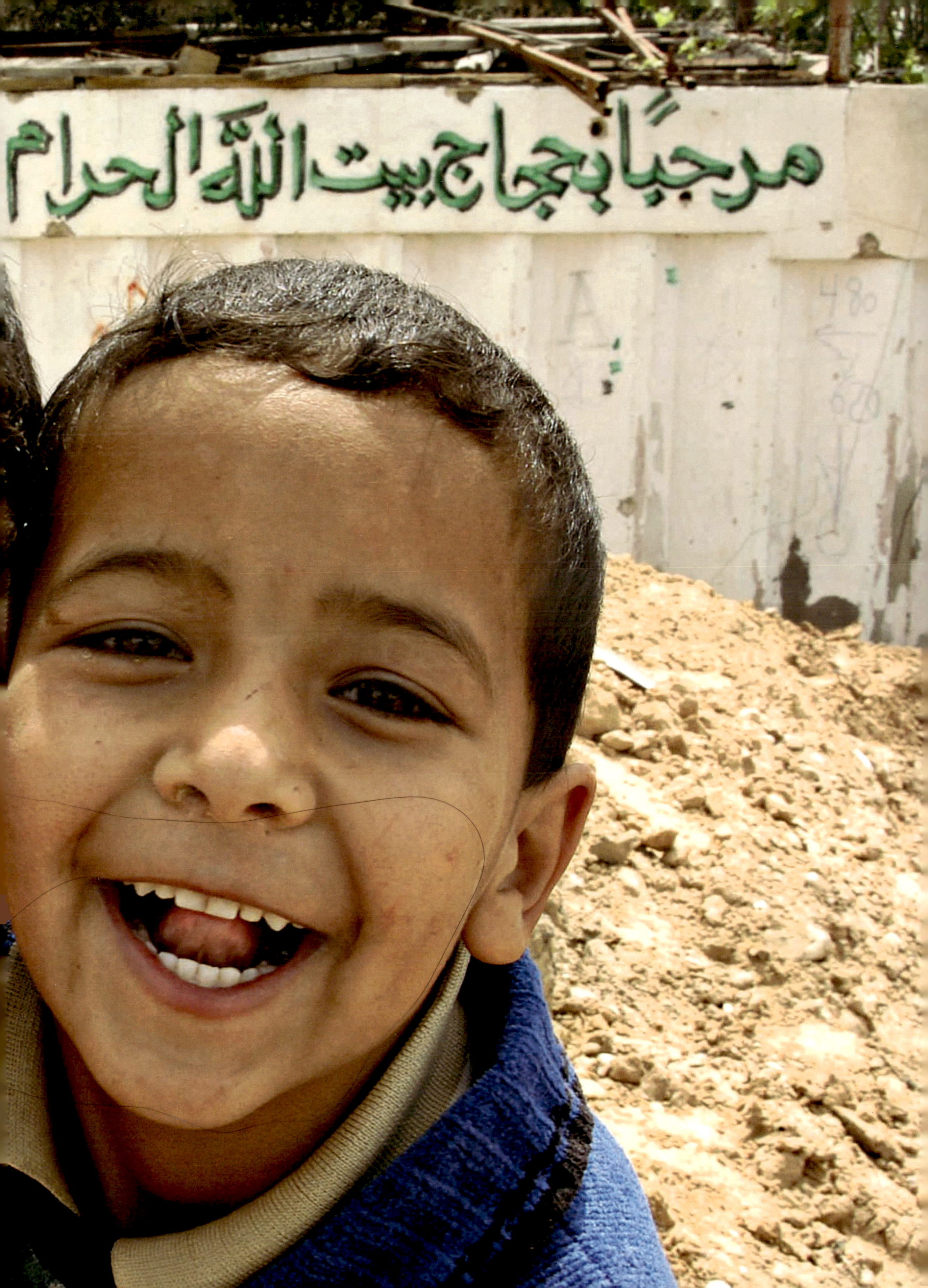

مرحباً بحجاج بيت الله الحرام

09 APRIL

It's a strange life here. The first job I did when
I arrived in Rafah, when we crammed into a
car, wearing orange jackets, responding to an
"emergency call", struck me as similar to British
emergency services. I actually felt like a fireman.

  Since then I have been on call 24 hours per day.
Right now I am on duty…my third night at Dr.
Samir's. I have my tools with me: striplight, orange
jacket and megaphone.

  Fuck it…something more important on my mind.
I have been away from England for almost 50
days…the best part of two months and I have done
a lot of stuff. Simply, I'm tired.
I have seen many impressive things. Some have
been moving and some awesome but it leaves me
looking to the future weeks. Am I going to achieve
anything more by being here?

  Maybe I just get bored easily. Maybe it's just the
constant adrenaline rush that has left me on a huge
come-down. And maybe it is the frustration of
being in the middle of various factions and their
hype and being unable to ascertain what the truth
is. That, I think, is the only reason I would have for
staying here.

  I have had my head filled with so much
propaganda and yet I know that in situations
like this half-truths can build on each other
exponentially to create a massive wrong conclusion.
People believe what they want to. Although I have
heard a mass of information, much of it credible,
none of it is first-hand. It would be easy to say that
because there is so much some of it must be true,
and even the smallest fraction would be damning to
the states of Israel and America.

  Likewise, things I have seen have been incredibly
powerful. Things have gone to shit in Palestine,
that is for certain. People die all the time and life is
cheap, but why? Some is justified, but the line for
me is when I see Israeli troops inflict unnecessary
pain. Bulldozing houses and injuring children in
assassinations provoke a huge, burning anger inside
me. But there is always the "What if?"

  The thousands of bullet-holes in south frontier
houses may have been in response to direct fire.
I know nothing about Dr. Samir's history.

  When it comes down to it, I have seen no
direct actions in major violations of the Geneva
convention. Hype can so easily make you lose sight
of that fact.

People too often mistake insanity
for reality's evasiveness
at the hands of a man
like all the rest of us,
but who has the strength not to follow.

That is the first step,
but again too often we are refused
by the accusations and hinderance
of the judgemental fools
who cannot accept diversity.

Tolerance is the height of patience,
so difficult to master,
impossible through want or effort,
it must be taught through hatred
and opposite expressionism.

09 APRIL
GAZA CITY

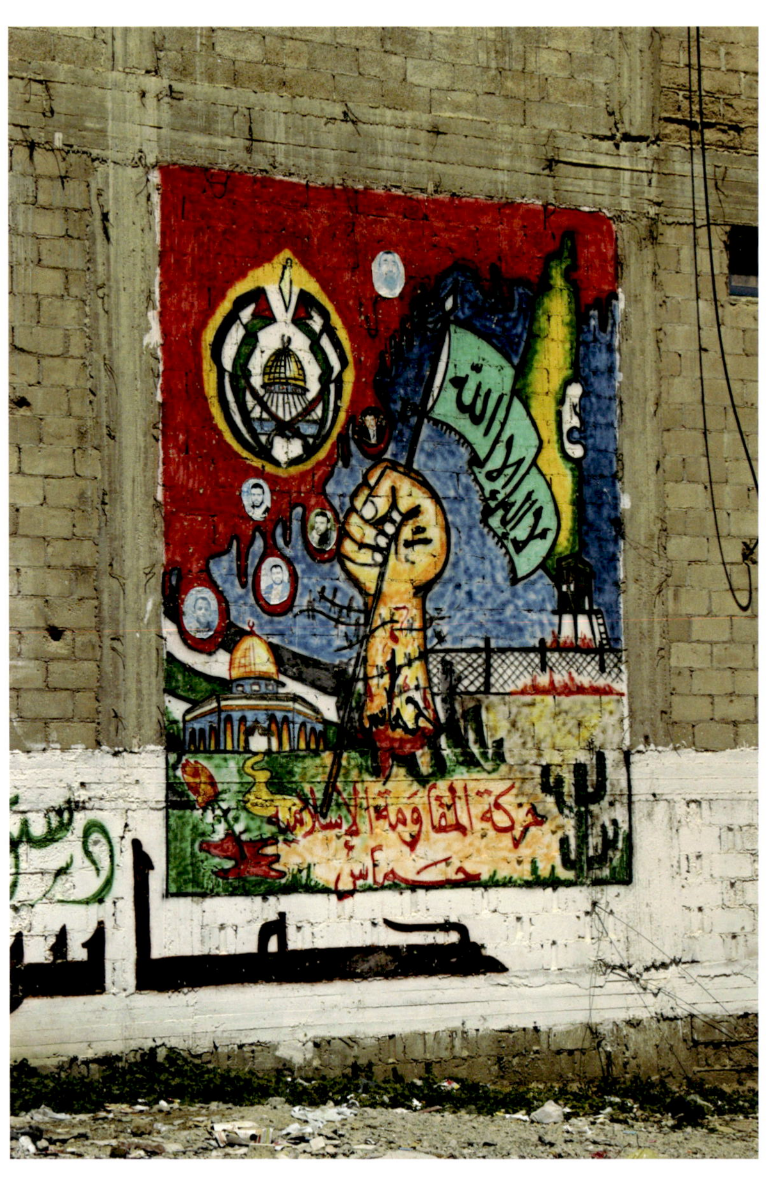

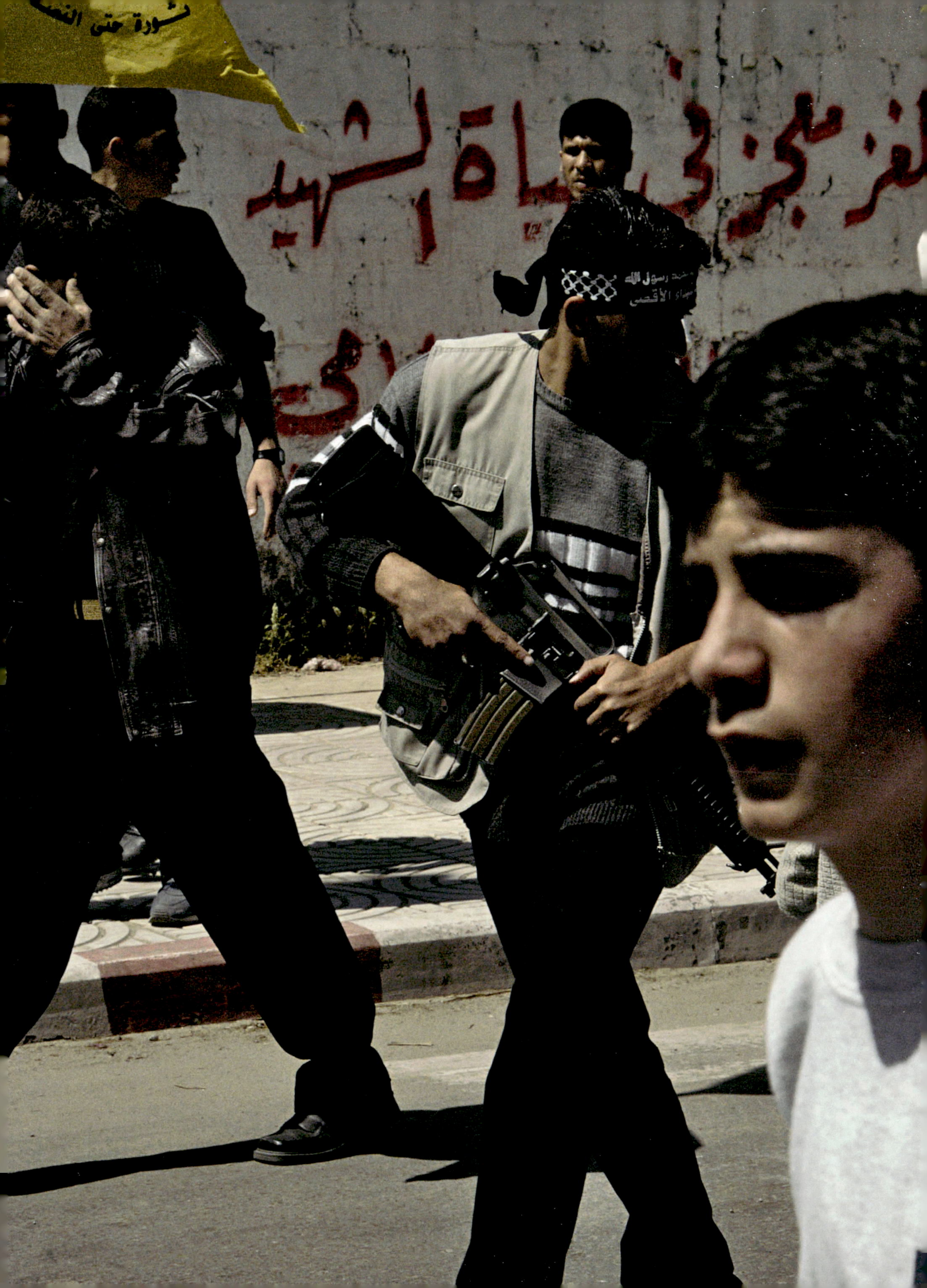

ثورة حتى النصر
الغز مجنى في حياة الشهيد
شهداء الأقصى

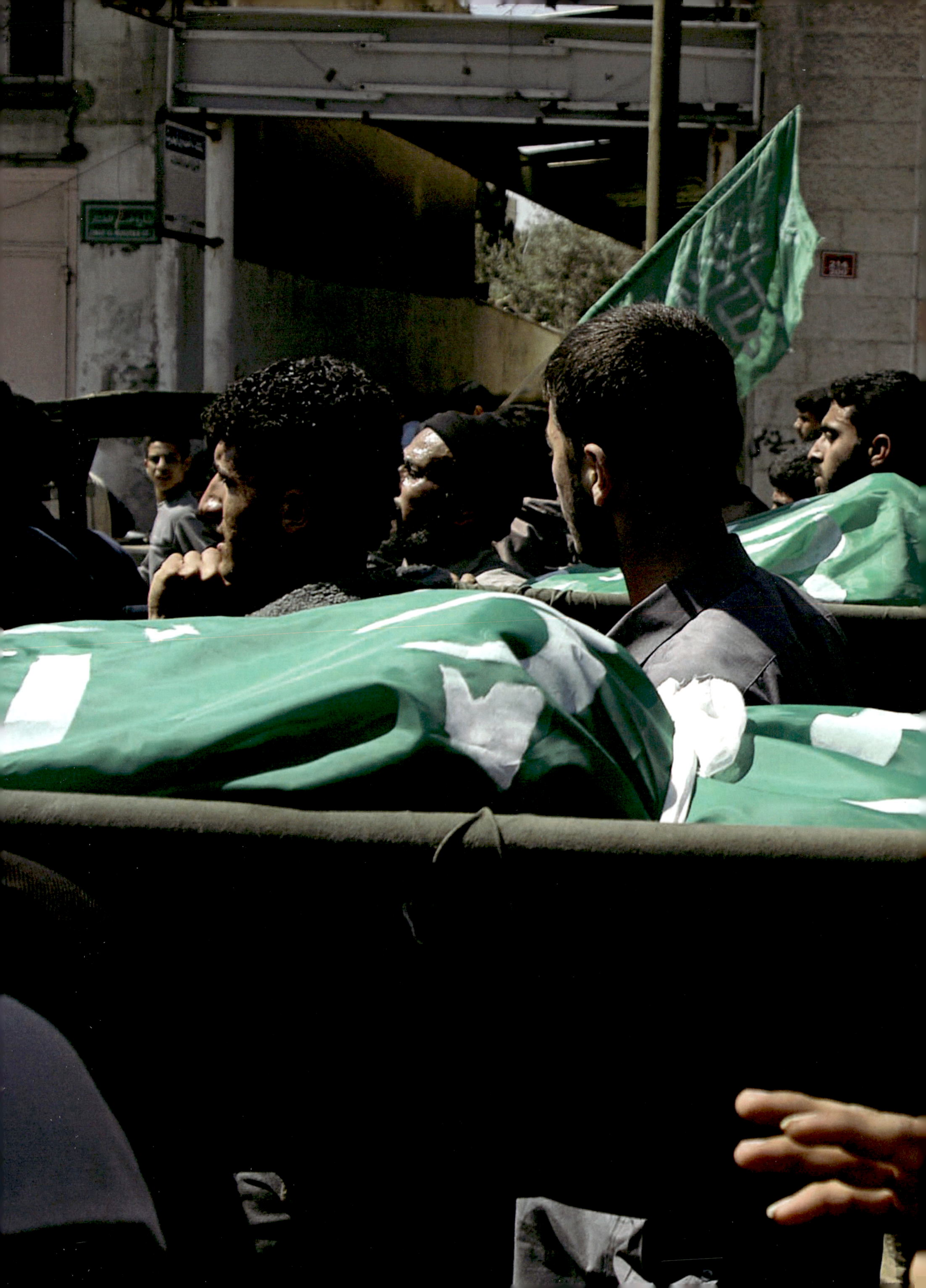
شارع الشهداء
SHAT AL SHUHADA ST.

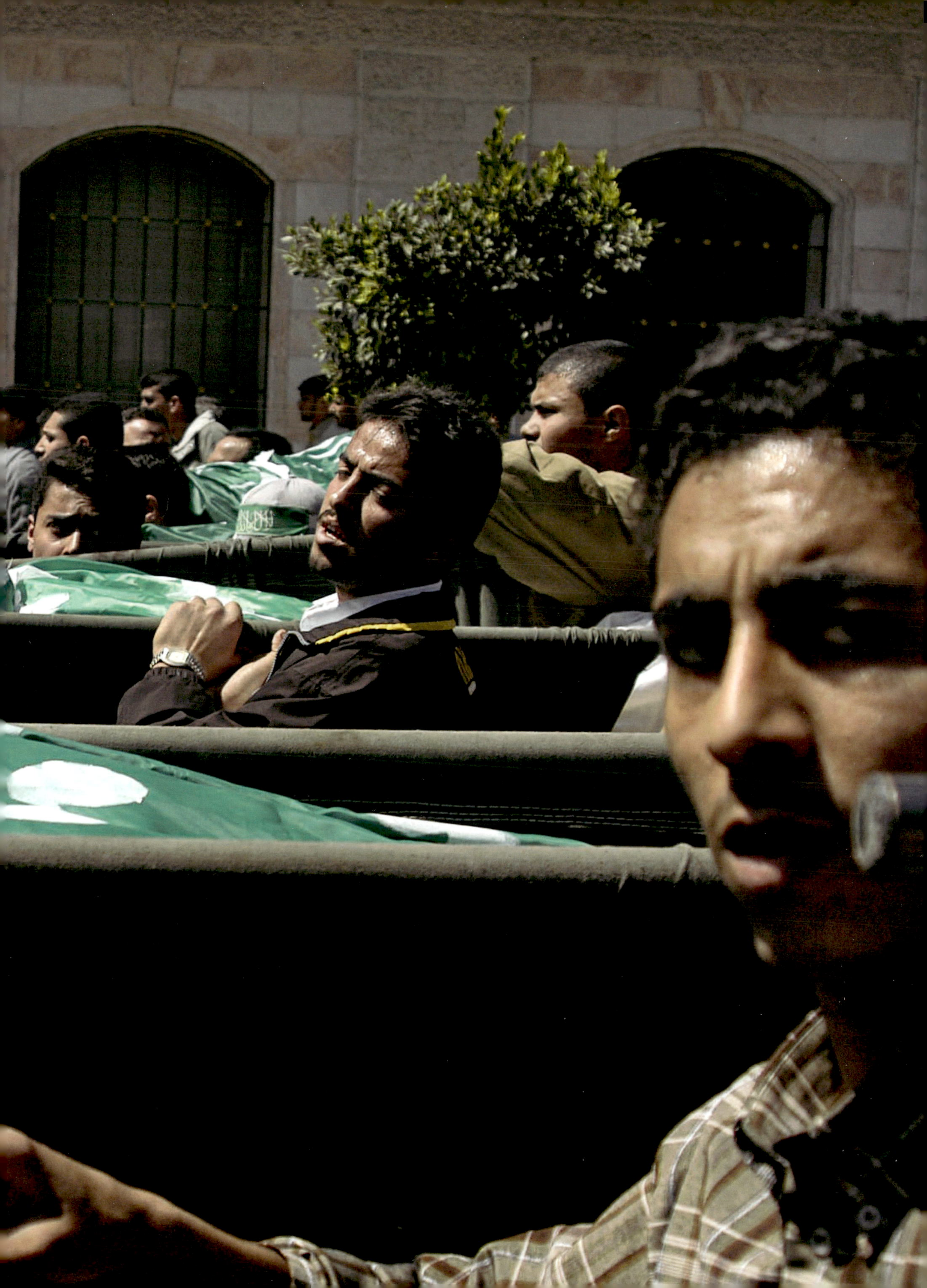

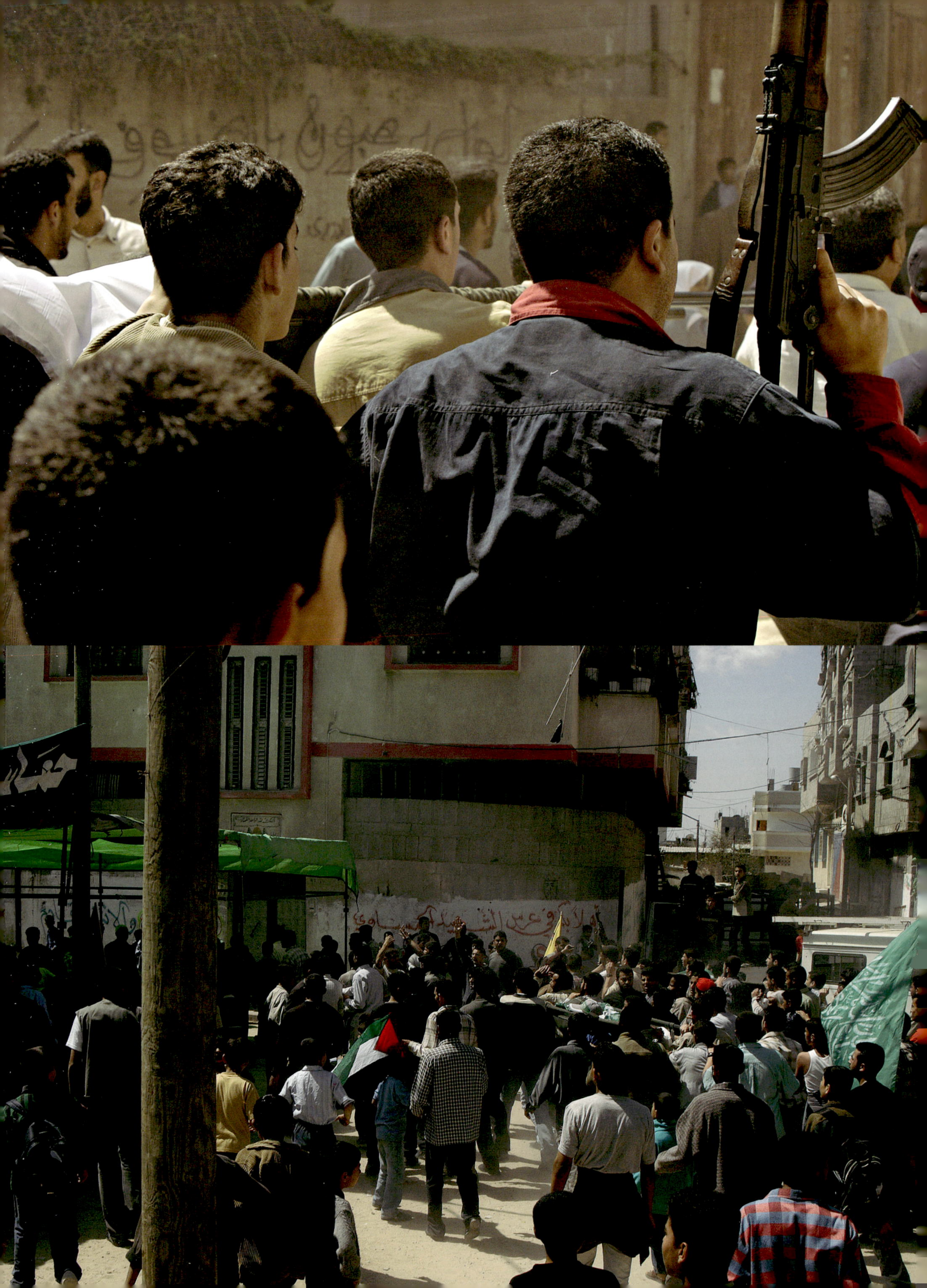

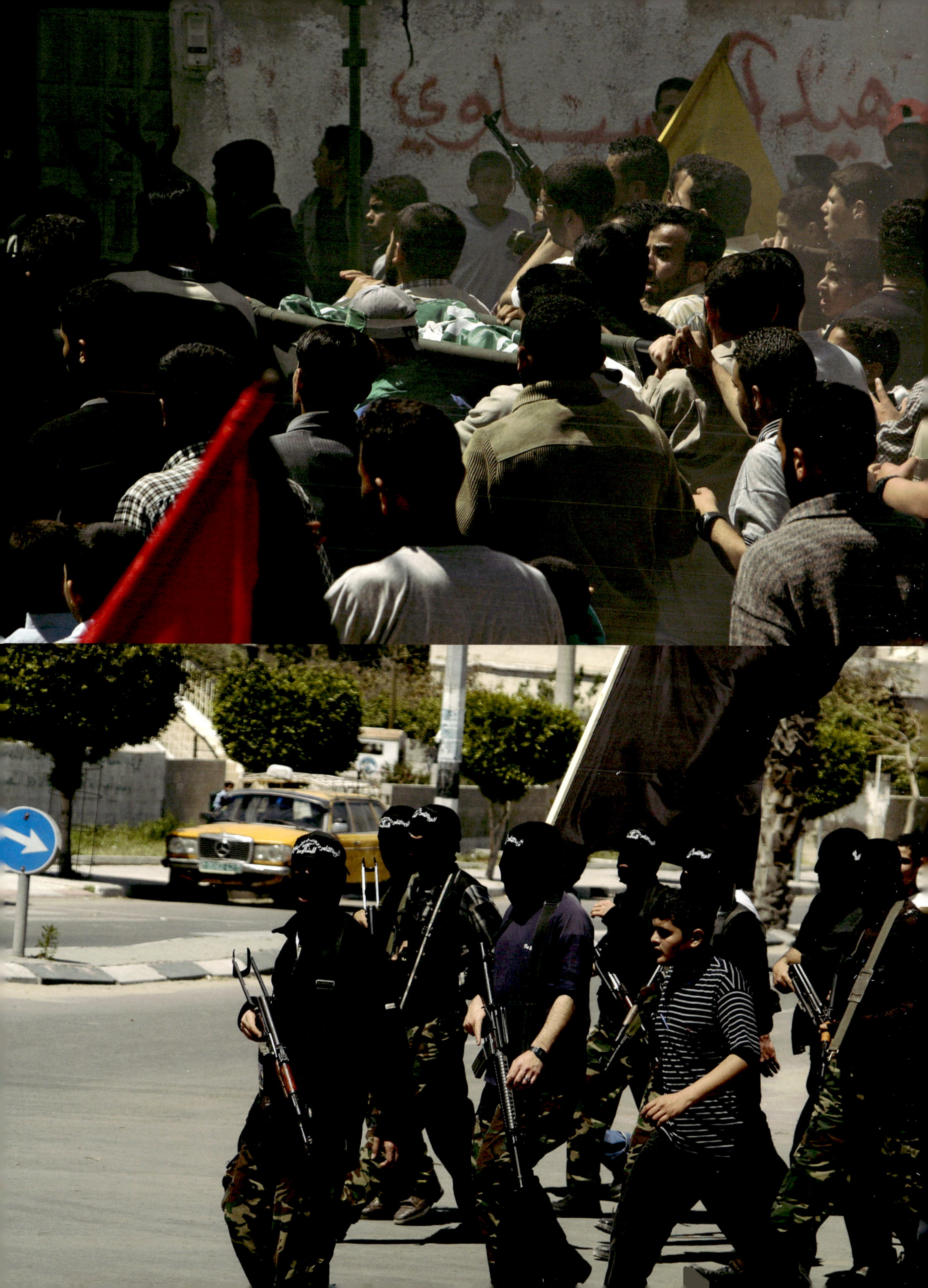

From: Thomas Hurndall <aqimaging@hotmail.com>
Date: 9 April 2003 15:01:14 GMT+01:00
To: ah@hurndalls.com, 6 more…

▶ 📎 5 Attachments, 195 KB   (Save ▾)   (Quick Look)

Afternoon all,

I took these this morning in Gaza City. For the people who didn't see the news last night, an F16 fired two rockets into the city in an assasination attempt on three Hamas and two Fatah members that Israeli intelligence knew to be in a car together. The first rocket missed, but the second hit, killing everyone in the car, and wounding three dozen civilians in the area (four of whom have died since). I spent this morning in Gaza City (northern end of the Gaza strip), visiting the site where the car was hit and the wounded in the hospital, and got caught up in the "march for the martyrs", where the family and many others carry the bodies through the street, running and generally making noise by chanting and shooting their guns into the air until they arrive at the "victim's" home and the family can mourn alone. It's kind of intimidating when you're the only non-Palestinian out of 850 and they're chanting "Kill the Americans and Jews, drive them out of Palestine". Anyway, of the images, 'arm-back.jpg' and 'HAM2.jpg' are of two Hamas members leading the run/march. 'IJ.jpg' is a group of Islamic Jihad members with a parallel intention. 'shout.jpg' is a Fatah "gunman" firing into the air, with the dead Fatah member on the stretcher in the background. And 'm2.jpg' is of the group carrying two of the dead Hamas members wrapped in the green Hamas flags.
 Well, I hope you all had a good day so far!
   That's it, hope you don't all mind me sending these out to everyone, but if you don't want to receive any more, feel free to ask me nicely, or just block anything coming from my address. On that note, I'm about to send some lovely pictures of kids in an e-mail after this one so if you haven't seen them yet you can just delete without looking.

   Have a nice day,
     Love Tom

P.S. Daniel and Ad C, you can come out from under the bed now, they're only photos!

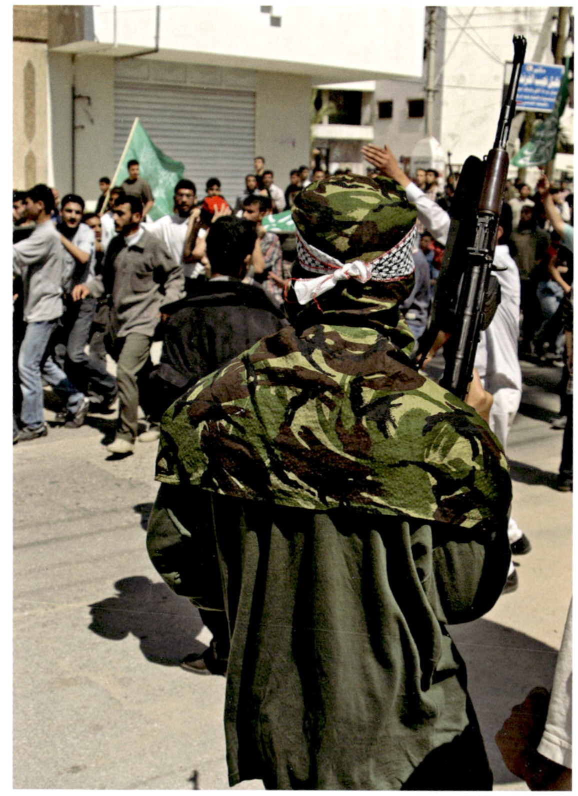

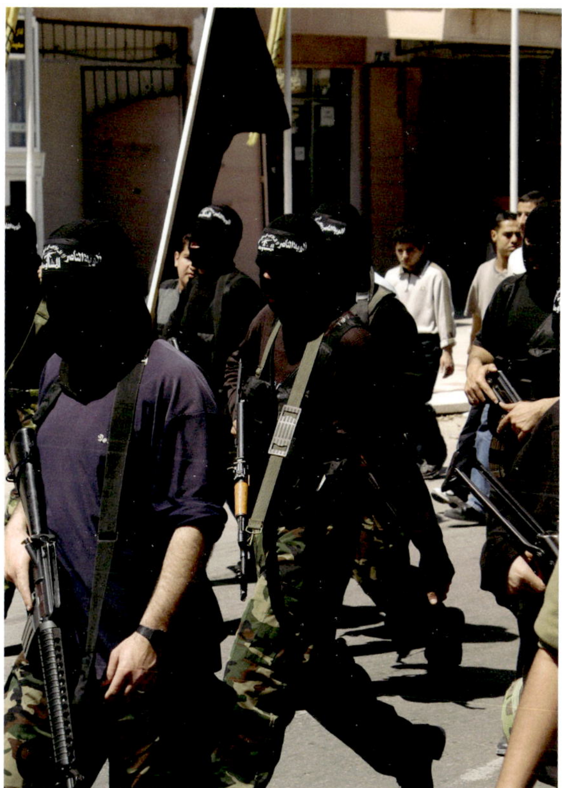

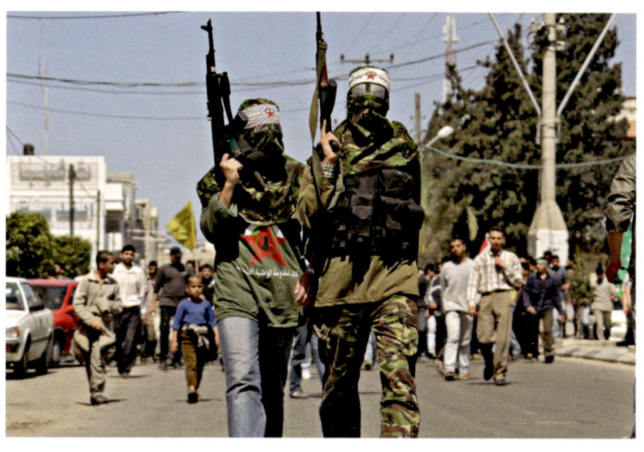

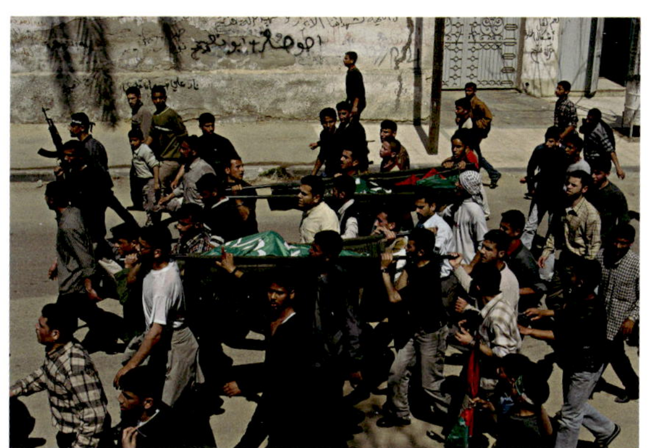

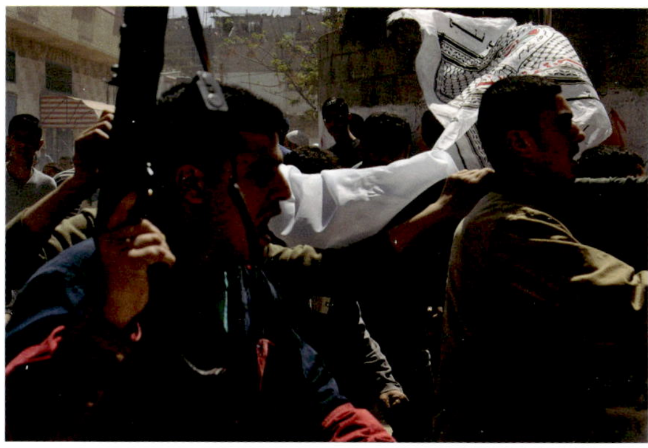

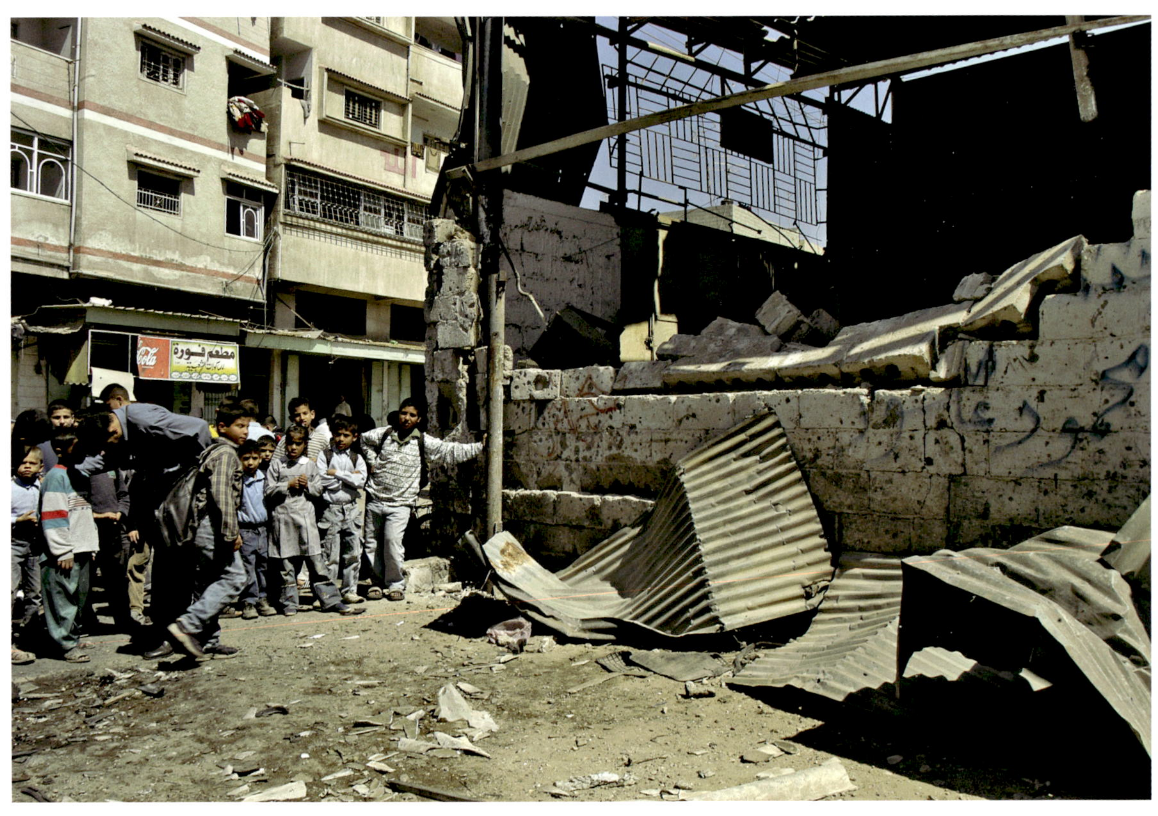

Destruction of metal workshop, Gaza City,
thought to be producing Hamas rockets.

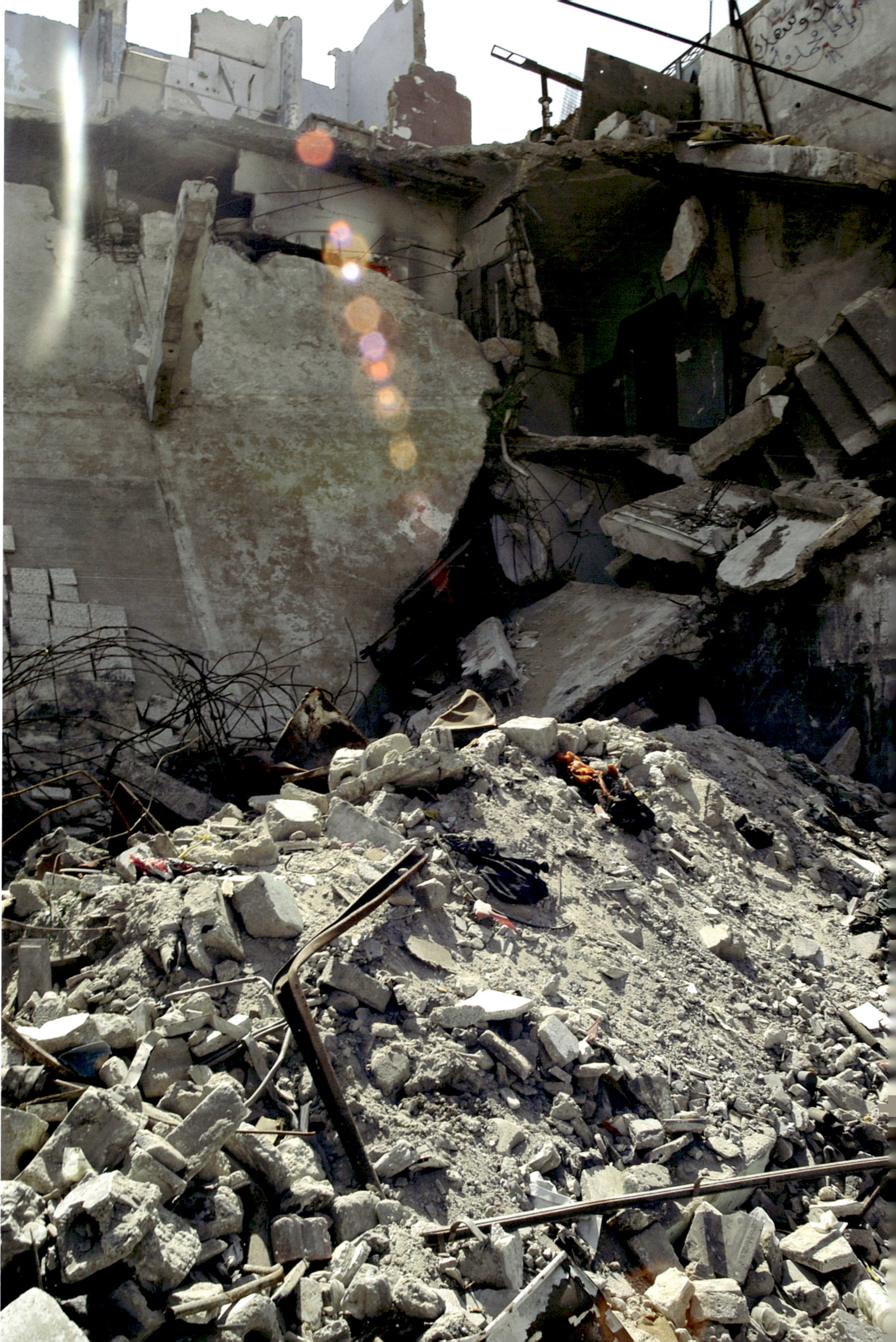

10 APRIL
DR. SAMIR'S HOUSE, RAFAH

Every morning, Dr. Samir's wife wakes me with
tea and bread and cheese.
   I don't feel like I'm doing enough for them. Guilt
is an underlying feeling I'm so used to that I don't
even know it's there any more.
I just feel shit and pride is only skin-deep.

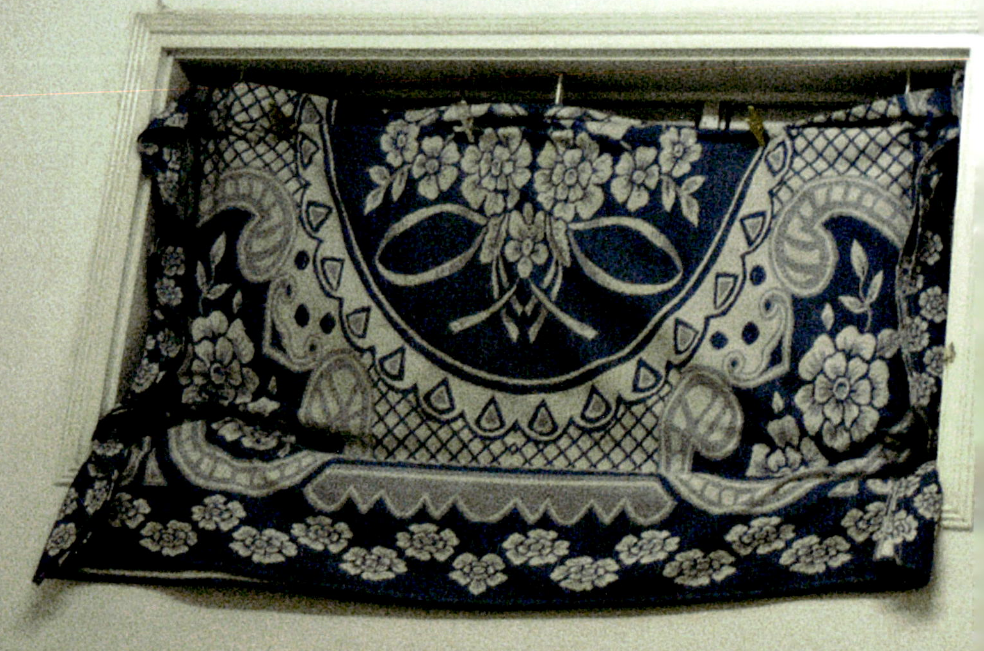

He revs his engines every now & then
to remind us he's still there.

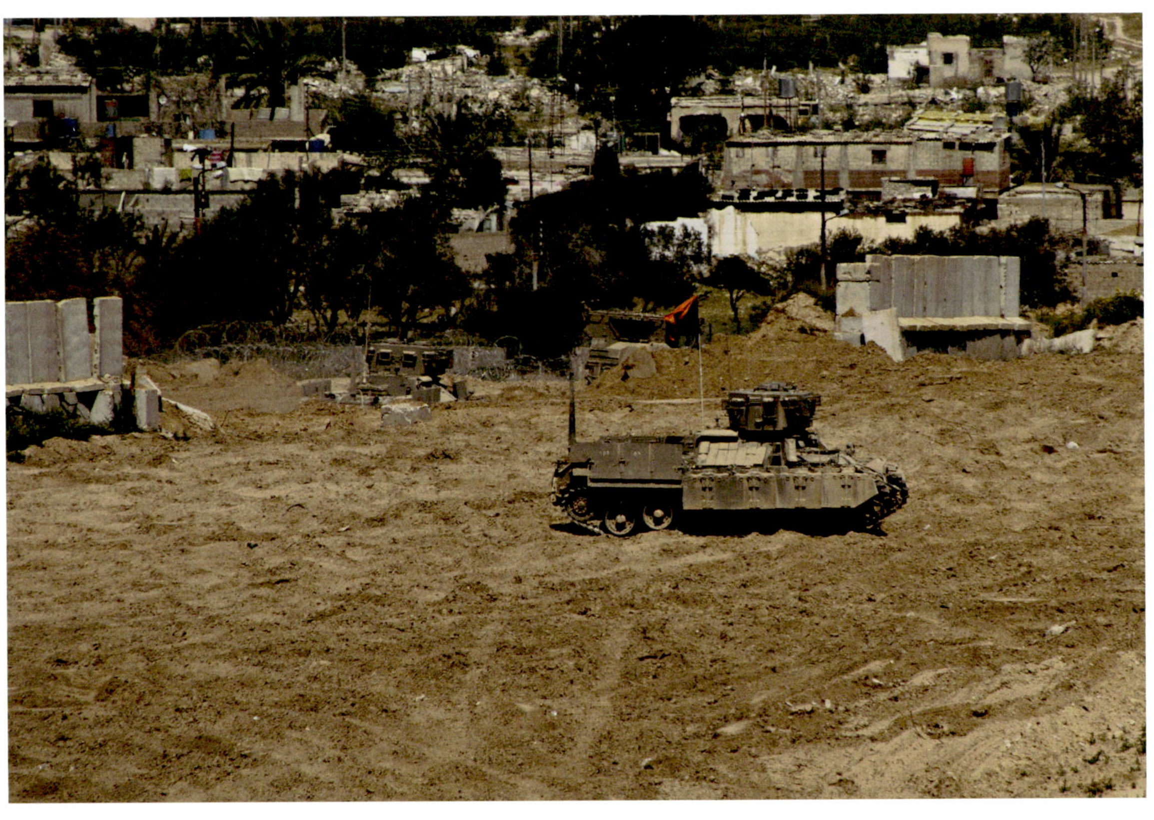

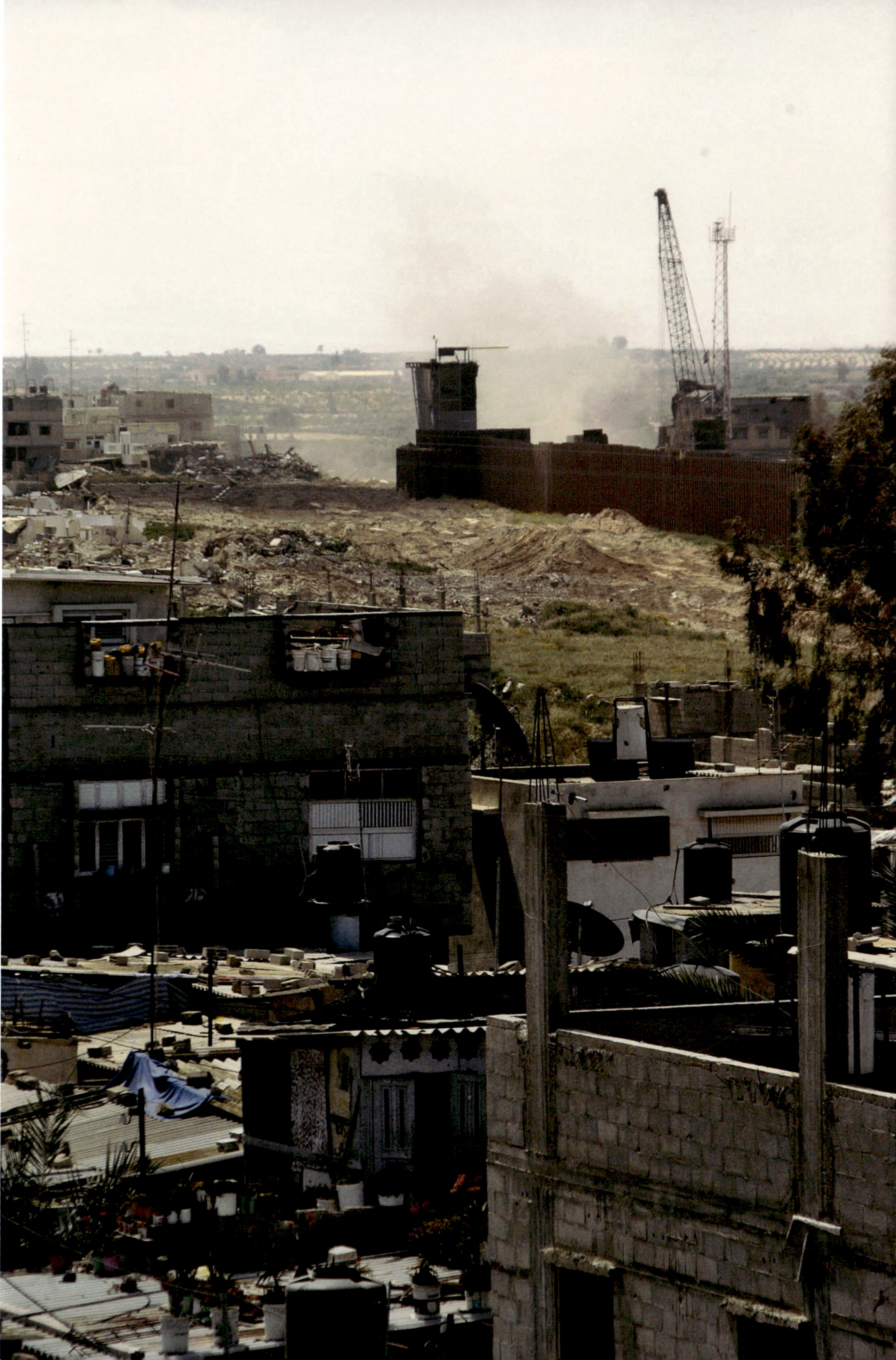

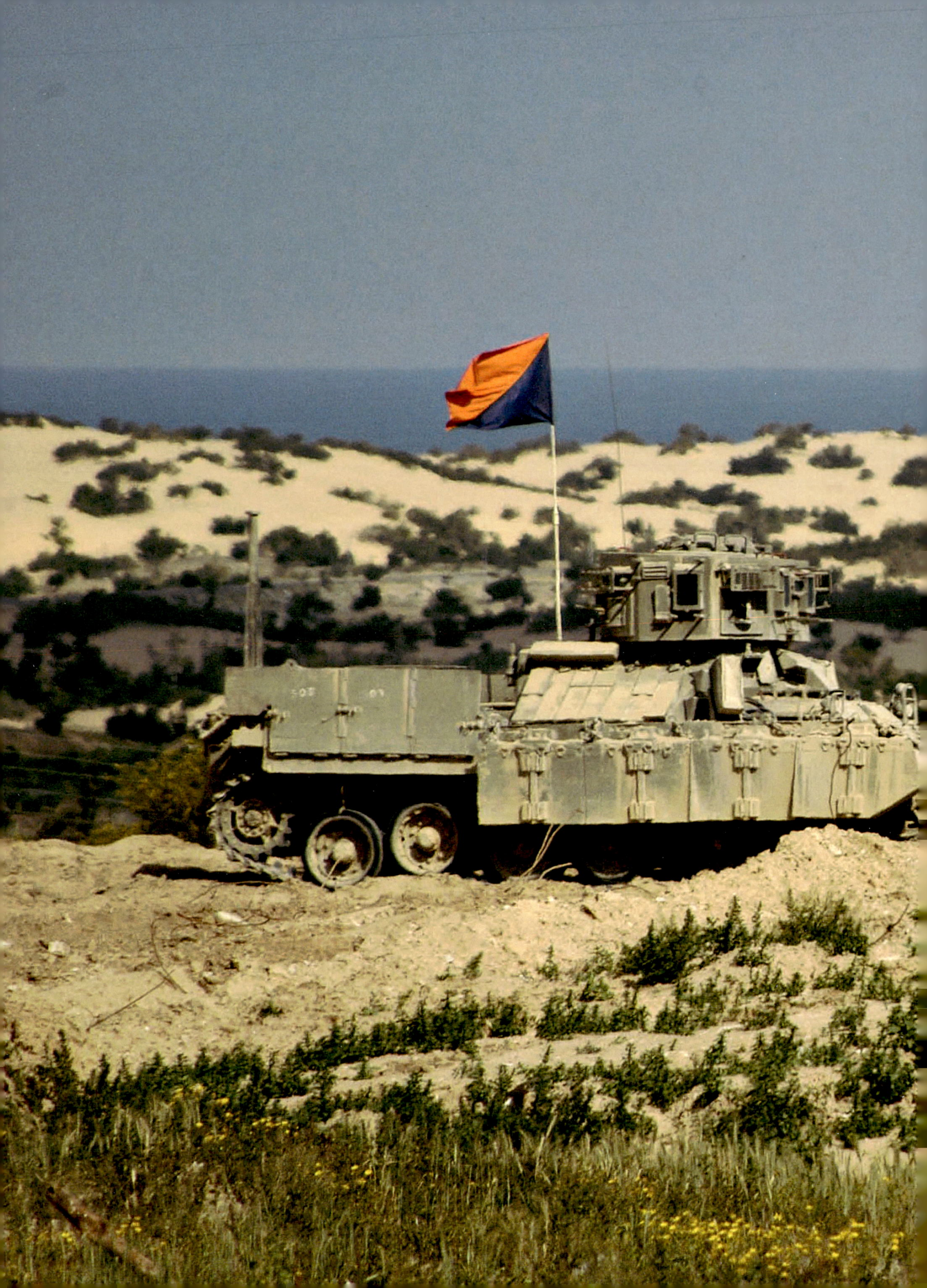

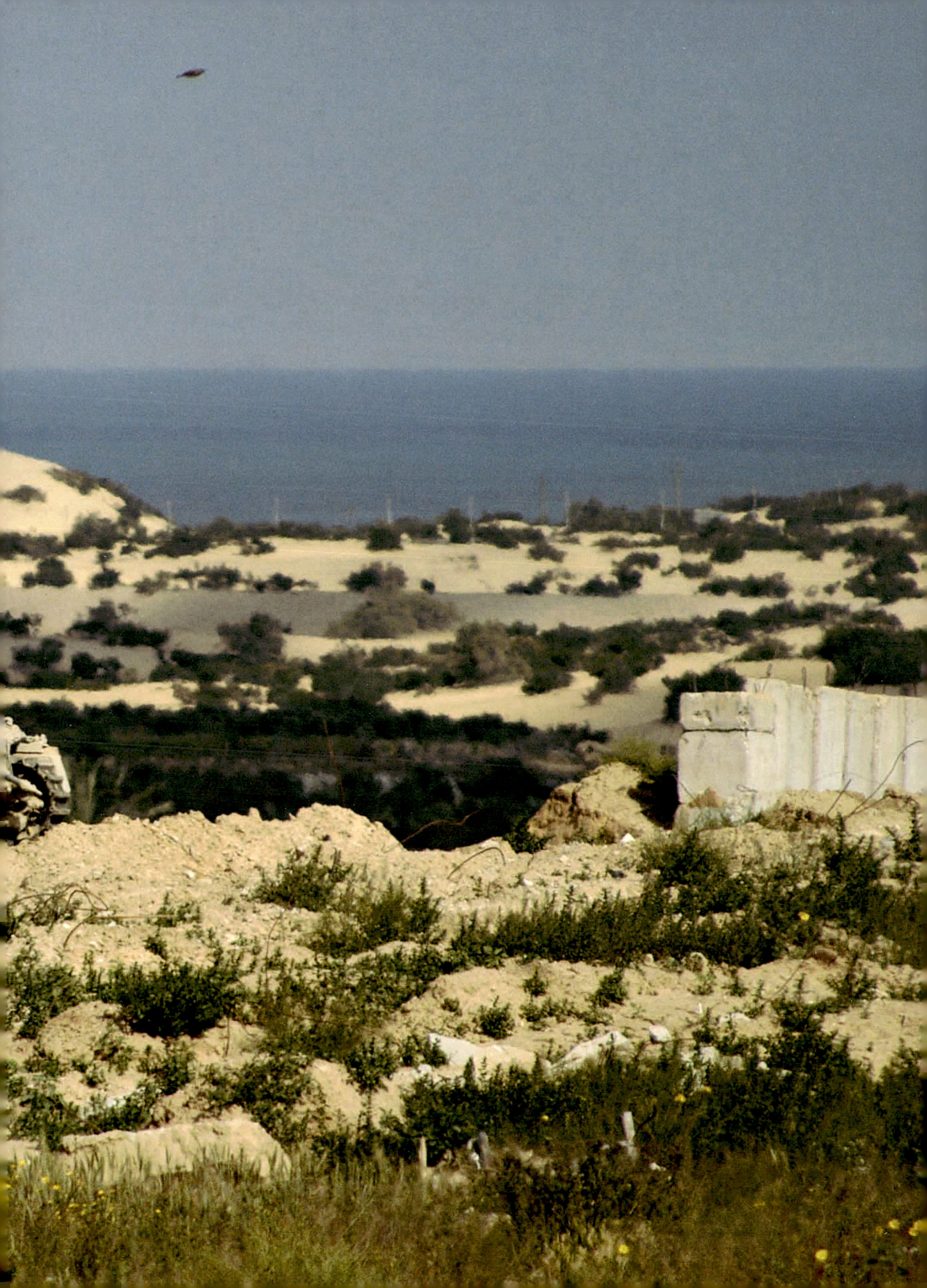

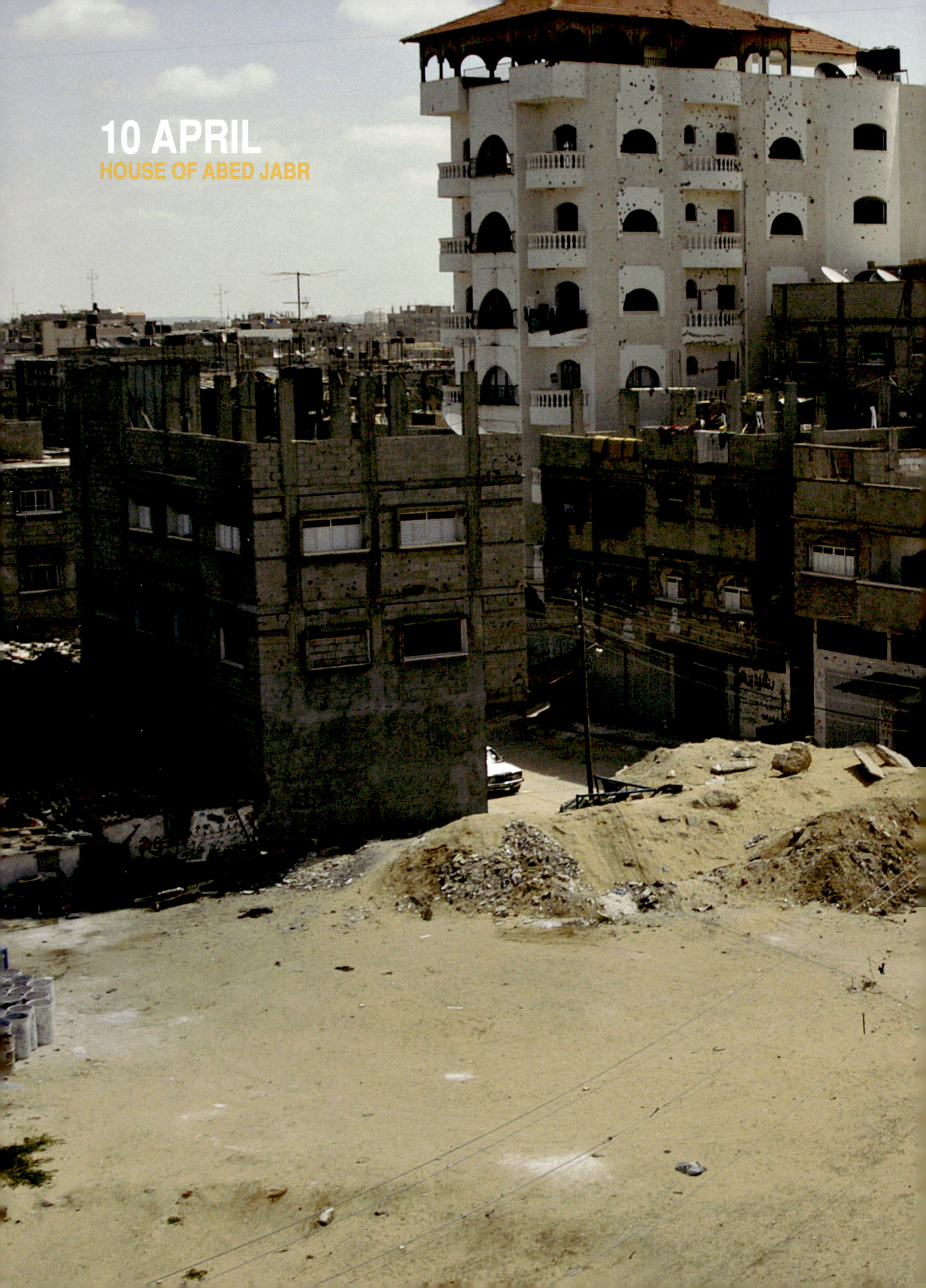

10 APRIL
HOUSE OF ABED JABR

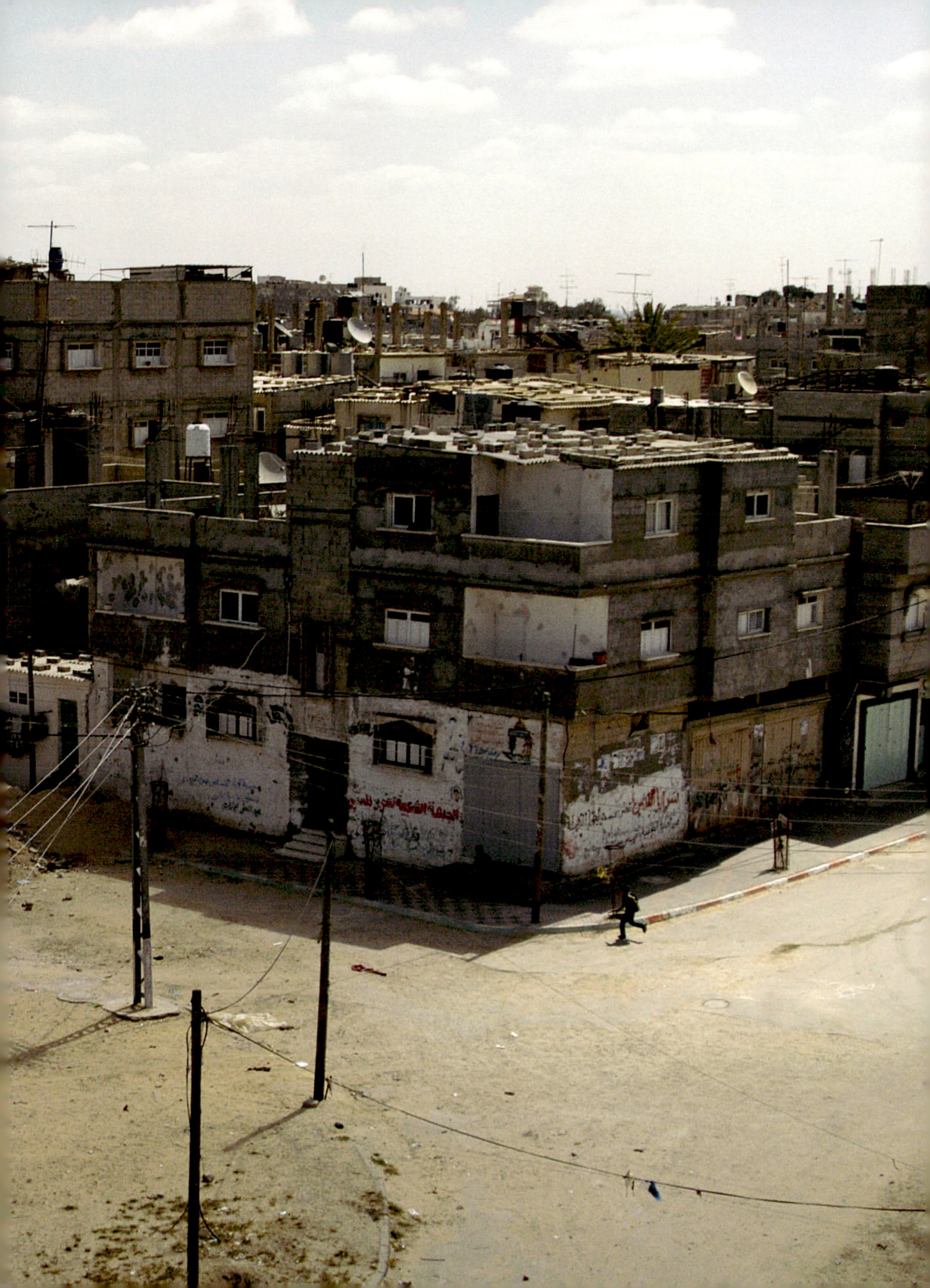

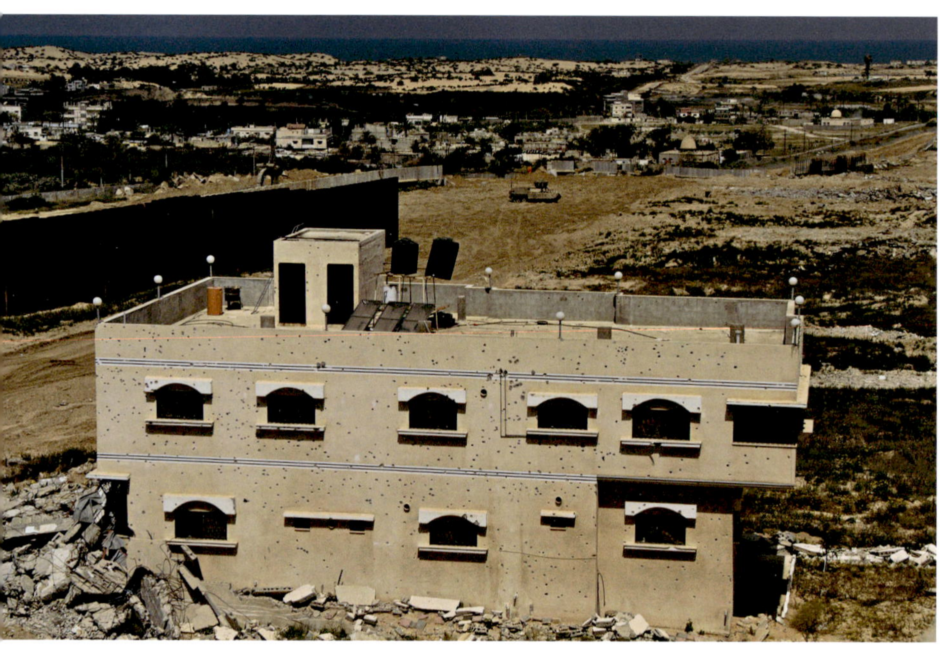 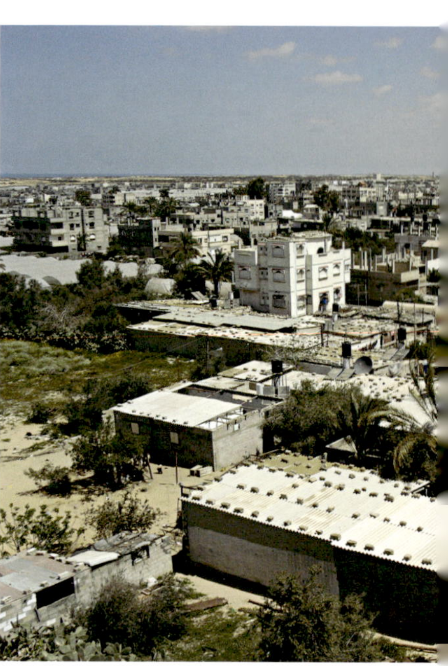

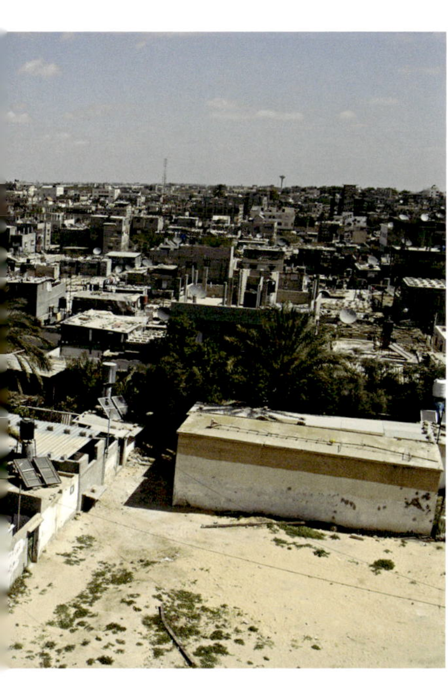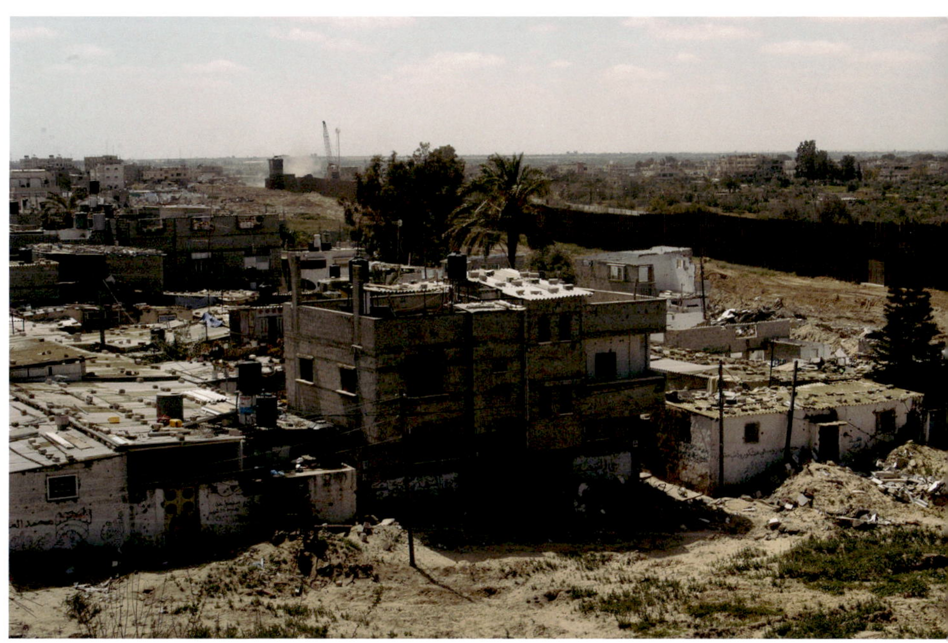

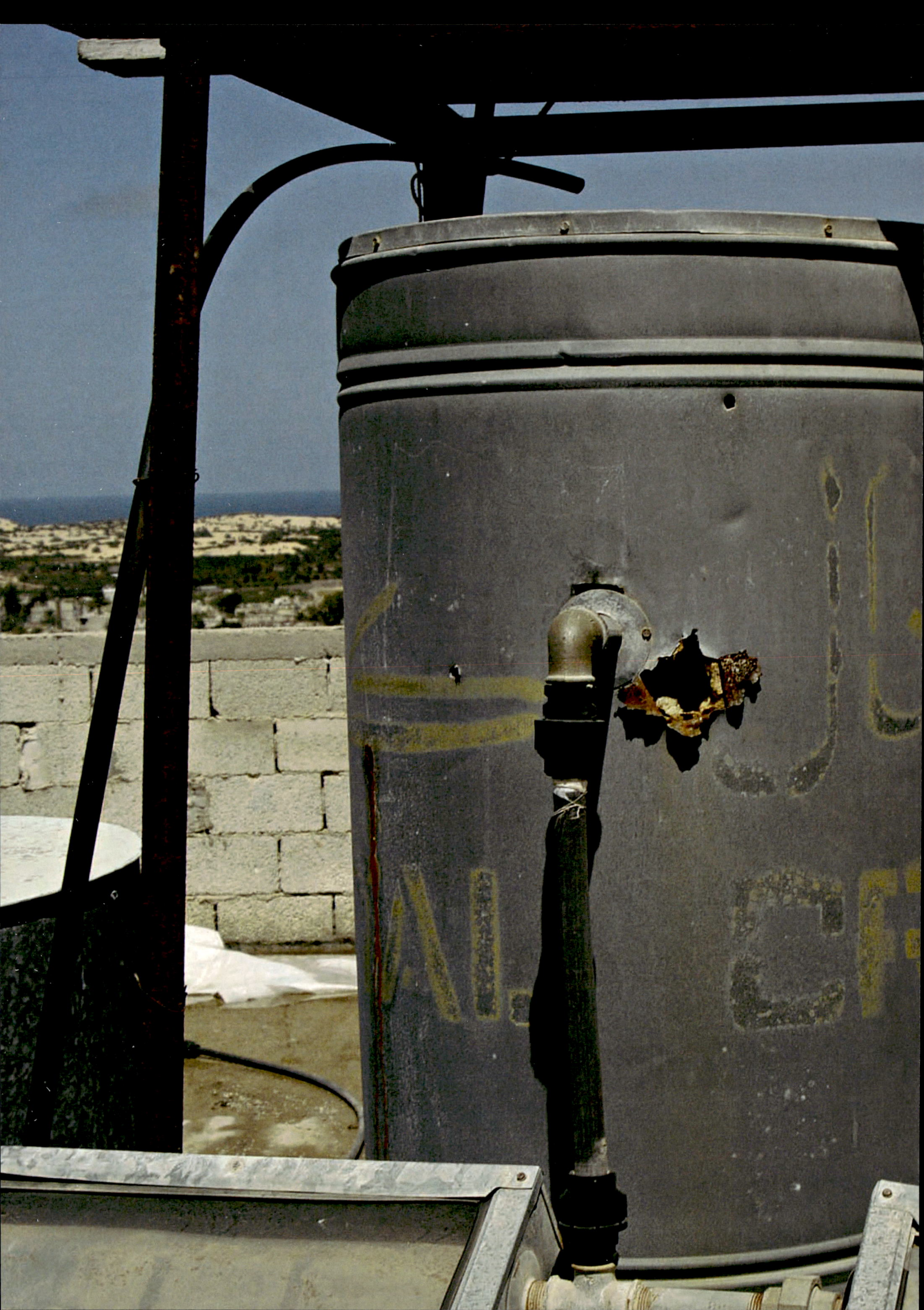

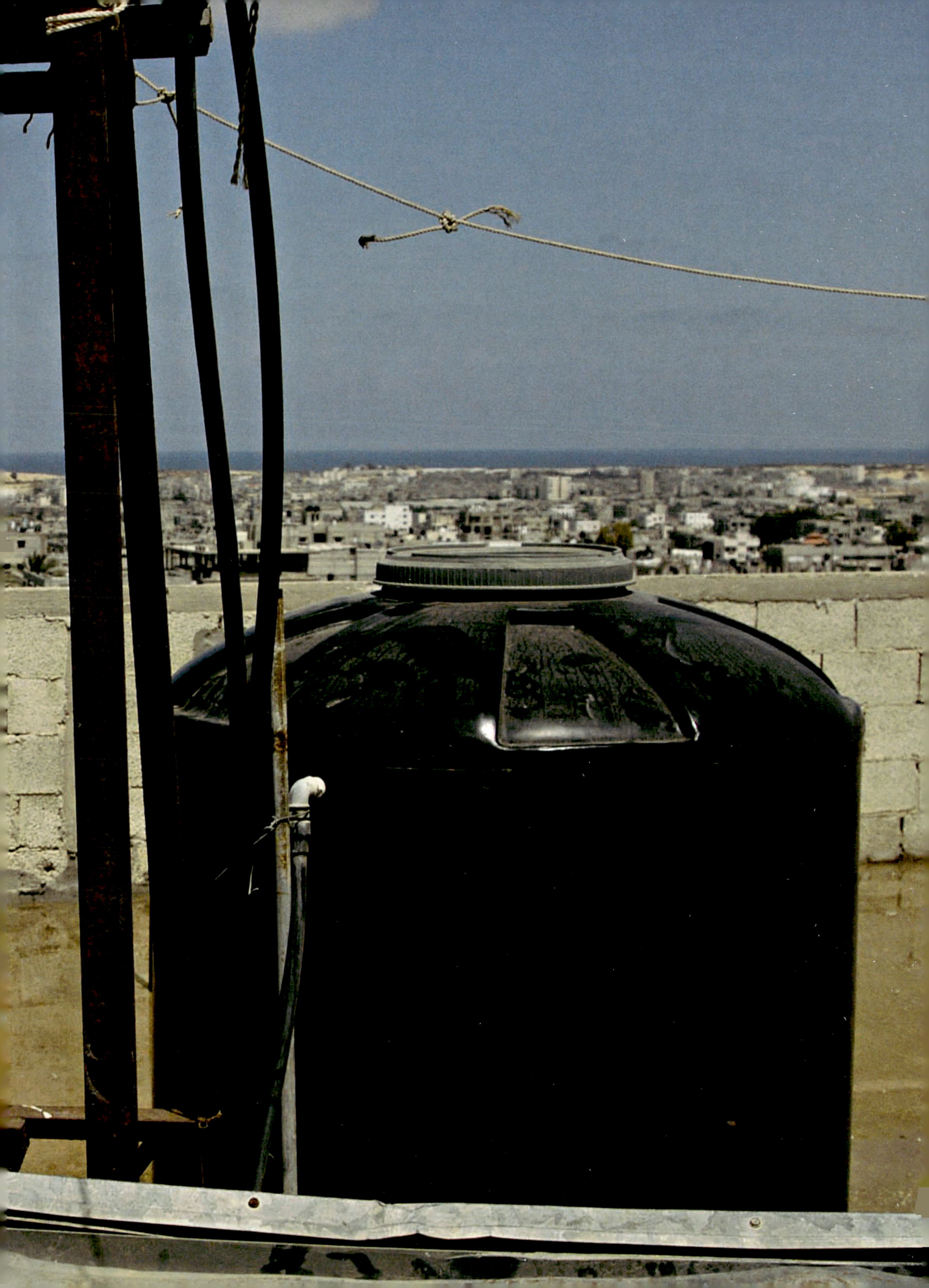

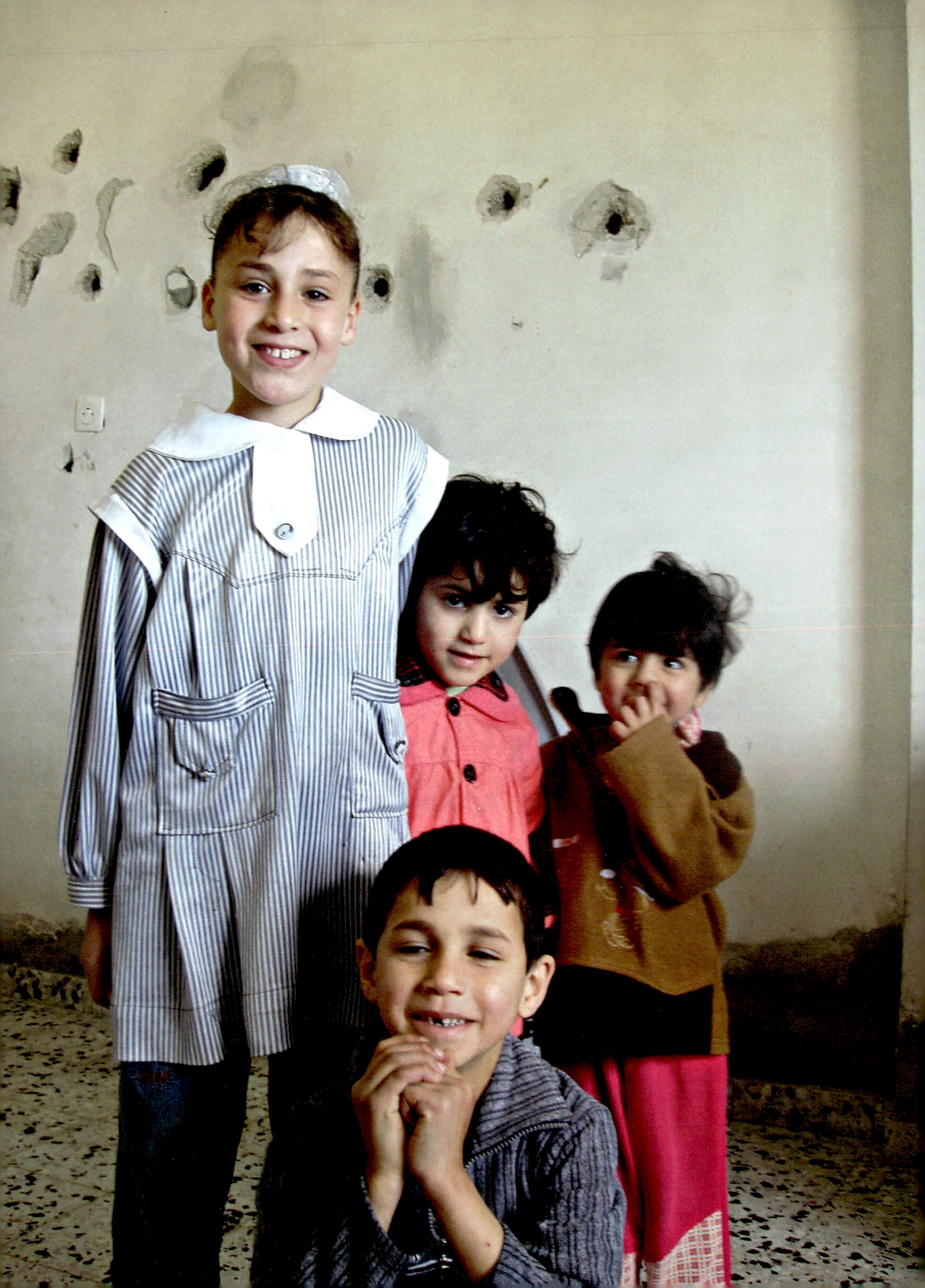

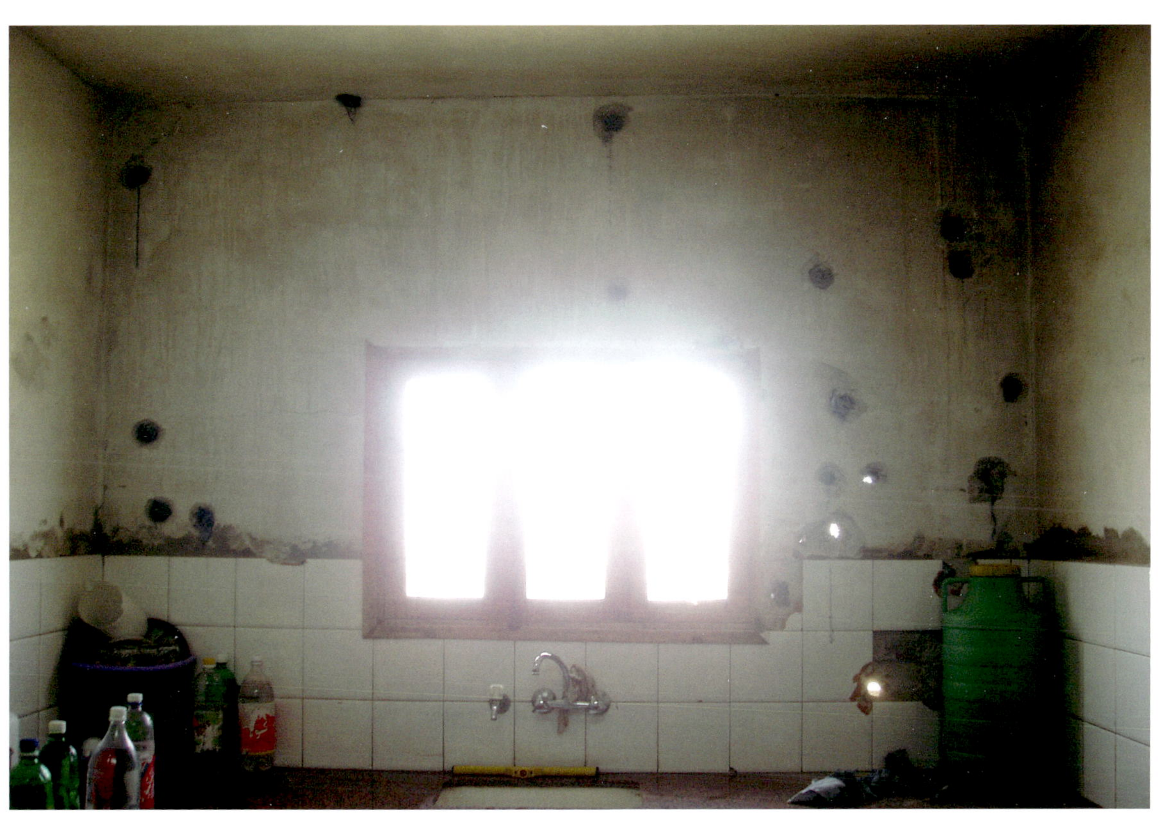

10.06.03
    4 families. 35 people - Yibna
    owned by Yassir.
    Two brothers shot. 1 in street, one in flat through
mashed glass. 1st in leg, 2nd in throat. 19 & 15 yrs.
last night.

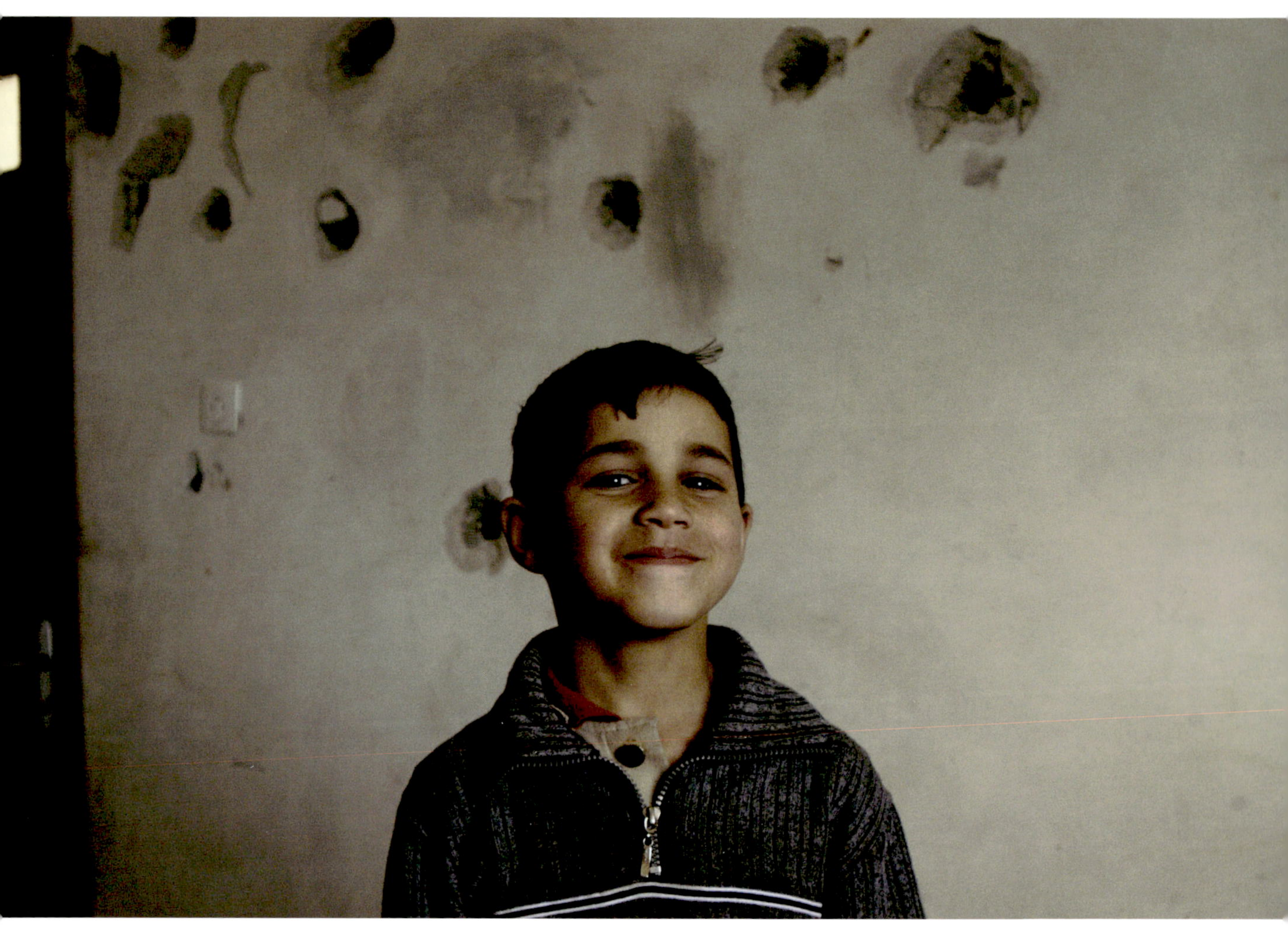

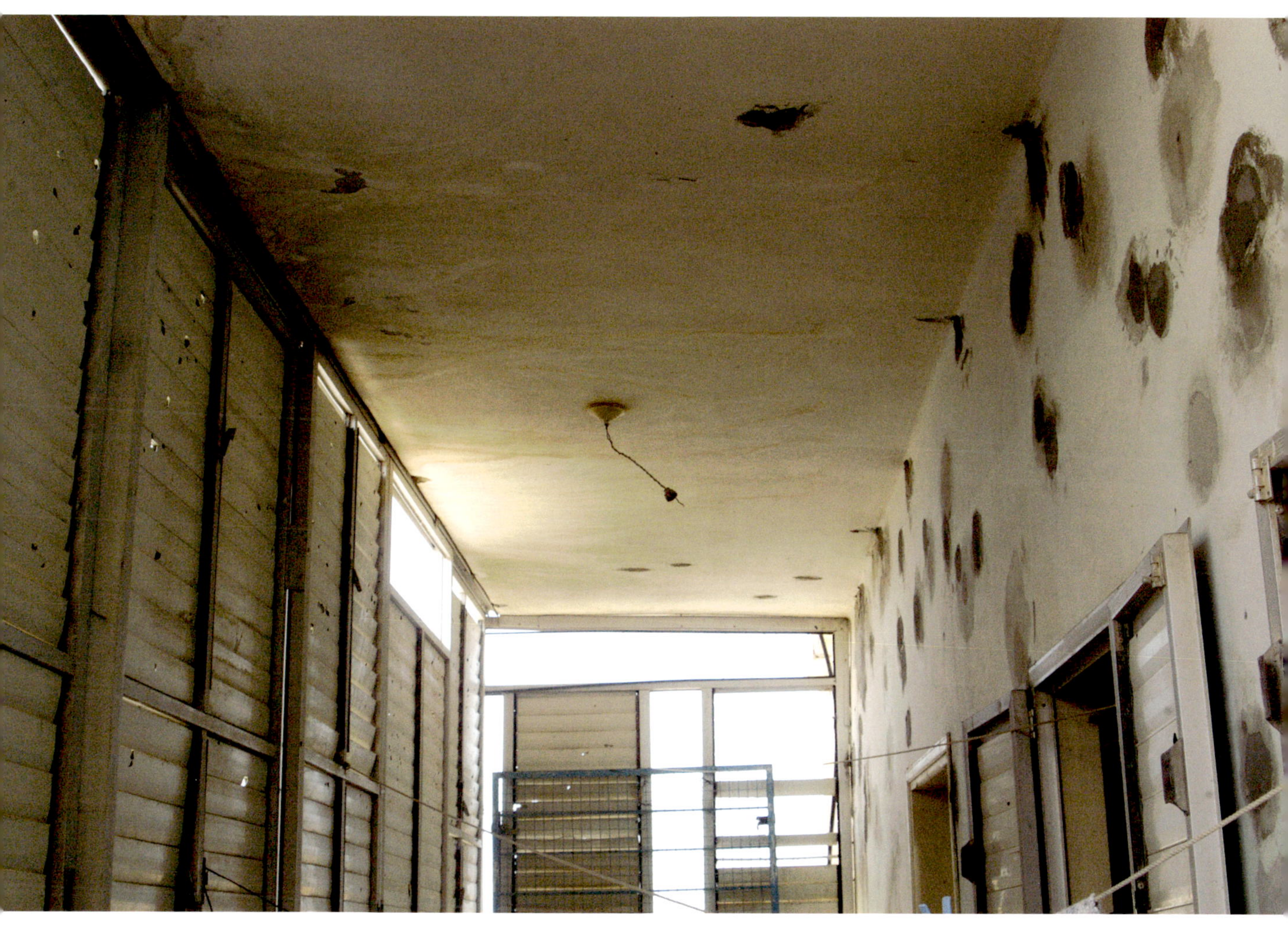

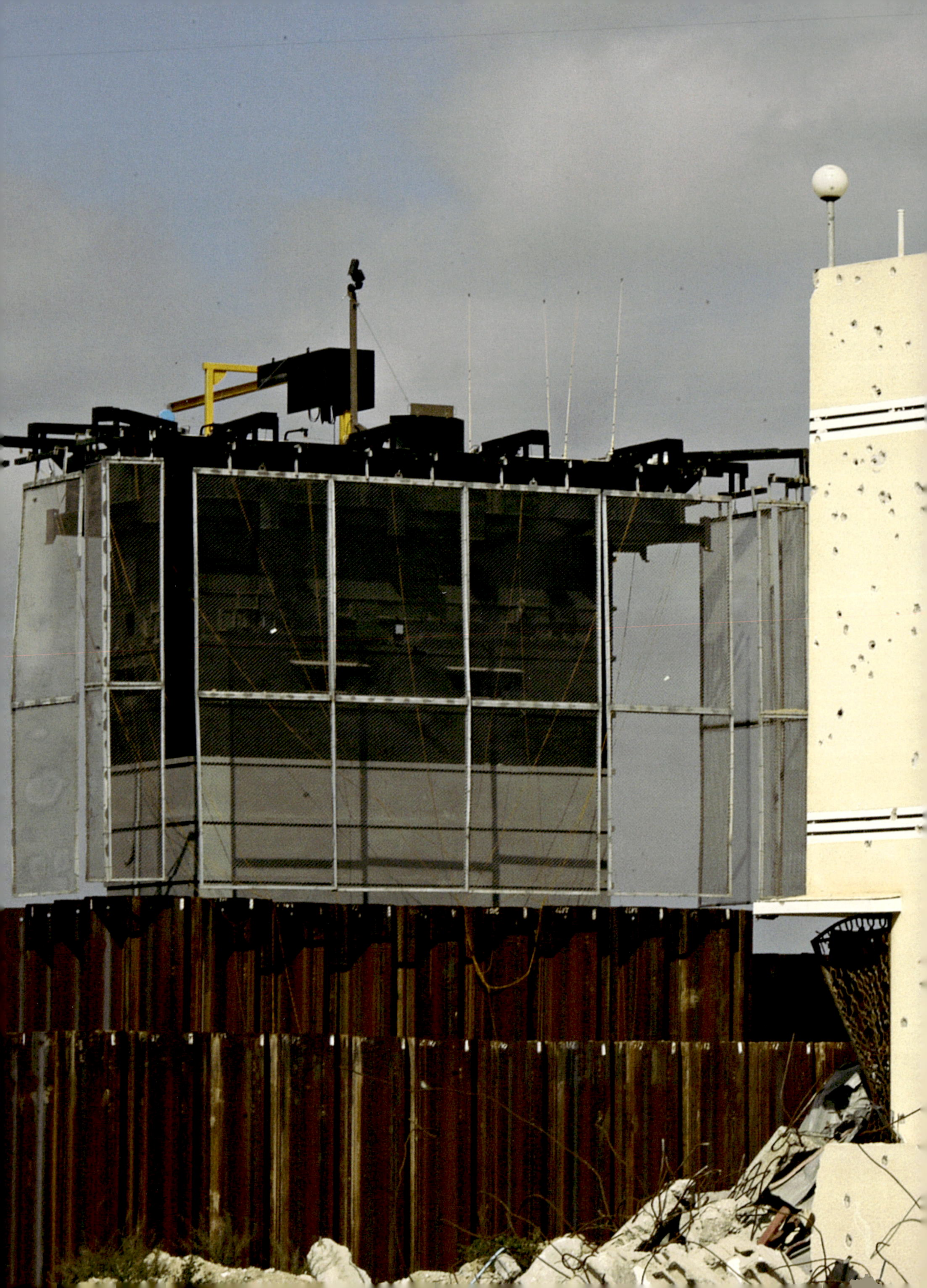

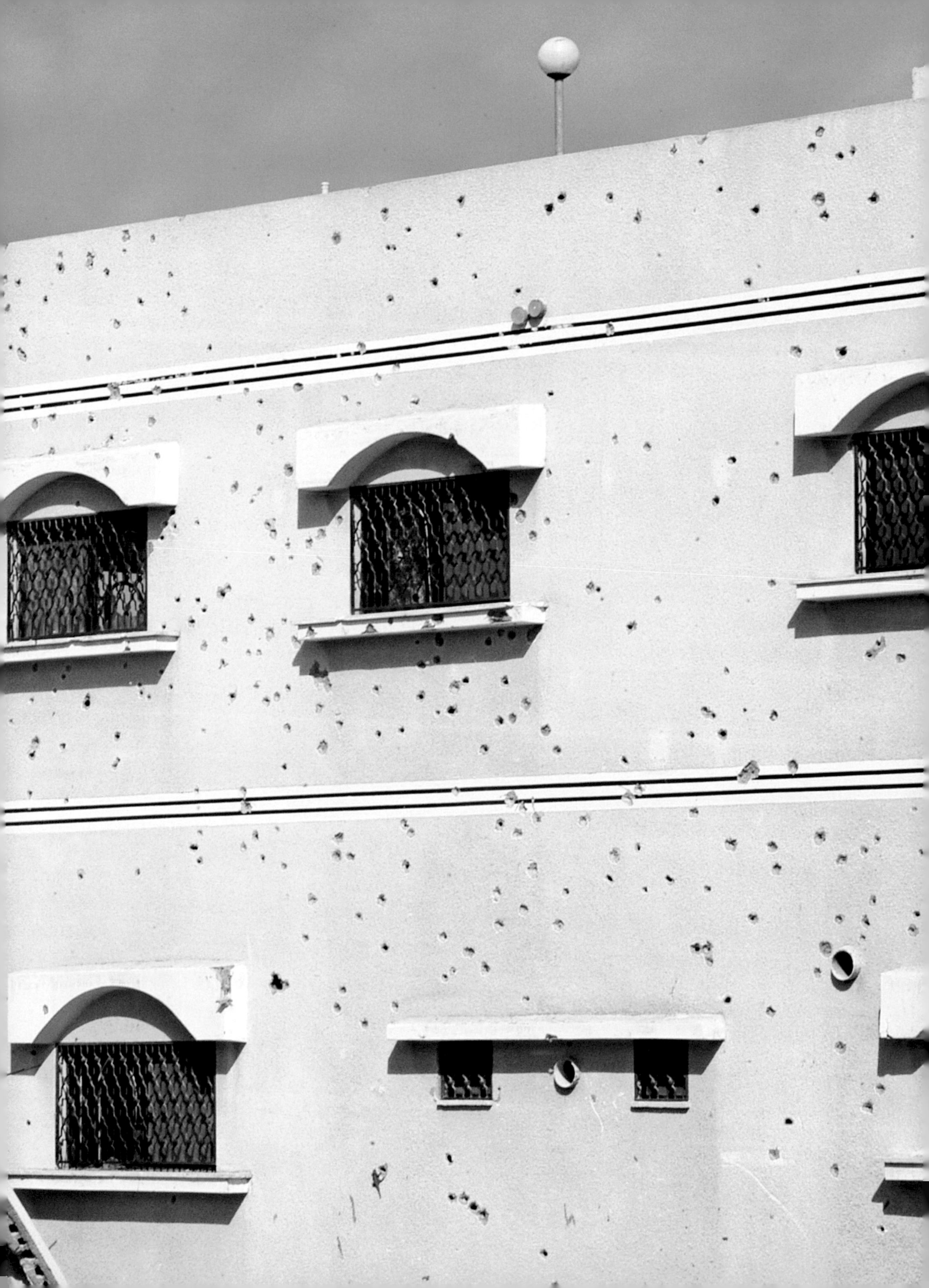

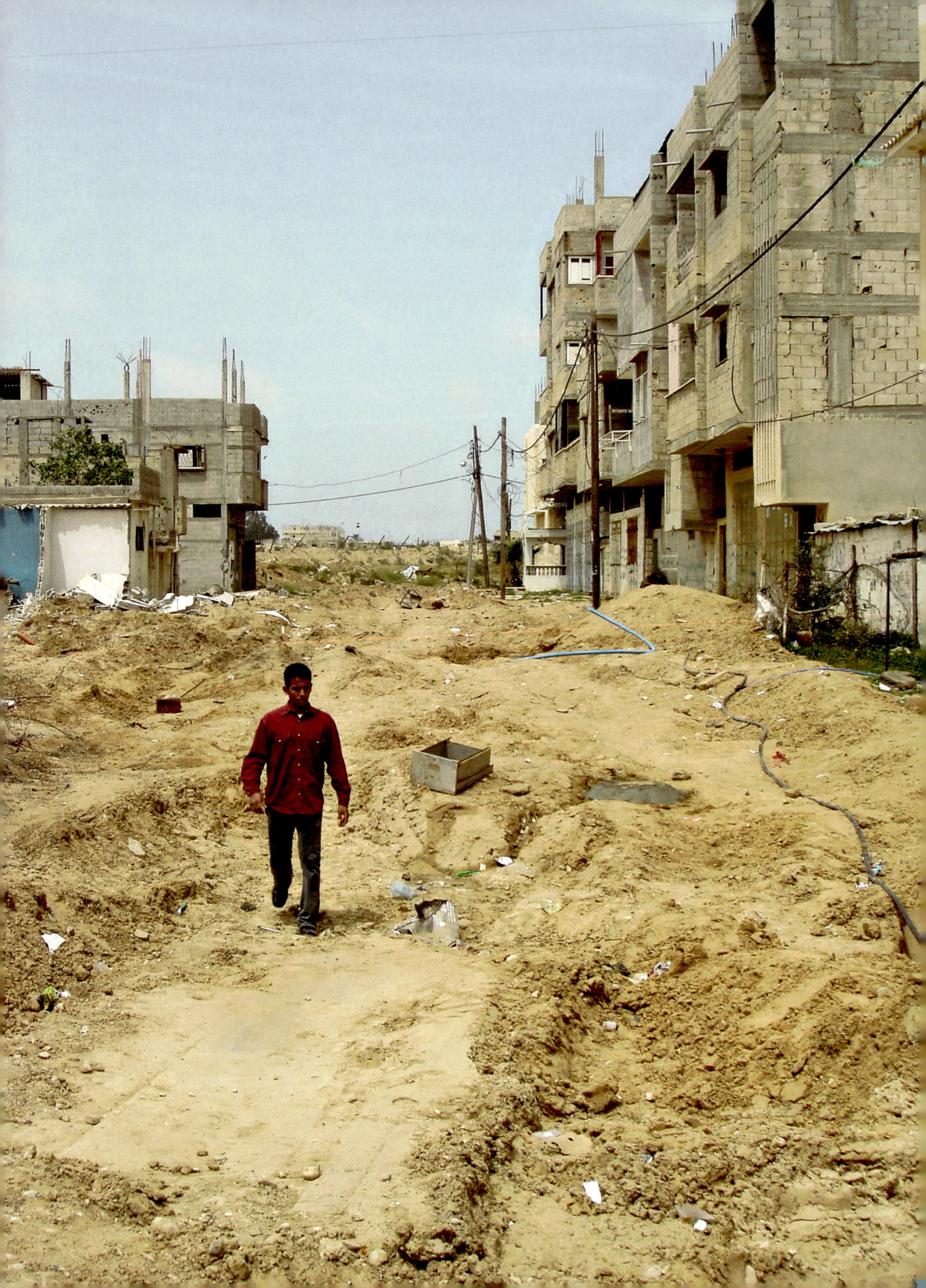

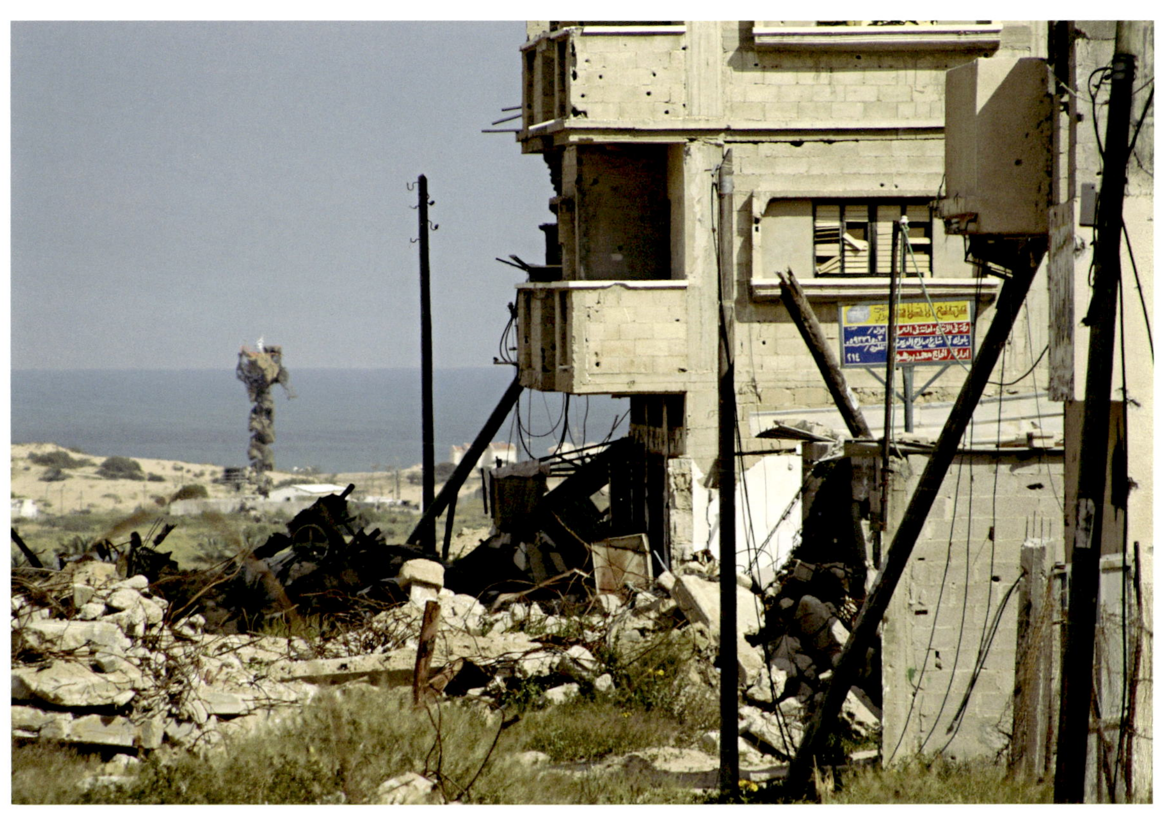

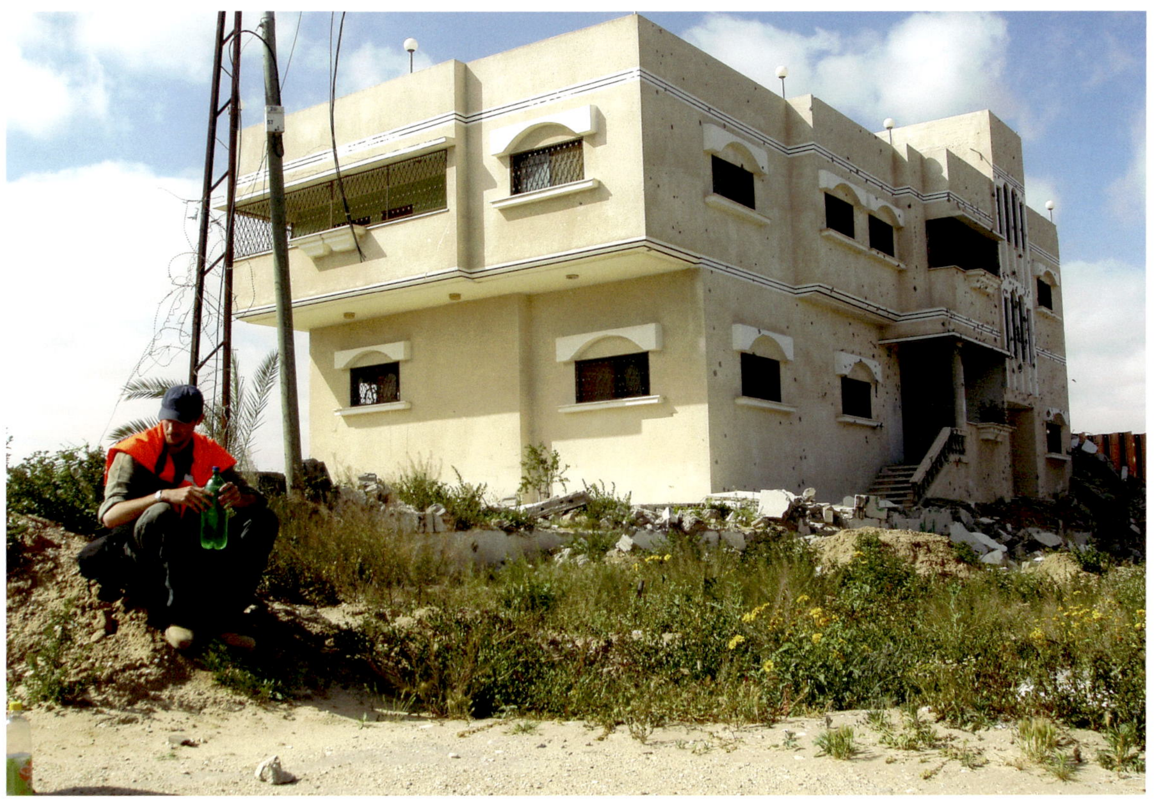

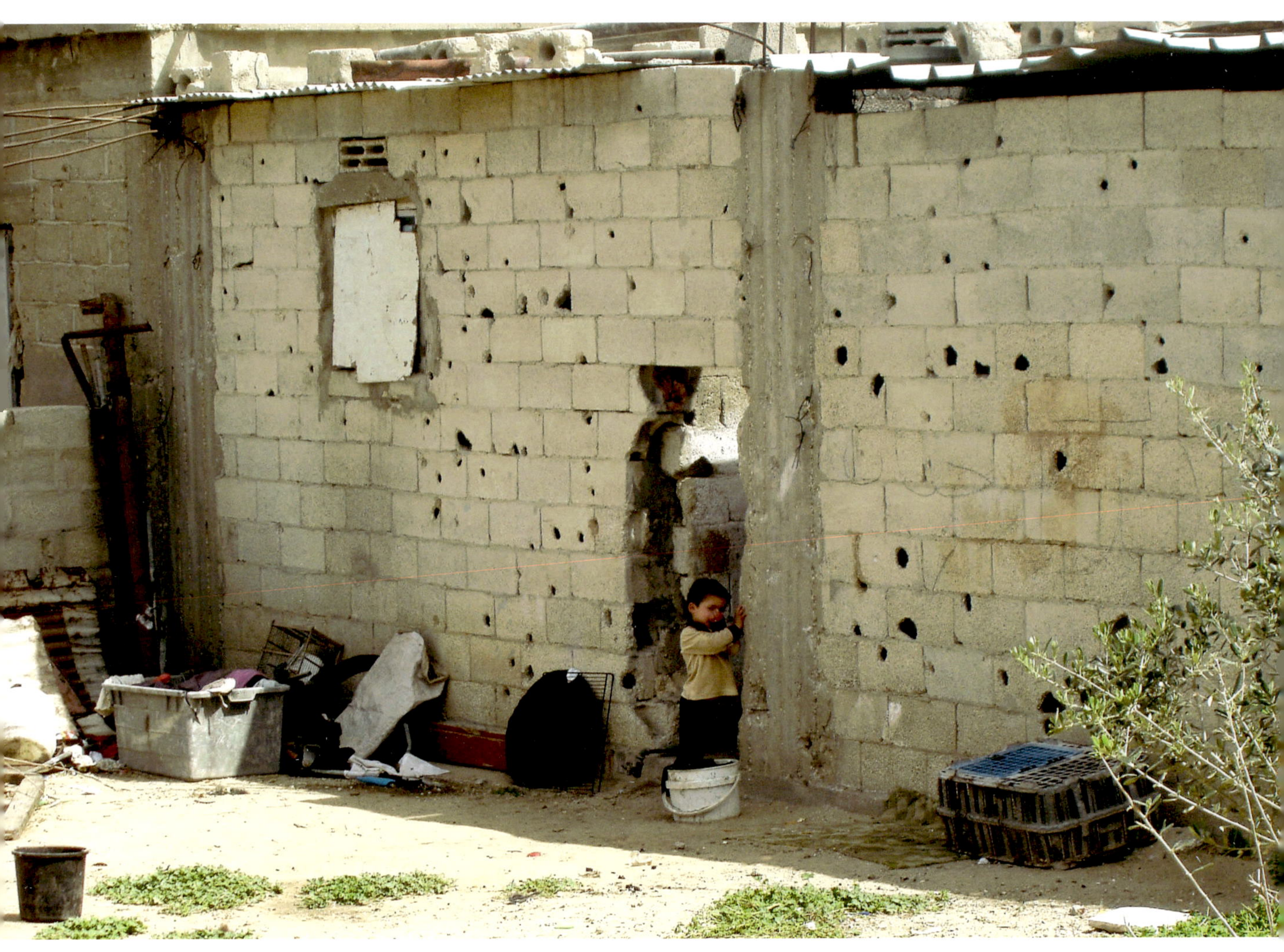

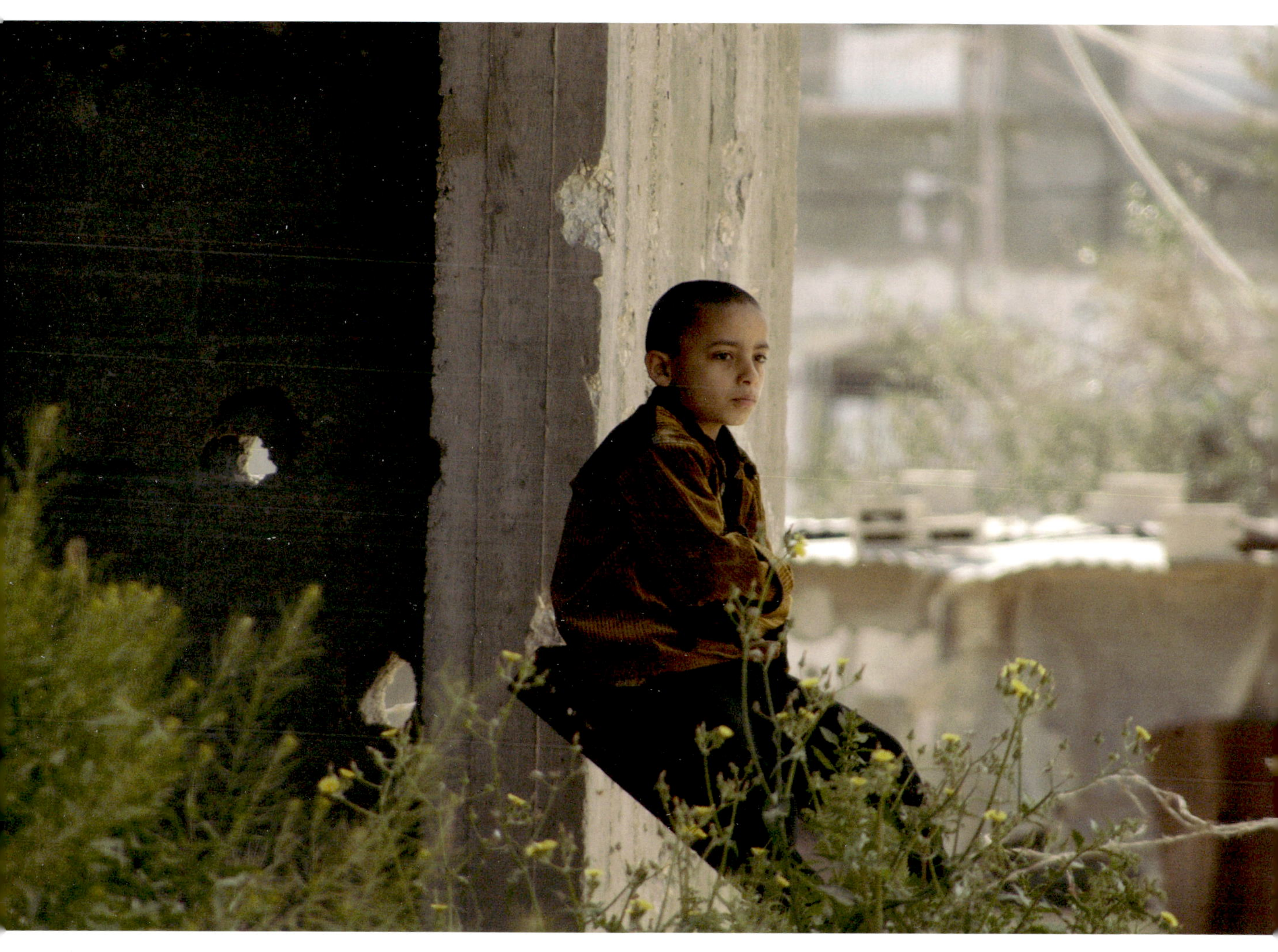

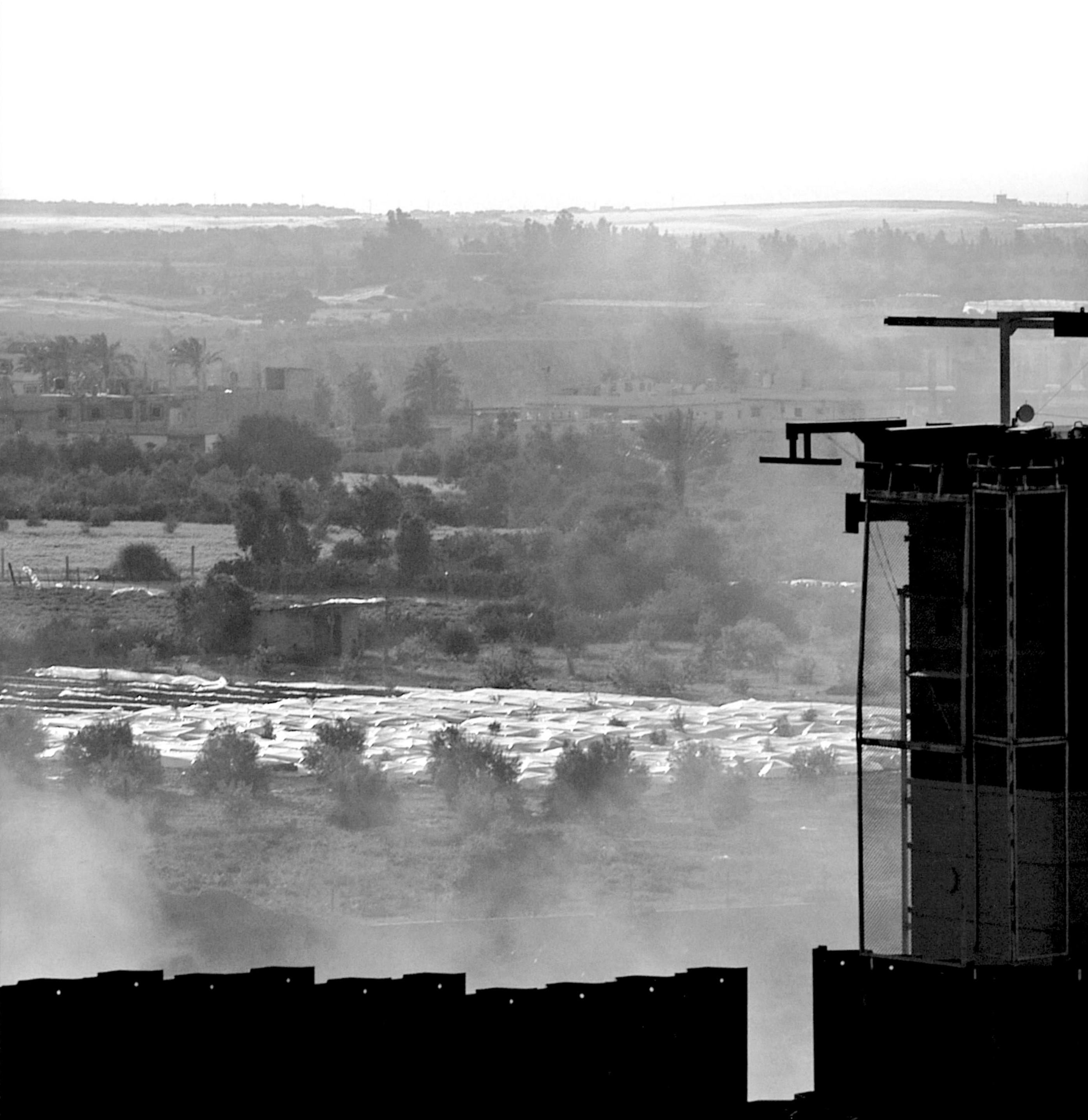

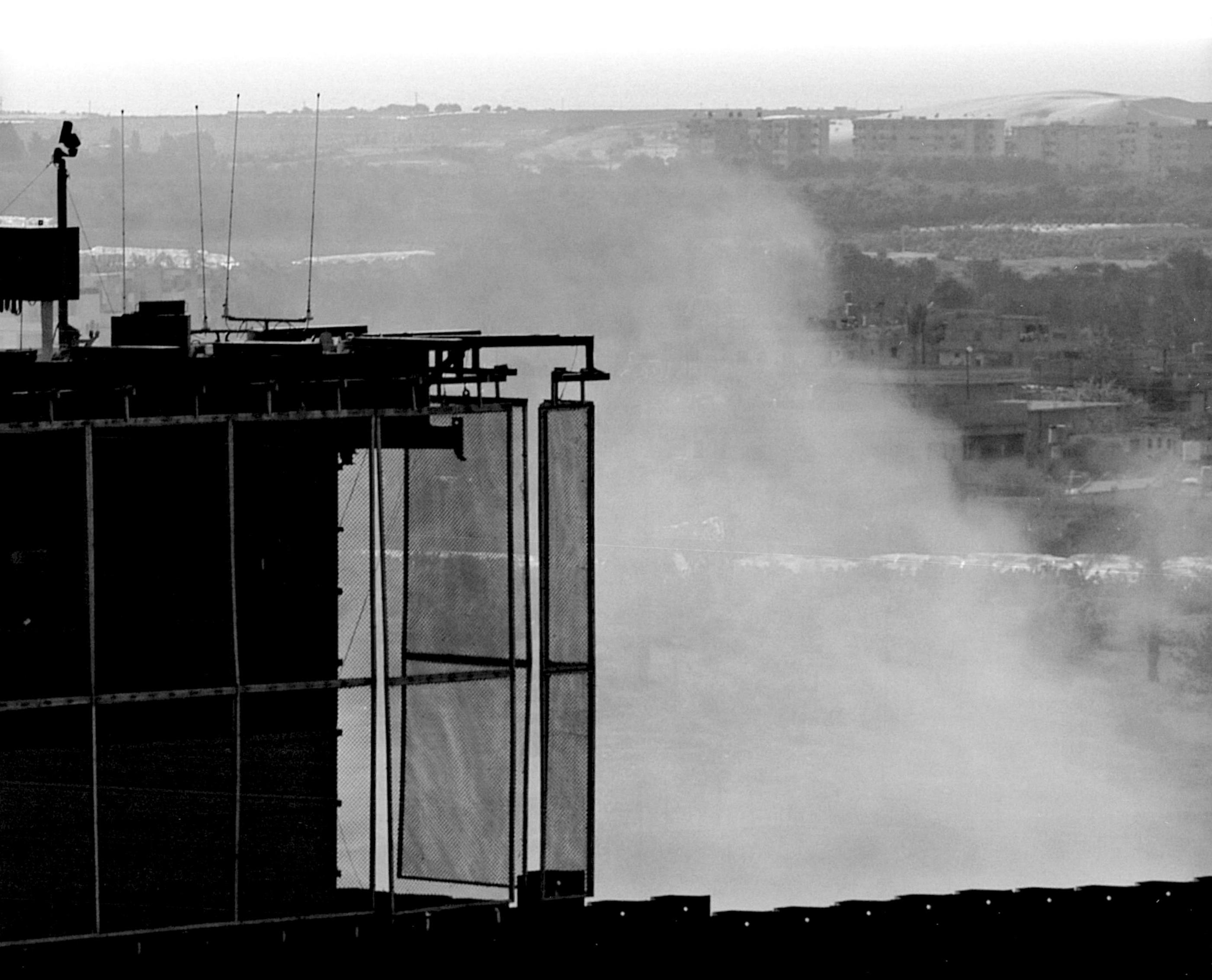

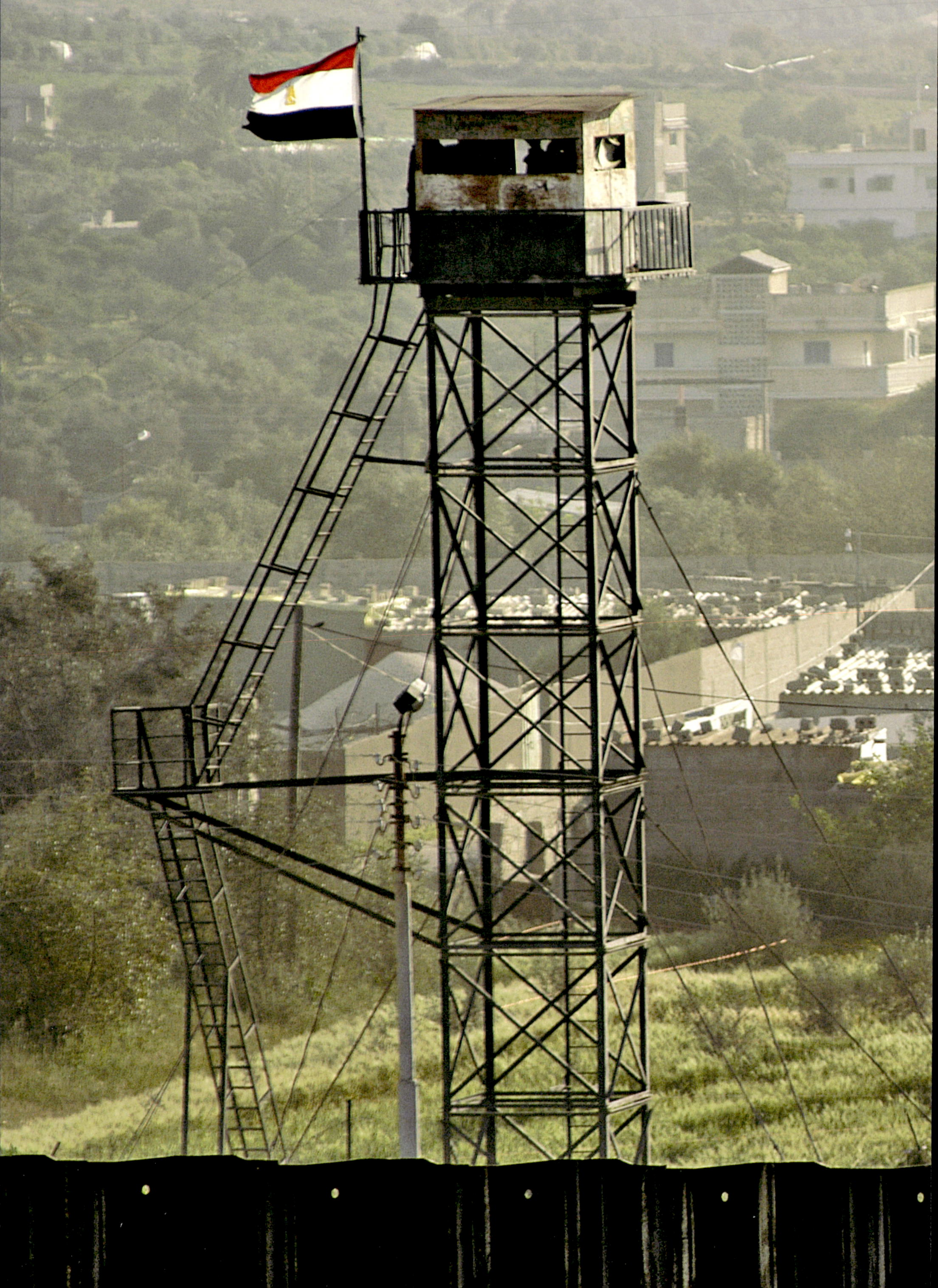

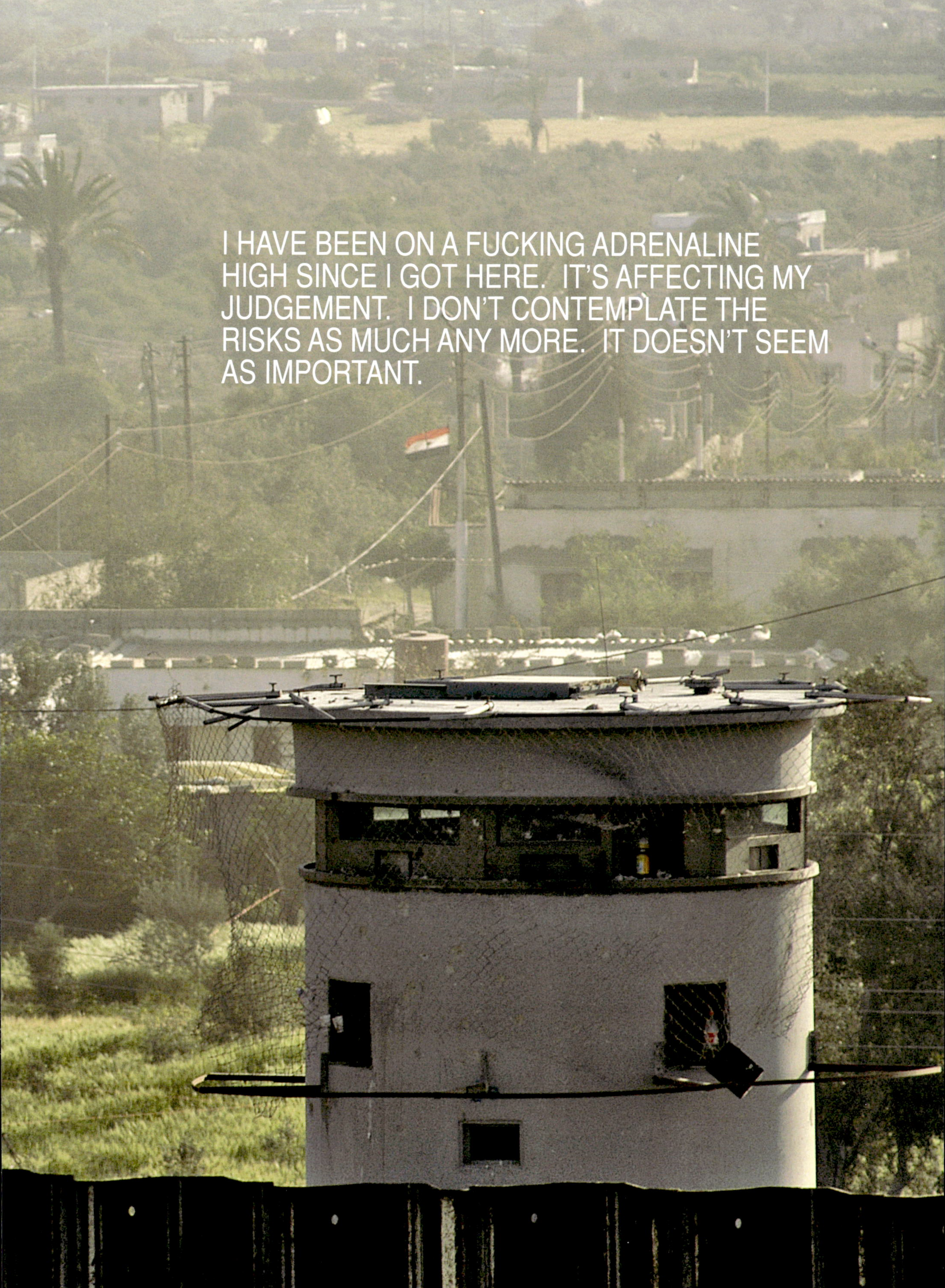
I HAVE BEEN ON A FUCKING ADRENALINE
HIGH SINCE I GOT HERE. IT'S AFFECTING MY
JUDGEMENT. I DON'T CONTEMPLATE THE
RISKS AS MUCH ANY MORE. IT DOESN'T SEEM
AS IMPORTANT.

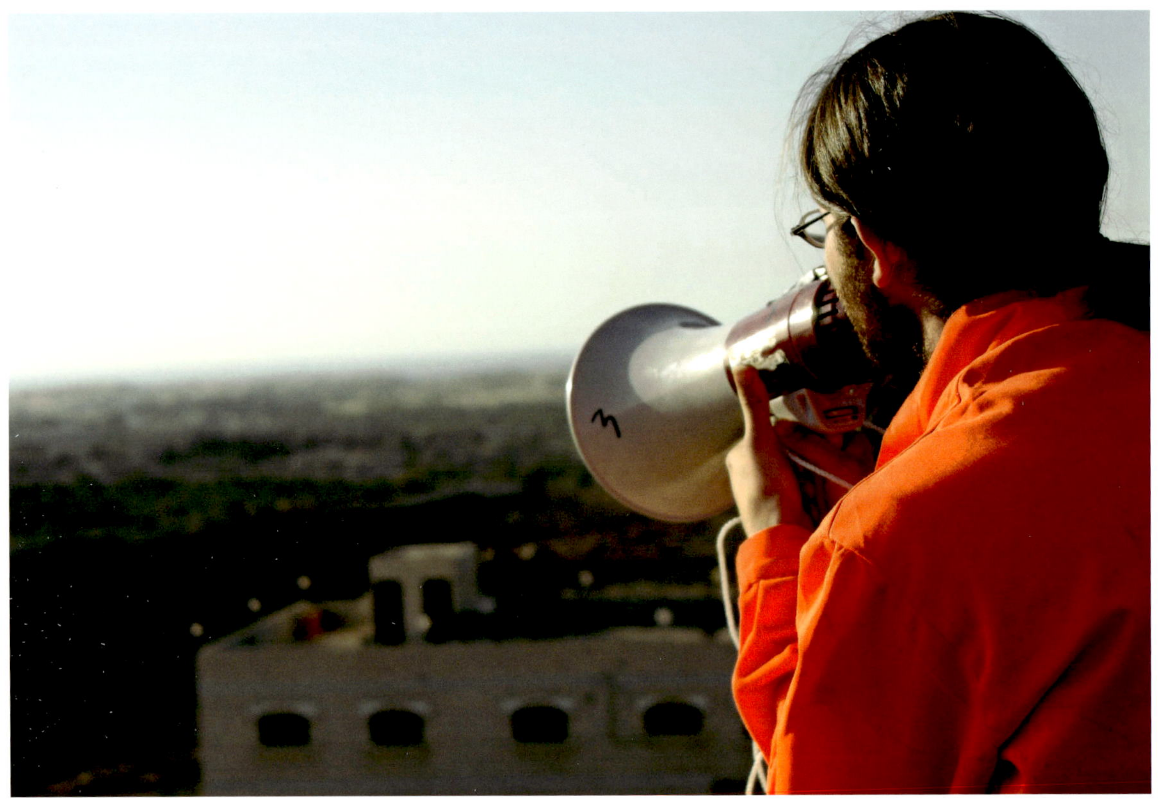
3

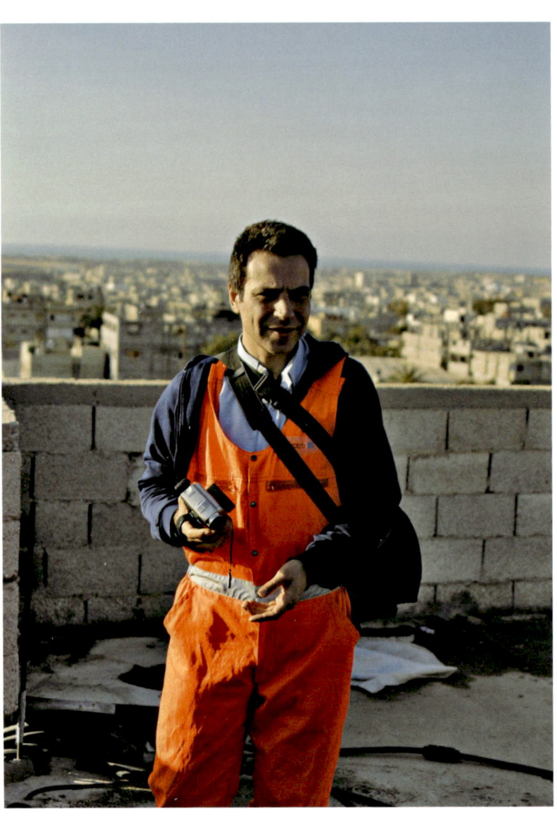

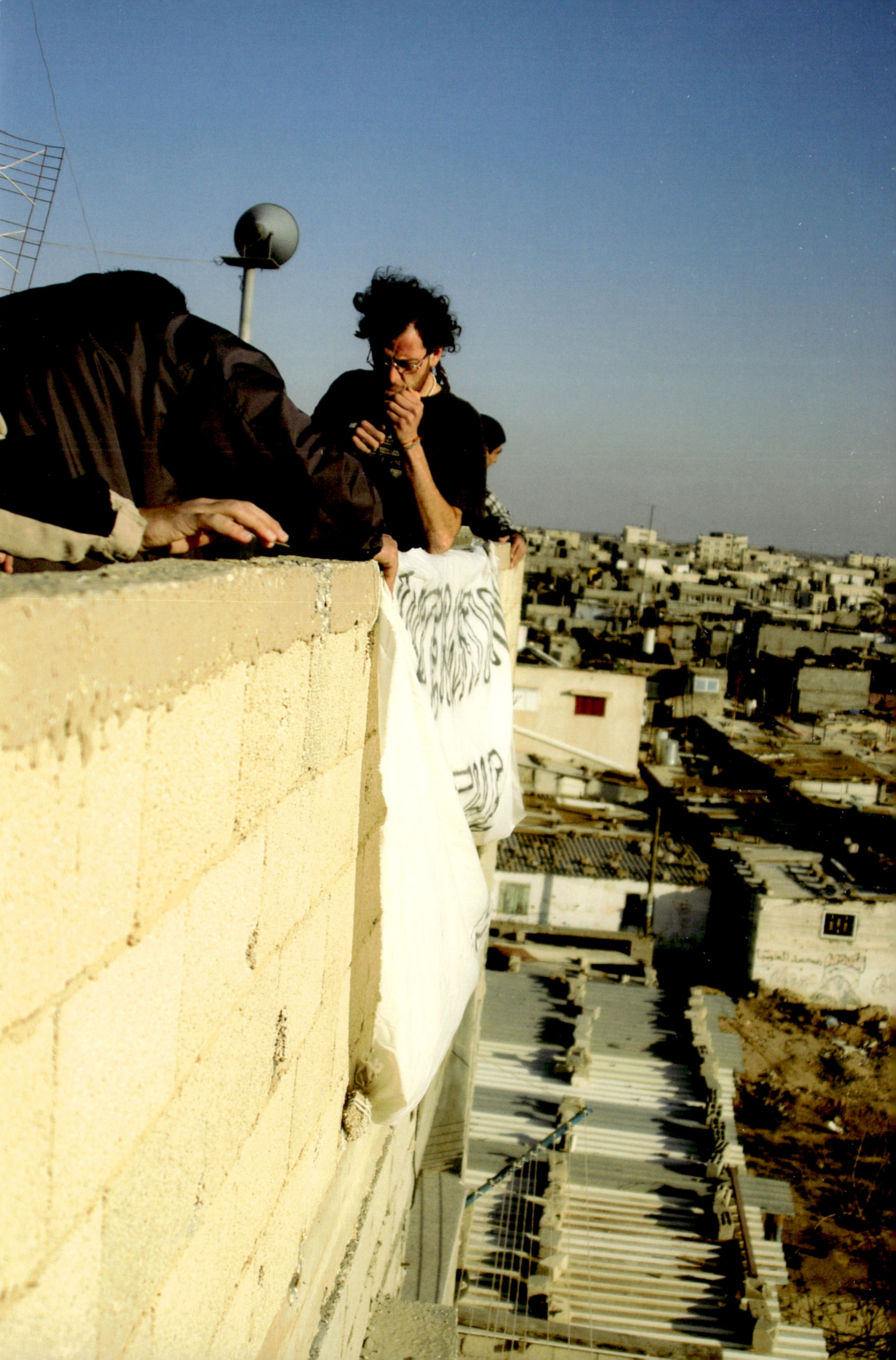

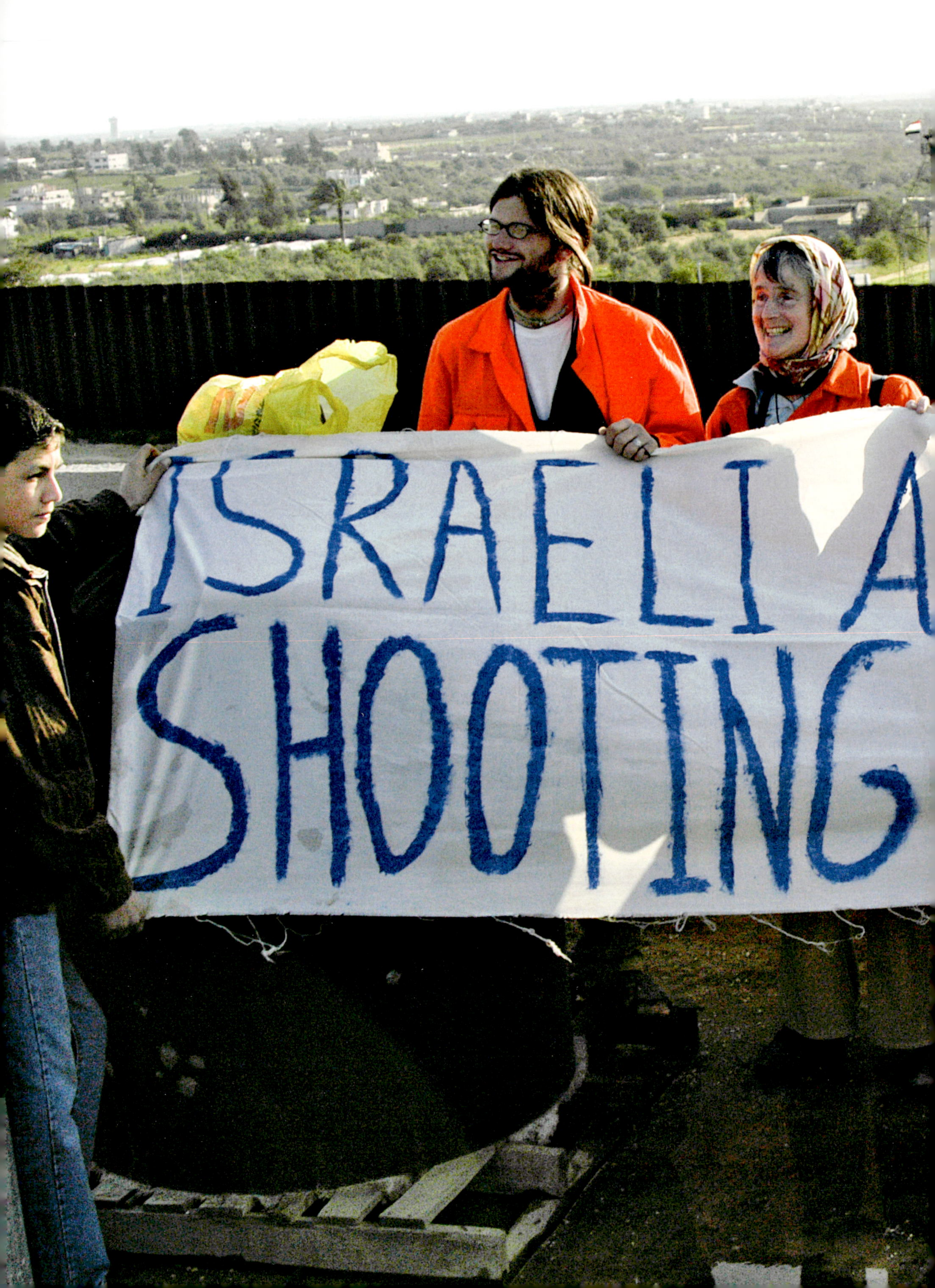
ISRAELI A
SHOOTING

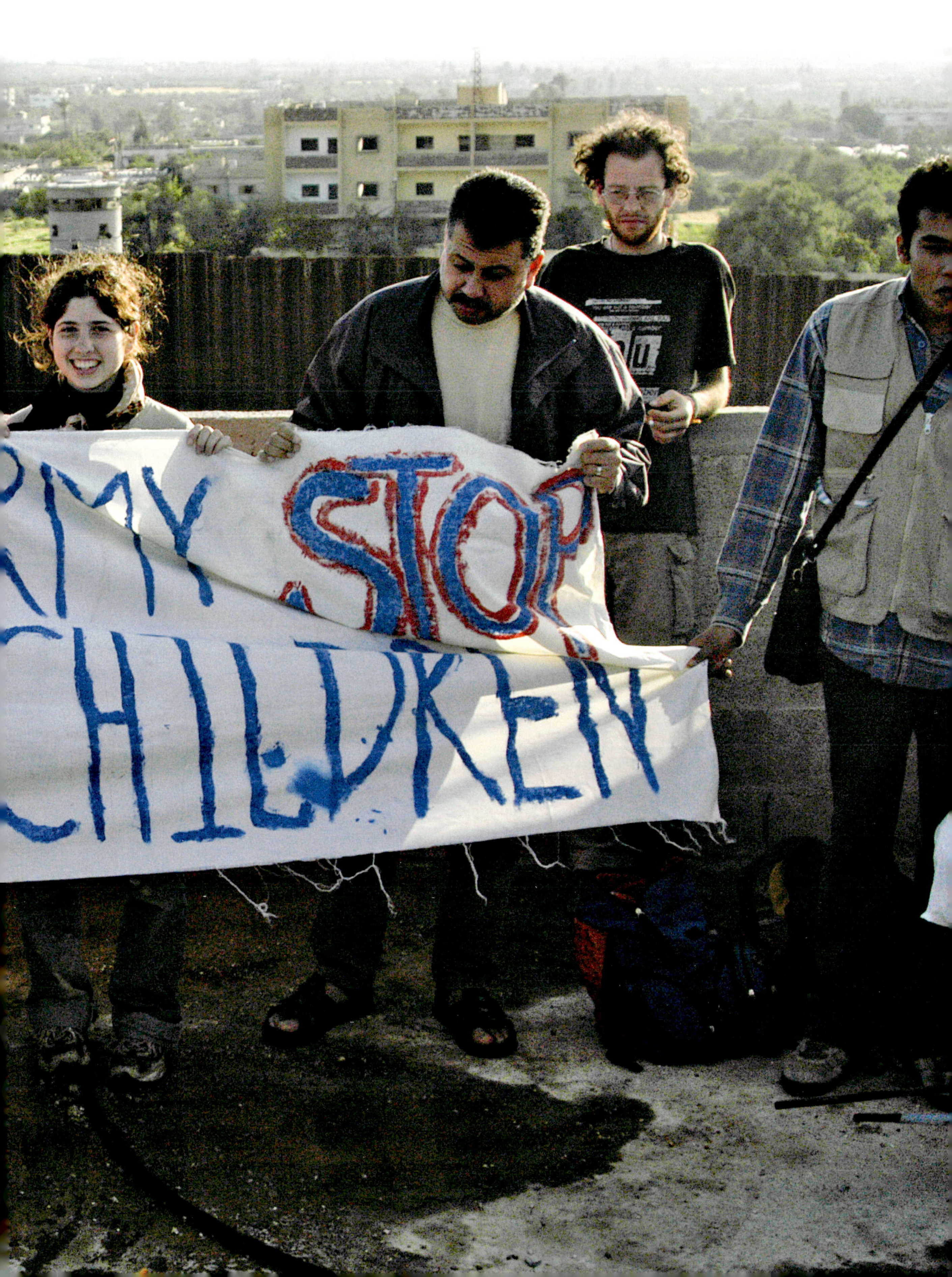

RMY STOP
CHILDREN

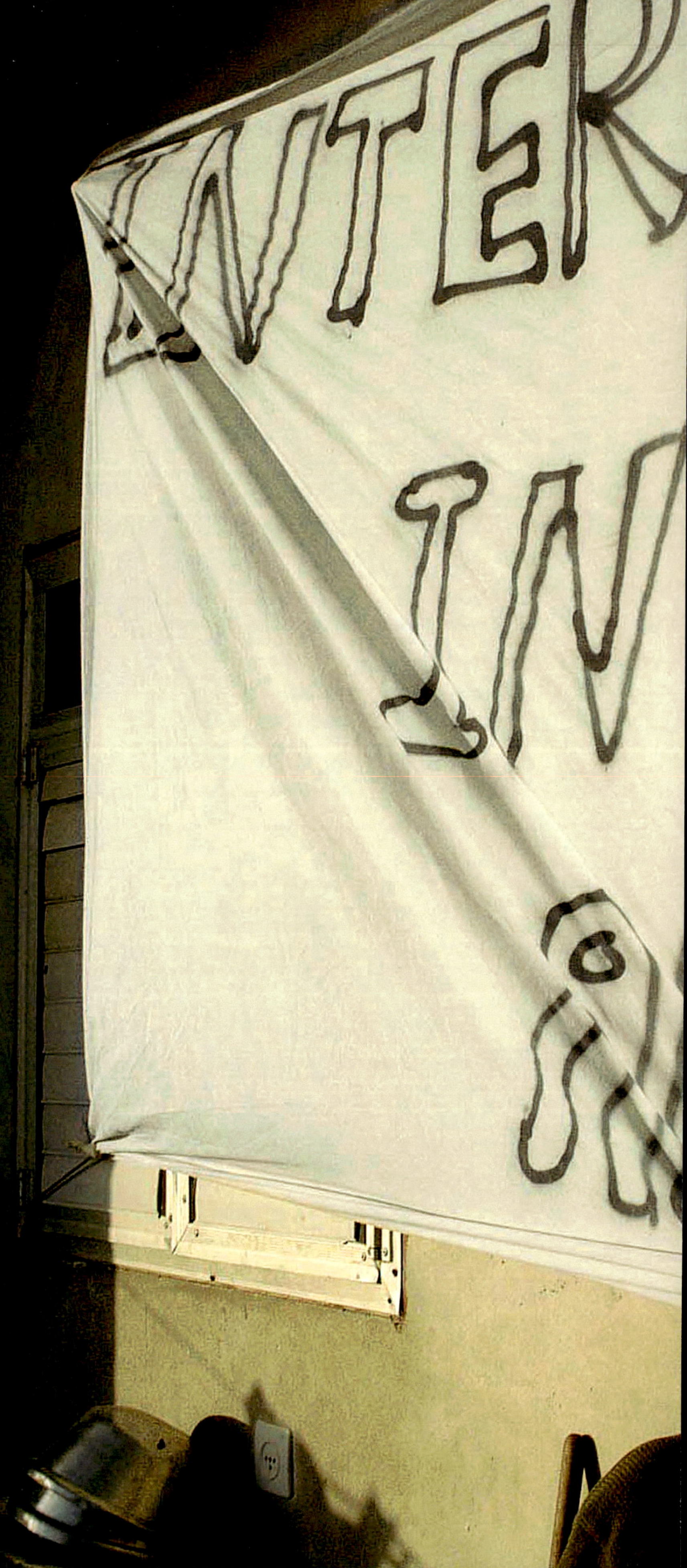
NTER
IN

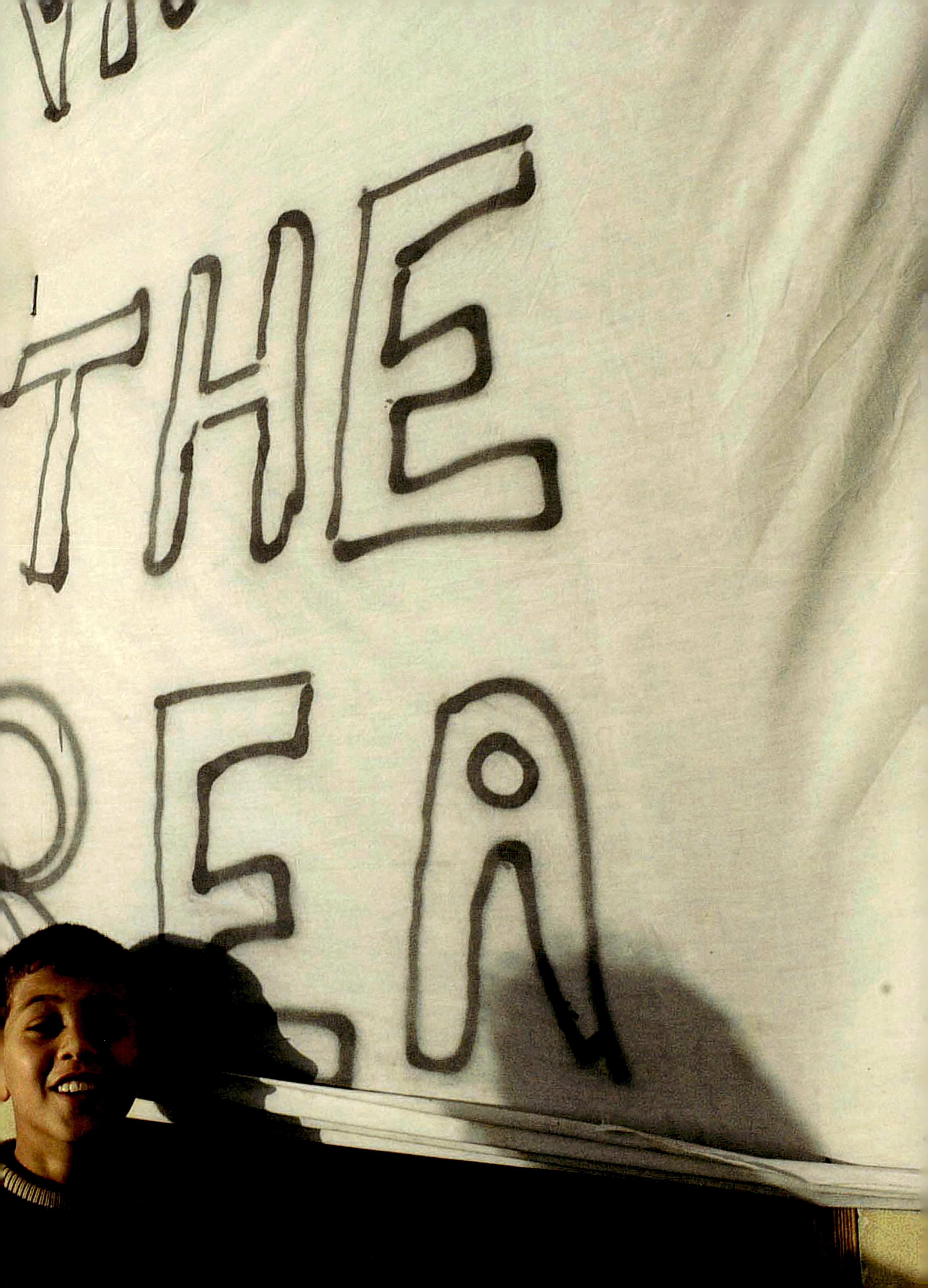
THE
REA

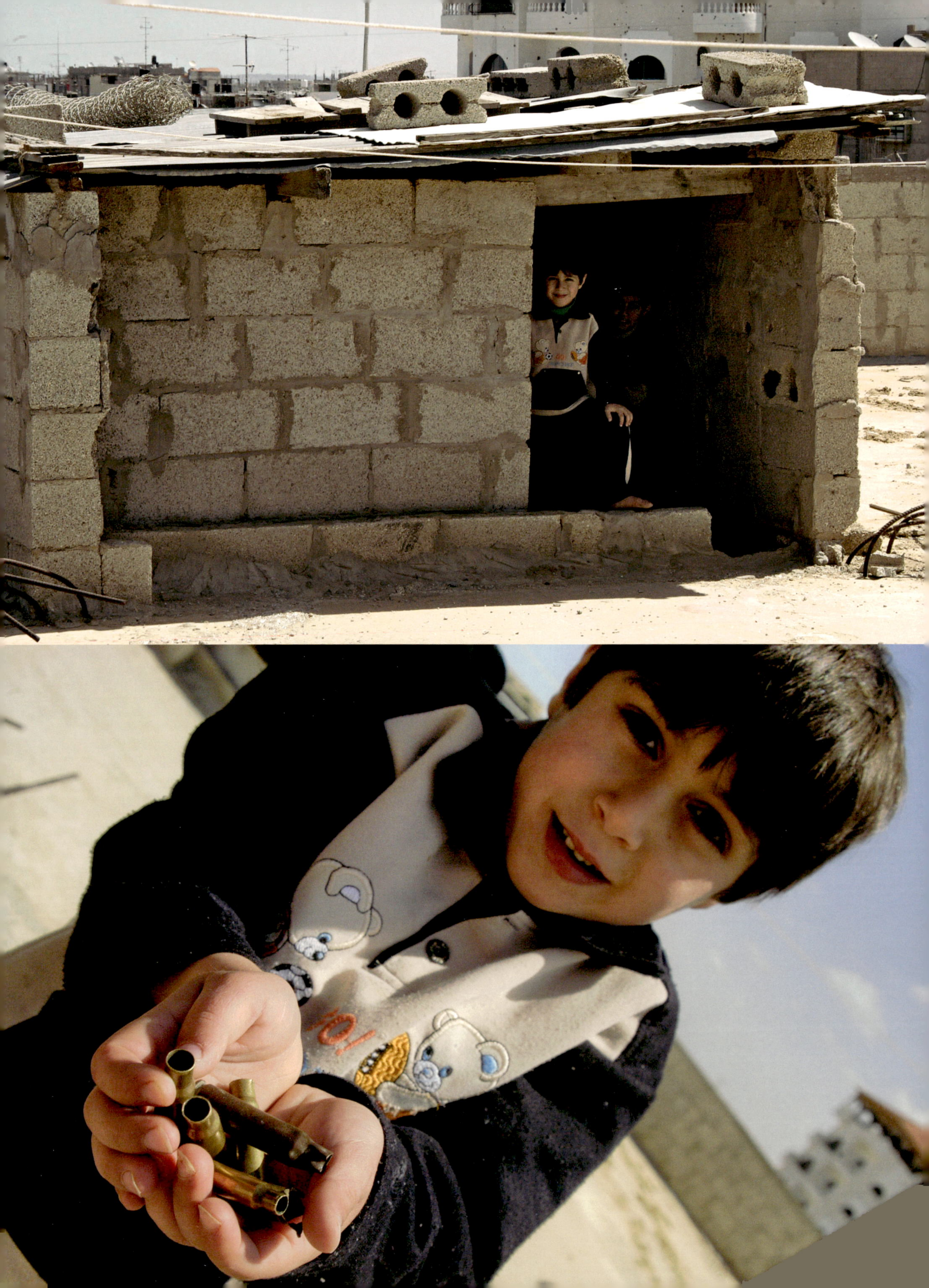

From: Thomas Hurndall <aqimaging@hotmail.com>
Subject: **more fun holiday snaps, yay!**
Date: 11 April 2003 10:13:20 GMT+01:00
To: ah@hurndalls.com, 6 more…
5 Attachments, 157 KB Save ▾ Quick Look

Hi all,

these are all images I've taken recently from one site "on the front line". There's a family living in a house (1st image) that is directly in front of a recently constructed IDF (Israeli Defence Forces) tower (2nd image). The IDF don't want anyone in the house, so they are using it for target practice (which is common practice, this house is one of hundreds). I've spent a lot of time there and there are no 'militants' or 'gunmen', just 35 people (30 of whom are women, under 16, or both) who have lived there for years. They are all extended family, as is common in the middle east, and are simply the families of the three brothers who own the house. Yesterday morning, two of the 'young' brothers were shot by snipers in the tower within two hours of each other. Both were from one of the three families. Mustafa, 19, was hit in the leg outside the front of the house, but should be alright. Rushdie, 15, was shot in the throat, while in the bathroom (through a misted glass window) and has been taken to a hospital in Gaza city. Ironically, his best hope for survival is if his family pay $4000 and apply to take him to Israel for treatment. They don't have the money, and Rushdie is still in critical condition. The next three photos are of the kids still there, as are most of those in the next e-mail. (notice in the 4th image of this e-mail, the water-tanks on the roof are often shot at, and when people go to fix them they, too, are targetted).
The last image in the next e-mail is just for your amusement... yes, ok, very funny, haha

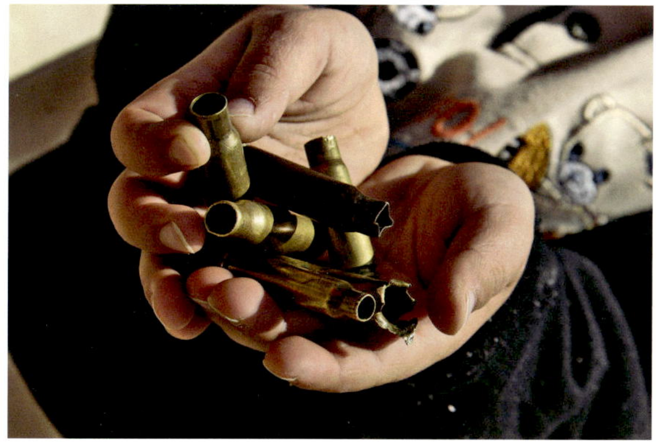

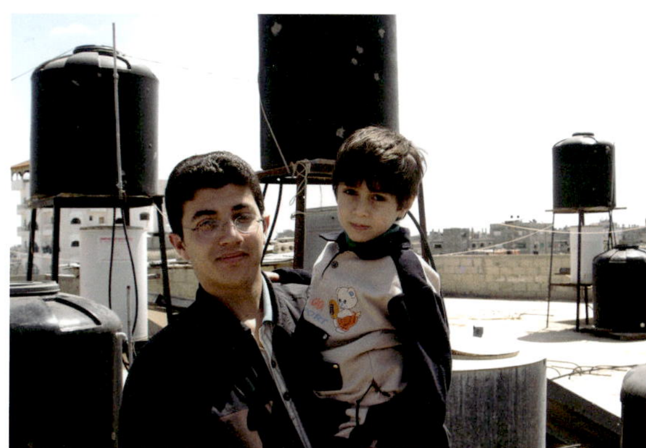

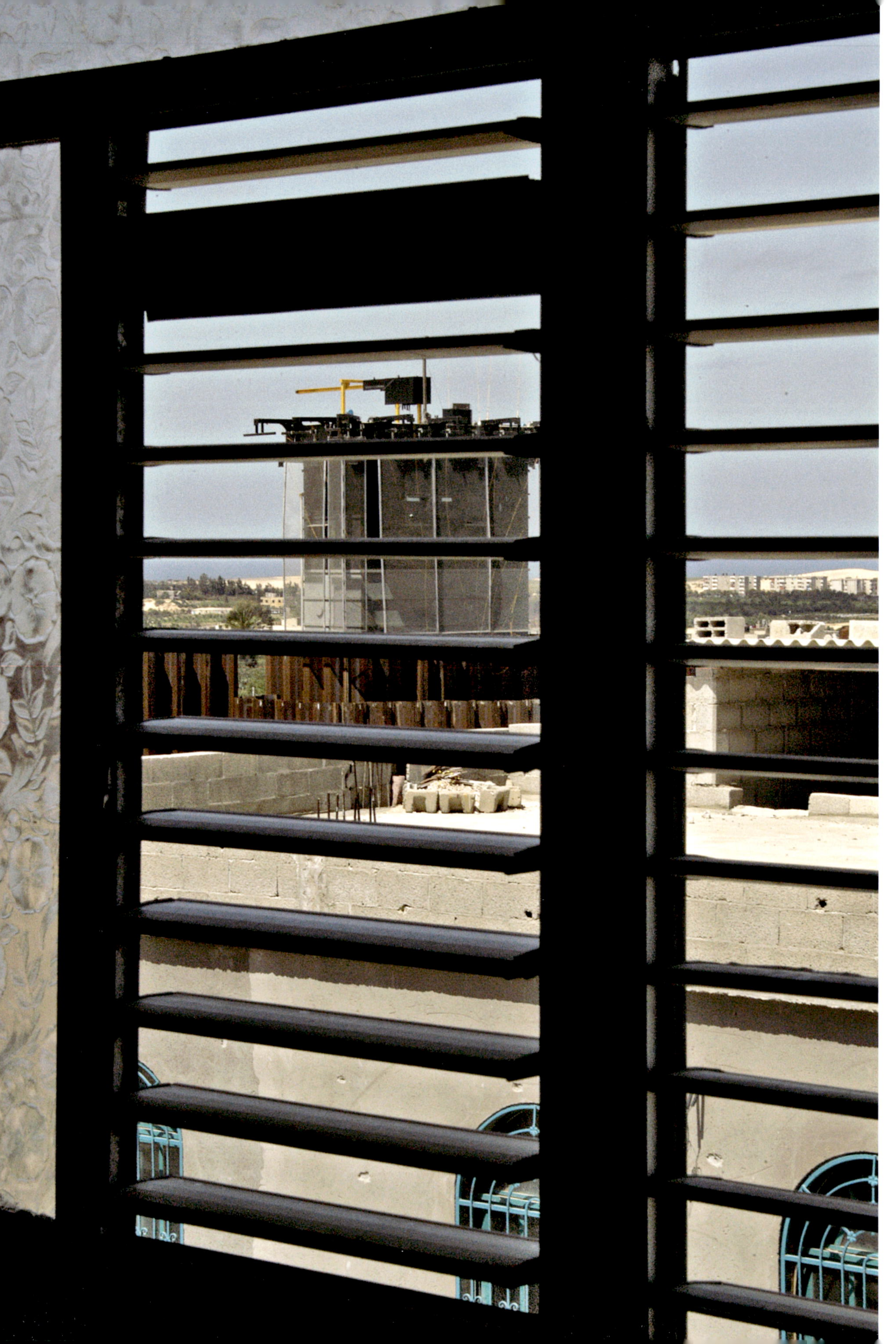

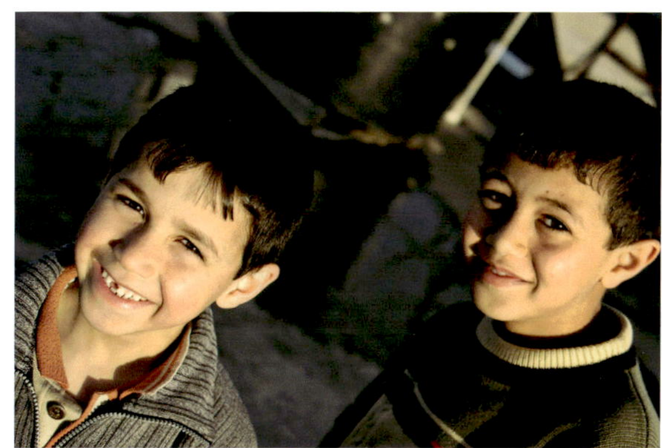
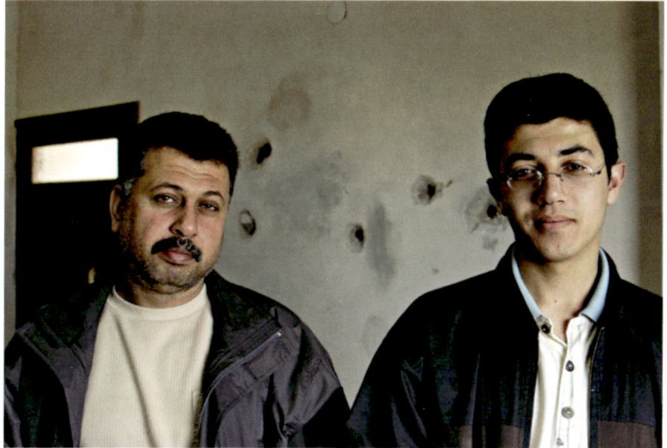
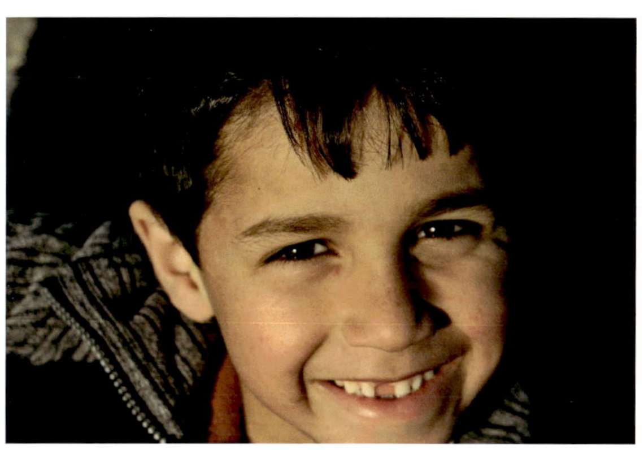
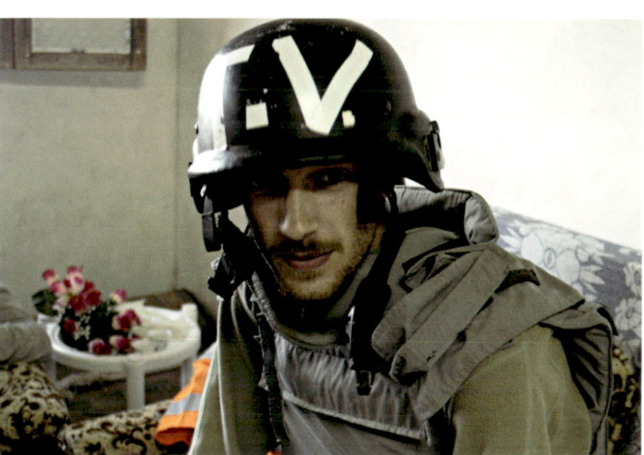

11 APRIL

There was pretty heavy fire last night.
   I was at Abu Jamil's and the IDF tower 50m
away came under mortar fire from 'resistance'.
The mortars wouldn't do a huge amount of
damage to the armoured towers, but all hell
broke loose in retaliation.

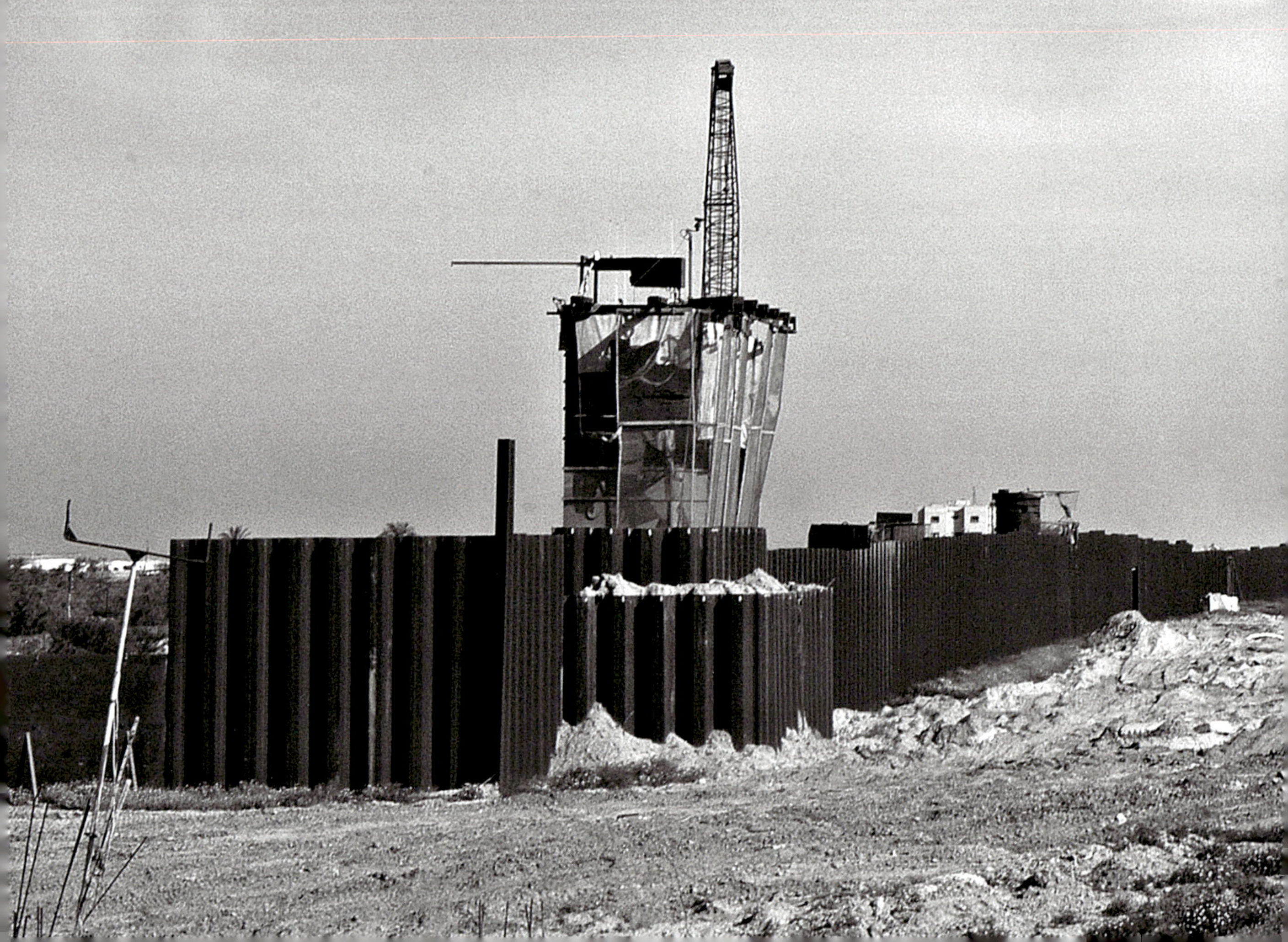

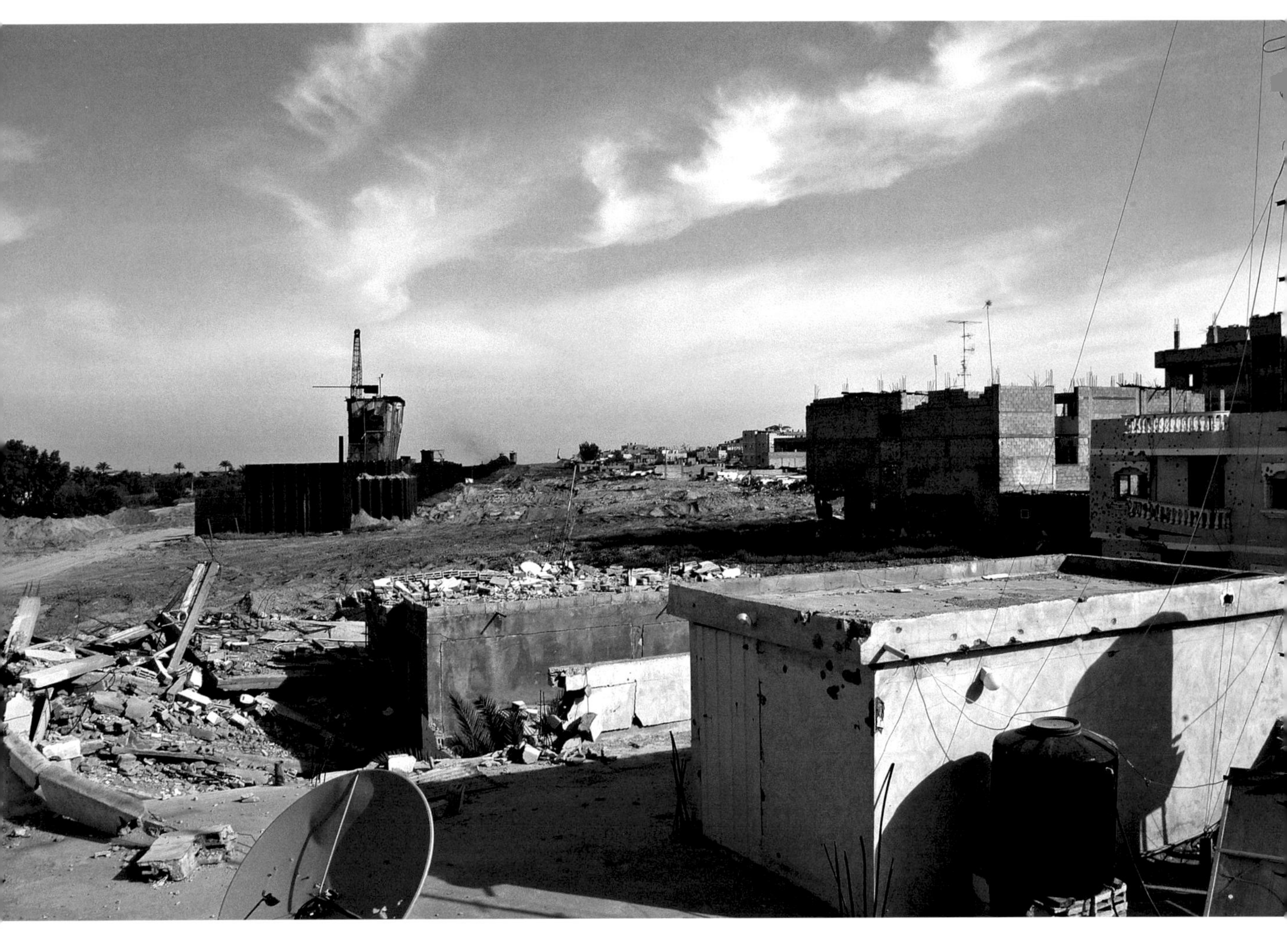

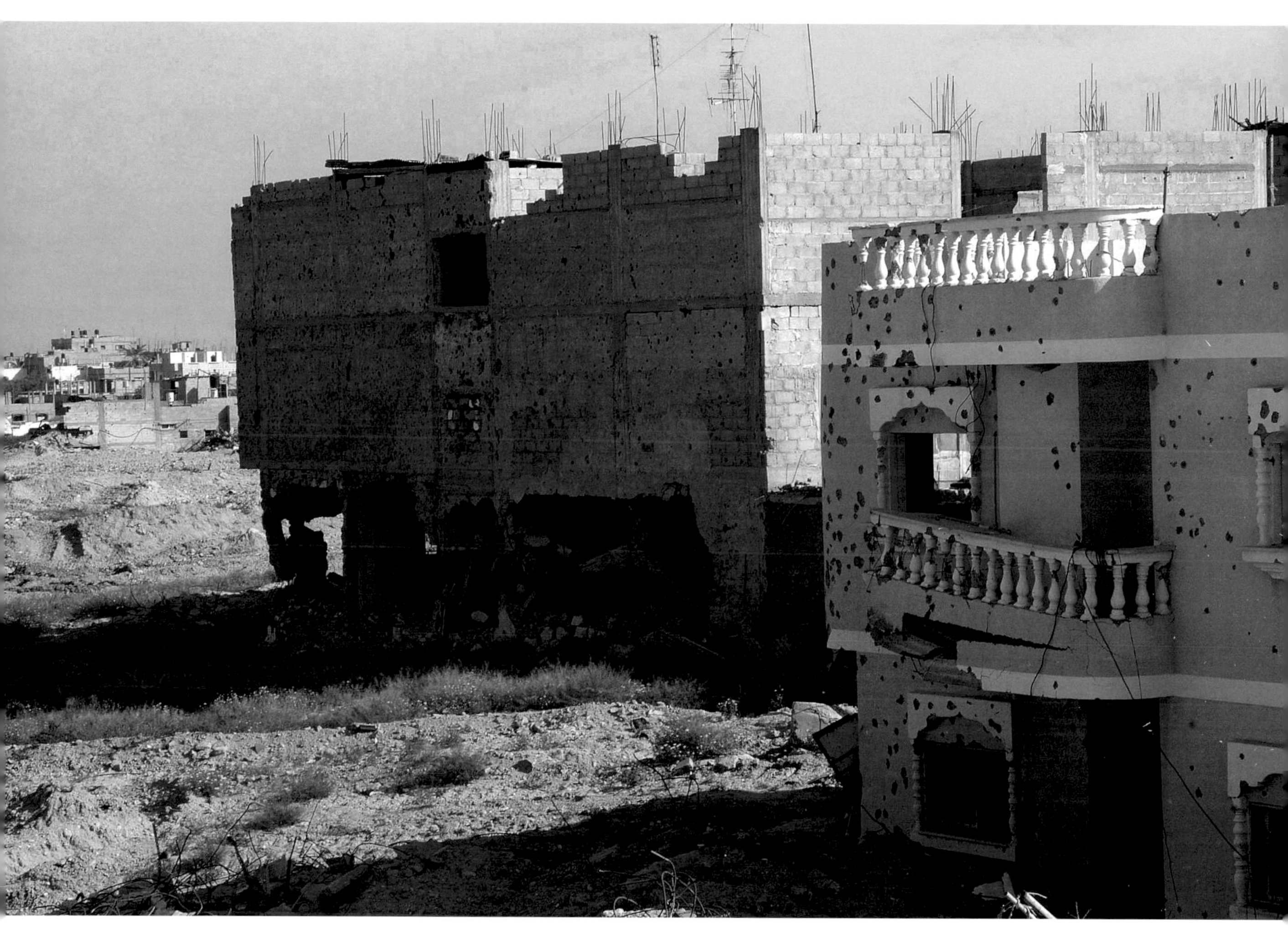

I peer over the edge,
but can't look down.
To lean over would be to fall
and I can only guess its height.

I have felt pain, but not my own,
I have seen power, superior or not,
its violence; an attraction,
not to be dismissed, but controlled.

The eternal fight of good or evil,
civil or primitive.
You can't run from the fight,
so hope says don't start it.

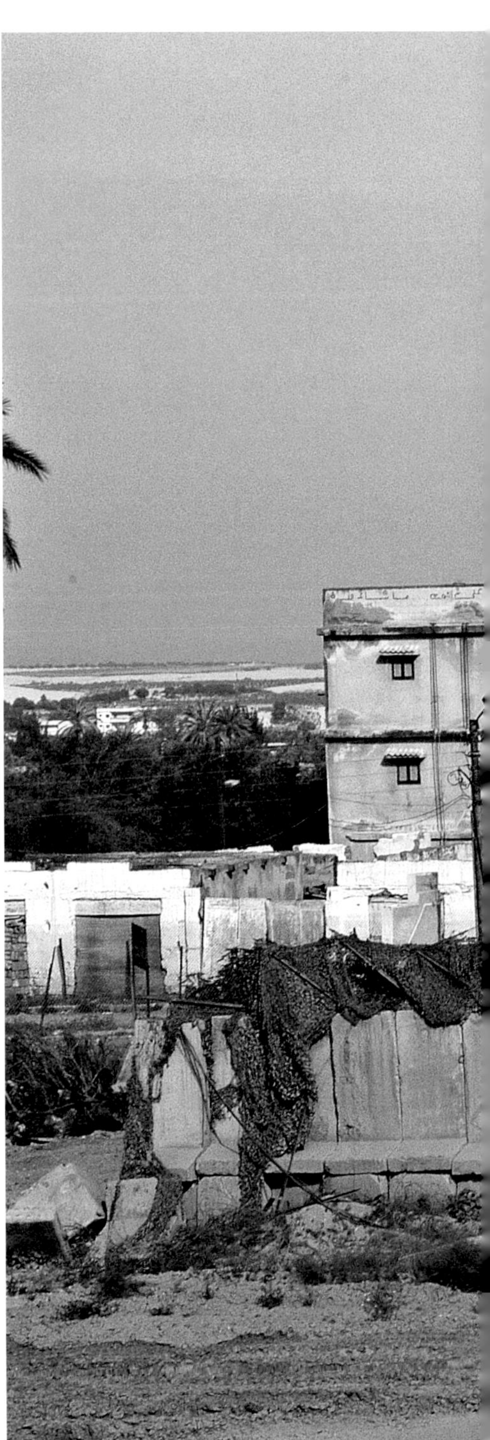

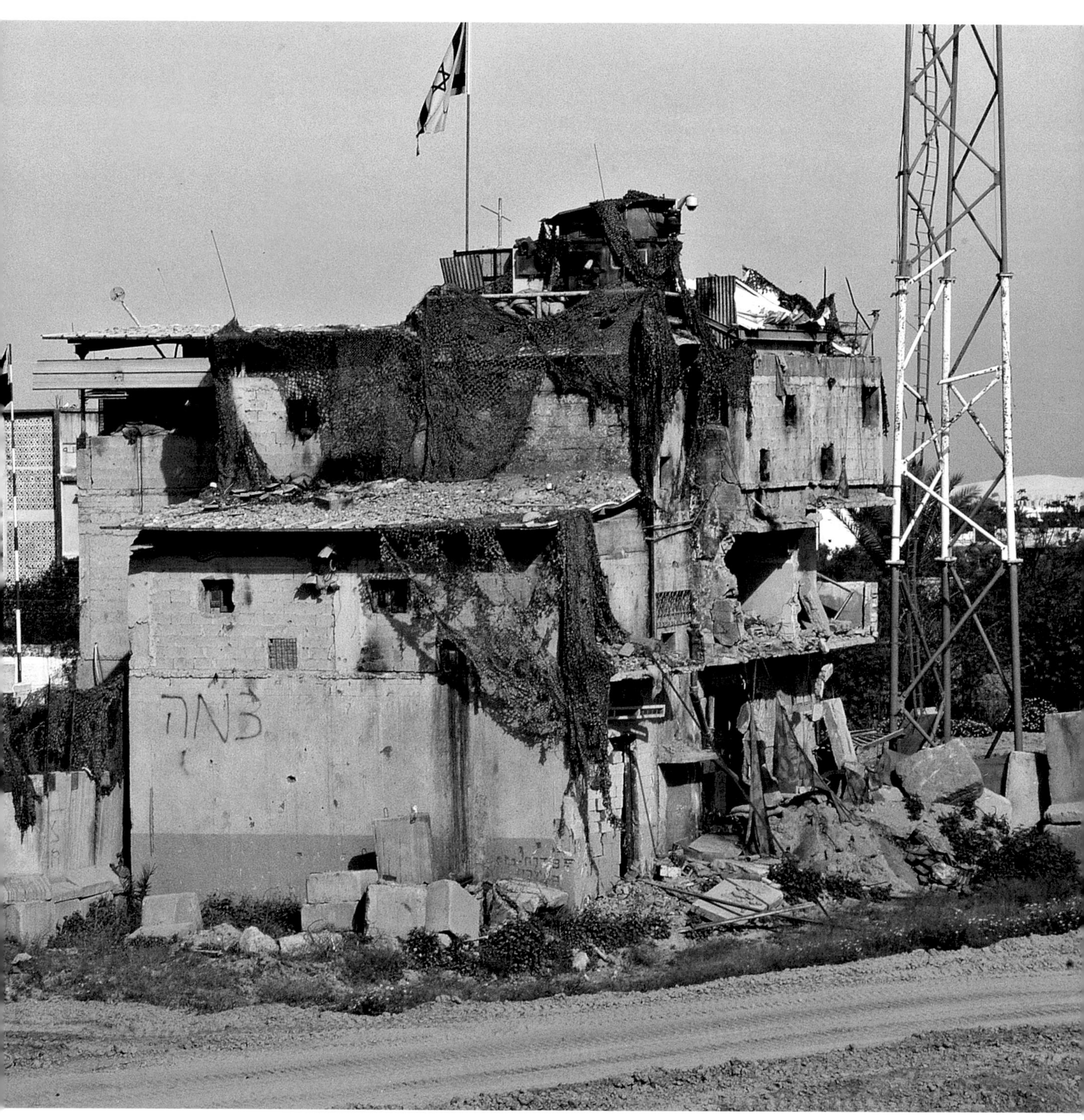

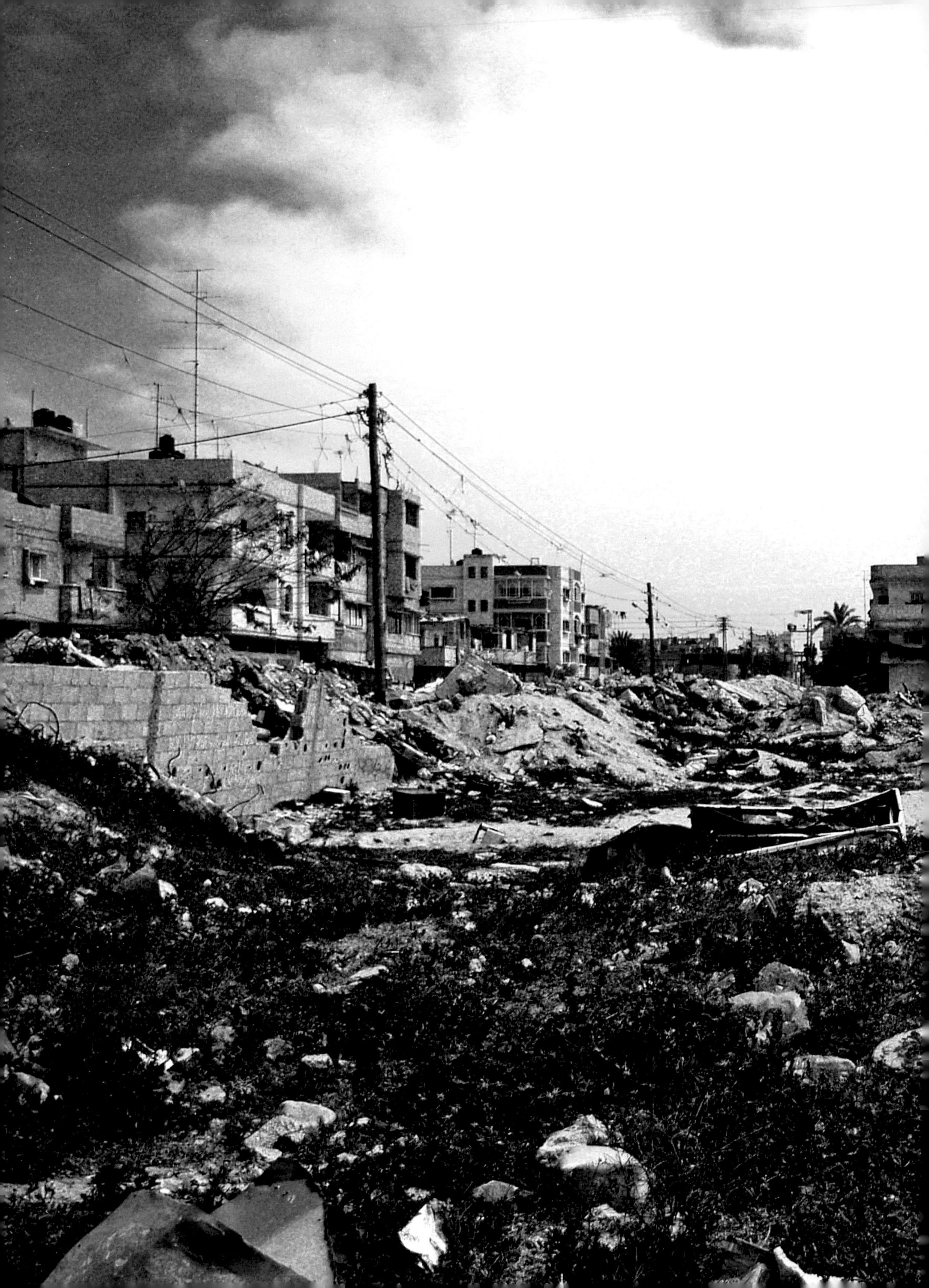

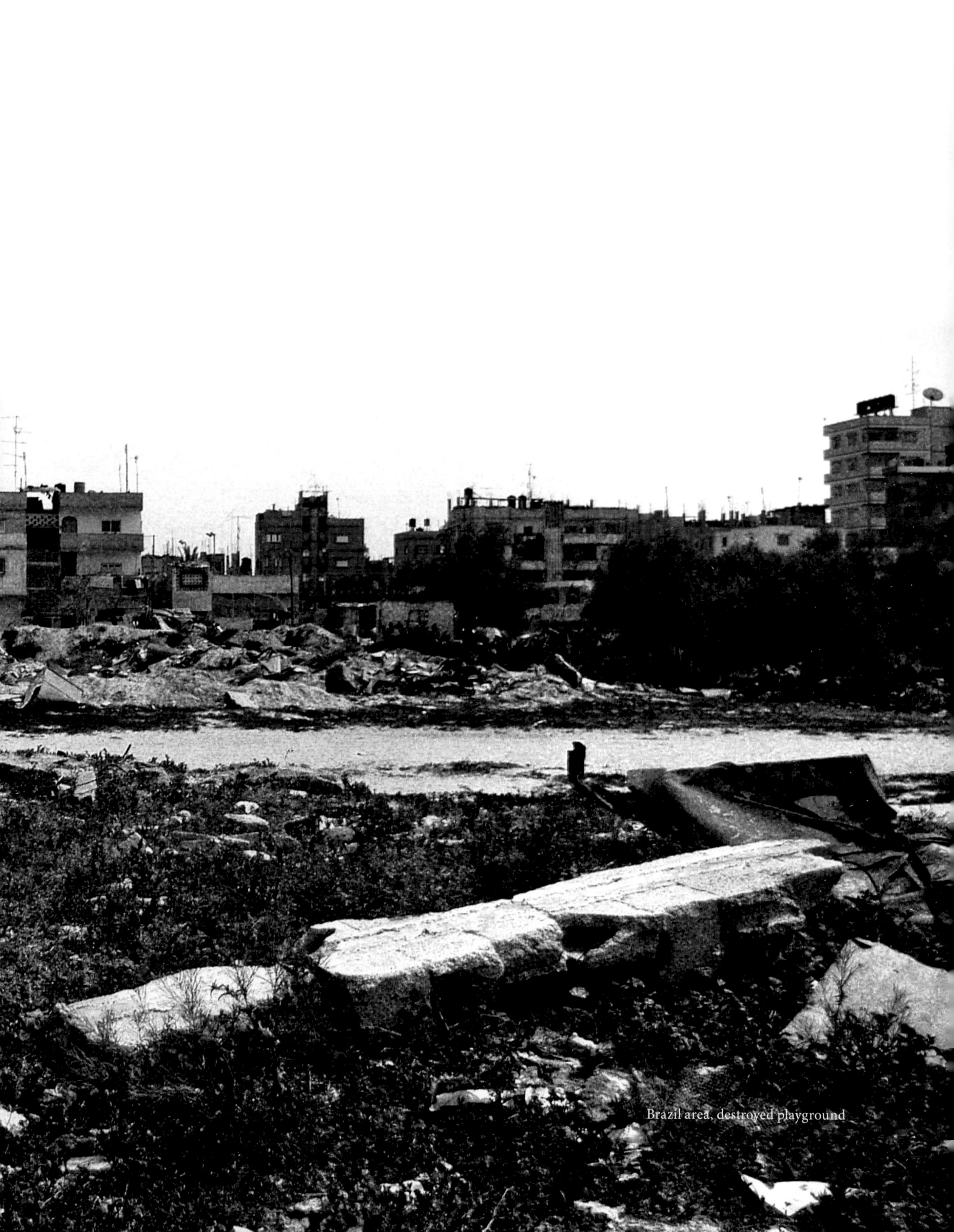

Brazil area, destroyed playground

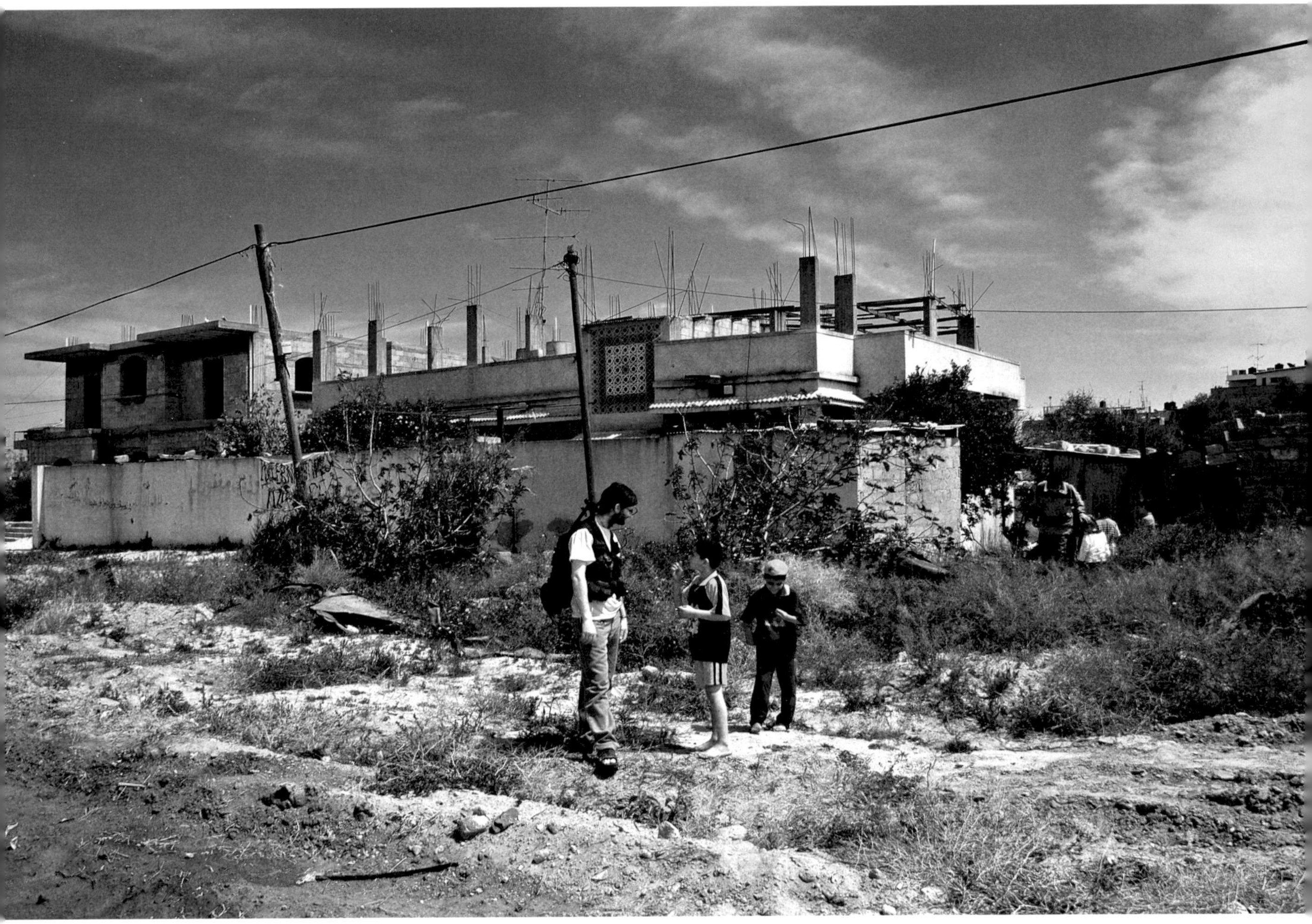

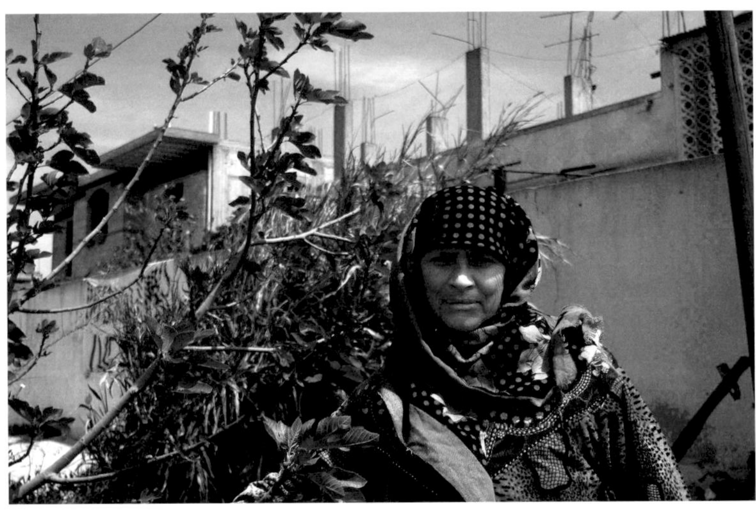

Above left and right: Foad
Al Shaer's farm
Below left and right: Foad Al Shaer's
mother and children.

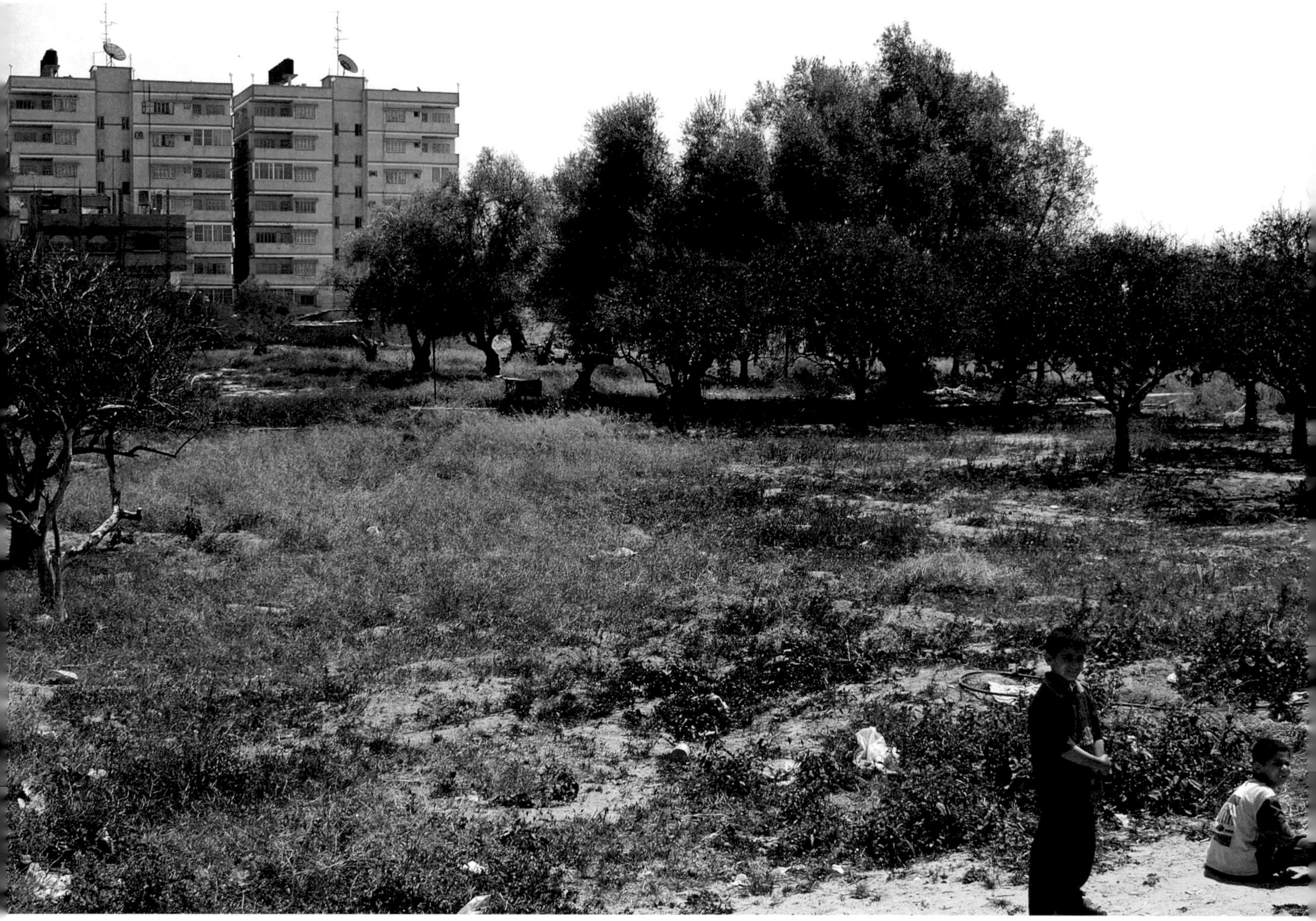

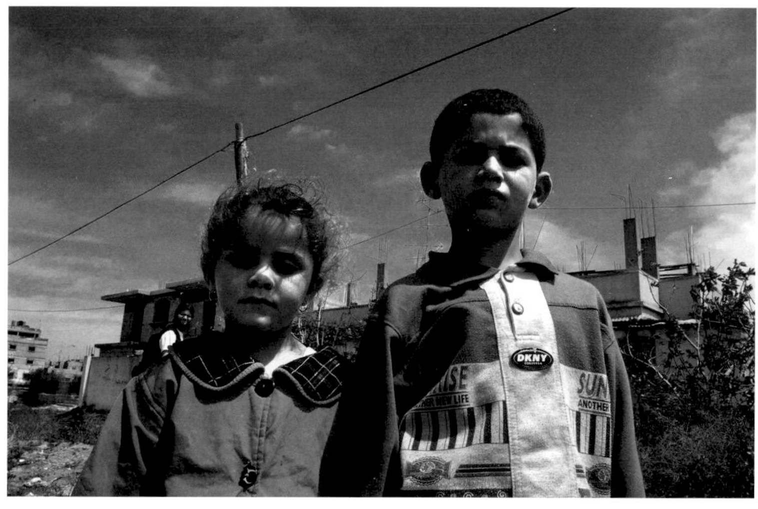

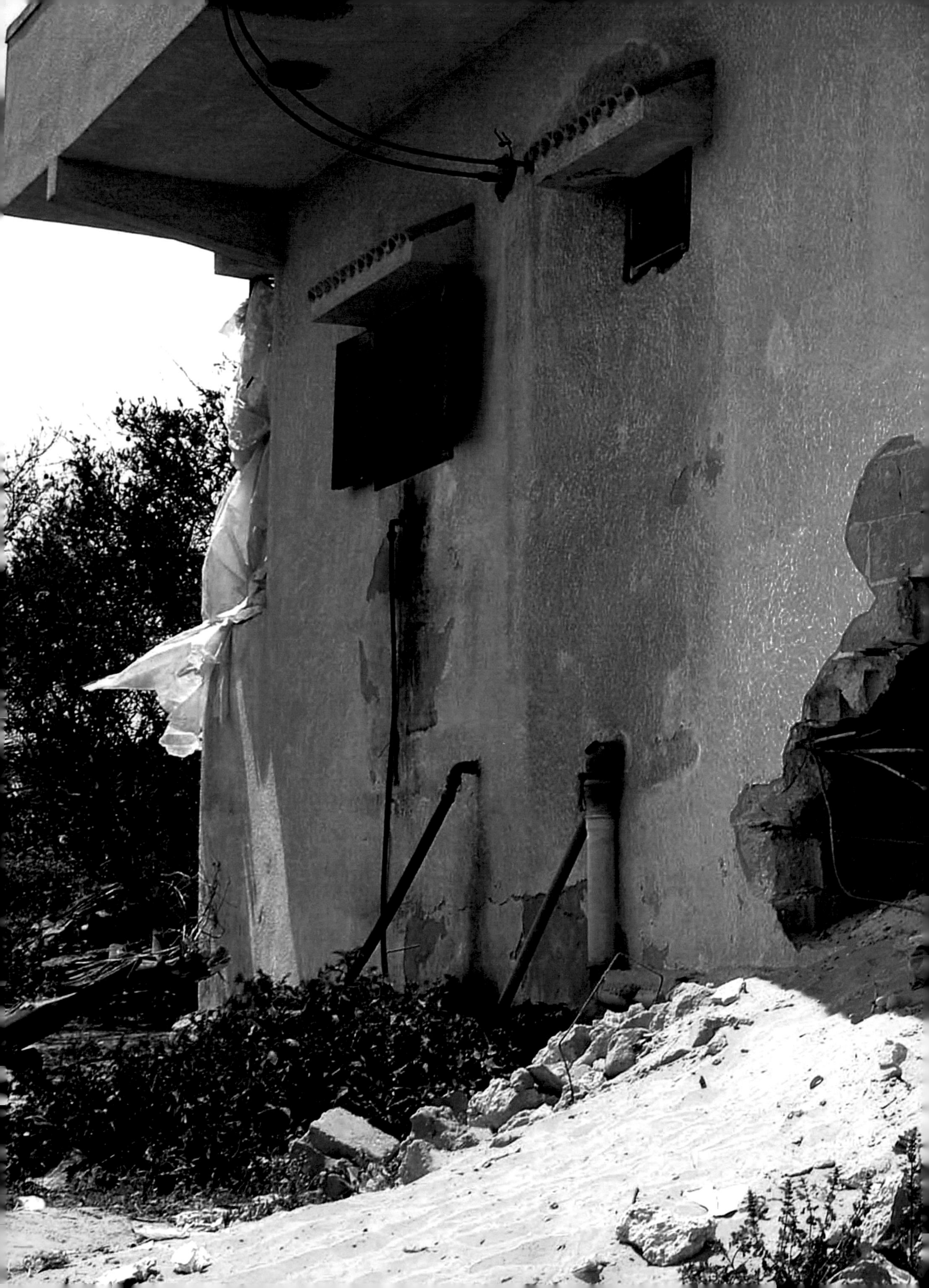

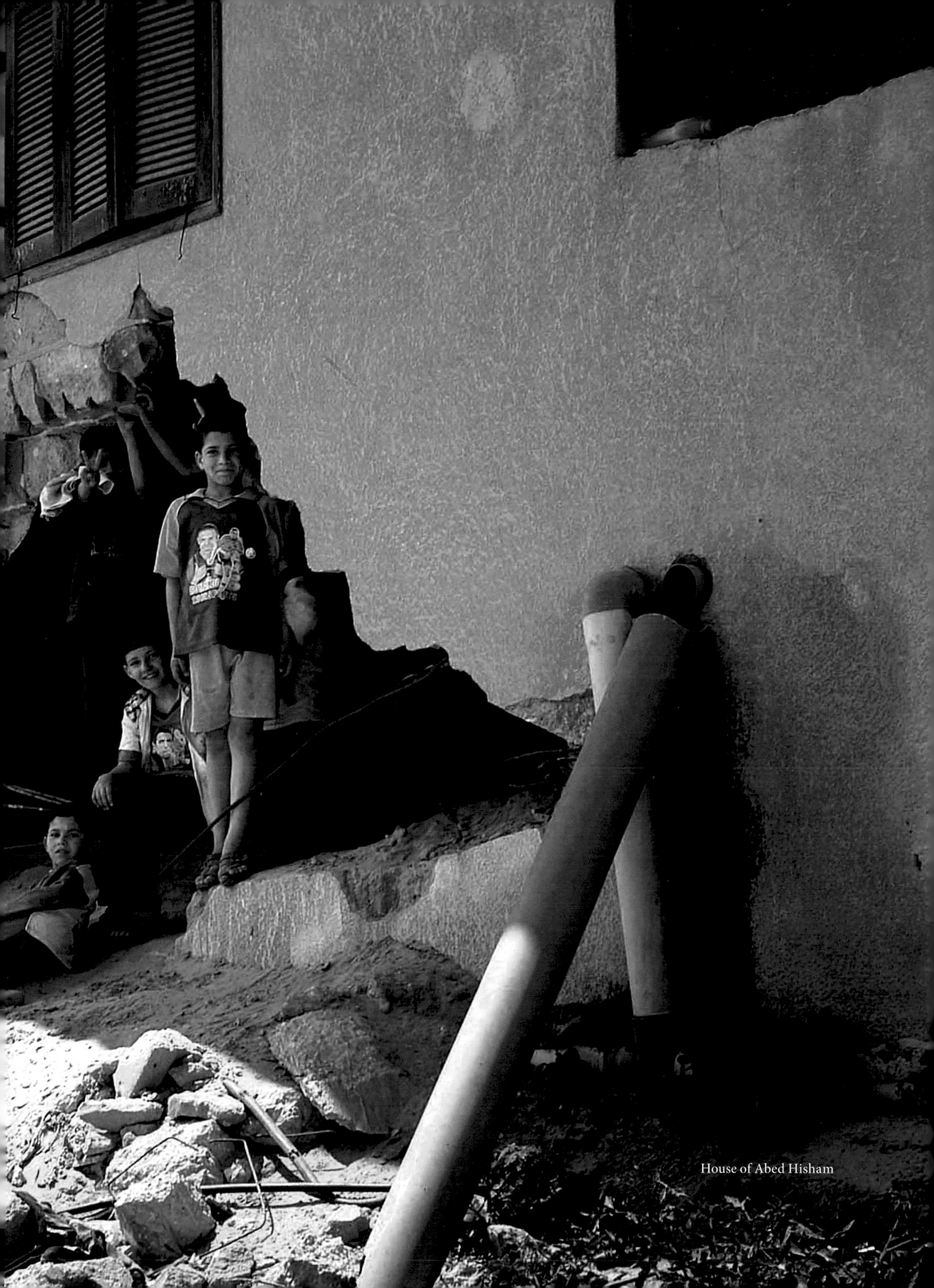

House of Abed Hisham

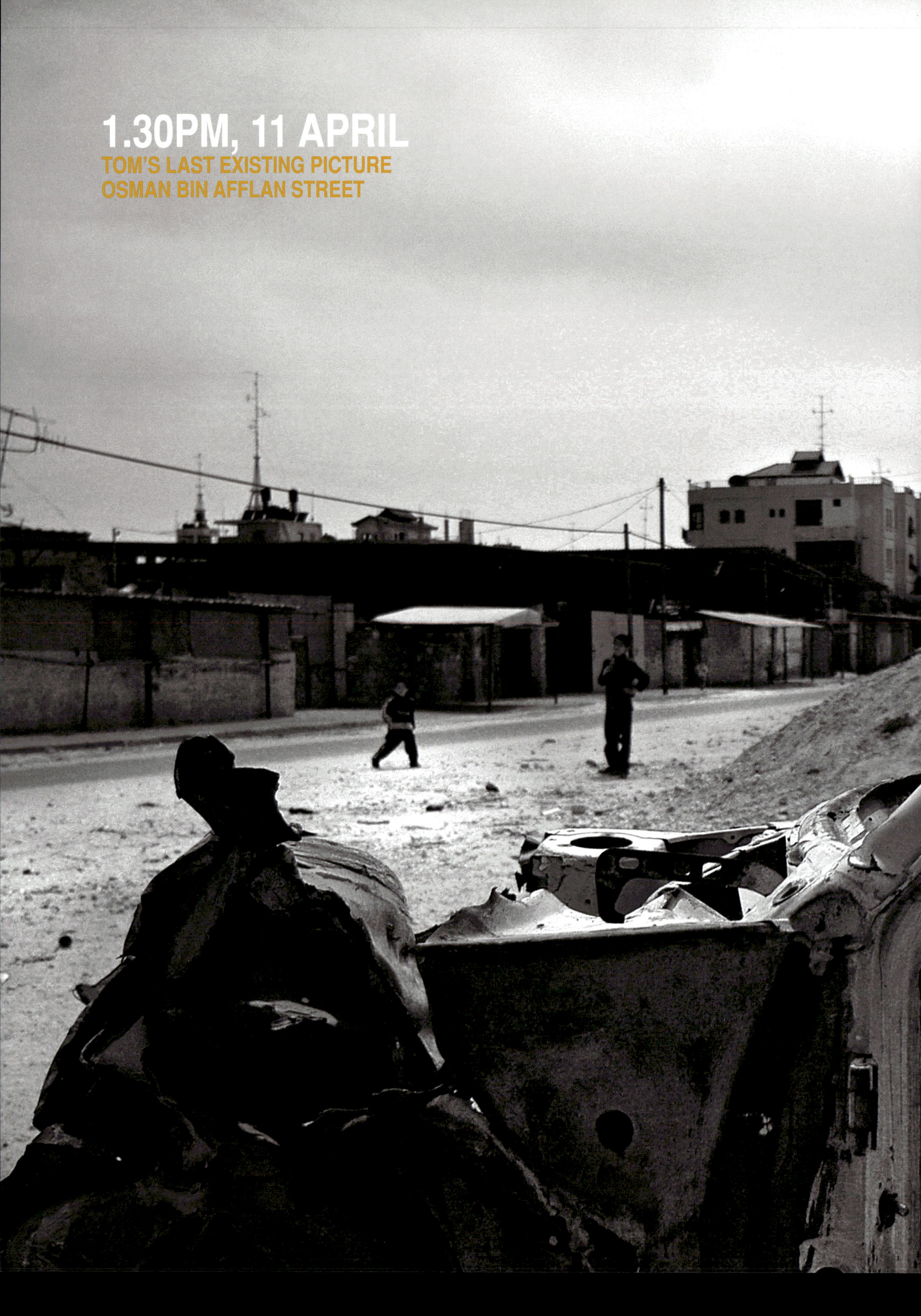

1.30PM, 11 APRIL
TOM'S LAST EXISTING PICTURE
OSMAN BIN AFFLAN STREET

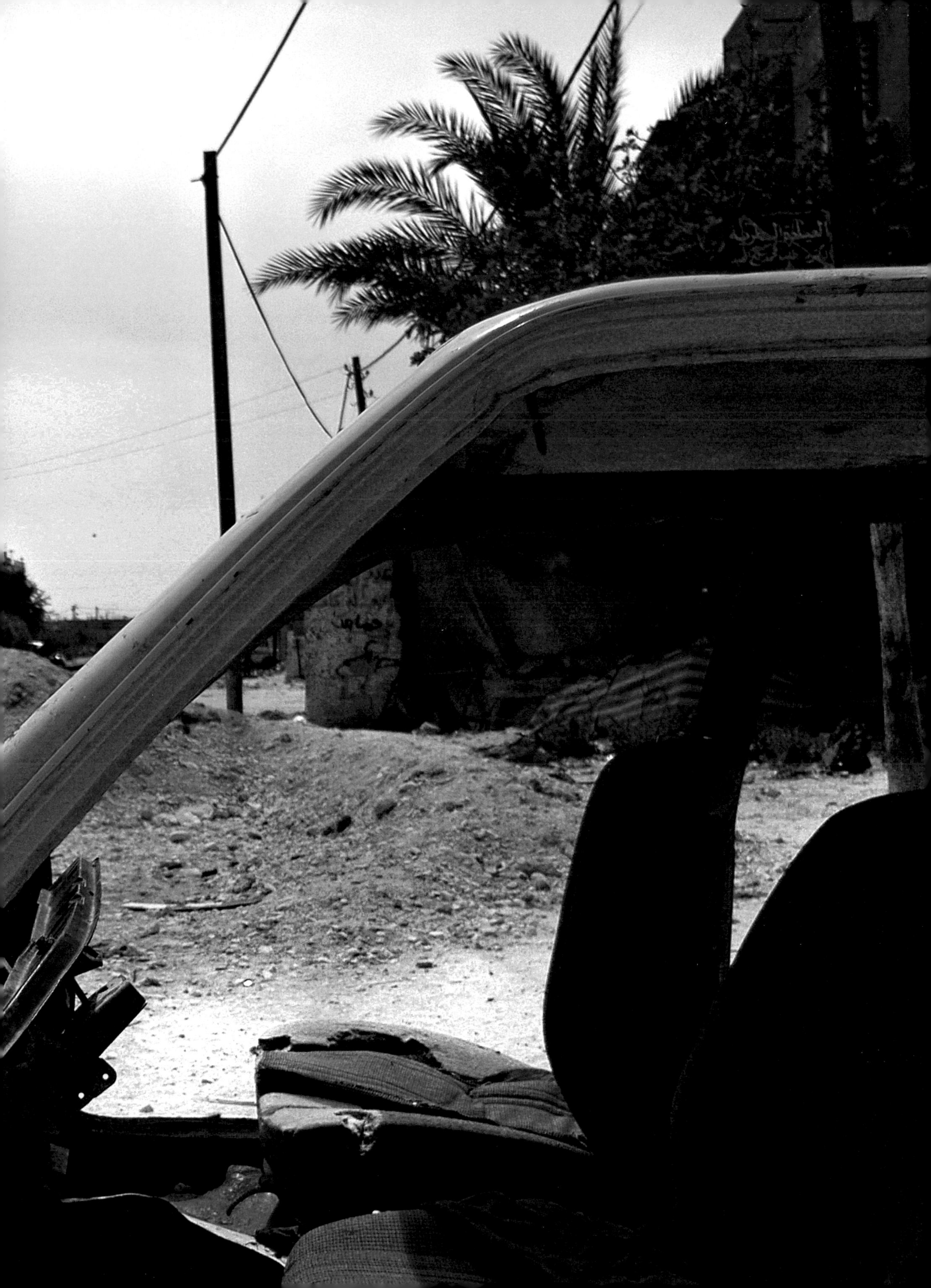

TOM'S LAST DAY

BY THE LOCAL COORDINATOR OF THE INTERNATIONAL SOLIDARITY MOVEMENT, RAFAH

As a Palestinian who grew up in the Gaza Strip under the oppressive Israeli military occupation, my mind has a lot of sad memories to recall and my heart has many loved ones to grieve. The 11th April 2003 marked a tragic day of my life.

I woke up in the morning feeling speechless. Strangely, I always felt that way shortly before something terrible happened, such as losing a dear friend or a family member.

On that unforgettable day, my colleagues in the International Solidarity Movement (ISM) and I were due to take part in a non-violent action which we had previously discussed and planned with the representatives of the local community. We aimed to help the residents of the Yibnah refugee camp in Rafah, to the south of the Gaza Strip, to overcome their fear of being shot dead at the hands of the Israeli snipers operating nearby along the border with Egypt.

The week had begun with a phone call from one of our ISM local coordinators in West Bank informing us that two new ISM volunteers were now in Gaza and would be joining the team in Rafah shortly. A few hours later, the new British volunteers Tom and Alison arrived and myself and another ISM colleague Raph went out to meet and bring them back to the office. Our next day began with a few complaints from Yibnah local residents about the practices of the Israeli troops. The most heartbreaking complaint was received from the Al-Abed Jabr family. They lived in the Yibnah refugee camp in a house located a few hundred metres from two Israeli sniper watchtowers. We learned that two of the family's children were seriously injured by Israeli sniper fire; one had been shot in the leg whilst playing in front of the house, the other had been shot in the neck inside, whilst drinking water in the kitchen.

We decided to pay a visit to the family to understand what had happened and to express our sympathy. As soon as we arrived at their street, we immediately realised how dangerous this area was under the Israeli army presence. They had watchtowers overlooking the Yibnah refugee camp and an armoured tank permanently stationed a few metres from the family house, right in front of the local mosque.

It was our intention to help the family and support the local residents of the Yibnah camp to find a positive way to cope with this frightening military presence. We agreed with the Al-Abed Jabr family to do nightly home stays with them. We discussed indicating our presence as international peace volunteers, so we obtained permission from the family to create and hang banners on the exterior of the house. We put up the banners, which clearly stated in Hebrew and English: 'Please do not shoot! International peace volunteers and innocent children live in this house.'

We stayed with the family for about two nights and they felt much safer with our presence. Our approach had actually worked and we noticed a change in the behaviour of the neighbouring Israeli snipers. The random gunfire that used to come from their watchtowers had relatively decreased.

However, the shooting from the stationary tank had never stopped, and the local residents' fear of being killed by stray bullets continued. We therefore met with the local community representatives to discuss the best approach to address this life-threatening situation. After prolonged debates we finally agreed to set up a tent near the house between the tank position and the main street. We agreed to do day and night stays in the tent and hang up banners indicating our peaceful presence. We believed that this action would not only help the local residents feel a bit safer, but would also help the soldiers in the tank to calm down and think before shooting.

On 11th April 2003, at about 12:00, all members of the group met in the ISM office to hold a final meeting to decide whether or not to go ahead with the tent action. The ISM activists had all arrived back from their routine home stays with local families. Our late British photojournalist student colleague Thomas Hurndall (aka Tom) had arrived from his home stay with Abu Jamil's family.

We held a long, final meeting and realised that we had different views and mixed feelings about the tent action. Some were concerned over safety issues and thought we could not trust the Israeli soldiers' reactions. But the majority felt we had an ethical responsibility towards the devastated local community and we should help them. At the end of this meeting, we finally decided to go ahead.

At about 14:00 a couple of ISM colleagues went along with the representatives of the Yibnah community to double check if the area was safe to carry out the tent action. Shortly afterwards, we received their confirmation that the rest of the group could make a move towards the location. We carried the tent equipment, the banners and a couple of megaphones with us. We also put on the standard ISM uniform of bright orange jacket and trousers. This was the outfit we always wore to clearly identify ourselves as international peace volunteers whenever we went on any non-violent protest/action.

We left the office on our way to the Yibnah camp. As we walked past a take-away restaurant on Sea Street, Tom stopped us to get some food. He had only been in Rafah for about five days, and I had hardly ever seen him eating. Tom was a very quiet person and I was surprised to see him stopping us to get two large shawarma sandwiches and a can of Coke. Some colleagues got annoyed as they were in a rush to catch up with the others, and continued slowly walking. I felt I should wait for him and ended up walking with him behind the rest.

On the way, we had the first proper conversation where I realised that he was a cool guy with a biting sense of humour and we could become good friends. Tom sounded relaxed, hopeful and confident about his motivation of being with us in the ISM. At some point during the conversation he must have felt that I was somehow anxious, so he smiled and put his hand around my shoulders and said: "What's up? Take it easy man, we are here with you people and will help with everything we can." His words were very touching and lifted my spirits.

At approximately 16:00, we arrived at the area where the tent action was going to take place. The general atmosphere seemed quiet and peaceful. Unlike most days, there was no Israeli shooting in the area and lots of local children were playing around a sand mound at the end of the street.

Suddenly, we heard gun shots being fired in our direction and into the street. It was clear these were sniper shots coming from the nearby Israeli watchtowers. Shortly afterwards, further gunfire opened in our direction from the nearby stationary tank. Everyone in the street got very frightened and ran to safety. We saw bullets striking the houses and doors around us, as well as the sand mound where the children were playing.

We noticed two children, a boy and a girl, screaming as they got trapped under fire behind the sand mound. None of us or the local residents dared to go in and rescue them. At that moment, I saw Tom stepping out to evacuate the two terrified children. He managed to reach them and firstly carried the boy to safety. He then went back to rescue the girl and, as he was attempting to carry her, he got hit in the forehead by an Israeli sniper bullet. I saw him falling on his knees with his arms stretched out to carry the girl.

I felt devastated as I saw the blood spilling from his head. I immediately realised that he had been seriously injured. We all ran towards him, and our colleague who was a trained medic offered him first aid. I started shouting: "Ambulance! Help! Ambulance! Help!"

He was bleeding heavily from the head and we were running out of time. We had no choice but to move him out of the direction of gunfire and put him into a taxi. We drove very fast to the Rafah Al-Najjar Hospital. It took us about five minutes to get there. In the car he was still unconscious despite the first aid he had been receiving. I sat in shock watching his face and crying. I recall him at this moment having a purely beautiful smile on his face. I strongly felt he was not with us anymore.

We arrived at the hospital and the doctors did everything they could to save his life, but shortly afterwards they decided to transfer him to another local hospital called the European Gaza hospital. Tom was transferred in a special Intensive Care Unit ambulance to the second hospital.

One hour later, the doctors informed us that he was critically wounded and needed to be transferred to the better equipped Israeli Soroka hospital in Be'er Sheva. We spent hours on the phone trying to contact officials at the British embassy and other diplomatic links in Israel to get them to organise Tom's transfer from Gaza to Soroka hospital.

Finally we managed to get an ambulance to be allowed to transfer Tom, but that was only the beginning of a long trip. When we reached the Israeli check-point we were subjected to extensive security checks for over an hour, following which they denied access to the doctor in the ambulance to proceed any further. Whilst waiting for another doctor to substitute him, there were more detailed security checks, again prolonging the experience. At last we were directed to a crossing terminal and told which route we were allowed to use to reach the changeover location between the Palestinian and Israeli ambulances, who would take him on to Soroka hospital, and where he was at last admitted. A few weeks later, his family decided to fly him home where he was admitted to a London hospital, and where he died nine months later.

Unfortunately, Tom was gone forever like many other friends and family members whose lives I have witnessed being taken since I was born and in the 60 years of occupation.

Nearly nine years on, I am writing these lines in the name of his unforgettable memory and courageous soul. Tom paid with his life to give life to others. His blood was unlawfully spilt on our roads, yet it has marked a step in the road to a free Palestine. Tom's soul and priceless sacrifice will always remain engraved in our minds and hearts. Dear Tom, rest in peace.

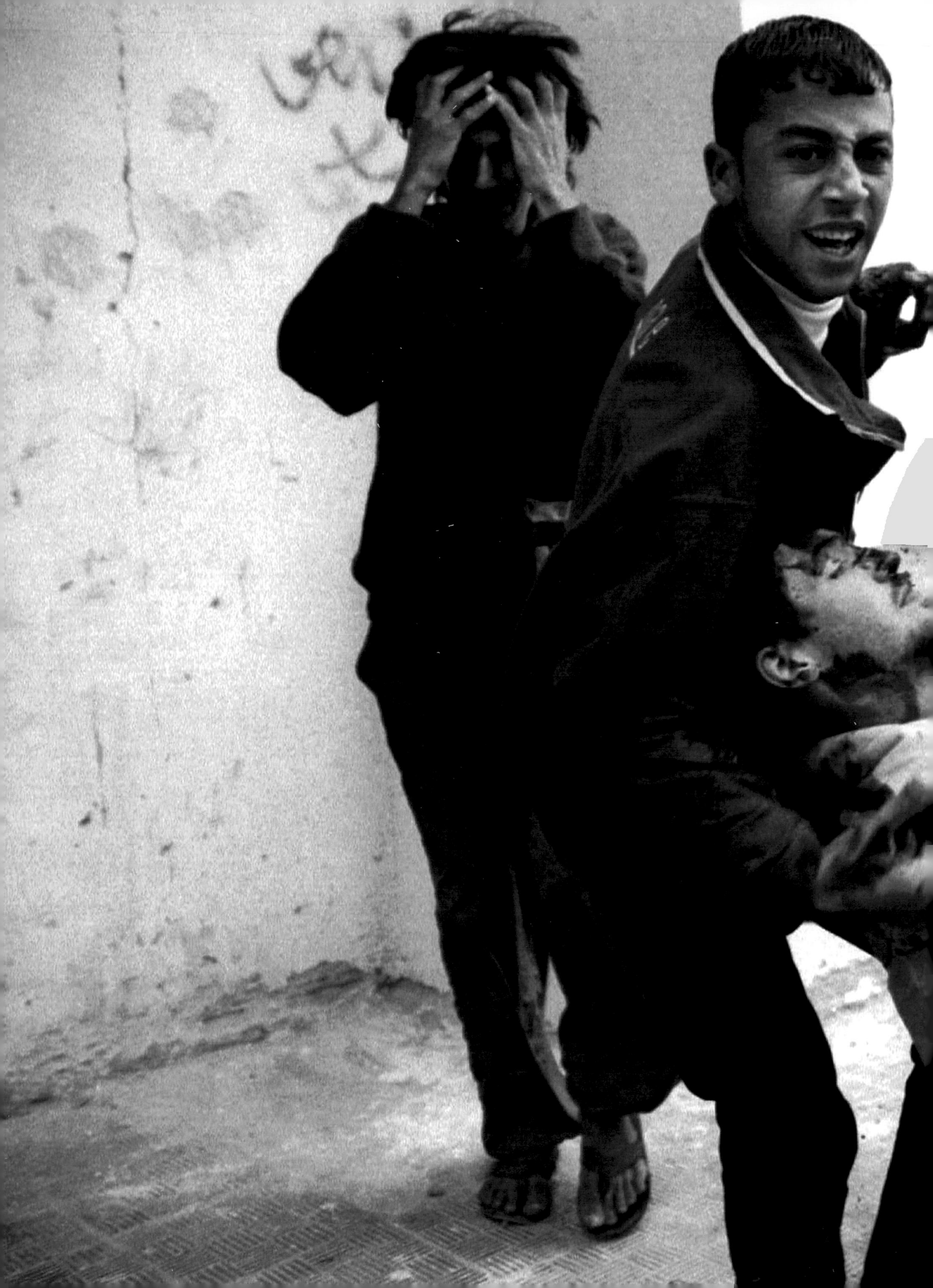

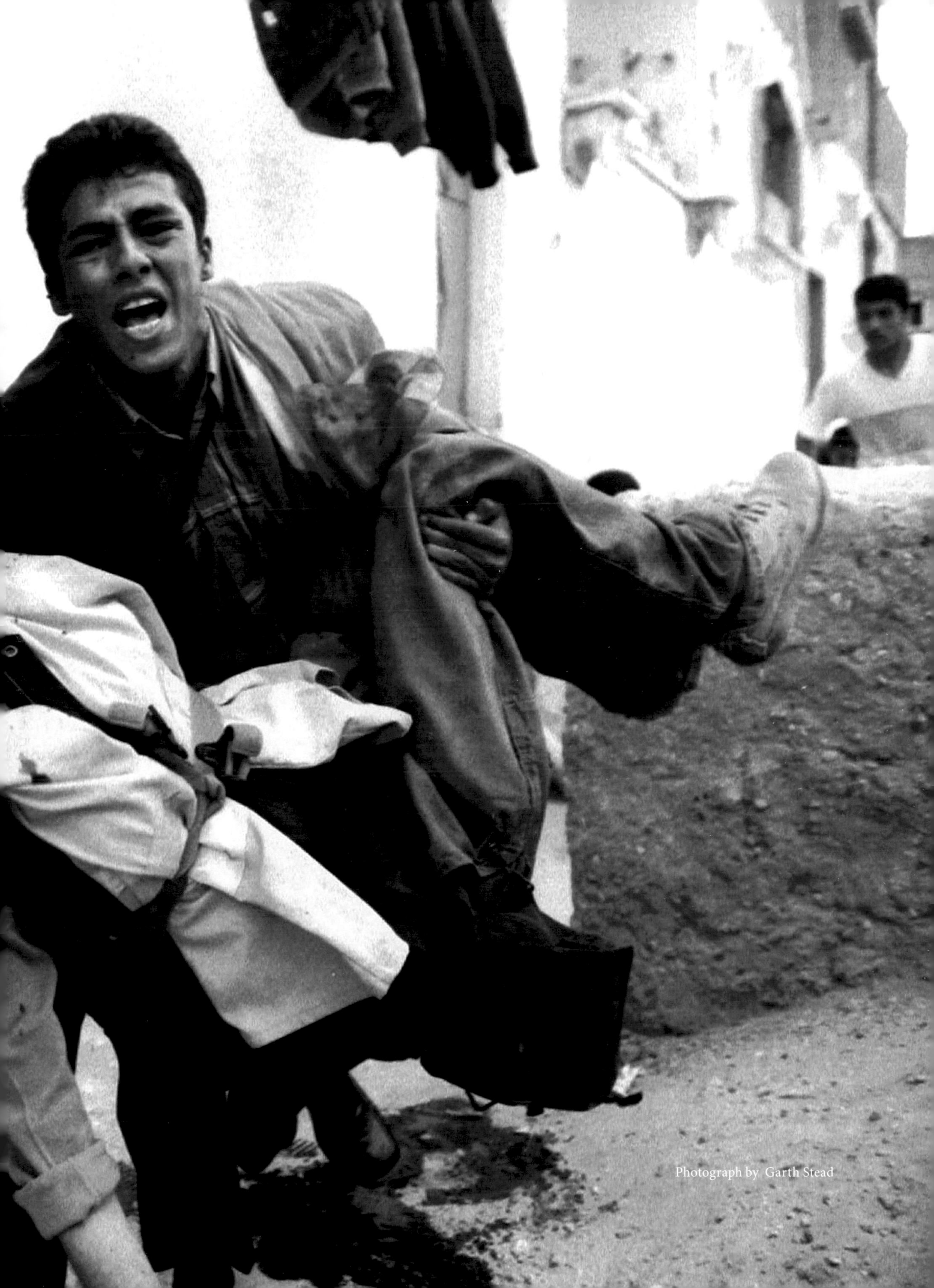

Photograph by Garth Stead

GLOSSARY

APC - Armoured Personnel Carrier

CPT - Christian Peacemaker Team

FPS - Facilities Protection Service

IDF - Israeli Defence Forces

ISM - International Solidarity Movement

TCN - Third Country National

ACKNOWLEDGEMENTS

That Tom's book has now been published, as close to his intentions as could be, is thanks to many caring and talented people. On behalf of Tom, our deepest gratitude is to Gigi Giannuzzi and Hannah Watson at Trolley Books who understood Tom's vision, his photography and writing. With their remarkable professional and creative skills they led us through the painstaking process of producing a book of Tom's work which reflects his passion to seek the truth, and which shows how his thinking developed. We are also grateful to photographer Kay Fernandes, who understood his photography and helped us select photos from thousands, and also with colour control. We appreciate with tremendous warmth how Tom's housemaster at Winchester, Rob Wyke, an important influence in his life, helped to edit Tom's book. Thanks also to Rowan Joffe, Simon Block and John Sweeney who generously gave their time to support the crowdfunding campaign. We hold in deep affection one special person who writes about Tom's final day but who cannot be named. We also appreciate the support of Frontline Club who held Tom's first exhibition of these photographs. Thanks also to Tom's friends who would willingly have had a greater role in the book and who are warmly remembered.

Jocelyn and Anthony Hurndall

Sincere thanks to the many generous people who helped make this book happen through our crowdfunding campaign, in particular:

Charles Armstrong
Conxa and John Ball
Tony Beaumont
Nina Berman
Bill Bows
Adam Chappel
Anne Foley
Katherine Hart
Hannah Haq
Norma Hashim
John Horsley
Simon Hyde
Linden Ife
Mona El Isa
Islington Friends of Yibna
Ian Jones
Nayema Khan
Gordon Klock
Ibrahim Koshy
Alex Leon
Per Lif
Costanza M.
MiCamera
Gaz O'Neill
Tayo Nelson
Libby Powell
Iyas AlQasem
Mariam Rosser-Owen
Jasmine Sailing
Christiane Schwarze
Amy Thurman
Harri Watson

and those who wish to remain anonymous.

Published in Great Britain in 2012
by Trolley Ltd

www.trolleybooks.com

ISBN 978-1-904563-51-8

Editor: Hannah Watson
Editorial production: Anna Stephens,
Carla von der Becke
Design: Fruitmachinedesign.com
Colour correction: Kay Fernandes

Printed in Italy 2012 by Grafiche Antiga